I0473613

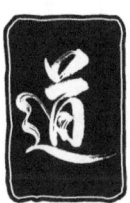

From *shodo*—"the Way of calligraphy"—to *budo*—"the martial Way"—the Japanese have succeeded in designing their traditional arts and crafts as paths to meditation. The names of these skills frequently end with the word Do, also pronounced Michi, which equals the "Way." When practicing a Way, we unearth universal principles that go beyond a specific discipline, relating to the art of living itself. Featuring the books of H. E. Davey and other select writers, works by Michi Publishing center on these Do forms. Michi Publishing's focus is on classical Asian arts, spirituality, and meditation, benefitting all cultures.

J THE
APANESE *WAY*
OF THE ARTIST

Living the Japanese Arts & Ways:
45 Paths to Meditation & Beauty

Brush Meditation:
A Japanese Way to Mind & Body Harmony

The Japanese Way of the Flower:
Ikebana as Moving Meditation

Three complete works on the
classic tradition by H. E. Davey

Michi Publishing ◆Albany, California

NOTE TO READERS

Published by Michi Publishing, 1053 San Pablo Ave, Albany, CA 94706

510-526-7518

www.michipublishing.com

This volume contains three works by H.E. Davey. Originally published separately, they are collected here in their entirety, except for a few updates, corrections, and omissions of duplicate elements; slight variations in design and word treatment that do not affect content or meaning have preserved. This anthology was originally issued in 2007 by Stone Bridge Press. The current edition is by Michi Publishing.

Living the Japanese Arts & Ways: 45 Paths to Meditation & Beauty

Photography, artwork retouching, and icons by Steve Aibel. All calligraphy and poetry translations by the author. Text, calligraphy, and illustrations © 2003 H. E. Davey.

Brush Meditation: A Japanese Way to Mind & Body Harmony

Some of the artwork reproduced in this book previously appeared in the following publications: "Ki" in *Furyu* (Spring–Summer 1995); "Mushin" in *Nichi Bei Times* (January 1, 1998); "Fudoshin" in *Hokubei Mainichi* (January 1, 1997). Interior layout and title-page lettering by L. J. C. Shimoda. Photography by Ann Kameoka. All artwork by the author, except the bonfire and poem on page 335 by Ohsaki Jun. Text, calligraphy, and photographs © 1999 H. E. Davey.

The Japanese Way of the Flower: Ikebana as Moving Meditation

Photographs © 2000 Stone Bridge Press, showing flower arrangements by Ann Kameoka. Originally digitally photographed in color by Canterbury Photographic, Berkeley, California. Process/flower illustrations by L. J. C. Shimoda, with acknowledgment to the many designers and artists whose work provided inspiration and guidance. Text © 2000 H. E. Davey and Ann Kameoka. Calligraphy and translations © 2000 H. E. Davey.

New introduction © 2007 H. E. Davey.

Printed in the United States of America.

First printing 2015

ISBN: 978-0-9904214-4-3

CONTENTS

INTRODUCTION

All Japanese art at its greatest level seeks to embody *wa*, or "harmony," which is a harmony of the mind and body, of the individual and the universe, and of artist and art. In the case of a few advanced teachers I've studied with, they have become the art itself. They teach the essential principles of their art not merely via words and writings but through their behavior. This unity of artist and art is perhaps not exclusive to Japanese *Do* forms, but it is distinctive of them. Do means the "Way" in the sense of a right and natural Way of living. Stemming from the Chinese idea of the *Tao*, or the "Way of the universe," ancient Japanese culture spiritualized a number of everyday activities, allowing them to become forms of moving meditation. Thus *cha no yu* ("tea ceremony") became *chado*—the "Way of tea." Likewise, *budo* became the "martial Way," *shodo* the "Way of calligraphy," and *kado* the "Way of flower arrangement." The designation Do indicates that these arts can help us realize deeper concentration, calmness, relaxation, and willpower in daily life. The Do in shodo, for example, suggests that artists can move from the art of brush calligraphy to the art of living itself. Using the word Do to describe seemingly unrelated activities also indicates that these arts are based on connected principles. Many aesthetics of Japanese dance, for instance, are also found in *sumi-e* ink painting, and the basis of correct posture in martial arts is the same in Japanese calligraphic art. The calm and immovable spirit underlying any one of the traditional arts of Japan underlies them all.

Living the Japanese Arts & Ways, the first volume in this compilation, identifies the universal principles that underlie all Japanese art forms and explains how such arts can be understood as forms of meditation that lead to calmness in action. These universal principles can be applied to everyday experience to allow us to live well, as opposed to merely existing. More than a guide to Japanese arts and crafts, the book is an exploration of what it means to live our very lives as art.

In the Beginning . . .

My first introduction to a traditional Japanese art form came via the martial arts. My late father, Victor, was one of the first Americans to study judo and jujutsu, which he began to practice in 1926. While living in Japan after World War II, his study intensified, and I began learning an authentic system of Japanese jujutsu with him when I was around five years old.

When I was in middle school, a friend in judo introduced me to a Japanese teacher of Shin-shin-toitsu-do, a unique system of meditation and physical development created by Nakamura Tempu Sensei in the 1920s. Nakamura Sensei lived in India, where he practiced Raja yoga—the yoga of meditation. When he returned to Japan, he combined this yogic wisdom with his past training in Japanese martial arts, healing arts, and meditation systems. He also drew on his previous studies of Western medicine and psychology to create Shin-shin-toitsu-do, the "Way of Mind and Body Unification."

This art is based on the idea that human beings arrive at self-harmony and realize their ultimate potential only when the mind and body are coordinated. These universal principles completely transformed and improved my martial arts practice, which by then included judo, jujutsu, and aikido. The breathing exercises and methods of physical development in Shin-shin-toitsu-do cured a severe and long-standing case of asthma as well.

More than this, however, Shin-shin-toitsu-do opened my eyes to the fact that universal principles actually do exist, connecting people all over the world and linking many different endeavors in life. In 1981, I established the Sennin Foundation Center for Japanese Cultural Arts in the San Francisco Bay Area, where I offered instruction in Shin-shin-toitsu-do and related healing arts as well as martial arts training in Saigo Ryu aiki-jujutsu.

While practicing at my childhood judo dojo (judo school), I admired pieces of Japanese brush writing hanging on the walls, leading to a desire to practice shodo or sumi-e. In the 1980s, a friend from Nagoya introduced me to Kobara Ranseki Sensei, one of the top shodo artists living in the United States. Sensei rarely accepted new students, but undeterred, I returned to his class in Oakland until he allowed me to join the Wanto Shodo-Kai (East Bay Shodo Association), a branch of his Ranseki Sho Juku school. Impressed not only with Kobara Sensei's artwork, but also with his peaceful and dignified demeanor,

I felt fortunate to practice with him. Upon receiving teaching certification, I began offering my students instruction in shodo, which like Shin-shin-toitsu-do and other Japanese arts, is a Way to spiritual realization.

A Special Dedication to Kobara Ranseki Sensei (1924–2005)

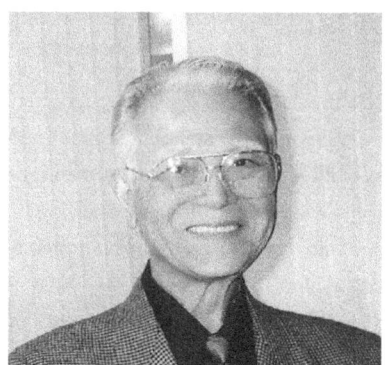

Kobara Ranseki Sensei.

As I was preparing to write this introduction, Kobara Sensei, the source of inspiration and anecdotes throughout *Living the Japanese Arts & Ways* and *Brush Meditation*, passed away. I dedicate this book to my late teacher not only out of gratitude, but because his life serves as an example of what *geido*—the "Japanese Way of art"—stands for, and because aspects of our lengthy time together illustrate the close teacher-student relationship needed to truly learn a Japanese art form. The calligraphic art in this book is based on his style of shodo and ink painting. His influence on this volume cannot be overstated.

Kobara Seiji was born on December 24, 1924 in Shimane Prefecture, Japan. His father was the priest of Myorenji Temple, and, like his forefathers, Seiji trained to become a reverend. He was devoted to Buddhism, but as a young man he found a second passion—shodo. He thus became a student of Fukuzawa Seiran Sensei, a famed artist teaching calligraphy at Kyoto University. Fukuzawa Sensei emphasized the study of the *Shin So Sen-Ji-Mon*, a very old 1,000-character classic that exists in several versions, one of them brushed by the Chinese monk/calligrapher Chiei. The calligraphy that you will have a chance to study in *Brush Meditation* is deeply influenced by Chiei's shodo masterpiece.

After World War II times were hard in Japan, leaving few people with time or money for artistic pursuits. Kobara Seiji was Fukuzawa Sensei's only private student then, visiting his home for one-on-one training each day. Eventually, Fukuzawa Sensei gave his student the name Ranseki, "Indigo Blue Stone," which included the *ran* character from his own pen name. The bestowing of *gago*, special names used in art, is common in Japanese disciplines, indicating that a student has come into his or her own as an artist. It also indicates the tight-knit relationship that must exist between student and teacher in these disciplines. Kobara Ranseki later received a Shihan-Dai teaching certificate from Fukuzawa Sensei, the top ranking in his school of calligraphy.

In 1947, Kobara Sensei wasn't just studying Buddhism and shodo. He worked in the prosecutor's office in Kyoto. Interested in new horizons, Kobara Sensei left his prosperous ancestral temple, taking a daring and uncertain path by moving to the United States in 1950. He enrolled at the University of Washington and studied at the Seattle Buddhist Church. After graduating, he transferred to the Buddhist Church of San Francisco in 1954. In 1960, Reverend Kobara retired from his church position and began a new profession with Japan Airlines. His successful career lasted thirty-one years until his retirement in 1991.

During his time with the Buddhist Church of San Francisco, Reverend Kobara learned that no one was available skilled enough to paint the names for tombstones at the Japanese cemetery in Colma, California. His experience in shodo made him the natural choice, and he brushed characters for engraving on over 150 stone markers. Kobara Ranseki's skill was obvious, and he was asked to teach calligraphy in San Francisco, where he founded the Ranseki Sho Juku, the Ranseki Calligraphy School, in 1966. This same year he also became the director of the San Francisco branch of the Urasenke school of tea ceremony. In 1977, with Ueno Chikushu Sensei he founded the Kokusai Shodo Bunka Koryu Kyokai—the International Japanese Calligraphy and Cultural Exchange Association—headquartered in Urayasu, Japan, with members throughout Japan, China, and the United States. As vice president, Kobara Sensei oversaw the annual International Shodo Exhibition in Japan.

During his long shodo career he received prestigious awards for excellence in Japanese art from the Japanese Foreign Ministry and from the prime minister of Japan. For years Kobara Sensei gave the primary address at the International Shodo Exhibition in Japan. So accomplished and distinctive was Sensei's style of traditional brush writing that even expert calligraphy teachers in Japan asked to become his disciples.

Kobara Sensei thought of himself as an artist, and emphasized his approach to shodo as an art form rather than as simple lettering. He spoke of the beauty of line, the mysterious luster of sumi ink, and the asymmetrical balance of shodo as transcendent creative elements common to many arts, and to which people of many cultures could relate. He insisted, "I'm not teaching *shuji* (handwriting), but rather shodo—the Way of calligraphy." Profoundly spiritual, Kobara Sensei viewed the practice of brush writing and ink painting as a path for refining character, and he taught that we could see the depths of our personality by observing our calligraphy.

Kobara Sensei's teaching style is widespread among experts who believe their art form transcends its utilitarian function. Tea ceremony instructors are more concerned with moving meditation than making tea; flower arrangement experts stress that their goal is harmony with nature more than mastering floral craft.

Sensei's distinctive style of calligraphy emphasizes Chinese characters and Japanese phonetic symbols that feature naturalistic, rounded, and flowing forms. Ranseki Sho Juku calligraphy is filled with uniquely graceful elements that rest in a sea of dignified serenity. Simultaneously powerful and calm, Kobara Sensei's shodo reflected his quietly resolute and dignified personality; in the years I spent around him—in class and in his home, at public demonstrations and in private, in Japan and in the United States—I never saw him lose his composure. Not once.

My teacher was an exceptional example of this quality, known as *fudoshin*, or "immovable mind," but it is a characteristic that all competent teachers of Japanese art should endeavor to display. Bear this in mind when you look for a qualified teacher of any Japanese art, and look for it within yourself as you practice.

During Kobara Sensei's numerous years of teaching, few students completed the 1,000 characters of the *Shin So Sen-Ji-Mon*, but when some of us finished the book, he helped us to study, copy, and learn the script of Ogishi, arguably the most celebrated calligraphic artist in China and Japan. However, instead of having us copy books of famous calligraphy, or a manual of his brush writing, Kobara Sensei chose to personally paint a lesson for each student, one lesson at a time, one person at a time. We then left for home, where we would repeatedly copy his artwork, absorbing its essence into our subconscious. In a couple weeks, Sensei would gently correct our best copy and give us the next lesson in his series.

Such a personal and labor-intensive approach is rare even in orthodox shodo, and as our teacher entered old age, we urged him to hand out photocopies of his artwork. He refused, spending long periods of time patiently teaching each student privately, one after another. Even in his 70s and 80s, he sat for hours at a time, painting continuously, until he finished with the students gathered on that day. Kobara Sensei insisted this fatiguing process was necessary to continue to train his mind and calligraphy. He rightly contended that it was better for his students.

Readers should bear in mind that classical Japanese arts are *shugyo*—a form of life-long spiritual discipline—and we get out of them what we put into them, for as long as we continue to put forth sincere effort. Kobara Sensei's effort lasted a lifetime. His calligraphy improved throughout his life, showing no decline in old age.

Several years ago, Kobara Sensei developed congestive heart failure, but due to his age surgery was not possible. He lost weight and his body weakened, but his gentle and indomitable spirit did not. Even in ill health, he continued to paint each day, and regularly traveled some distance to teach his students outside of San Francisco.

Since shodo, budo, kado, and other arts take decades rather than days to learn, they can cultivate immense self-discipline and perseverance within any student. We can all develop these qualities in ourselves if we sincerely study a Japanese art under a competent instructor. I hope this book will lead you in that direction.

A Final Tribute and a Farewell

Early in 2005, Kobara Sensei and I presented a calligraphy exhibition in San Francisco's Japantown in honor of Sensei's thirty years of teaching in Oakland. We demonstrated shodo for the public, as we had on many occasions over the years. The event was a resounding success, and Kobara Sensei was frail but joyful. Later in 2005, he gave his last speech at the International Shodo Exhibition in Urayasu, where he was acknowledged by Japan's top shodo artists for his contributions to the art.

On November 17, 2005, Kobara Sensei received Kyokujitsu Tanko Sho—the Order of the Rising Sun (with Silver Rays)—from the Japanese government for his years of promoting traditional Japanese art and culture. This rarely bestowed medal of honor was presented to Kobara Sensei by Yamanaka Makoto, Consul General of Japan. Surrounded by his wife, children, and grandchildren, he quietly thanked his spouse, Kazuko, and his family for their support. He took no credit for his achievements, insisting that his accomplishments were due to his longevity, the love of his family, and his late shodo teacher. This humility, this quality called *shoshin*—"beginner's mind"— is common among advanced practitioners of Japanese art, and is essential to our ongoing development. Once we think that we've mastered shodo or any art, our growth stops.

Sensei was touched by this decoration that so few people have received, and he shyly showed us his award at one of his last shodo classes. He was at peace and delighted by how his life had turned out. At their highest levels the Do stress realizing a state beyond all attachments, including fame and even skill in the Do itself. Kobara Sensei exemplified this peaceful satisfaction.

Shortly after he received the Order of the Rising Sun, we held an end of the year party for Kobara Sensei. As I sat with him and his wife, Sensei softly said he was very happy, but that it was hard for him to breathe. He radiated contentment at the close of the event, when he bid what would be his last goodbye to his students.

During a family holiday in Hawaii, I received a phone call from Kobara Kazuko telling me that her husband was in intensive care. I immediately phoned his other senior students and returned to California. The day before our plane landed, Kobara Sensei passed away.

On January 6, 2006, I helped his family members carry his casket into the Buddhist Church of San Francisco. He was famous throughout the Japanese community in Northern California for his contributions to traditional Japanese culture, and the outpouring of grief was massive. Nearly five hundred people crammed into the church.

After the tolling of the temple bell, I offered incense with his family before his open coffin. The Consul General of Japan and many dignitaries from Asia and the United States attended the funeral. Many of the telegrams and faxes that flooded the Kobara home were read at the service, including condolences from the current and past headmasters of the Urasenke tea ceremony school and from the chief director of the Kokusai Shodo Bunka Koryu Kyokai. A large number of people who had never studied tea ceremony or shodo with Kobara Sensei spoke of him as their teacher, their sensei for life.

They spoke of his deep compassion and patience. One mourner told me that whenever he met Kobara Sensei, he saw his beaming smile and felt a wave of benevolent warmth rush over him. I'd felt it too, many times and in many different ways. In a sense, my teacher's kindness was not only the hallmark of his teaching style; it was the very foundation of his life.

It was a life honed like the edge of a razor-sharp Japanese sword through endless shodo practice. The Ways are not always easy, and legitimate training can be severe at times. Individuals devoting their lives to these disciplines know all too well the difficulties that sometimes arise along this path. Having lived through and conquered many such obstacles, Kobara Sensei displayed great tenderness for his fellow travelers in shodo and kindness toward others in general. All those who have penetrated deeply into meditation, or into Japanese arts practiced as meditation, arrive at this same river of compassion.

On January 9, 2006, Sensei's family and I again acted as pallbearers as we carried his coffin into the crematorium. Few people were present—just myself, his wife, his children, their spouses, and his two grandchildren. Before the cremation, I bowed before my sensei's body for the last time. Kobara Sensei had been my friend, supporter, and teacher for twenty years.

After the cremation service, Kazuko took us to the graveyard where her husband's ashes would reside. It was the same tiny cemetery in Colma where his artwork first achieved recognition over fifty years ago. His daughter Rumi rode in my car, and as we pulled into the parking lot, she asked, "Can you see Father's calligraphy?"

We walked to the Kobara plot, tall tombstones filled with Kobara Sensei's singular calligraphy surrounding us. As my teacher's body was leaving this world, I walked through a vast forest of his art.

This Book and the Legacy of Kobara Sensei

I've described Kobara Sensei's unique calligraphy as elegant, graceful, and refined. It's all of these things, but I've realized that it is something more. The most distinctive quality of Kobara Sensei's artwork—the tree from which all other branches of its beauty arise—is compassion. Kobara Sensei's calligraphy looks the way it does because of a well of kindness, which he realized from his lifelong study of the Way. His artwork was an expression of this. Kobara Sensei and his art had become one.

Sensei expressed wisdom through verbal instruction, but his deepest teachings were nonverbal in nature. Whenever I studied with him, I felt uplifted, not by what he said, but by his very presence. He demonstrated a means of teaching that embraced and encouraged those around him without the need for words. It is an uncommon and unteachable gift, and its expression in ink is Kobara Ranseki Sensei's true legacy. It's a legacy that I have pledged to preserve.

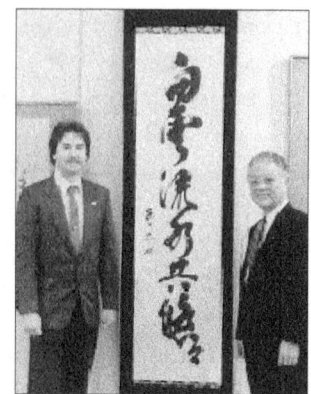

H. E. Davey and Kobara Ranseki Sensei in Japan at the 1989 International Shodo Exhibition.

After I received the name Hiseki, "Flying Stone," from Sensei, we were sitting alone in his own home in San Francisco. He told me that I had the ability and motivation to perpetuate his form of shodo after he was gone, and he asked me if I would do him this favor. I assured him that I would. This book is a step in that direction.

In writing this introduction I've realized that to genuinely continue my teacher's legacy, I must further find within myself the profound tenderness and kindness that Kobara Ranseki Sensei showered upon me for over twenty years.

Acknowledgments

While Kobara Sensei greatly influenced my life and books, this new volume wouldn't be possible without my training under several teachers of Japanese cultural arts. I'm grateful to the many talented people I've studied with.

In jujutsu, I'd like to acknowledge Victor Davey Sensei and Sato Shizuya Sensei. In Kodokan judo, I'm grateful to Lloyd Yonago Sensei, Richard Yamamoto Sensei, Fukuda Keiko Sensei, Maki Katota Sensei, and numerous past teachers. Likewise, in aikido and other martial arts I once practiced, I've trained with skilled instructors from Japan and the United States, and I'm indebted to all of them.

In Shin-shin-toitsu-do, I've been lucky to study the original version of this art and one of its modern offshoots from Hirata Yoshihiko Sensei, Tohei Koichi Sensei, Hashimoto Tetsuichi Sensei, and Sawai Atsuhiro Sensei. In recent years, Hashimoto Sensei and

Sawai Sensei, senior representatives of the Tempu Society in Japan, have been especially helpful. In particular, I'd like to acknowledge Sawai Sensei, a native of Kyoto, who unselfishly brought his advanced knowledge of Shin-shin-toitsu-do to my school in California, and who tirelessly helps me translate rare writings of Nakamura Tempu Sensei.

Ann Kameoka, my wife and coauthor of *The Japanese Way of the Flower*, also deserves my thanks for helping me write this book. Without her flower arrangement certification from the Ikenobo Headquarters in Kyoto, *The Japanese Way of the Flower* wouldn't have been possible. She also deserves credit for putting up with my attraction to all things wheeled; as I write this, British and Italian motorcycles, German and Japanese sports cars, and racing bicycles from Italy threaten to overrun the garage and invade our home.

Wayne Muromoto, my fellow teacher of traditional martial arts, wrote the foreword to *Living the Japanese Arts & Ways*. Mr. Muromoto is an advanced practitioner of Ura-senke tea ceremony and Takeuchi Ryu jujutsu. A member of the Shudokan Martial Arts Association's Board of Advisors, he is also the editor/creator of www.furyu.com, and I'm grateful for his friendship and his foreword.

Last, but in no way least, is Peter Goodman, Grand Poobah of Stone Bridge Press and my friend/editor. Without his continued belief in the value of my writings, you couldn't have purchased this big book with a tiny price that you're now reading.

A Final Note

The ancient Japanese art forms are becoming more accessible to Westerners, and I hope my books are contributing to this phenomenon. It's one reason I wrote them. Anyone can study Japanese calligraphy, martial arts, and other disciplines as I have, and you can benefit from their practice as much as I have. If you're sincere and hardworking, there's a good chance you can surpass what little I've accomplished in these old and fragile disciplines. For the sake of their preservation, and for the benefit of humanity, I hope that some of you will undertake this lifelong task. The rewards are innumerable.

H. E. Davey
Green Valley, California

A NOTE ON THE JAPANESE LANGUAGE

Japanese is the international language of the Japanese arts and Ways, and even a modest knowledge of the Japanese language can open certain doors and lead to a deeper grasp of Japan's culture, thus making the practice of its cultural activities more meaningful. Knowledge of the language also allows the Western enthusiast to more easily interact with both Japanese experts and genuine Western authorities (many of whom have spent time training in Japan) without embarrassment. In fact, my knowledge of Japanese art terminology has proved to be a common bond between me and non-English-speaking artists from other Western countries. It's possible to read the Japanese words in this book and avoid embarrassment over mispronounced terms by following the guidelines below:

a is pronounced "ah" as in father
e is pronounced "eh" as in Edward
i is pronounced "ee" as in police
o is pronounced "oh" as in oats
u is pronounced "oo" as in tune

Doubled consonants (as in *kappa*, for example) are pronounced with a brief pause between syllables. The Japanese *r* is pronounced so that it sounds like something between English *r* and *l*. Further, Japanese doesn't have a plural form: thus *yubi* ("finger") can refer to one or more than one finger, depending on the context. The special orthographic signs called macrons, used in some books to indicate extended vowel sounds in Japanese, are not used here.

Last, according to traditional Japanese practice, it is customary to refer to a person by family name first and given name second. This custom has been followed throughout this volume. Sensei, a title of homage meaning "teacher," is always placed after an instructor's family name: Tanaka Sensei, for example.

LIVING THE
JAPANESE
ARTS & WAYS

45 PATHS TO MEDITATION & BEAUTY

H.E. DAVEY

FOREWORD BY WAYNE MUROMOTO
ILLUSTRATIONS BY STEVE AIBLE

Michi: Japanese Arts and Ways

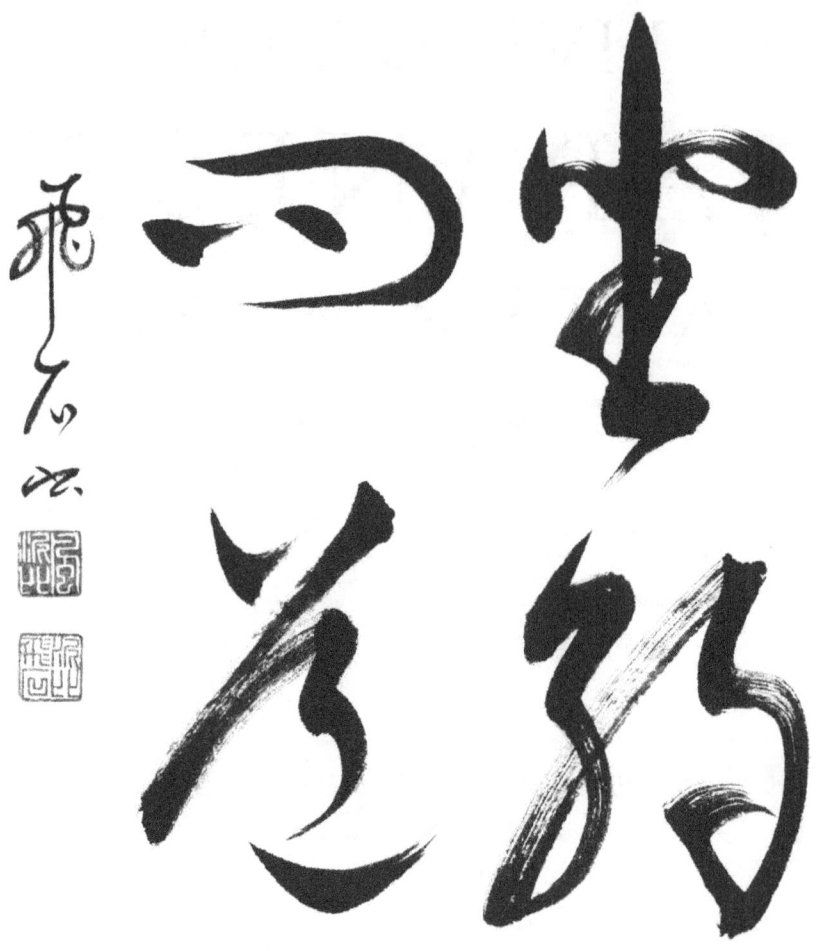

Cho ni za shite michi o toi.
"Sitting in the morning and searching for the Way."
CHIEI

From tea ceremony to flower arrangement, every Do form ultimately amounts to an inquiry
into the Way of the universe. The line is from Chiei's Sen-ji-mon. Calligraphy by H. E. Davey.

CONTENTS

FOREWORD

I have thought long and hard about how to introduce readers to this book. All Japanese artistic Ways offer numerous benefits to the Western practitioner, and they utilize a wide variety of similar principles. Picking exactly which principles and benefits to discuss in this limited space wasn't easy, especially since I wanted to communicate the essence of all Japanese arts ranging from tea ceremony to martial arts. But then I remembered a story I like to tell.

It's about how I met my martial arts teacher, Ono Yotaro. Although this book isn't about martial arts, the story hints at something that goes beyond martial activities to include the essence of every Japanese art or Way. It begins after a rather hilarious martial arts demonstration in Ono Sensei's backyard training hall (largely at my expense). He'd invited me to join him over snacks and beer left from a party thrown for carpenters refinishing his house.

Ono Sensei and the rest of us students walked to his front yard in the dim moonlight. We sat on chairs and old stone grinding wheels strewn about his yard, which overlooked northern Kyoto, the ancient capital of Japan. It was only my third evening in Japan, and I was suffering from culture shock and jet lag.

Ono Sensei took out a bamboo flute and played the loveliest, loneliest melody on it, which stuck to my homesick heart. The song represented the forlorn calls of deer in the winter, seeking each other in the snow. Then he laughed and bade us to enjoy more food and drink as he grilled me about my personal background.

Upon discovering that I had studied Japanese literature in college, he said, "Do you understand *furyu?*"

I shook my head. "It's a literary concept used by the Heian courtiers of Kyoto . . . but I could never grasp what it meant. It was a very complex term."

"Not really," Ono Sensei said. "Furyu—wind and flowing waters. The literati loved

4

life, but their lives were fleeting and often full of sorrow. Happiness can be as elusive as the wind or the waters of a river running through your hands. Furyu is what underlies our martial arts and all classical Japanese arts. It's a fleeting kind of beauty."

Ono Sensei continued. "Look, it sounds complicated, but it's really simple. The reason it's hard to explain logically is that it's a feeling, not a logical concept. Sitting here, in the dark with only candlelight, the stars and the city lights out there in the distance, talking with new and old friends, knowing that this moment will never come again . . . that is furyu. Simple as that."

Simple as that. And yet, like much of Japanese traditional culture, seeming simplicity hides a deepness and a complexity that takes decades to comprehend. In my case, after years of studying various Japanese arts, I still find myself learning anew the seemingly basic concepts and movements: how to hold a tea scoop properly, how to grasp an opponent's wrist, or how to pull a Japanese plane to shave off a hair-thin layer of wood. . . .

In this day and age, one is often asked what "good" is there in pursuing a particular pastime, as if everything in life has to be measured and quantified like a statistic. Yet even the Bible notes that there is no profit in gaining the entire world if one loses one's soul. There may be no direct worldly profit from pursuing the Do arts of Japan, but it gives us an opportunity to gain insight into our very soul.

H. E. Davey, an old friend and fellow traveler on the Way, has written a series of books pointing out the winding road that meanders up the Taoist Ways. In this book, he lays out the first steps. He is surely one of the few writers in the English language who is qualified to describe the general lay of this land. Davey Sensei has studied Japanese systems of calligraphy, yoga, healing arts, and classical martial arts for most of his life. He therefore goes beyond an academic, clinical survey of such arts, and also beyond a narrow, technique-oriented "how-to" type of book to give us the spiritual and conceptual foundations of the Do arts.

Finding such a teacher, who can verbalize such concepts, is a rarity even in Japan. This book will be of great service to people studying any of the Japanese arts, or anyone curious about what such study entails and offers the student.

Priests and warriors of old Japan once took to heart the study of these arts, placing mastery of seemingly effete and elitist disciplines like tea ceremony or flower arrangement on the same level as mastery of martial arts. So while a study of the Ways may not win you fame, fortune, or glory, it will offer you intangible benefits that those ancient people were all too cognizant of.

Tread lightly, dear reader, for such arts and their serious practitioners are rare. Finding a legitimate teacher takes some searching, but this book will be a wonderful start. If even a bit of the Way's true flavor can be tasted and passed on through you, then the dreams of our teachers will have been met: that their cherished Ways would be of service to us all, across cultures, across centuries, and across generations.

WAYNE MUROMOTO
Honolulu, Hawaii

WAYNE MUROMOTO, *a college instructor of journalism and graphic arts, grew up in the Japanese cultural arts. He graduated with a BA in Japanese literature and languages from Cornell University and holds an MFA in Fine Arts from the University of Hawaii. He publishes and edits Furyu: The Budo Journal, writes freelance, and has won several national poetry awards. He has studied traditional papermaking under Fujimori Yoichi Sensei in Japan, and he is an advanced practitioner of chado, the "Way of tea." He received comprehensive instruction at the Urasenke Foundation in Kyoto, where he lived and studied chado full-time. A longtime student and teacher of martial arts, he is a Shihan-Dai (Associate Professor) in the ancient Bitchu-den Takeuchi Ryu, which specializes in jujutsu grappling and weapons training. His permission to teach and issue rank was granted by Ono Yotaro Sensei, the Headmaster of this over-450-year-old art. Wayne Muromoto is the only American ever to receive this certification.*

6

PREFACE

Japanese arts and Ways have been growing in popularity around the world for decades. In the West, many people practice flower arrangement, bonsai, tea ceremony, shiatsu, and martial arts. Despite their wide popularity, however, Japanese arts (geido) are often misunderstood and distorted in the West. There is consequently a real need for literature that goes beyond the typical examination of the history and outward techniques of a single art form and that also exposes the lesser-known arts. What is most needed are comprehensive guides to what these arts are, where they came from, and how Westerners can successfully engage in them. Such guides are unfortunately rare. Writings that explore the more esoteric but immensely important aspects of these arts are rarer still. What are the underlying aesthetics of the Japanese arts? Some arts are touted as effective forms of "moving meditation," but how exactly do they function in this manner? What about the oft-mentioned but usually unexplained "spiritual dimensions" in the Japanese arts?

These esoteric aspects not only are inseparable from the technical and physical parts of practice, but they are also the elements of these arts that are most universal and applicable to the daily lives of non-Japanese practitioners. The lack of information about these universal principles masks the fact that, at their deepest levels, such arts as tea ceremony (chado), flower arrangement (kado), calligraphy (shodo), and martial arts (budo) are closely related. This book is intended to reveal, among others, this important aspect of these disciplines and to fill an important gap in the relevant literature.

Harmony of Mind and Body

Despite outward differences, Japanese arts share certain aesthetics; and more important, they demand the acquisition of related positive character traits for their successful

7

performance. Notice that many of the names for these arts end in the Japanese word Do. Do means "the Way," and its use in these names indicates that an activity has surpassed its utilitarian purpose and been raised to the level of art, that its students are practicing it as a Way of life. In sum, a Do is an art that allows us to understand the ultimate nature of the whole of life by closely examining ourselves through a singular activity of life: to arrive at the universal through studying the particular.

Many artistic principles and mental states are universal to all Japanese Ways. One of the most meaningful and fundamental is the concept of mind and body coordination. Although few of us are required to use a calligraphy brush, Japanese sword, or tea ceremony utensils in daily life, learning how to use them skillfully can enhance our mental and physical health. Moreover, skill in these arts comes from integrating the mind and body. The important relationship between the mind and body and how to achieve mind-body harmony is also a principal theme of this book.

In Japanese calligraphy, teachers speak of a "unity of mind and brush" and declare that "if the mind is correct, the brush is correct." In Japanese swordsmanship (kenjutsu), it's usual to speak of a unity of mind, body, and sword. Mind and body coordination can be thought of as self-harmony. This integration is necessarily one of the mind and body in action, a central element for mastering any classical Japanese Way. But even if we aren't practicing a Japanese art or Way, we can all benefit from the principles of mind and body unification underlying the various Do.

It is absolutely true that practicing one of the Ways can lead to an understanding of the art of living life itself. Yet the teacher or book that can effectively demonstrate how the study of calligraphy or floral art can lead to spiritual understanding is rare; most simply pay lip service to showing the Way but fail to really offer clear explanations and effective techniques. It is commonly assumed that just throwing an opponent or manipulating a brush will somehow magically produce insight. Mere action will not lead to insight.

What to Expect from This Book

In fact, it's the manner in which we approach the Ways that determines what we learn from them. I've spent the majority of my life studying various Japanese arts, and

8

speaking as someone who was once an excruciatingly shy, overweight, uncoordinated, and severely asthmatic child, I can confirm they offer a tremendous potential for self-transformation. The deliberate, conscious practice of Japanese Do forms *can* result in the cultivation of the mind and body. But they provide that potential; they don't guarantee it.

In order to fruitfully approach the tea ceremony, Japanese dance, or other arts as meditative acts, it's important to see exactly how they can lead to understanding. Many people arrange flowers, make tea, or practice the martial arts without any sudden insights into the nature of living taking place. I have attempted in this book to show principles and practices that will allow readers to directly experience these arts as meditation.

It's also important to keep in mind that cultural props like traditional dress and bowing are not inherently spiritual. Simply wearing a kimono or bowing does not express a meditative nature; it is the manner in which you bow, for example, and the invisible spirit of your practice that makes a Do a Way. This spirit and its importance is another topic addressed in this book.

Although all who write about the Japanese arts and Ways are themselves students of their disciplines, it's important to share the knowledge and insights one has gained for the benefit of others, and that has also motivated me to write this book. At the same time, while I want to share with readers my experiences and thoughts concerning the Ways, it would be a mistake if others view me as a spiritual authority or expert. I am not interested in an exalted status or celebrity.

To look to another for the truth is to bypass the Way of the universe that's right before our eyes. It is trying to see through the eyes of another and thus fated to result in delusion: the follower thinks she or he has seen the truth—whereas it is at best only a reflection of it—and the leader figures he or she must be doing something right because of the worshipful demeanor of the followers. The connection between such leaders and followers is, unfortunately, shared delusion. Still, many opt for following others, because looking for the truth invariably involves a leap into the unknown. And it's a leap we each must make by ourselves.

All of my books deal with meditation and spirituality in a Japanese context. Nevertheless, in these books I've tried to avoid telling readers *what to do*. Instead, I hope to offer readers a means to discover for themselves *how to do it*. It's not my place, or anyone else's for that matter, to tell you how to live, and although I write about spiritual and meditative arts, I'm not qualified to be anyone's "spiritual master." I doubt if anyone is so qualified. My aim in writing this book is simply to share meaningful techniques of mind and body coordination with others. I've learned a great deal in writing this work, and I hope my readers, too, will find the book a catalyst for their own growth.

Since many Japanese Ways involve physical activity to some extent, it's possible to sustain injury if you practice incorrectly or if you have a preexisting medical condition. It is important, therefore, to consult a medical professional before embarking on training of a physical nature. Practicing under the supervision of a qualified teacher is also advisable. As always, you are responsible for your own physical and psychological well-being.

How This Book Is Organized

To make this book easy to understand, I've arranged it logically. I start with the Chinese concept of *Tao* and explore how it became the Japanese Way; how, in other words, Japanese culture has interpreted the Chinese Tao. I also make a point of outlining exactly how the Ways of Japan function to lead us from the particular to the universal, and I discuss the nature of the Japanese Ways today.

In subsequent sections, I cover aesthetic principles found in the Japanese arts and give detailed information about their spiritual counterparts—ideas such as ki ("life energy"), *hara* ("abdominal centering"), *fudoshin* ("immovable mind"), and others. From this, you will discover how these artistic ideals and spiritual principles connect all of the Japanese art forms together. Whether you're interested in karate, tea ceremony, or flower arrangement, you'll find informative material that makes the study of these arts easier and illustrates how they're linked by a common set of little-understood principles. Better yet, you'll receive knowledge about these concepts that you might be able to positively incorporate into daily life.

To illustrate these aesthetic and spiritual principles, I take examples from a wide variety of Japanese arts and Ways, such as tea ceremony, flower arrangement, calligraphy, and others. They are merely representative examples, however. If I mention how a particular concept relates to the martial arts, for instance, the idea is rarely limited to that

The glossary-style sidebars throughout this book present brief descriptions and definitions of Japanese Arts & Ways and words. The following icons are used at the ends of these to indicate what area of endeavor each belongs to:

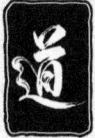 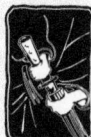 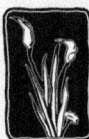 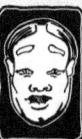 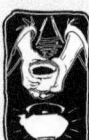

| Ideals of the Way | Martial Ways | Artistic Ways | Performing Arts | Traditional Crafts |

specific example and finds expression in other art forms as well. And though I may discuss how the substance of the Way expresses itself in the martial arts, that doesn't make this a martial arts book; the same can be said for examples taken from dance, Japanese gardening, and other classical arts.

Toward the end of the book, I discuss what to expect if you undertake the study of a classical Do. The number of people practicing flower arrangement, tea ceremony, ink painting, martial arts, and similar endeavors outside of Japan is vast. Unfortunately, so is the dropout rate. I could have included this section based simply on the great number of people who are studying, have studied, or are thinking about studying one of the Do. But when considering the relatively large turnover of Western students, I felt addressing how to study a Way and combat "culture shock" was something I needed to do here. These aspects have rarely been properly discussed in other books. I also include valuable information about what a traditional teacher will expect from you and how to successfully negotiate the hurdles faced by many newcomers to the Japanese Ways. An appendix includes important information about finding such a teacher.

Throughout the text are sidebars containing summaries of many of the traditional Japanese crafts, arts, and Ways mentioned in this volume or that you may run across in your further studies; these have been placed in alphabetical order, glossary-style, so that you can find them easily.

I occasionally cite Japanese poems and sayings for illustrative purposes. All translations are mine, some more literal than others.

Beauty is in the eye of the beholder and so is how we define Japanese aesthetics.

There isn't a universally agreed upon standard in Japan, and not everyone will concur with my explanations. Remember that this book's orientation is on the spiritual and meditative aspects of these concepts, which has influenced my interpretation of them.

You might enjoy my other books under the Michi: Japanese Arts & Ways imprint. *Brush Meditation: A Japanese Way to Mind & Body Harmony, The Japanese Way of the Flower: Ikebana as Moving Meditation,* and *Japanese Yoga: The Way of Dynamic Meditation* all discuss the nature of the Do—the Way of the universe. It's a Way I've been following since childhood. And although I miss the Way as often as I hit it, my writings aim at encouraging others to look directly at the actual nature of existence and see the Way that underlies all creation. I hope we can discover it together.

Acknowledgments

Although writing is ultimately a solitary activity, this book would not have been realized without the help of a number of people.

Peter Goodman, my publisher, editor, and friend, suggested this project to me not long after we first met. He seemed to think the book would be something I could write with authority. I appreciate his confidence in me, his friendship, and his support of my writing. The staff of Stone Bridge Press has also been a big help to me.

Ann Kameoka, my wife, has always supported not only my book projects but me as well. I'm very fortunate, and I'll always be grateful.

My late mother, Elaine, and my late father, Victor, both backed my lifelong involvement in the Japanese Ways. My dad, in fact, provided me with my first introduction to a traditional Japanese art. Our debt to our parents can never be repaid.

I'm also grateful to my friends Dave Lowry and Wayne Muromoto. Dave has written numerous books and articles about Japanese culture and martial arts. Several of his books gave me information that was useful in writing this work. Wayne publishes *Furyu* magazine and has written for the *Hawaii Herald,* a Japanese-American newspaper. I'm fortunate to have such knowledgeable friends who have given me fine feedback on my ideas and endured my long-distance phone monologues for years.

My students Terri Brown and Sean Souders posed for this book's illustrations. I appreciate their time and help. Sean started studying Japanese yoga and martial arts at my dojo when he was just four years old. He is now one of my best adult students.

Steve Aibel, another of my students, is an excellent artist. I'm grateful for his fine illustrations.13

Finally, I couldn't have written this book without studying a variety of Japanese arts and Ways. In Shin-shin-toitsu-do (a system of Japanese yoga), budo, shodo, and other arts, I've had many outstanding teachers—too many to name in this limited space.

This book is dedicated to my *sempai* and *sensei* (seniors and teachers), both in the United States and Japan.

H. E. DAVEY
Green Valley, California

THE 45 PATHS TO
MEDITATION & BEAUTY

Attributes of the Way

Harmony
Asymmetrical Balance
Artlessness
Impermanence
Unity with the Universe

See p. 74.

The Essence of the Japanese Arts & Ways

Spiritual Aesthetics in the Japanese Arts & Ways

Mind & Body Unification in the Japanese Arts & Ways

Traditions & Personal Relationships in the Japanese Arts & Ways

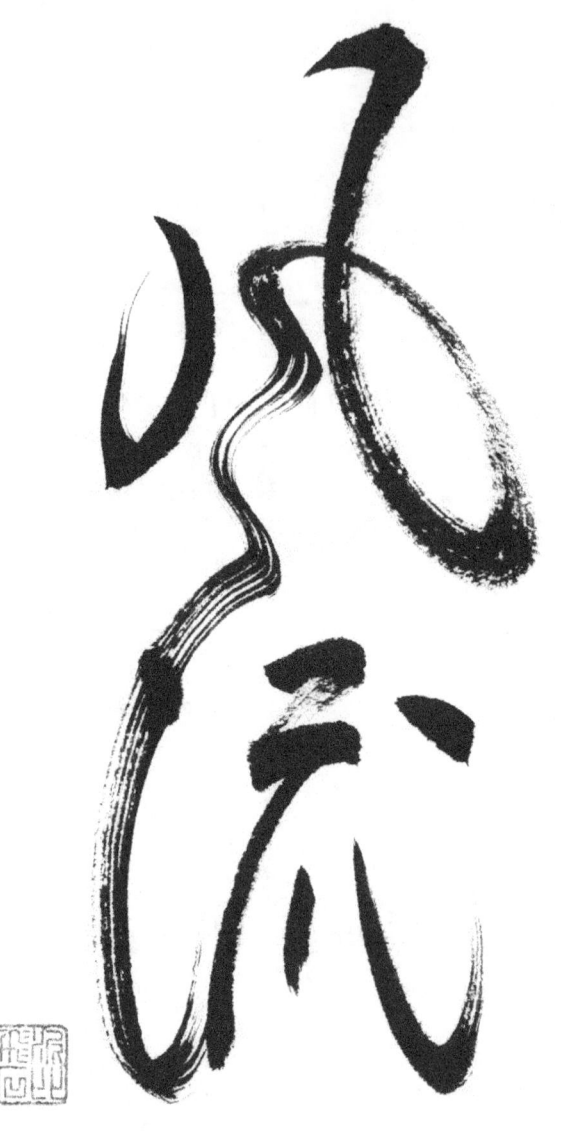

FURYU: *Furyu is composed of two characters: "wind" and "flowing." A renmentai shosho, or "connected cursive," script was used in this artwork to suggest flowing action. Like the moving wind, furyu can be sensed but not seen. It is both tangible and intangible in its suggested elegance. And like the wind, furyu points to a wordless ephemeral beauty that can only be experienced in the now, for in the next instant it will dissolve like the morning mist.*

Chapter *1*

THE WAY

Japan's long history of importing, synthesizing, and recreating aspects of other cultures continues to this day. The primary source of such cultural borrowing in Japan's early history was China, whose civilization existed for centuries at a high level hardly seen in other parts of Asia. Chinese religions and spirituality had an immense impact on Japanese society and the Ways of Japan. Chinese religious development is marked by diversity and was heavily influenced by native as well as Indian beliefs. This diversity can be found in the multiform tradition known in the West as Taoism.

The Chinese Tao

> Something mysteriously formed,
> Born before heaven and earth,
> In the silence and the void,
> Standing alone and unchanging,
> Ever present and in motion.
> Perhaps it is the mother of ten thousand things.
> I do not know its name.
> Call it Tao.
> TAO TE CHING [1]

Taoism is based on the concept of the Tao. Most basically, Tao means "road" or "path"; in a spiritual context, it refers to "the Way." Taoism was (and is) grasped and

Aikido

The Way of union with the life energy (ki) of the universe, a modern martial Way founded by Ueshiba Morihei Sensei and derived from Daito Ryu aiki-jujutsu and other influences.

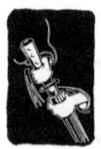

practiced in many forms, each reflecting the historical, societal, or individual circumstances of its disciples. This variety can be confusing, but some claim it explains the resiliency of Taoism. Its versatility has allowed it to evolve in accordance with the particular character of its followers.

Confucianism was the primary moral and ethical tradition in China. And, whereas Taoism has a relationship to Confucianism, it has avoided being absorbed by this major tradition, with which it has coexisted for generations. Taoism's persistence is remarkable in that Confucian traditions served as the moral and sacred bedrock of Chinese institutions, etiquette, and rites. Throughout Chinese history, people have tended to embrace both teachings, sometimes at different stages in life or according to individual disposition and preference. The phenomenon is not unlike the widespread embrace of both Shintoism and Buddhism in Japan. This long-standing phenomenon in China and Japan probably says as much about the Asian mindset as it does about Asian spirituality.

It is said that Taoist philosophy was established by Lao-tzu (literally "Old Master"), who is believed to have lived during the fifth century B.C. He is believed to be the compiler of the Tao Te Ching, or the Classic of the Way and Its Power. The sage Chuang-tzu, who lived in the third century B.C., contributed greatly to the evolution of Taoism through his philosophical tract known as The Chuang-tzu. The teachings of both men represent a reinterpretation and elaboration of an already rich Chinese heritage of beliefs based on veneration of nature and divination.

Both men lived during a period of cultural discord and religious unbelief. They advanced an idea of the Tao as being simultaneously the origin of all creation and the life power behind all action in nature. Both the Way and its power are beyond the limits of intellectual comprehension, but they can nevertheless be observed in the endless manifestations of nature. Within these natural manifestations and the Tao itself, Lao-tzu and Chuang-tzu saw evidence of a spiritual approach to being.

Further, owing to the social upheaval of the time, early Taoists envisioned Taoism as a means to establish a united and permanent secular order. The order in nature and the Tao was seen to be more reliable and timeless than the state and other societal fixtures and their underlying concepts created by humans. Thus, life could best be lived in agreement with the Tao, which, in essence, is a Way of living that is natural, simple, and free from all conditioning. The first Taoists taught that living prosperously was synonymous with harmonizing with the natural Way of the universe. This approach of noninterference and harmony was termed wuwei, "nonaction," or action that doesn't conflict with nature. In Japanese, this is called mui. It will be explored over the course of this book.

Confucian teachers were often seen in China as insightful, scholarly, and models of high moral character. Taoist *hsien*, or advanced mystics, were insightful in a related but radically different manner. (These advanced mystics were called *sen* or *sennin* in Japan; *sen* is the Japanese pronunciation of Chinese *hsien*.) Chuang-tzu wrote of savants who were, for example, craftsmen and woodworkers. Although humble in status, these artisans captured not merely the enigma of artistry but also the art of living. The Taoists viewed the artists' understanding of the essence of artistry and living well as arising from a concentrated mind, a mind existing in the moment, one that has transcended attachment to relative states and objectives such as wealth, fame, and power. The sages described in the *Tao Te Ching* and the *Chuang-tzu* embraced an art and a Way of life that accorded with the cycles of creation and destruction that pervade the absolute universe instead of merely following the transitory and relative values of society.

Although Chuang-tzu wrote of men who embraced the Tao

Aiki-jujutsu

"Jujutsu based on aiki." A martial art that's ultimately derived from the oshikiuchi combat techniques of the Aizu clan and popularized by Takeda Sokaku Sensei, disseminator of Daito Ryu aiki-jujutsu.

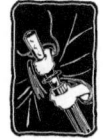

but remained in society, living with wives and children, it was common throughout Chinese antiquity for people tired of civilization and its trappings to withdraw from their social milieu and retreat to rural settings and join with the artless elegance of nature. Such seekers might create poetry about the cosmos or paint naturalistic scenes of splendor; Taoist breathing exercises and forms of meditation were practiced too—all were used to secure the life energy (*chi* in Chinese, *ki* in Japanese) that is inseparable from nature itself.

These sennin, variously described as "Taoist immortals," "sages," and "mystics," figure prominently in the Taoist universe, more so than is sometimes recognized. The Chinese character for sen is composed of a component representing "person" and one representing "mountain," indicating the Taoist inclination to retreat to the mountains in search of enlightenment.

> Religious Taoism stressed the idea of eremitism, which is implicit in the character for immortal, combining the characters for mountain and man. The rejection of the world of strife to live as a hermit is one aspect of the search for an ideal life of quietude. The quest for immortality and the pursuit of eremitism provided the abiding appeal of Taoism over the centuries.[2]

Mountains, owing perhaps to their lofty and awe-inspiring nature, occupy an important place also in the native Japanese Shinto religion. The sennin can be seen as equal parts man and myth, both aspects of which will be explored shortly.

Within China, a distinction between what might be called "original Taoism" and "popular Taoism" has never been clear. For our purposes, however, such a distinction is useful. Popular Taoism had (and has) a tendency to stress magic, fortune-telling, and related activities. Original (or perhaps "philosophical") Taoism, as explained in the Tao Te Ching, stresses universal harmony and natural action rather than magical rites for personal or material gain. Its concern is thus the human rather than the mystical component of the sennin. Popular Taoism, furthermore, gradually evolved a group of eight sennin, known in English as "the Eight Immortals," who were modeled after the Eighteen Arhats found in Buddhism. These eight sennin were advanced Taoist adepts who were believed to have attained immortality. This later claim of immortality was perhaps an attempt to successfully compete with the advancing influence of Indian Buddhism in China. In ancient Japan, some of the populace also embraced the lore of the Eight Immortals.

Taoist themes and art can be partly attributed to inspiring the Chinese love of nature and the tendency to abandon society in an attempt to gain enlightenment. They also encouraged a confirmation of life and health in the form of pursuits of vitality, long life, and even exemption from death. Lao-tzu reexamined and recast in a natural light the age-old deification of nature and the secret arts. Nevertheless, esoteric rites seeped back into Taoism as a desire to strengthen health and prolong life. Taoist alchemists searched for herbs and chemical compounds that could guarantee imperishability. Taoists sought the legendary mountain-dwelling sennin, who were regarded as either enlightened practitioners or actual immortals. In their pursuit of well-being and vigor, they explored herbal potions, developed principles of cooking and nutrition, and developed methods of exercise, healing, massage, breathing, and meditation to keep the mind and body youthful.

Said to be able to cure sickness, see into people's souls, and read the future, the sennin were viewed as mavericks, with their own set of values and way of life; yet, the stern moralistic retaliation of the Taoist gods actually fortified the conventional social mores. Thus, although Taoism was an alternative to Confucian-

Bonsai

Japanese dwarf trees, which vary from a few inches to several feet in height. Different approaches to cultivation exist, but they share common Japanese aesthetic qualities. Among these are simplicity, naturalness, harmony, and artlessness.

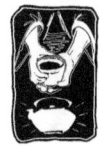

Budo

*Martial ways; combat
forms of personal
growth derived from
koryu bujutsu. See
also koryu bujutsu.*

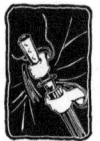

ism, it rarely endangered the established social structure. Some scholars suggest it was an important safety valve in the Chinese social order and a conduit for alternative ideas. Yet to an individual who clearly sees the actual nature of the Way—a nature that is primordial, universal, uncreated, and unconditioned by mere thoughts and beyond relative cultural values—the genuine Tao is much more than a social safety valve or system of magic whose end is the delusional elixir of immortality.

Considering ancient Japan's heavy borrowing from China's advanced culture—the Chinese system of writing and Buddhism are two prime examples—it was probably inevitable that Taoism and Taoist esoteric practices would be imported to Japan.

Tao into Do: Japanese Interpretation of the Way

Like many aspects of Chinese culture, Taoist shamans and concepts were eventually brought to old Japan. Taoist teachings, referred to in Japanese as Dokyo (do, meaning Tao, and kyo, "teachings") gradually influenced Japanese society and arts. Direct influence took place through interaction with Taoist adepts, while more indirect influences occurred via Chinese arts and practices shaped by Taoist principles, and through the wide introduction of Chinese Zen Buddhism, which also bore a Taoist influence.

> Do, of course, is the Japanese pronunciation of Tao, the metaphysical force of the ancient Chinese religion of Taoism, as much a ritual of alchemy as it was a philosophy that encouraged "going with the flow" of nature. Fused with Confucian concepts of etiquette, respect, and a devotion to tradition and learning, the seeds of the Tao were germinated in Japan, where they emerged not so much as

a distinct religion but as ideals applied to the performance of native arts and crafts, evolving them into something much more.

The list of the Do forms in Japan is considerable. Occidentals are familiar with some that have been transplanted, more or less successfully, like judo and kado, or as it is better known, ikebana (flower arranging). But many others are virtually unheard of. There is kodo, for instance, the Way of incense appreciation, and togeido, the Way of pottery. Some are even more esoteric, such as shiseido, the Way of femininity.[3]

After Taoism was transplanted to Japan it quickly became "Japanized." The sennin lore of popular Taoism spread and was transformed in its new, fertile ground.

Gama was one of the mythical sennin embraced in certain sectors of Japanese society. He is usually depicted in Japanese art with a white, three-legged toad, whose form he could assume. Gama was also associated with Tekkai, who, like Gama, was said to be immortal. He was believed to be able to leave his body, an ability that on one unfortunate occasion had disastrous results: while his spirit was wandering about, his followers discovered his deathly body and burned it; Tekkai was then forced to occupy the body of a diseased beggar (perhaps a warning against unnatural practices!). Carrying an iron crutch, he was believed to help with the transmigration of souls.

Chokaro, another sennin, refused to serve the government in times of corruption. He is shown in art with a white mule that could carry him thousands of miles. Even better, Chokaro could fold his mule up like paper when it was no longer needed. Another sennin, Kinko, was a musician who rode on the back of a giant carp. One of the native Japanese sennin, Kume, could fly. These

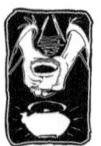

and other mythical Taoist adepts are depicted in many Japanese art forms, from painting to sculpture.

In China the label sennin (hsien) was applied not only to mythical personages but also to advanced Taoists. This distinc-tion hasn't always been clear in Japan; nonetheless there have been in the past and still are today those who practice Taoist-oriented forms of spiritual cultivation. As Michio Kushi writes:

> Among these people, those principles led to the develop-ment of cosmically universal consciousness, along with health and longevity, and they were often called Sen-Nin, or "free men." There is much evidence including records, documents, and legendary stories about their unusual abilities.
>
> In the present there are still some people who train in this ancient macrobiotic way, Shin-Sen-Do, especially in the oriental countries—Japan, China, India, and oth-ers. Their existence, and these practices, are not widely known among modern civilized societies.[4]

Kushi, an ardent proponent of macrobiotics, refers to the Sen Do Ren, a group in Tokyo that studies Dokyo-based mind and body exercises known as Shin-Sen-Do (Shin: "gods" or "divine beings"; Sen, from sennin; and Do:"Way,"). Sen-do, Sen-jutsu, and Sennin-do are other designations used in arcane circles in contemporary Japan to indicate spiritual disciplines that trace their origins to esoteric Taoism. Associated healing arts are some-times nonspecifically termed Sennin Ryoji, and though particular versions of these disciplines are fairly close to Chinese Taoist prac-tices, many have widely diverged from their origins.

E. J. Harrison, a writer who lived in Japan in the early 1900s, detailed his impressions of Taoist influences in early twentieth-century Japan:

. . . closer inquiry reveals the presence in society of a type of occult operator called by the Japanese Sennin—a word which I am inclined to render as "yogi" or "adept." While some of these yogi are known to pass their lives in the forests, or mountains, cut off as far as possible from communion with their kind, there are others who, although they have attained a high degree of occult development by persistent introspection, are yet content to pass the rest of their lives in the busy haunts of men and even pursuance of normal avocations.[5]

Many modern Japanese, however, know little of Dokyo and even less of Sennin-do (which is even misconstrued to relate to "1,000 people," based on the word for "thousand," sen, which, although pronounced the same, is represented with a different Chinese character). For this and other reasons, not all Taoist-inspired Ways in Japan directly acknowledge this debt in their names, histories, and literature. This is the case with, for example, the Shin-shin-toitsu-do system of Japanese yoga, which I practice and from which the mind-body exercises that will appear shortly are derived.

On the other hand, it is a mistake to think that every art whose name includes the designation Do has a deep or specifically Taoist origin. The Japanese Do has long since come to be used in a generic manner, and though it does have origins in the Chinese Tao and carries a similar meaning, in many Japanese arts, that is the extent of the connection. In any case, it's my belief that the Taoist connection is not always fully explored or acknowledged in writings about the Ways of Japan.

And what of Confucianism? Certainly along with Buddhism and a writing system, Confucianism was a cultural artifact the Japanese imported from China in a big way.

Bunraku

Bunraku, with Noh and Kabuki, is one of the three forms of traditional Japanese theater. It makes use of captivating puppets, each of which is animated by three black-clad puppeteers. The classical Bunraku repertoire often includes retellings of historical events as well as tragic love stories. A Bunraku troupe of puppeteers follows many traditional Japanese practices of the Way, such as strict training, observance of respect, and hierarchy, and lifelong devotion to seamless execution of technique.

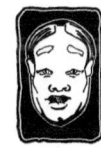

The Confucian Influence on the Japanese Ways

The impact of Confucianism—which continues to this day—on Japanese social mores, etiquette, government, and nearly all aspects of Japanese society was profound.

Historically, although the emperor usually reigned, he didn't always rule. For a significant portion of Japanese history, the shogun (military leader) and the bakufu (military government) held feudal Japan in an iron grip. Starting in 1603, after years of internal warfare, the bakufu of shogun Tokugawa Ieyasu ushered the country into a more peaceful era. The Edo period (1603–1867) was dominated by the autocratic Tokugawa family, whose bakufu made use of imported Confucian doctrines to provide ethical legitimacy to its administration. These doctrines still influence Japanese social strata, including the different Do. Confucianism, in its deep concern with societal behavior, has also affected the reigi, or formal etiquette, associated with a number of the Ways. (I discuss this in detail in chapter 4.)

The Tokugawas selected concepts from the conservative Chu Hsi style of Confucianism, ideas dealing with social decorum and filial piety, typically emphasized in Confucianism but also serving to bolster the Tokugawa view of a social order that ensured allegiance to the bakufu. Eventually, however, resentment of the Tokugawa brand of Confucianism (and the Tokugawa family itself) arose in several segments of society.

Bakufu administrators created a list of Confucian principles that were officially ratified by the government. These precepts were drawn from the teachings of Chu Hsi (1130–1200). His philosophy is known as Shu-shi or Tei-shu in Japanese. Its emphasis on loyalty to parents, social alliances, and duty to one's ruler made it an ideal means of promoting social cohesion and fidelity to the Tokugawa bakufu. In addition, however, the Neo-Confucianism of

Chu Hsi stressed investigating the universal by means of the particular, which is a central idea in all the Ways.

As dissatisfaction with the bakufu and its variety of Confucianism expanded in Japan, another form grew to rival Chu Hsi's doctrines. This new type was termed Oyomei in Japan and was based on the system of Wang Yang-ming (1472–1529). In opposition to the intellectual orientation of Chu Hsi, Oyomei stressed intuition and personal development. More important in relation to the evolution of the Do forms, Oyomei emphasized control of the mind through a process of systematic bodily disciplines such as what we now associate with the Ways. Wang advocated that virtue would result from such disciplines and felt that disciplined activity would give rise to a unity of thought and action, mind and body, an ideal that still lies at the very heart of the Japanese Do forms. He urged that action, more than words, was the way to self-perfection. Oyomei exhibits a simple and direct spirituality that has some similarities to Zen, but, unlike Zen, has seldom been credited in the West for its large role in shaping the Japanese arts and Ways.

Unfortunately for the Tokugawa bakufu, Oyomei also stressed individual worth over hereditary position. In any case, Oyomei Confucianism, closer to Taoism than orthodox Confucianism, clearly influenced the Do forms and had a historical impact on them as large as or larger than mainline Confucianism.

The Ways evolved and were influenced by both Confucianism and Taoism. But the Japanese seem to have been less inclined to think in metaphysical terms than the ancient Chinese, and their interpretation of the Do tends to be pragmatic and more concerned with social relationships. They were, in other words, as influenced by the Confucian Tao as they were by the Taoist Tao. Japan's societal conditions, feudal ruling class, and two influential religions—Shinto and Zen Buddhism—nonetheless modified both ideas.

Butoh

A present-day avant-garde Japanese dance form, initially performed in 1959. It blends dance, theater, improvisation, and Japanese established performing arts with German Expressionist dance and performance art.

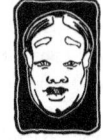

Shinto and Zen Influences on the Japanese Ways

Chado

The Way of tea; also known as sado. The archetype of drinking powdered tea was brought to Japan from China in the twelfth century; chado was developed by Sen Rikyu in the sixteenth century. The tea used in chado comes from green tea leaves that are steamed, dried, and ground into a powder using a tea mill. Greatly influenced by Zen, chado emphasizes ideals of harmony, respect, purity, and tranquility. A central teaching is ichi-go, ichi-e, "one encounter, one opportunity," which expresses the idea that a gathering for tea is a unique event that can never be repeated and so one should value every moment of it.

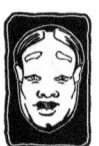

Zen and Shintoism have for centuries had a great impact on the entire Japanese cultural matrix, and both have likewise influenced the Ways. Shinto, which refers to the indigenous Japanese religion, means roughly "the Way of the gods." The term is thought perhaps to have originated in China, and indeed it can be found in ancient Taoist and Confucian writings. With no originator or original scriptures, Shinto centers on a reverence for all aspects of nature, including one's ancestors. Central to this concept is the idea that all parts of creation, animate and inanimate, have their own kami, perhaps best translated as "divine beings." The kami are believed to have protective capacities, and seeking their favor is a major part of the many Shinto festivals.

From Shinto, the Ways drew their traditional emphasis on purity and different purification practices (*misogi*). Purity is, in fact, one of the four maxims of the tea ceremony: harmony (*wa*), respect (*kei*), purity (*sei*), and peaceful solitude (*jaku*). Related to purity is the Shinto accent on cleanliness. Whether you visit a martial arts dojo or a school of calligraphy in Japan, it's common to see students engaged in *soji*, ritualistic cleaning of the training hall or practice room. Shintoism's focus on a reverence for nature has also formed an influence in the naturalistic emphasis of the Ways—in the form of practice, the style of the physical practice itself, and the aesthetics of the Do. *Sabi* ("rusticity") and *wabi* ("simplicity"), two fundamental elements in the aesthetics of the Ways, although also inspired by Zen, have profound Shinto overtones. These two elements are associated particularly with the tea ceremony, which, again, clearly shows influences from Zen.

The Zen Buddhist sect originated in India in the sixth century. Its originator is generally considered to be the monk Bodhidharma (Daruma in Japanese). Shortly after establishing Zen, in

about A.D. 520, he left for China, where, according to oral tradition, Daruma sat facing a wall for nine years until he attained
enlightenment.

The word "Zen" is the Japanese equivalent of Chinese
"Ch'an," which in turn comes from the Sanskrit Dhyana. The
monks Eisai (1141–1215) and Dogen (1200–53) introduced
Zen into Japan from China. Japan's martial ruling class promptly
adopted it along with Shingon Buddhism, and with its message of
deliverance through meditation, it rapidly made inroads into most
aspects of Japanese existence. Zen's accent on being unobstructed
by intellectual questioning and realization of oneness with the universe affected all of Japanese culture, and many aesthetic qualities
have a historical relationship to Zen. Owing to its sweeping historical influence in Japan, Zen has touched most Japanese arts—
the tea ceremony, flower arrangement, and brush writing are a few
examples. Chado, or the Way of tea, one of the most important
Ways, has in particular had a long relationship with Zen and a
major impact on the other Ways.

Zen, in its link of meditation to daily activities, has made a
deep impression on the Japanese Do; indeed, the Ways have been
described as "plastic Zen." Zen stresses the avoidance of self-
deception, and the Ways have long served as a "reality check."
It's possible to imagine that we've achieved complete imperturbability while sitting alone in meditation; yet, if this same Zen
state cannot be demonstrated in Ways such as shodo or budo,
real imperturbability has not been attained. If a student of shodo
cannot remain detached, even when his or her ink-laden brush is
about to cause a character to bleed, or if a kendo practitioner can't
remain calm in the face of a rapidly approaching bamboo sword, a
Zen-like imperturbability has not been genuinely realized. In Zen
is the idea that no matter how skillful our physical technique in
tea ceremony or the martial arts may appear, if the mind is not

at peace, the technique isn't representative of the Way. It is this Zen-related emphasis that allows the Ways to go beyond a particular activity and become arts that are capable of transforming all aspects of a person's life.

Although Zen is often mistakenly viewed in the West as the only body of spiritual teachings to significantly influence the Ways, a view that overlooks other important influences (like Esoteric Buddhism and Shingon Buddhism), it has indeed had a very deep and lasting impact. Perhaps the best source for a detailed discussion of Zen's relationship to the Do is the classic *Zen and the Ways*, by Trevor Leggett (see the notes and references at the end of this book). It covers the topic in far greater detail than is possible here and is recommended for interested readers.

Many Paths, a Single Way

Zen, Shinto, Confucianism, and Taoism all aided in the transformation of everyday Japanese arts and activities into viable spiritual paths. Nonetheless, an intellectual study of these religions will not result in an understanding of the Japanese Do forms; only actual participation will succeed. And when you deeply grasp one, you grasp them all.

To illustrate, when I began to study Japanese calligraphy and ink painting, I had already been involved in different Do since childhood. According to my teacher, Kobara Ranseki Sensei, I made unusually rapid progress. He regularly joked with me and the other students that I was a *meijin* ("genius"), but he once told me he really was baffled by my advancement. Eventually, when we were in Japan to show our work at the International Japanese Calligraphy Exhibition, I explained my background in other Do. I didn't want Sensei or my fellow students to believe that I thought

I was "special" because I was a teacher of several Do. Only at this point, after a few years of studying shodo, did I feel comfortable explaining my previous training to him.

Kobara Sensei, acknowledged in Japan as one of the preeminent traditional calligraphers outside of Asia, nodded in recognition. Now, as he explained, he understood "my secret." As Kobara Sensei understood, and this is widely echoed in the Ways, if you genuinely grasp the essence of even one Do through firsthand experience, you have access to the sum and substance of all of them. This of course does not mean that a calligrapher will know the techniques of judo, for example, but it does mean that, on a very elemental plane, he or she will perceive the principles, aesthetics, and mental states common to all the Ways.

On another occasion, I heard my friend Shimbara Koyo Sensei, a high-ranking judo exponent, talking to a local student of Zen.

"What were you guys talkin' about?"

"Oh, we were just discussing the essence of Zen."

"I didn't know you were even interested in Zen."

"Well, I haven't read anything about its history, if that's what you mean . . . but I've practiced judo most of my life. We just figured out that we have a lot in common."

And what students of the Ways have in common is the Do itself, which isn't merely a particular way of doing a specific thing, but is actually the Way of the universe.

Do

The Way, a spiritual path (or michi), originally derived from the Chinese concept of the Tao. The names of many Japanese arts end in this designation, indicating their ultimate objective.

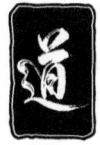

From the Particular to the Universal

Since all Japanese arts share the same aesthetics, the study of one Do can heighten the understanding of others. The same feeling of balance needed for skillfully "sculpting" a flower arrangement is needed in Japanese brush writing, in which every character exhib-

Do Chu no Sei

*Do is "movement,"
while sei compares
to "calmness." Do
chu no sei describes
"stillness in motion,"
or calmness in the
midst (chu) of action.
When Do forms, such
as the martial arts
or tea ceremony, are
portrayed as forms of
"moving meditation,"
it is this quality that is
being expressed. Many
Ways involve activity,
often in relationship to
others. They are usu-
ally performed with
the eyes open, and as a
result, when practiced
as dynamic medita-
tion, they relate closely
to life. They can also
help us translate seated
meditation into
activity.*

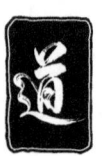

its a dynamic balance. In *odori*, or Japanese classical dance, and the martial arts, participants likewise master a dynamic balance that is analogous to the balance aimed at in Japanese calligraphy.

The identical unity with nature stressed in flower arrange-ment is also accentuated in martial ways like aikido and *aiki-jujut-su*, while shodo demands an intense attention to detail and brush form that is not incompatible with the methodical exactitude culti-vated by disciples of ikebana. *Cha-no-yu*, or the "tea ceremony," is based on wa-kei-sei-jaku ("harmony-respect-purity- solitude"), and both Japanese calligraphy and flower arrangement seek to manifest related capabilities. Wabi and sabi are specific expressions of the philosophical foundation of the tea ceremony, and they are also artistic, even spiritual, attributes universal to all the Japanese arts.

In short, a thorough study of a particular Way allows us to assimilate these qualities and apply them to the practice of unlike art forms. The opposite is also true: many Western students of miscellaneous Japanese cultural arts commonly miss out on the consequence of these ideas, and in the end practice a pale imitation of the authentic art that they are studying.

Japan has traditionally excelled in "spiritualizing" activities like brush writing, dance, drama, and flower arranging. The ulti-mate goal in these Do is to see the whole of life through a particu-lar practice or individual part of living. Master calligrapher, Zen expert, and founder of Muto Ryu swordsmanship, Yamaoka Tes-shu, said that one of his principal teachings was "the practice of unifying particulars and universals." D. T. Suzuki, author of many books on Zen, in like manner referred to "the One in the Many and the Many in the One."

A certain procedure or copying exercise, for example, can be considered as a "particular." In *sumi-e*, ink painting, the aim in copying the teacher's rendering of a branch of bamboo is not to make merely a flawless duplicate; rather, the goal is to discover the essential quality, contained inside a given lesson or particular technique, of all techniques. We copy and study a particular model to lay hold of the universal principles that allow the technique to operate in the first place and that will at last empower us to rise above form to discover the formless. In so doing, it is often possible to perceive that these universal principles comprise something much greater than the singular art we're studying, that they amount to indispensable lessons in living.

On a more penetrating level, ikebana experts speak of achieving a state where they discern the actual characteristics of the blossoms they'll be arranging. They merge with nature, so that the particular (the arranger) unites with the universal (nature). Martial artists also speak of becoming one with their opponent and even the universe itself. The ultimate aesthetic running through every Japanese Way is a naturalness in which the difference between the individual and the universe softens into oneness.

The Japanese Ways Today

There are many Japanese arts and Ways, and while it's beyond the scope of this book to explore all of them or offer complete descriptions of the ones chosen for brief depiction, it is important in a volume of this sort to offer an overview of prevalent Japanese arts, crafts, and Ways.

What's more, although all of the Ways can be thought of as art forms, not all Japanese cultural arts are inevitably being practiced as Ways. Deplorably, not all bona fide Do forms, especially in Western countries, but also in modern Japan, are really being studied as Ways. Their proponents have often allowed the program of instruction in these Do to become purely physical and/or superficial in nature.

33

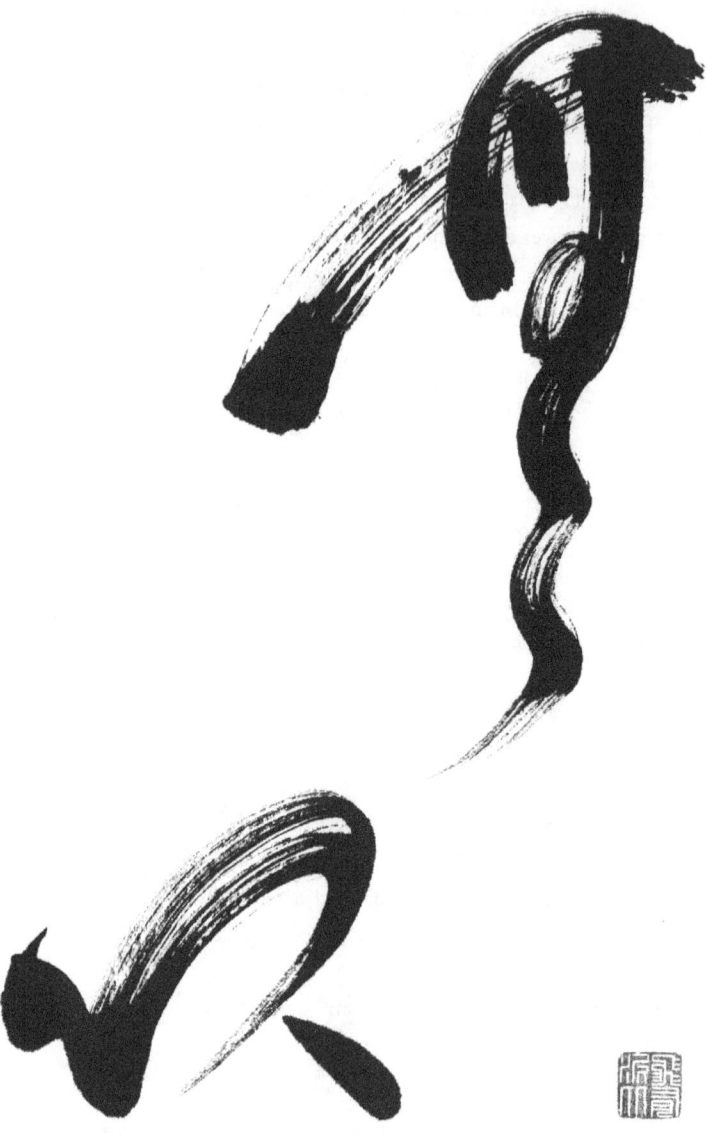

MUI: *"Do nothing." Mui is painted in the cursive and abstract sosho style of Kobara Ranseki Sensei.*
It refers to a state in which nothing is forced, contrived, or out of harmony with nature.

Chapter 2

AESTHETICS OF
THE WAY

Certain philosophical and aesthetic standards are shared by all Japanese arts. From the martial arts, to Japanese dance, to flower arrangement, distinctive artistic codes are held in common. These aesthetic codes have had a profound effect on the unfolding of the Ways. If they are not absorbed, no great appreciation of any Japanese cultural art is likely.

The large body of terms and theories allied with the aesthetics of Japanese art is beyond the reach of this book, and indeed, legitimate mastery of these principles comes only through individual, hands-on experience. But I would be remiss if I didn't note here at least the more significant of them. All of these principles connect to one another to form the harmonious totality of the Japanese arts and Ways. The descriptions of some terms and concepts thus sound similar: they are simply different methods of describing aspects of a singular entity—the Way.

The following list of attributes, which will be elaborated upon at the end of this chapter, represents a summary of my understanding of the aesthetics of the Way:

- Harmony
- Asymmetrical balance
- Artlessness
- Impermanence
- Unity with the universe

Some observers of Japan have noted that it is a culture of contradictions, and the same can be said for the aesthetics of the Japanese arts and Ways. Noh drama, for exam-

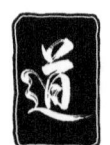
ple, mirrors the Japanese affection for artlessness, understatement, subtle expression, and representative motions. But Kabuki drama employs larger-than-life mannerisms, passionate oration, and dazzling stage effects. Consequently, like any generalizations, these five attributes are not invariably applicable, but they do offer a beginning point for examining Japanese aesthetics. And I hope, as you read through this chapter, you will discover that the Way lies in embracing and transcending duality, thus entering a state in which all contradictions dissolve.

With these attributes in mind, then, let's examine the most important principles underlying the Japanese arts and Ways.

Wabi

In the West, or the United States at least, it is difficult to pinpoint a universally accepted definition of beauty. I exaggerate only a little when I say this isn't the case in Japan. In Western countries few people pay serious attention to aesthetics, aside from professionals working in artistic circles. True, an interior decorator may have a specialist's sense of what looks good in your house, but this rarely extends to your garden or your car. And we look for a car that appeals to whatever sense of style we subscribe to, but few long-lasting, overriding aesthetic principles guide this type of purchase. The generic, four-in-a-box, everyman appeal of the typical economy car isn't mirrored in the metallic insect on wheels, newfangled hot rod look of the Plymouth Prowler—automobiles that both have their fans. We can say the same for our taste in houses, furniture, and other items.

In Japan, however, most classical arts and Ways have shared common aesthetics for generations. Through the practice of nearly ubiquitous disciplines, the Japanese populace has been exposed to an almost universally acknowledged set of aesthetics. Although these aesthetics are frequently missing in the urban concrete sprawl of cities like Tokyo, nonetheless, in backdoor bonsai, a cherished antique in the home, the design of traditional clothing, and countless other forms, the Japanese is aware of a commonly affirmed aesthetic. Not only is there a common awareness but also there is widespread participation among Japanese in arts devoted to classical concepts of elegance and beauty.

Ride a train any evening in Japan, and you'll see it filled with women in kimono coming from tea ceremony class, students carrying kendo swords and armor, elderly people with samisen instruments—the list is long. At times I've wondered if every person in Japan is studying, or has studied, some traditional art form, and my experience is that in fact most people have or are doing so.

Owing to this widespread proliferation of traditional arts and Ways, the Japanese have come to embrace universal aesthetics, or bigaku, that first arose around A.D. 700 in the rarefied lives of the Japanese priesthood and royalty. These aesthetics soon filtered down into the everyday lives of ordinary people, and into the Do forms. They affect everything in Japan, from the way a house is decorated, to its outdoor garden, to the color of the car in the garage.

True, Japan has embraced Western artistic ideas, but they have often been modified by the Japanese sense of beauty. And of course not every Japanese thinks about such matters in the same way, or at all, but most have a clearer idea (but not necessarily a deep understanding) of what their traditional aesthetics are than is found in the West. One of the most important artistic sensibilities in Japan is wabi. Wabi is one of several key terms in the vocabulary of Japanese aesthetics. This vocabulary is called fuzei and refers to words that describe particular artistic feelings, sensibilities, and ways of seeing. Wabi is also a term that strongly resists easy definition.

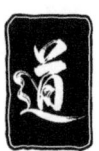

In wabi art, we find elegance with a feeling of austerity. Wabi is the recognition that beauty can be found even in the depths of poverty, and that beauty isn't limited to expensive, formal works of art produced by recognized masters. In fact, objects of great elegance can be constructed out of simple, inexpensive components. (It is interesting to note that tea ceremony utensils, which originally exhibited a rustic wabi style, can be extremely expensive nowadays.) A traditional Japanese wooden house is an example of the unpolished appeal of wabi.

On the other hand, Sen no Rikyu, who promoted wabi-style tea ceremony, once remarked that a tea caddy, owned by an acquaintance and made by a famed craftsman, was lacking in the spirit of wabi. The caddy was later broken into pieces and skillfully repaired. Upon a subsequent visit to his friend's house, Rikyu spied the restored caddy and promptly declared it a work now imbued with wabi.

In the Japanese arts and Ways, simple and natural don't necessarily equate to quick and easy. In calligraphy, for example, although a work might look like it was dashed off in a frenzy of artistic inspiration—characters about to leap off the paper—it was likely the result of hundreds of dry runs and failed experiments. And even if it was brushed in only a few moments, the skill that allowed art to be produced in a brief time was the result of years of training.

Simplicity can be achieved when skill is present, but being able to consistently hit this "sweet spot" can take years of experience. In shodo, the character for *ichi* ("one"), which consists of nothing but a single horizontal line, is considered to be among the most difficult characters to paint effectively. Likewise, when a martial arts teacher downs an opponent with just a small step forward and a slight motion of the arm, you're seeing budo at a high level. Defeating an attacker with many movements and an exaggerated display of technique is actually the crudest approach to combat, while ending the encounter with just a single glance, before any physical action takes place, is one of the ultimate goals of the Japanese martial Ways. Such simplicity has great depth, and it is inspired in the martial arts, shodo, flower arrangement, and other Do by consciousness of wabi.

The literal meaning of wabi is "poverty," but in aesthetics what is understood is a poverty of superficiality and artificiality. Wabi lies in finding that intangible, but valuable, "something" within ourselves and our art that defies trends and is timeless. To find value on the inside and in the soul of things, rather than in their monetary worth—or in monetary worth itself—is to cleave to the spirit of wabi. There is a Zen saying:

> *Ware tada taru o shiru.*
> I don't know much. I only know that I'm perfectly satisfied.

This expresses the essence of the wabi attitude of acceptance, in which being at peace in nature is valued above luxury, wealth, and opulence.

Once this understanding of our innate nature, as well as our innate unity with nature itself, is firmly recognized, then every moment and aspect of our lives is transformed. Whether at home, outdoors, in the city, or in the country, our lives can reflect an essential naturalness, simplicity, and ease of living that are our birthright. This is *wabi-zumai*, or "a wabi lifestyle," and it goes beyond a mere preference for an uncomplicated, unaffected, natural mode of living. Wabi-zumai is as much about *what we are* as it is about where we are, what we wear, and other externals. This natural Way of being, along with the principles of mental and physical harmony that can lead to it, will be discussed in chapter 3.

Fudotai

"Unmoving body." Refers to a stable posture that appears unmovable and is the physical expression of fudoshin. See also fudoshin.

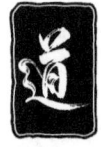

Fuga

Refinement of living. The concept stems from a wabi-sabi sensibility and correlates to a profound appreciation of and closeness to nature. Basho described it as being "a companion of the four seasons." See also furyu.

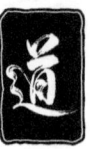

Sabi

As I look about,
The flowers and maple leaves
Have long since vanished—
Just thatched roofed huts by the sea . . .
Merging with autumn twilight.

Hundreds of years ago, the poet Fujiwara Sadaie composed this ode to a singular austere moment . . . a moment that was gone before his ink-laden brush touched paper, and a moment that is still echoing through endless time. In this waka poem (Figure 1), both the view and the viewer have merged into a solitary unit. Fujiwara hints at an ageless sliver of eternity, in which the individual and the universal melt into a sole, absolute one that's resting motionless and unconditionally alone. Encompassing everything and thus nothing, endlessly fluctuating and therefore unchanging, swallowing up all creations and containing all things to form the absolute one that dissolves duality: it is the totality of existence.

By its very nature, it is utterly alone. A singularity containing every speck of time and space within infinite borders, it is unaccompanied but never lonely. Fujiwara sensed, and then portrayed, solitariness and detachment, but without a trace of lonesomeness, a condition totally autonomous and yet still linked to all things . . . but not clinging to them. It is a feeling of embracing while letting go. In the Do, this is called sabi, and it allows life to disappear back into itself without remorse or longing.

D. T. Suzuki was one of the first writers to explore in English the spiritual complexities of two elementally simple concepts—wabi and sabi:

Just to be tranquil or passive is not sabi nor is it wabi.

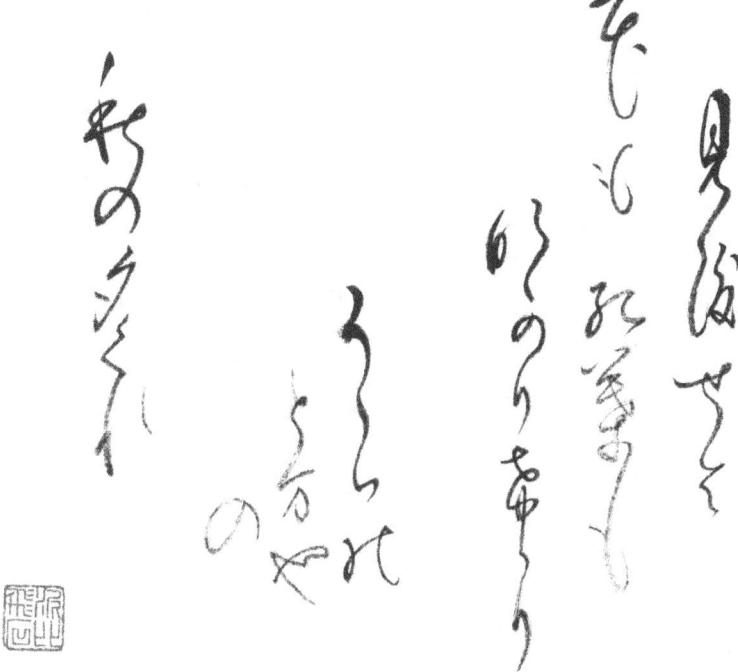

There is always something objective that evokes a mood to be called *wabi*. And *wabi* is not merely a psychological reaction to a certain pattern of environment. There is an active principle of aestheticism in it; when this is lacking poverty becomes indigence, aloneness becomes ostracism or misanthropy or inhuman unsociability. *Wabi* or *sabi*, therefore, may be defined as an active aesthetical appreciation of poverty. . . . Nowadays, as these terms are used, we may say that *sabi* applies more to the individual objects [of the tea ceremony, for example] and environment generally, and *wabi* to the living of a life ordinarily associated with poverty or insufficience or imperfection. *Sabi* is thus more objective, whereas *wabi* is more subjective and personal.[6]

41

Funi

Non-duality, where the Creator and the created can be distinguished from one another but ultimately cannot be divided. Funi hints at the true nature of existence, which transcends cultural and relative distinctions. It points at a state in which the separation between us and others, between life and death, dissolves. And with the dissolving of duality comes the transcendence of fear as well as conflict of every kind. The Ways offer a means of experimenting with the nature of funi.

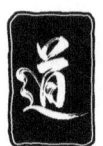

We shouldn't, however, take these comments in too literal a manner. Sabi can also make reference to a spiritual quality and a psychological state. It isn't used exclusively to describe individual objects. Plus, not all Japanese practitioners of the arts and Ways use the terms here in exactly the same manner. In short, no universally accepted and precisely delineated definition of wabi and sabi exists in Japan. And Rikyu, perhaps history's most famous advocate of the wabi-sabi aesthetic in chado, wasn't a poor man who lived far from his kind, alone in a hut—far from it. While wabi and sabi can be lived out literally, they point to the spirit of living in a certain mode, with a particular sensibility, as much as to the specifics of location, house, or occupation.

Along these lines, we can say that in Japanese art circles, wabi tends to refer more to our lifestyle (wabi-zumai), while we might describe an elegantly simple vase as having a "sabi feeling to it." Nonetheless, the aesthetic sense evoked by both wabi and sabi suggests that the terms are interrelated, although the distinction and usage pointed to above are typical among Japanese artisans devoted to the essence of wabi-sabi.

Sabi, like wabi, contains simplicity and austerity in its aesthetic makeup, and the two terms can be used together, so that it's possible to speak of something as having a wabi-sabi feeling to it. Nevertheless, sabi has its unique implications, such as the sense of solitariness mentioned above. In chado, sabi makes up one of four basic principles, in which case it is pronounced *jaku*. (The others, mentioned previously, are wa, "harmony," kei, "respect," and sei, "purity.") Jaku implies peacefulness, and this is also a central aspect of the sabi sensibility. In this sense, sabi refers to a spiritually independent state, a condition that is connected to all things while being absolutely alone and unaffected by the myriad creations of the world. This solitariness is called *sabi-shiori*. Such a state of timeless, solitary serenity lies at the core of sabi.

The aesthetic of sabi is also one of melancholy, summoned by, for example, verdigris and patina. It is the antique, rustic appearance of things after lengthy and loving handling—but before old age fully consumes them. In Japan, such a patina is often appreciated since it indicates that a work of art has passed through many hands, an extended succession of human hands. Blemishes and age spots give the object a humanistic property, a certain personality, and consequently make it more aesthetically inviting.

In the West, our enchantment with science and industrialization have made us fans of the modern and the automated. Our tendency has been, therefore, to miss the beautiful patina of age or to avoid objects that appear imperfect. Asia, in contrast, was less overwhelmed by either the scientific advancement succeeding the Renaissance in Europe or the engineering progress following the Industrial Revolution in the Western world. Following the Renaissance, Western art grew apart from its traditional link to human enterprise. In Japan, however, art and existence remained more integrated. Westerners have been inclined to concentrate on the sciences and commerce, leaving the practice of art to individuals designated as artists. The Japanese, on the other hand, have had a greater inclination to remain close to the arts and directly involved in them. Because art in Japan was more integrated into daily life, slight differentiation was made between the beautiful and the usable, an idea that ties into the sabi aesthetic. As expressed in this aesthetic, even everyday things became both elegant and practical.

Certainly the preceding observations are general, and exceptions can be found in both the East and West. And they pertain to a traditional orientation that is, however, being rapidly altered. From the late nineteenth century, the East and West began a period of mutual influence that continues today. Nonetheless, the

Furabo

Related to fuga and furyu, indicates a person who roams about, unattached, carried like a slender piece of cloth fluttering in the wind. See also furyu.

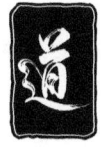

generalizations about Japan point to a context in which aesthetics such as wabi and sabi evolved.

Sabi beckons to us in objects that evoke the resonance and unevenness that time bestows. In the classical Japanese garden (*niwa*), certain areas may at first appear as if nature has taken over, but if we look more closely, we see how human creativity has actually merged with nature to give birth to a sabi effect. Sabi is best expressed by the use of natural objects. In the garden, much use is made of bamboo (for fences, for example), rocks, straw, tree bark, moss, and the like. All of these things are incorporated into the design of the garden so that as they age and settle into the landscape they will express sabi. Gradually these things are altered by their inescapable advance toward dissolution, and this too is incorporated into the niwa, hence the melancholy appeal of sabi.

Rustic objects, autumn and winter, sunsets and twilight, the willing embrace of solitariness, like an evening spent trapped alone in a cabin in the backwoods by a sudden cloudburst, welcoming the charged stillness—all express sabi, which in turn expresses a self-governing beauty. It is an elegance that is consummated not just by human beings but by the universe through its natural course.

Mono no Aware

Mono no aware has been said to describe a sentiment of pathos relating to the fleeting nature of our relative world. In addition to a feeling of life's fragility, mono no aware relates to seeing beauty in this fragile, impermanent nature, and even grasping that without impermanence, genuine beauty cannot exist.

Nothingness is permanent, and everything is momentary. Accompanying this recognition is a moment outside of time, a moment that lasts throughout eternity, a moment that passes before we can absorb the words I've just written.

Experiencing the fragility of life affirms the worth of living. Beauty fades as quickly as it is experienced and thus it lives forever. And the moment passes so instantaneously that it cannot be contained by the intellect, making it everlasting. Mono no aware embraces all of these assertions.

These aspects might appear opposed—as in fact they are—but they are not contradictory. Let's look at them one by one.

First, though we might wish to believe otherwise, all living things are vulnerable to dissolution. Whereas the life force continues, the relative, changing aspects of us—our physical selves—are impermanent. This of course applies to all objects of creation. And it is the beauty of things, the beauty in their fleeting nature, and the evanescence of beauty too that are evoked by mono no aware.

When we see a dancer unexpectedly leap into the air with incredible grace, the beauty of the action captures the mind in an instant—and in the next instant it's gone. We glimpse the elegant movement of tall trees curtsying in the wind, but this too lasts only a moment. This sudden awareness of a fleeting beauty is well illustrated by a shooting star. Even a painting, which we can look at over and over again, often has its greatest impact when our gaze is first frozen by its magnitude. While we might look at it many times after, the real impression of beauty in its fullest force occurs only once—unless we grasp the art of seeing.

To wholly see beauty (or any aspect of living), the mind must be in the moment. Physical existence is now, with the past and future functioning as ideas rather than actual reality. Experience of beauty, and of life more generally, does not happen in the future, which is an imagined time that might not ever take place, or in the past, which no longer exists. The full experiencing of life and art must be now or not at all.

Furyu

From two words meaning, "wind" and "flowing." It suggests an elegance both tangible and intangible, an inexpressible, ephemeral beauty that can be experienced only in the moment, for in the next instant it will dissolve like the morning mist. See also furabo.

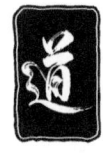

Yet the mind clings to the known, to the past, out of a striving for security. We eat a wonderful dinner or see a fantastic sunset, and the mind seeks to hold onto and sustain the wonder, awe, and happiness. Unfortunately, a mind that's caught in the past, that compares now to before, rarely experiences the present in a full way. By constantly comparing what we sense now versus what we once felt, we deaden all of our present experiences. The beauty expessed by mono no aware is a beauty of only this instant.

Like the past, which is only a memory, the future is an idea, not reality. The now, however, genuinely exists. This instant is real, but it is fleeting. And experience of the present instant cannot be used to predict the next instant. Just because we have started each day with a shower for the past twenty years, we have no contract with the universe that assures us the hot water will be working tomorrow.

Like the sense of security that stems from clinging to the past, "knowing" is an illusion. Reality lies in the unknown. If we realize and embrace this fact we discover that the only security in life comes from accepting and adapting to the instant, to a moment that is brief and transitory. To embrace change and the unknown is in the spirit of mono no aware. Mono no aware relates to harmony with the constantly changing universe and with universal cycles of creation and destruction.

A mind that resides in the instant can encounter beauty in its greatest breadth, from instant to instant. Although the beauty of a painting is often completely experienced only upon first sight, this need not be the case. If the mind abides in the moment, and then lets that instant die, and rests fully in a new instant, that beauty can again be fully appreciated. We can encounter a work of art, a food, or a natural landscape many times without diminishing its splendor. To understand mono no aware, we need to grasp that beauty and life exist in the instant. In mono no aware, we let the past dissolve, realizing that destruction is ultimately a positive act of creation. This realization manifests in a number of ways in the Japanese Do forms.

Shoshin

Shoshin means "beginner's mind," and it is believed to derive from Zen. It isn't so much an aesthetic concept as it is a state of mind. Nonetheless, this mental condition is needed to understand mono no aware and other aesthetics, which is why it is included in this chapter.

Shoshin describes a consciousness that's always fresh, never bogged down by its own past. In the condition of shoshin, we look at each lesson or practice session in a given art as if it were our first time to experience it, and this should be true even in the case of techniques and exercises that have been practiced thousands of times. With the shoshin mindset, we can continue to learn year after year, never reaching the point where we think we've learned all there is to know about a certain art or facet of that art. Thus, we assure a never-ending growth and development in an art that never grows tiresome.

Still, shoshin goes deeper than avoiding the complacent assumption that all there is to know has already been learned. Authentic shoshin is encountered in a mind that doesn't cling to the past and experiences the present wholeheartedly. It's this mind that retains a bona fide beginner's attitude, recognizing that past training is no guarantee of present success or even of an appropriate understanding. Every instant is ultimately different, and art, beauty, and success must be found right in that instant or it will not take place.

Let's look at an example. Shodo calligraphy students spend

Gagaku

One of the ancient forms of Japanese music. In 701, the Imperial Court Office of Music was created. Gagaku, "imperial court music," was the result. It is still performed under the direction of the Imperial Household Agency.

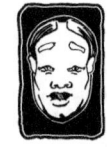

47

Go

An ancient game played on a square board divided into 361 squares. Two players take turns placing small, round, black or white stones on the board. The objective is to enclose as much area as possible. The person who surrounds the biggest section wins. Go is valued as a means of enhancing concentration and learning strategies that some claim are applicable to daily living. As in the modern martial Ways, players of go are promoted through a series of ranks.

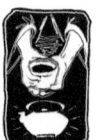

many hours each week copying from *tehon*, which are models of characters brushed by advanced artists. Over the years that I've studied shodo, I've heard many novices remark that, even after making dozens of copies of the tehon, the first copies are the best; the more they practice, the worse they do. Is there something killing the realization of skill? Indeed there is.

As I noted, it's not uncommon for beginners to complain that practice results in a lessening of quality, and the natural question is why—why would more practice cause worse skill? Part of the answer lies in the mind's tendency to intrude the past into the present.

When we first copy a work of art, it's new. Our reactions to what we're attempting to reproduce are also new, and so are our successes and problems with the particular tehon. But as we continue to copy, layer upon layer of the past piles onto the current moment, making an accurate perception of what we're really looking at, and what we're actually doing, difficult. Soon, we're no longer looking at the piece we're trying to faithfully copy, but rather we're seeing only our *own representation of reality*. This representation contains all of our impressions, beliefs, prejudices, fears, desires, etc., that relate to the observed object and our effort to skillfully copy it. The more experiences we have with the object and the act of attempting to copy it, the more we tend to filter what we see through this veil of conditioning.

For instance, making a straight line in shodo or ink painting can be difficult. The line often wavers. This isn't necessarily a problem, as with practice most people can make a fairly even line. The mechanics aren't that complicated, but the mind can certainly complicate matters, and this typically takes place when we initially meet with failure. Then, if the mind clings to this failure, each time we try to create a straight line, we see that line through the veil of past failures. Since the mind controls the body, when we

48

retain images of past wavering lines, our present line also wobbles. In short, we "psych ourselves out."

Avoiding this common tendency requires nonattachment, a state in which we live through each moment completely and let it dissolve, rather than clinging to it. And a mind that isn't in the moment inherently clings to the past. By practicing Japanese arts and Ways, we can discover a mind that rests in the instant, in a moment that is timeless. In this condition, each time we see a tehon to be copied, a sunset, or even our own house, the experience is fresh and new. We see what is instead of *our representation of what is*.

Donald Richie, a longtime resident of Japan and observer of its culture, makes the following observation about this nonattachment:

> By sacrificing an urge to immortality, and through a knowing acceptance of himself and his world, he [the Japanese] stops time. He has found a way to freeze it, to suspend it, to make it permanent. He does this, not through pyramids and ziggurats, but by letting it have its own way.[7]

Richie points to the timeless permanence in constant change that is revealed in the traditional Japanese garden. In the niwa, flowers bloom in the spring and leaves flutter to the ground in autumn, but the rocks, water, and essential landscape—the garden's structure—are invariable.

> The Japanese garden is like a still picture—a frozen moment which is also all eternity. It remains the same no matter the season because the seasons are acknowledged, and this acknowledgment is spiritual, a combination of idea and emotion.[8]

49

The present is outside of time. No matter how quickly we say that we're aware of the present, the moment has already past. It can't be clung to or measured. Thus, a full experience of beauty, indeed of all things, is possible only in the moment, and since the moment cannot be contained or clung to, beauty is found in an instant that is dissolving.

Clinging to moments that have passed precludes knowing the newness of each moment. The aesthetics of mono no aware and shoshin reveal the understanding that reality exists in an instant beyond time . . . and so it lasts forever. Beauty is indeed beautiful and fresh precisely because it is always new, spontaneous, and in the moment. It's special because it can't be preserved or recreated. With this comprehension comes the ability to see beauty in every fragile facet of life, even in the fading of a flower or the aging of a friend.

In this way, shoshin, mono no aware, wabi, and sabi are related. Shoshin is a beginner's mind that sees each moment in life as the first and only time that moment can be experienced. Mono no aware is an awareness of the fleeting and fragile nature of life, the fact that all created things deteriorate and dissolve back into the universe. Wabi-sabi correlates to an appreciation of this gradual dissolution, finding beauty in the rustic patina of age. In a material sense, the wabi-sabi aesthetic finds elegance in such a patina, while mono no aware recognizes that this patina is the result of inevitable natural corrosion, and even deterioration can be beautiful to a mind that doesn't compare the present to the past, the new to the old. This mind recognizes mono no aware rests in the present and perceives the indivisibility in birth-death, creation-destruction, and duality itself. It grasps a beauty that is absolute, that has no opposite, that contains no conflict between the inevitable and the wished for.

The element common to these principles speaks ultimately

to an acceptance of ourselves. For to accept ourselves completely, we must also embrace our own mortality.

Furyu

Furyu is composed of two elements: "wind" and "flowing." Like the wind, it can be sensed but not seen. It is a quality both tangible and intangible in its suggested elegance. Furyu points to an ephemeral beauty that can only be experienced in the now, for in the next instant it will dissolve like the morning mist.

> An ancient pond
> A frog leaps—
> The sound of water.

Basho's most famous haiku, in fact the most famous haiku (Figure 2), describes a moment of furyu that is at once simple and yet easily missed by those lacking in the furyu spirit. Think of it as a poetic snapshot, a split second in nature in which time ends.

Basho taught that the spirit of haiku is the spirit of *fuga*. Fuga means, "refinement of living." Yet this refinement isn't merely a matter of education, breeding, and financial stability, as is often assumed in modern times. Basho's fuga stemmed from the wabi-sabi philosophy of old Japan, and it correlates to a profound appreciation of and closeness to nature. Basho described it as being "a companion of the four seasons" in his *Yoshino Journal*. He further described his fellow poets, who were imbued with the character of fuga, as *furabo*—people who roam about, unattached, fluttering like slender pieces of cloth swept by the wind.

The second component in furyu, which can mean "flowing," can also mean "waters" and "to be washed away." Imagine the wind rustling tree leaves above a brook of crystal-clear water. For

Hacho

"Intentional unevenness," one phrase for expressing asymmetrical balance, a distinctive feature of Japanese arts. Japanese poetry, for instance, has uneven, asymmetrical numbers of lines per verse—three for haiku and five for waka poems. In Japanese flower arrangement, the application of unevenness is endlessly changeable and calls forth a charismatic feeling of movement and life, a feeling of naturalness.

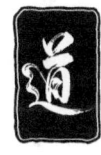

51

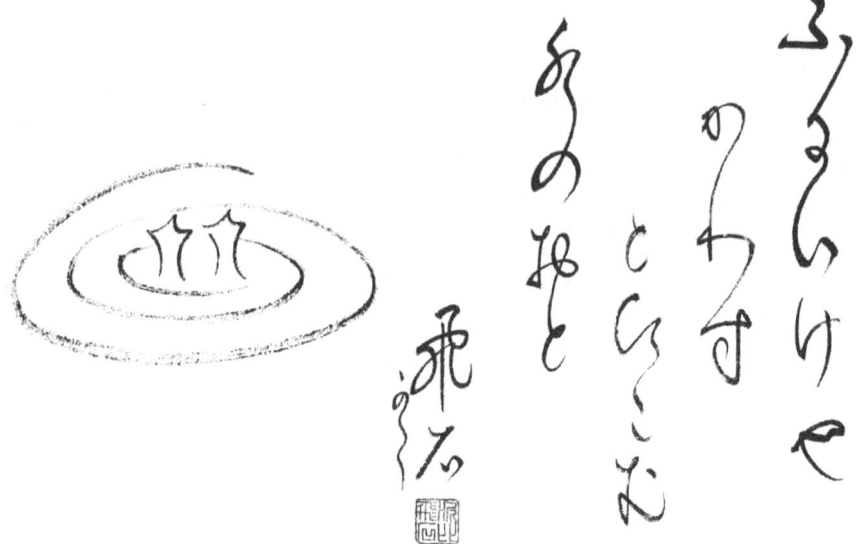

FIG 2.

Furu ike ya \ kawazu tobikomu \ mizu no oto.

"An ancient pond \ a frog leaps— \ the sound of water."

Basho's most famous poem, painted in the style of Kobara Ranseki Sensei.

an instant, the sun shines through the moving leaves, catching a ripple just so, and the glittering water, framed by a mosaic of shadow and light, is extraordinarily beautiful—and then the moment is gone, "washed away" by the changing patterns of light and movement. Furyu describes the heightened awareness of that moment and of the universe that affords a glimpse of that flash of beauty.

Japan has a number of traditional experiences thought to be capable of calling forth the spirit of furyu. Moon viewing and springtime cherry blossom viewing, the contemplation of classical gardens of rock and raked sand—such activities are said to be "furyu experiences." In Japan, those who fail to have such experiences are traditionally thought to be uncultured. Of course there's an important distinction between actually encountering the deep pathos and beauty of creation-destruction in an instant and using the word "furyu," regardless of the actual state of mind, in response to viewing the moon because such an experience is *supposed to be* one of furyu.

Furyu is not solely an appreciation for nature; it is also a detached connection with nature. Detachment—the word hints at but does not fully describe the state of mind alluded to here—allows one to connect with all parts of the natural experience and not just aspects commonly assumed to be pleasant. It was this component of furyu that allowed cultured Japanese to sometimes write a poem just before death, which was once a fairly common custom.

Furyu relates to a sensitivity and heightened connection with nature, and it can therefore occur in moments or settings outside its traditional associations. In his book *Tea Life, Tea Mind*, Sen Soshitsu XV, the head of the Urasenke tea school, recalls:

> Once, at the home of an American acquaintance, I found hanging in an open window a pair of metal chopsticks, the kind used for arranging a charcoal fire. When I asked my friend why they were there, I was told, "When the wind blows they strike each other and make the most beautiful sound." I was delightfully amazed; they were his wind bell. A Japanese would never use them in any way other than to handle charcoal, but here they were serving a completely different purpose. This insight was so perfectly furyu that I almost did not take notice of it, and with that realization I experienced a twofold surprise.[9]

The word "furyu" has been used in Japan since the Heian period (794–1192). Unlike other periods in Japanese history, the Heian age was an essentially peaceful one, characterized by a love for the rich, ornate, and elaborate. Yet shadowing this romantic, and at times even pretentious, Heian aesthetic was another, very different way of looking at beauty, one that drew its inspiration from the fleeting, simple magnificence of wind and water—furyu. And although aspects of Heian culture were influenced by Chi-

Haiku

Short poem arranged in three lines of five, seven, and five syllables. A haiku captures the essence of a brief, transient moment in one's life and the universe. The composition of haiku is believed to lead to an enhanced state of sensitivity and closeness to nature.

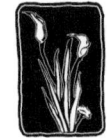

53

Hara

Refers to the lower abdomen, a point of mental focus and stabilization from which correct bodily movement originates.

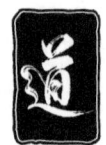

nese civilization and art, furyu appears to be a wholly Japanese concept. It was embraced by the samurai, who, given their at least potentially violent and short-lived existence, were drawn to ideas like mono no aware and furyu. Although furyu dates far back into Japanese history, like many aspects of the Way, it is concurrently ancient and immediate.

In addition to describing the flash of intensity in which time ceases, furyu indicates that we should flow (suggested by "ryu") through life as the wind moves through the myriad aspects of nature, touching everything fully but not clinging to any one thing.

Furyu embraces the ever-changing, fleeting character of life, beauty, and nature. Yet it doesn't imply resignation. Resignation relates to defeat and giving up, and the acceptance contained in furyu is one that takes place when we realize our essential unity with the transient universe, and in this state, there is no defeat, nothing to fight against. In embracing absolute acceptance and harmony with the constantly changing universe, furyu is ultimately positive.

In the Ways, furyu describes an instant in which the mind experiences the poignancy of a brief moment of fragile beauty, a moment so overwhelming and intense that words can barely hint at it—cherry blossoms caught by the wind, and for the briefest moment . . . cascading . . . hanging in a cloud of pink.

Shibumi

Balanced imbalances, artlessness, solitude, antiquity—all are fundamental to classical Japanese sensibilities. They also relate to wabi and sabi, which in turn have a kinship with the concepts *shibumi* ("elegance") and *shibui* ("elegant"). Shibumi also relates

54

to something astringent in taste, while shibui indicates that which is unaffected or refined.

An unripe persimmon is traditionally said to have a shibui taste. In ikebana, a shibui flower arrangement elicits a feeling of coolness during a scorching summer and warmth on a chilly day. Shibumi is quiet and subtle. It is soothing and fulfilling to the soul in a manner unrelated to reasoning. It is the sensibility of "not too much," the use of aesthetic restraint in the highest sense. It is suggested by the English phrase "in good taste," but its reverberations widen and join other Japanese aesthetic and spiritual principles like wabi-sabi.

Shibui and shibumi are artistic ideals that suggest a timeless, beautiful elegance that transcends a particular style or trend. Shibui items aren't showy (in coloration, for example), but rich in quality. Such items are called *shibui-mono*, literally "shibui things." Unpolished silver or gold, or the hue of ashes or bran, can produce an unpretentious, yet elegant and tranquil shibui effect. The classical color arrangement of a woman's kimono, a traditional martial artist's costume of quilted *gi* (cotton garment) and *hakama* (full, skirted pants), the color design of a Japanese guest room, the garments and utensils of the tea ceremony—all evoke shibumi.

Terms that relate to the shibumi ideal are *hade* and *jimi*: If a painting is hade, it is too loud (for example, in color) or even garish. On the other hand, artwork with a naturalistic, subdued, and subtle character is deemed jimi. A piece of calligraphy, an ink painting, or a kimono that is jimi approaches shibumi.

The collection by many Japanese of *suiseki* ("art stones") provides an interesting example of the pursuit of shibumi. Suiseki is the art of symbolizing natural phenomena, from countryside to the universe, using a stone a few inches to a foot or more in dimension. The art begins with the acquisition of stones in nature

Hyoshi

Hyoshi describes "timing" and "rhythm." In the martial Ways, timing is clearly vital. Likewise in shodo, the brushed characters, sitting motionless on the paper, should nevertheless look like they're moving. This is "motion in stillness." Art that displays a visible rhythm in the manner that music gives off an audible rhythm can only be achieved in shodo, and in other Ways like budo and chado, by means of relaxation. Relaxation allows us to achieve calmness in action and action in calmness. We are only able to find timing and rhythm when we stay calm despite outward movement.

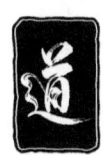

GA: *"Graceful elegance."* *Grace, elegance, simplicity, and naturalness are embodied in most Japanese folk crafts and arts. Aesthetic concepts, such as shibumi, also hint at this state of grace.*

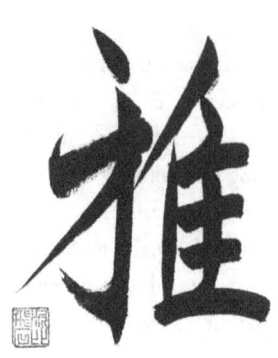

and consummates in a sensation of beauty and spiritual connection between the fancier and the stone.

Collectors look for simple lines on their suiseki, since these are evocative of shibumi. Stones shaped like faraway mountains, or *toyama*, and dark-hued stones are also examples of shibui suiseki. Suiseki that have an abundance of shibumi give off a sense of reserve, refinement, and serenity. Shibumi is particularly noticeable in a suiseki's texture. Shibui suiseki have a texture and character marked by understatement.

An authentic niwa garden is another good place to witness a manifested shibumi. Tendencies characteristic of Japanese art and art objects—such as lack of clutter; simple, reserved backdrops and undecorated surfaces; uneven numbers; lower, as opposed to higher, denominations; subtle suggestion; rounded and natural forms—hint at the subtle elegance of shibumi, a quality we can discover by observing nature and direct participation in Japanese classical arts. The similarity of this aesthetic to wabi, sabi, furyu, and others only mirrors the holistic nature of life itself.

Shibumi itself expresses this synthesis. A Japanese aphorism relating to this aesthetic and the use of color states that an artist needs to comprehend only the roles of white, black, and crimson, which form an understated synthesis and ultimately one hue. All other uses of coloration, including the decreasing of strength or graying of tone, will happen naturally with this comprehension. The expression of this adage is seen in brush writing and ink painting where the sole speck of color is a scarlet accent, the signature stamp (*inkan*) of the artist. In the niwa, a similar red accent is found in the *maku*, the felt covering on a viewing bench.

Subtle elegance also arises from suggestion. Although colored ink is common in sumi-e today, traditionally artists used black ink (*sumi*). This monochrome wasn't because of a dislike of color or a lack of comprehension of its use; rather it stemmed from the artists' awareness of the power of elegant suggestion—the power of shibumi. A flower painted purple will be forever purple, but one rendered by a few strokes of ebony ink can be any hue the viewer's imaginativeness solicits. Similarly, a few brush strokes can suggest a flock of birds and a single stroke can indicate a stalk of bamboo.

This shibui aesthetic of suggestion focuses on beginnings and endings, whereas much of Western art concentrates on a "climactic instant." For instance, everyone enjoys a dazzling spray of flowers in full bloom, and the Japanese artist is no different, but in Japanese aesthetics, scarcely opened buds and scattered flower petals resting on the earth are also deeply appreciated. They feature prominently in flower arrangement. And although the climactic moment suggested by fully blooming flowers may be awe-inspiring, it also precludes an opportunity for the elegant engagement of the imagination.

Shizenteki

Shizenteki implies "naturalness," and reverence for nature is a central aspect of Japanese art and traditional culture. Japan is, after all, a country whose inhabitants once sliced holes in the roofs of their farmhouses in order to avoid chopping down a tree. And such farmhouses were often built to fit in the curve of the countryside rather than the other way around.

Nonetheless, Japanese art is more than the mere celebration

Ichi-go, Ichi-e

"One encounter, one opportunity." Refers to the emphasis in the Ways on being fully present in the moment based on an awareness of its ephemeral nature. Due to the fleeting nature of each instant, every moment is precious, and it is the only moment that genuinely exists. By focusing on the past or the future, and only encountering the present fully during times such as a crisis situation, we sleepwalk through life. The Ways emphasize activities that require the full, unified force of the mind and body—a force brought to bear in the present and in a flash.

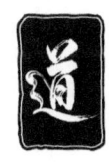

57

and preservation of nature. Ikebana, for example, isn't simply the appreciation of flowers in their natural state; no, the flowers are clipped, bent, positioned—they are arranged—in a manner that embraces their natural tendencies *but also recognizes the natural artistic tendencies of the artist.*

Japanese people, like people everywhere, love forests and flowers. Yet, if you visit a Japanese garden, you won't see a spontaneous grouping of trees, but a meticulous arrangement of them in the garden. And, although arranged, the grouping appears unforced and beautiful. The arrangement appears unaffected and artless, but there is something more.

A bonsai tree offers a good example. We marvel at how the bonsai seems like a replication of a tree in nature, only in miniature. But if we look longer and more carefully at an exquisite bonsai, we note a curious fact: *the tree looks more distinctive and striking than a tree in nature.*

A distinctively twisted, aged, and yet beautiful tree can be found in nature, but not often, and this same tree, only dwarfed, while found occasionally growing from a crag in some remote wilderness, is rarer still.

Bonsai (and suiseki) thus isn't simply nature as it is; it is nature in a super concentrated form, a form that is squeezed, compacted, and multiplied in intensity. In the case of bonsai, and even ikebana and other crafts, we can think of Japanese art as nature reinterpreted and intensified, a distillation of its essential quality.

Thus, the painstaking pruning and wiring of bonsai are not meant to reproduce nature as it is but to produce something beyond what is usually found in nature: simply to copy nature pales in comparison. It is when the life force and creativity of the artist—the human being as a functioning part of nature—merge with the essence and rhythm of nature that something wondrous results. That result is art—not Japanese art—but art.

Although not alone in this recognition, Japan has refined it over centuries to a high level. Japanese art has united an awareness of nature with an innate predilection for formally established ways of doing things. These established forms, or kata, are widespread, but their use accords with the idea of shizenteki. (I say more about kata later in the book.) Although Japanese art has specific, long-established rules that contribute to its recognizably Japanese style, these rules generally work within the natural order.

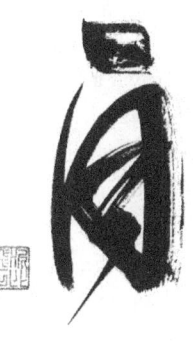

ONOZUKARA:
Brushed in the cursive sosho style of the monk Chiei, this character can mean "self" when pronounced ji and "naturally" or "naturalness" when pronounced onozukara or inozuto. Naturalness lies at the heart of all the Japanese Ways. And in these Ways, the individual self and nature are not separate.

The ideal of asymmetry is one example. Just as flowers do not grow in neat rows in the wilderness, symmetry is avoided in a Japanese garden or in ikebana. Nature is "arranged" in the traditional Japanese arts, but the arrangement accords with the intrinsic movement of ki in nature. Thus, in general an ikebana artist will bend a flower, but not so much that it will be forced into a shape it would not exhibit in nature.

Relating to this idea is *sashiai*, which can be unsatisfactorily translated as "reciprocal interference." Sashiai embodies the idea that less is more. By reduction and elimination, by leaving certain elements of a design empty, specific aspects of nature can more successfully be brought to the viewer's attention. For instance, it is common to find in the small hut used in the tea ceremony a simple, seasonal arrangement of flowers. Wandering through the garden leading to the hut, you are likely to notice something unusual—no flowers. This deliberate act of reduction and elimination serves to heighten the effect of viewing the few flowers sim-

Ikebana

Literally "living flow-
ers." Refers to the tra-
ditional art of flower
arrangement. Also
known as kado (the
Way of flowers), its
origins are in Buddhist
floral offerings.

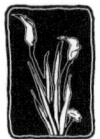

ply yet carefully displayed in the hut. It concentrates attention on them, and expresses the essence of the garden itself and even the character of flowers as a whole. Using less to intensify an effect, and intensify it in harmony with nature, is the essence of sashiai.

The same effect can be observed in ink painting. A large blank area may be left in a painting. But this void isn't really emp-ty; it is filled with itself and defines, for example, the small figure wandering up a mountain path, surrounded by vast emptiness. In sumi-e, the deliberate absence of form actually supports the struc-ture of the painting and draws attention to specific parts of the painting.

Sashiai leads to *mitate*, a new manner of seeing. Many of us just glance at the world, usually through the eyes of the past, and in the example above, the absence of flowers in the garden leading to the the tea hut encourages observers to genuinely see and con-nect with the flowers in the arrangement. With the mitate that comes from sashiai, the observer is able to make a deep, immedi-ate, and intimate connection with specific aspects of nature that have been arranged by the artist. Ultimately, it is a connection with the universe itself.

In some ways, this reverence for nature has entered the realm of mysticism, a "natural mysticism," as certain Western scholars have stated, as opposed to a "spiritual mysticism" conceived in a Judeo-Christian context. In this natural mysticism, nature isn't perceived as merely plants and animals, as something bestowed on humankind by a separate Creator. It is essentially a nondualistic perception in which nature is the visible aspect of the Creator on earth, part of the Creator in the same way that legs are part of the body and not separate from it. Nature is perhaps better described as the Creator himself/herself, as the absolute, or the absolute uni-verse.

Thus, in the Do, oneness with nature is more than harmony

with the natural physical environment; it is union with the absolute universe itself. But shizenteki in the Ways implies still more than this. It means to embody natural principles in the way we function, and this embodiment can occur in any environment—urban or naturalistic. It isn't about *where we are* but *what we are*, and how we act. (More discussion of shizenteki and the concept of naturalness is in chapter 3.)

We practice one of the Do to reveal for ourselves and to ourselves the principles inherent in nature. In the Way of the flower, the classical strata are heaven, earth, and humanity. Certain elements will represent heaven, or perhaps God, others the earth, and still others, branches for example, humankind. Humans are placed between heaven and earth in kado, not only as an intermediary but also as a means for us to absorb the teachings of the universe itself. The same can be said for other Ways, and in studying such Ways we have a chance to directly and intimately experience and experiment with the principles of the universe in a microcosm.

Ma

More than an aesthetic standard, ma specifies a technical principle inherent in many of the Japanese arts and Ways. Ma means "interval" or "space." In budo, or the martial Ways, ma (or *ma-ai*) refers to a proper combative distance. The person that controls the distance and space in combat controls the entire encounter. Position yourself too close and the opponent can strike you at will, without even having to take a step (Figure 3). Remain too far away and no sense of connection with the opponent is possible. Furthermore, no combatant will intelligently attack from across the room. In many systems of jujutsu, aiki-jujutsu, and aikido, the fundamental ma-ai is one in which the opponent can't hit or

FIG. 3. A ma-ai (distance) in jujutsu that is too close.

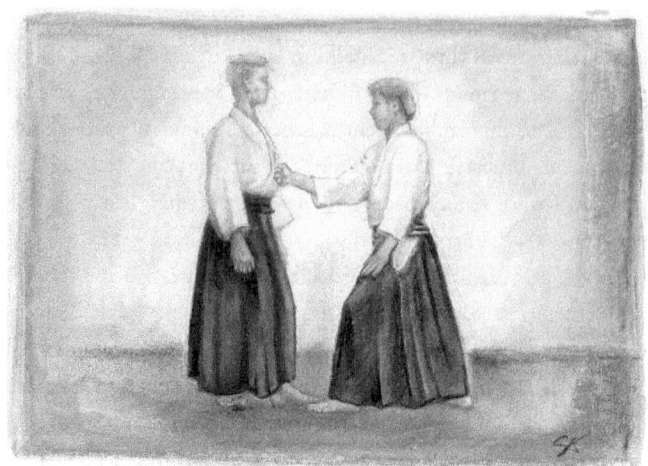

kick you without having taken at least one step. This distance can be roughly gauged as that at which the fingertips of two extended arms just barely touch (Figure 4), and a similar distance is used in Japanese swordsmanship, in which the sword tips nearly touch (Figure 5). By having to step in to attack, the assailant is forced to commit to the assault, and he also must make a larger, slower movement, which tends to "telegraph" the attack. Ma is thus of vital importance in budo. Not too close, not too far away.

This idea of just the right distance also applies in human relationships. The sort of closeness expected and welcomed from an intimate would likely be deemed uncomfortable from an acquaintance or stranger. Appropriate physical and psychological distance thus obviously varies according to the person and circumstances. This is also true in the martial arts, where we might stand closer than the standard ma if we feel that an opponent isn't especially skilled, but move farther apart than usual when dealing with a particularly fast and powerful attacker.

That a highly developed awareness of ma would have evolved in Japan is easily understood once we consider its geographical and

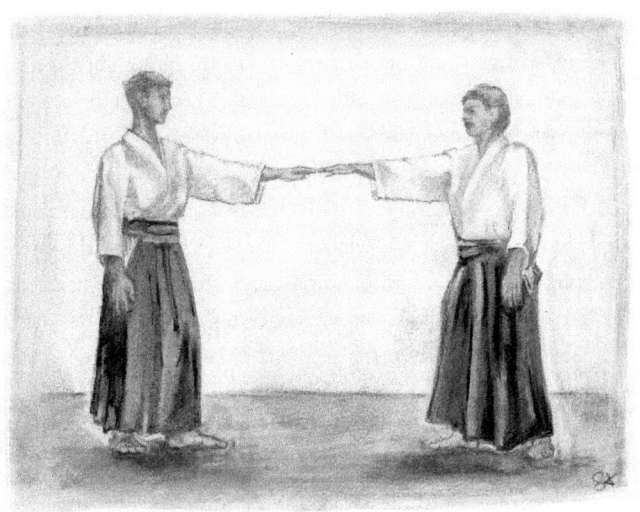

FIG. 4. A ma-ai (distance) in jujutsu that is correct (where the fingertips just touch).

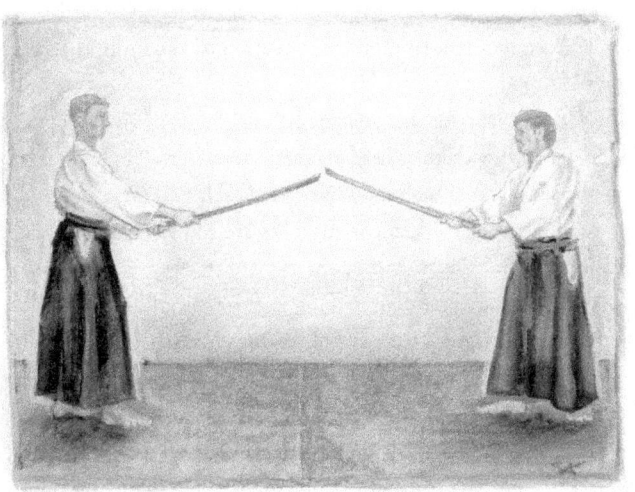

FIG. 5. A ma-ai (distance) in kenjutsu that is correct (where the sword tips nearly touch).

historical circumstances. Japan is a small island nation that has long been densely populated. Over the centuries, if for no other reason than to avoid conflict, the Japanese had to cultivate a sense of ma, had to literally "give each other some space." But, despite the crowdedness of the environment, the aim was not to keep others away, which would have adversely affected group cohesion in this group-oriented culture; rather, correct ma embodies space but not excessive distance, and it will vary by person and situation in both martial and social relationships.

Each of us gives off a certain "presence." We say that some people have a big presence, whereas others do not. And this presence, like ma, varies according to time and situation. For instance, we often note that actors appear larger on stage than off stage. This is said to be due to the fact that they're projecting to the audience during a performance. The big presence that is projected is sometimes described in Japan as ki, "life energy" or "spiritual force." A dynamic, positive mental state gives rise to a powerful outward expansion of ki—a big presence. Conversely, a negative, withdrawn state of mind creates a concurrent withdrawal of ki. Thus, from moment to moment, situation to situation, the radiation of ki modulates.

Correct ma can be imagined if we think of two people as magnets, each with an aura of magnetic force. If we gradually bring the positive ends of each magnet toward each other, we can get an impression of ma. When the magnets are too far apart, we can't feel the magnetic aura, but at the right distance we can perceive the two fields of force touch. This is correct ma. Likewise, if we force the two magnets past this point, too close, they start to push away from each other. Where magnets give off magnetic energy, people give off ki. Ki is sensed through the hara, a natural and immovable center inside human beings. The concepts of ki and hara are explored at greater length in chapter 3, which examines the spiritual aspects of the Ways, but it's important to note here that ma pertains to both the body and the spirit.

Ma can also be seen in Japanese visual arts such as shodo. The brush strokes that form a character must not be too far apart

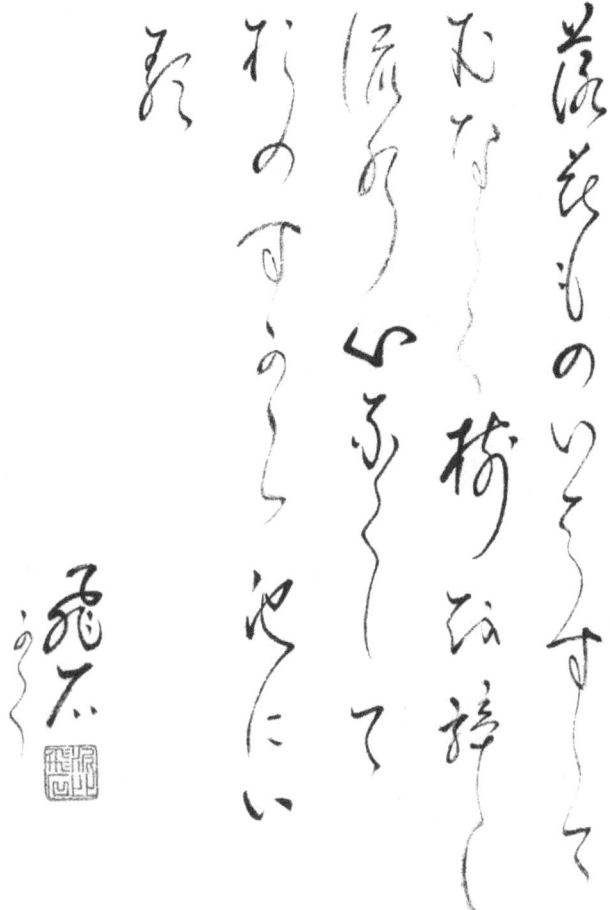

or it will not hold together, and placing the strokes too close to each other only creates a cramped feeling. Similarly, the space between characters should be not too close nor too far—just like people in society. In the same vein, the lines of a poem must con- nect with each other in a harmonious way. When a poem is to be written in uniform, vertical lines, it is called *fujidana* in design, and a correct ma is relatively easy to arrive at (Figure 6). How- ever, when a *chirashi*, or "scattered," arrangement is used to cre-

FIG. 7.
*Omoi demo / Hakanaki
mono wa / Fuku kaze no /
Oto ni mo kikanu / Koi ni
zo arikeru.*

"It's ever fleeting, / like
the echoing wind's voice,
/ that's no longer heard.
/ Love only truly exists
/ In the flash of the
moment."

This poem from the
*Nishi Honganji Sanjuroku
Nin Shu* aptly sums
up Japanese attitudes
to impermanence and
reflects elements of
mono no aware and ichi-
go, ichi-e.

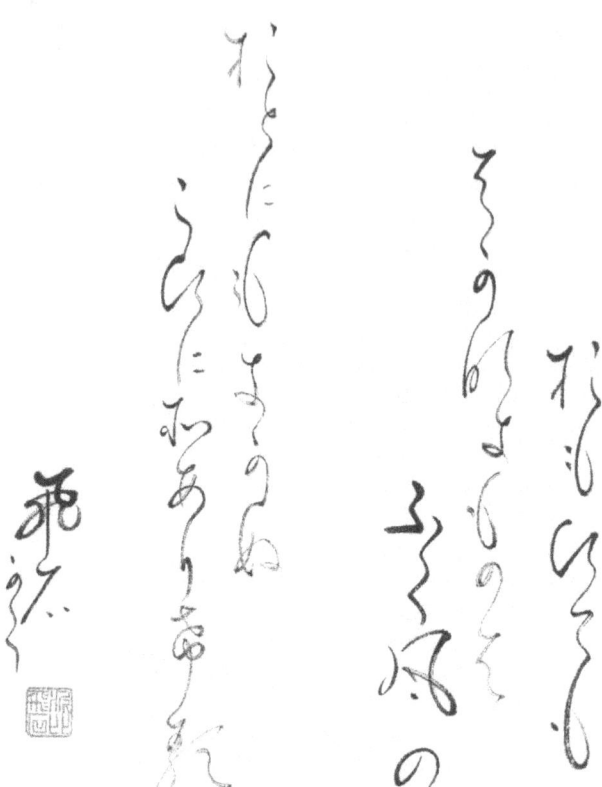

ate asymmetrical balance, ma is much more challenging (Figure
7). Note that in Figure 7 I've painted the characters to form more
than one "island." If the groupings are too close, they cease to
function as islands and run together. Too far apart, on the other hand, and there is a lack of cohesion. The ki of each grouping
must touch but not repel. Thus, the sense of ma and of balance in
shodo are intimately connected.

In sumi-e, the lines applied by the brush are frequently
incomplete. The incompleteness allows the mind's eye to com-

plete the composition, thus drawing the observer into the work. In this minimalist approach, the empty space is important. This space is ma. In Western painting empty space is designated "negative space," and students are usually urged to "fill up the space." But in Japanese visual arts, from sumi-e to flower arrangement, empty space isn't seen as something negative. I often advise people interested in Japanese calligraphy to look at the white space instead of the lines of black ink when copying sample characters. When I engage in brush writing, I regularly think of outlining the white space as opposed to drawing lines on blank paper. Ma is space, but the space isn't empty.

In-Yo

In and yo are commonly known in the West by their Chinese equivalents, yin and yang. Their origins are related to Taoism, in which they refer to the basic, complementary, and inseparable dualism that is evidenced in the relative world.

In the Tao Te Ching, the canon of Taoism, Lao-tzu described yin and yang thus:

> Is and is not are mutually arising;
> Difficult and easy are complementary;
> Long and short arise from comparison;
> Higher and lower are interdependent;
> Vocalization and verbalization harmonize with
> each other;
> Before and after accompany each other.[10]

Although the Chinese origins of yin and yang are well known, few realize that ancient Japan offered parallels in its native Shintoism. In Shinto mythology, at a moment before time, the

Inro

The classical Japanese apparel, the kimono, had no pockets. A sash tied the robes together. Objects carried were held on a cord tucked under the sash. The hanging objects (sage-mono) were secured with carved toggles (netsuke). A sliding bead (ojime) was strung on the cord between the netsuke and the sagemono to bind or slacken the opening of the sage-mono. The best known accessory was the inro, a little box used for carrying medication and seals. Inro are beautiful art objects that are still carved and widely collected. See also netsuke.

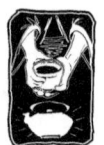

universe existed as an undifferentiated whole, without form or substance, absolute life energy (ki) that contained no dualistic or relative aspects—pure oneness. Suddenly, by means of a spiral movement, the ki of the universe began to divide, with one aspect swirling centrifugally upward to become heaven and the other corkscrewing downward with infinite centripetal force to form the earth. Into this swirling mass of ki were born Izanagi and Izanami, male and female kami, divine entities, whose birth herald-ed the creation of the relative world. Duality manifests throughout Shintoism.

Thus, in Japan in and yo and their origins in native Shinto and Taoism have, among other influences, formed the contempo-rary cultural matrix. The concept of in and yo, although clearly discernible in Taoism and Shinto, is in fact a universal one, embodying the essence of existence itself.

In-yo, preferably linked rather than split by "and," literally describes "light" and "dark." Since we can recognize light only because of dark, and vice versa, in-yo cannot be separated. Oppo-sites—front, back; up, down; heads, tails—can be known only in relation to one another. Heads and tails are inseparable parts of the same coin, which is ultimately the universe itself. And though opposites, they are not in conflict.

Attempts to ultimately and fully divide aspects of existence are doomed to end in failure, delusion, and discord. The abso-lute—and that is the key word—universe is one, and its essence is ki—or God, kami, the universe, nature, etc., whatever might be preferred. While this absolute ki has divided to form the world in which we live, our relative, dualistic world is never separate from the absolute universe. It is, rather, a manifestation of it. This is expressed by the Zen phrase, "not one, not two."

In-yo is not one, not two, and this holds true for all parts of reality. In-yo makes the absolute, undifferentiated nature of the

68

universe visible, just as distinct phonemes make language possible. Mind and body are one, for instance, and discerning where one ends and the other begins is impossible. Nevertheless, we still speak of mind *and* body, since communication requires such distinctions. We must, however, realize that speech is an artificial construct that mimics nature; it isn't nature itself, and words are not the things they describe.

Moreover, if the two parts of in-yo are not separate and not separable, then they point to something with apparent dual parts that are actually linked "beneath the surface." That something is our relative world. And in the relative world, we see up/down, rich/poor, gentle/severe—endless dichotomy. In seeing these opposites, it's easy to conclude that life is conflict.

A more encompassing view allows us to glimpse the source of these opposites, and the fact that they cannot exist apart from each other. With this observation comes the realization that all opposites form a single whole that is the absolute ki of the universe.

What's more, just as the dual aspect of life does not negate its underlying oneness, seeing this oneness does not eliminate the relative nature of our world. To believe that only harmony exists is a worldview that is flawed, just as is the belief that conflict between opposites is the nature of life. Neither assertion is complete, and both ideas are based on a dualistic viewpoint that engenders conflict in and of itself.

Looking at one aspect of human nature, men and women represent opposites. But these opposites are complementary, thus the natural attraction between them. A specific man and woman join to create a child. From two, we have one; and from the dual, we move to the singular. This child, male or female, finds its opposite. From one, we return to duality. These two in turn give birth to a child. And duality becomes one again.

In-Yo

*Japanese equivalent
of Chinese yin and
yang, a Taoist concept
that refers to the basic,
complementary, and
inseparable dualism
evidenced in the rela-
tive world.*

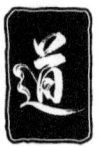

Not one, not two. This is the essence of existence, the com-prehension of which has a revolutionary effect on human con-sciousness.

Funi

D. T. Suzuki, lecturer and writer on Zen, often spoke of "the One in the All and the All in the One." He stated that in this seemingly simple phrase could be found the essence of Zen and Japanese art. Haiku authority Yoel Hoffman has written of the "haiku moment," a nondualistic moment in which the separation between subject and object, self and other, grows blurred. Every-thing is revealed as it is, for in well-crafted haiku the moment is now, time and place cease to exist, becoming any time and every place.

In a similar vein, Yanagi Soetsu, author of *The Unknown Craftsman*, expounded on a quality known as *funi*:

> What, then, is Enlightenment? It is the state of being free from all duality. Sometimes the term "Oneness" is used, but "Non-dual Entirety" (funi) is a more satisfac-tory term because Oneness is likely to be construed as the opposite of duality and hence understood in relative terms.[11]

Funi is a term that may stem from Japanese Buddhism. In its aboriginal Sanskrit, it is *advaitam*, and it is found in the Yui-ma Sutra. But its relationship to the Japanese arts and Ways goes beyond specific religious affiliation.

In funi, or nonduality, the Creator and the created can be distinguished from one another, but they cannot ultimately be divided. Likewise, in the Japanese Ways the artist and the created art cannot be separated. Nonduality, in fact, is more than a Japanese artistic construct and hints at the genuine nature of exis-tence, which transcends cultural and relative distinctions. Funi then points to a state in which the division between ourselves and others, between life and death, dissolves. And with the dissolving of duality comes the transcendence of fear as well as conflict of every kind.

In relation to the Japanese arts and Ways, funi is the lack of separation between what we in the West might typically think of as beauty and what we perceive as ugliness. Japanese art regularly includes asymmetry and irregularity. Embodied by the wabi-sabi concept, this inclusion of the "imperfect" in the Japanese aesthetic of beauty is, at least potentially, an expression of the unity of oppo-sites, an expression of nonduality. In such a case, beauty is not the opposite of ugliness. Rather, beauty lies in a state beyond and includes all opposites; beauty is thus found in naturalness.

For the artist in harmony with nature, no effort or contriv-ance is needed to produce wabi-sabi elegance. Existing in a state transcending distinction, a state in which the duality separating the artist and the universe has dissolved, the artist allows the ki of nature to flow through her or him and into the art being created. Nature, the artist, and the creation form a "nondual entirety." The result is a beauty that does not distinguish between ugliness and its opposite.

Ichi-go, Ichi-e

Ichi-go, ichi-e means "one encounter, one opportunity." It emphasizes that every second is alive and moving; it does not stay in place and it doesn't last. Because of its ephemeral nature, every moment is precious—it is the only moment that genuinely exists.

Judo

The Way of yielding and pliability, a modern martial sport founded by Kano Jigoro Sensei in 1882.

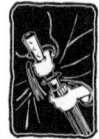

By focusing on the past or the future and encountering the present fully only during times of great intensity, such as a crisis situation, we sleepwalk through life. In the Ways, from tea ceremony to the martial arts, there is an emphasis on the full, unified force of the mind and body, a force brought to bear in the present and in a flash.

In ink painting, for instance, owing to the variable character of the paper, brush, and ink, it's not possible to know exactly how the bristles will twist or turn in contact with the paper or how much ink the paper will absorb. Depending on these variables, sometimes the brush must move more quickly and sometimes more slowly. And judgments must be made as the changing conditions are observed; adjustments must be made right then and there. The artwork that results is one of a kind, as is the singular instant that produced each action in its creation. An exact reproduction is impossible.

Moreover, in shodo and sumi-e "touching up" or redrawing aren't allowed. Erasing isn't possible. The only option is to adapt to the moment at hand, as it takes place, and if things don't go as planned, the sole choice is to move forward. You can't go backward or stop the flow of events, and "do overs" don't exist.

If this sounds a lot like life, it is not a coincidence, and this parallel is one of the ways that the various Do function as lessons in the art of living. The Do are tools to help us see into our nature and the nature of living. When properly practiced, they offer a device to help us wake up to the essence of life, to realize that living is now or not at all.

Ichi-go, ichi-e as a concept also gives the Japanese arts some of their distinctive "Japaneseness," or perhaps the unique character of these arts has given rise to ichi-go, ichi-e. Regardless, the mutual influence is profound, and it serves to distinguish Japanese art from its Western counterpart. For example, where sumi-e is based on a quick, simple brush stroke that is not preceded by a sketch and cannot be touched up later, European oil painting is often built up, altered, and repainted until the desired result is obtained. As the artist and creation are one, this difference represents more than a variance in technique. In sumi-e, we see the spirit of ichi-go, ichi-e directly manifested as technique.

Another example of ichi-go, ichi-e can be found in the martial Ways of Japan. Budo is derived from the hoary traditions of the *bushi*, the warrior of feudal Japan. For a bushi—or more familiarly known as a samurai—facing death was an everyday consideration. The bushi's life was likened to the cherry blossom, whose vibrant color and beauty remain only briefly before being scattered by the wind. Bound to give his life in the service of his homeland, clan, and lord, the bushi knew that he could be required to lay down his life, without faltering, at a moment's notice. By resolving to live each day as if it were his last, he discovered how to experience life completely, without indecisiveness or regret.

For the bushi to be able to have a positive attitude in the face of possibly imminent death, he learned not to worry about either the past, or particularly, the future. This ability is also indispensable for the modern student of the Ways. If the mind remains in the now, it's impossible to worry. People worry solely about an event that's come to pass or one that may take place in the future; the current moment contains no time or space for worry.

The past is forever unalterable, and fretting over the future weakens our ability to fully grasp the present moment and could even condemn us to live through an event twice, first in the imagination and again in reality.

Keeping the mind in the now, unless we consciously want to contemplate the past or future, it's possible to face life without fear. There are then no thoughts of past failure or future hurt, and a positive mental state results: fudoshin, the "immovable mind."

Jujutsu

The art of yielding and pliability, Japan's oldest martial art, used by feudal warriors as a minimally armed form of combat.

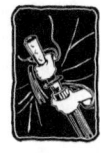

73

Five Attributes of the Way

Kabuki

An ornate form of theater said to have originated in 1603. Features elaborately costumed male actors who play both male and female characters. Accompanied by samisen, flutes, and other instruments, actors employ highly stylized expressions in historical portrayals of nobility, samurai, and commoners.

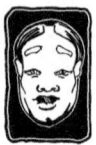

HARMONY

Harmony underlies the Ways. In kado, for example, you must understand the character and growth patterns of the plants you're working with. Yet mere comprehension of the temperament of a given flower isn't enough to arrive at wa, or harmony, in ikebana.

The tranquillity and directness of a flower are mirrored in the eye of the artist, once she surrenders to its blossoms. The scalloped edge of the mountains in the distance, if they can be seen from a window, should be in harmony with the flower arrangement inside the home. The season, too, should be brought into the composition in ikebana, and the artist's ki and creativity are linked to this to give birth to a harmonious trinity. Structure and hue, blossoms and branches, buds and foliage combine with the vase and home, the time of year, and the ki of the adept. Harmony is attained in kado through a refined composite of understanding and reverence. This harmonious condition is reflected in the kado expert's relaxed and gentle treatment of flowers, even when shaping their stems.

Similarly, the more accomplished one becomes in the Japanese martial Ways, the greater the ability to recognize and understand an opponent's intentions. Through correct, hard training, the martial artist arrives at an unflappable alertness that allows him to literally comprehend the opponent's very mind. Nevertheless, this enhanced sensitivity is insignificant unless it is accompanied by a spirit that respects the opponent's intentions. Forcing people in budo, or plants in kado, seldom equals a practical or efficient use of ki. When both understanding and respect coalesce, harmony is brought about in budo; and in this harmonious state, an expert can lead and control an assailant.

74

Harmony is a critical aspect of brush writing as well. In shodo, harmony is expressed through dynamic balance. Balance is asymmetrical, which causes a feeling of action within the characters. It could be likened to a photograph of a sprinter, whose inclined running stance has been frozen by the camera. The snapshot gives a sensation of motion (as opposed to one of a person standing still). But this feeling of movement is unlike that in a photo taken of a runner at the moment she has tripped and is stumbling forward. Both images show bodies in motion; the crucial difference between the two is balance.

Dynamic balance in shodo is also achieved through a natural variation of heavy and light brush pressure, which produces a fluctuation of thick and thin lines of ink. Brush strokes of uniform thickness create a work that is awkward, artificial, and dead.

Although harmony is expressed differently in kado, budo, and shodo, the principle of harmony is a constant element in all the Ways.

Kan

Intuitive perception; also connotes the idea of "quickened insight," the ability to perceive what is about to take place even before, for example, all the action has played out. In the Ways, it refers to learning through direct experience, personal discovery, and intuition, and by means of the cultivation of heightened intuitive perception itself.

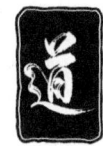

ASYMMETRICAL BALANCE

Asymmetrical balance is another distinctive feature of the Japanese arts. It is sometimes known as hacho, intentional unevenness, which is an especially distinctive feature of Japanese culture. Japanese poetry, to give just one example, has an uneven number of asymmetrical lines of verse, three lines of five, seven, and five syllables in haiku and five lines of five, seven, five, seven, and seven syllables in waka poems.

Asymmetrical balance can also be clearly seen in kado, where it elicits a feeling of naturalness. Since nature itself is ever changing, kado shuns a dead, static impression, which is precisely what is produced by rigid, symmetrical balance. Unevenness suggests endless change and evokes a feeling of charismatic move-

75

Kan Geiko

Rigorous training in one of the Do that deliberately takes place during the coldest time of the year. While it can be misinterpreted as an exercise in masochism, kan geiko is actually a form of "spiritual forging"— a quality commonly identified as one of the primary reasons for participating in the various Do forms. The Do value and cultivate a positive and indomitable attitude, the real motivation for training long hours with no heat in the dead of winter. See also shochu geiko.

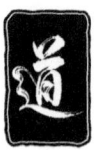

ment and life. Thus, a relatively long branch placed on one side of an arrangement will not be balanced on the other by a matching branch; rather, something exhibiting a contrasting texture or shape will be used to create a dynamic, asymmetrical balance. Kado also uses in particular an unequal triangular balance. Many compositions consist of three central elements that represent heaven (*ten*), earth (*chi*), and humankind (*jin*), with humankind assuming an intermediate balance between the other two.

"The Way of flowers" also makes ample use of empty space, which tempts the mind's eye to complete the arrangement, drawing the observer into the work. In other words, the incomplete asks to be completed; that which is unfinished is in harmony with life's dynamics of unchanging change and evolution. This expression of asymmetry does not inevitably denote a lack of balance; rather, in kado, the union of opposites creates a form of balanced imbalance. An unbalanced balance in kado mirrors the nature of a Zen koan, a metaphysical question that rises above the conditions of logical thought.

The manipulation of asymmetry, incompleteness, and unevenness are also found in Japanese ink painting, brush writing, and even classical architecture. Like harmony, asymmetry is a ubiquitous feature of the Ways.

ARTLESSNESS

As discussed earlier, the Ways have been influenced by philosophies and religions that include Zen and other forms of Buddhism, Shinto, and Dokyo. In the Ways and Taoism, less is more, and noninterference with nature allows the creative course of the universe to flow through the artist.

In order to grasp the concept of artlessness, an understanding of aesthetics such as wabi and sabi is necessary.

As stated previously, the poverty of wabi is, in the tea ceremony for example, a poverty of ostentatious display and the human attachment to things; it speaks to the suspension of intellectual entanglement and all forms of self-regard and affectation in the pursuit of the unadorned truth of nature underlying all relative phenomena. As nature is asymmetrical, spontaneous, imperfect, wabi expresses a purity of natural imperfection. It evokes the nobility of artlessness, of even "deformity." When this artlessness merges with a simple antiqueness, Japanese artists describe this as sabi. In certain instances sabi, literally "solitariness," suggests an effortless quality.

The aesthetic concepts of wabi, sabi, and shibumi underlie and inform the ideal of artlessness in the Japanese Ways, but they also, at their deepest level, touch something in the human heart that is universal.

Karate-do

"The Way of the empty hand," a Japanese martial Way imported from Okinawa that emphasizes striking techniques and is often practiced competitively.

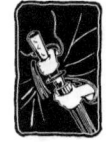

IMPERMANENCE

Sabi also relates to the universal impermanence in life; it expresses the fleeting nature of existence. To blend sabi into life is to recognize that relationships, even those we cherish, are fleeting. They exist in the moment, and once this is seen with our whole heart, every moment becomes precious, stretching beyond the boundaries of time.

Sabi as an expression of impermanence in art means that, whether we participate in cha-no-yu, view another's flower arrangement, or create our own arrangements, the mind must be in the present, knowing we will never again have the chance to encounter that moment.

Not only sabi but indeed all the aesthetic principles of the Ways describe, in their different emphases, a universal Way. Each Do represents a different path to the same spot. Proponents of

Kata

Traditional, formal exercises designed to preserve and communicate the essential principles of an art. Kata are found in some form in most Japanese arts.

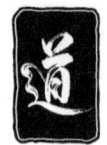

the Japanese arts universally regard transience as a respected aesthetic, if not spiritual, element. Releasing self-consciousness and completely experiencing a single, fleeting moment is equal to the realization that life exists only at this instant, and we'll never have another chance to live it again.

Utsuroi is another word that relates to the impermanent nature of the universe. It suggests the ephemeral quality that exists like a reflection in a mirror . . . appearing one second, and disappearing the next . . . with nary a trace left on the reflective surface. It describes in kado, for example, the understanding on the part of the artist and viewer of the profound meaning and beauty inherent in the impermanence of the flowers in an arrangement. Think of the gossamer colors of falling petals. People who see futility in the careful composition of flowers that will soon shrivel and die miss this understanding and suffer under the illusion that some form of everlasting art exists.

The acknowledgment and expression of impermanence is found in many aspects of Japanese culture. Historically, straw sandals were worn out and traded at each stage of a lengthy trip. Clothing often consisted of a small number of widths of cloth loosely sewn together for wearing, and later unsewn for washing. In the traditional house, paper shoji panels were re-covered twice each year. Likewise, straw tatami mats were renewed each autumn. These and other examples reveal the Japanese comfort with impermanence.

Impermanence, nonattachment, living in the present, uniting mind and body in a moment transcending time—all find expression in such aesthetic ideas as the solitude of sabi and the "sentimental melancholy" associated with mono no aware (or simply, *aware*), ideas that make Japanese art clearly unique but that, at the same time, point to something transcendent: creation and destruction each leading inevitably to the other, the never-ending dance of in-yo, the unborn and undying indivisible absolute that lies within the eternal pulse of life and death.

UNITY WITH THE UNIVERSE

Awareness of our inborn unity with the universe or nature is the common point that ties the above principles together. Human beings are no more disconnected from the universe than a wave is independent of the sea. Each wave is unique, and exists, if only for a moment, but every wave originates in the sea, rises from it, and returns to it. The sea and its wave are one.

In like manner, humans are one with the universe. We contain the essential mark of the universe, ki, within us; each individual is a microcosm of the universe. But to know this basic unity requires going beyond hearing or reading of it. You cannot feel the wind by reading about it; further, a theoretical understanding alone, without firsthand experience, without authentic embodiment, only encourages a split between mind and body, a conflict in which the mind "knows" but the body cannot do. It leads to a phantom of comprehension instead of harmony with an absolute universe that is timeless and infinite. In this state of harmony, we directly perceive our own limitless and eternal nature. As between the sea and its wave, harmony with the universe means no beginning, no end, no fear, and no suffering. It is a moment that is unending, beyond the bonds of time, beyond duality.

Harmony in kado, for instance, is arrived at when the artist perceives the growth patterns and attributes of the plants that are being arranged. It is a perception, however, of not only the character of particular plants and flowers used in a flower arrangement but also, on a deeper level, the spirit, or ki, of nature itself.

In bonsai, suiseki, and the arrangement of a traditional garden, Japanese art aims to capture the essential nature of tree, stone,

Keiko

"Practice," but not practice as we think of it in Western terms. Practice in the Do isn't a matter of "beginning a course," or "taking a class." Instead, students of the Ways run through actions that they have repeated hundreds of times in the past. Learning takes place, but frequently on subconscious and intuitive levels.

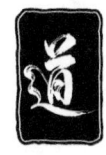

79

landscape, to create a work of art that exemplifies the very core of these things, and ultimately, the substance of nature itself. This aim begins with a recognition of the fundamental character of the thing the artist is working with and progresses to a "sculpting" of the material to intensify the expression of its intrinsic character. A Japanese gardener works "with the grain," and as he prunes and shapes, he reveals an aspect of beauty that is born in nature but that nature has hidden in its abundance.

Japanese art aims to discern and then liberate what has always been present. And who are we to assume that such liberation is needed? Humanity is a part of nature. We, like the flowers in ikebana and the trees or shrubs in the niwa, are part of the infinite variety that is the universe. We are transitory and timeless, existing in the eternal present, just like the aspects of nature we create with. In perceiving and freeing aspects of nature that have always existed, we ultimately see into our own nature.

In Japan, native arts both humble and dignify their participants. Humankind is forced to recognize its mortality and the fact of impermanence. But in seeing our smallness in the universe, we discover our link to something infinitely large, eternal, and awesome.

Such ideas aren't always directly articulated in Japan, but they are, and have been, present in most Japanese arts and Ways. They are living notions passed down for generations, and as part of a living tradition these ideas are subject to wide variance of expression, interpretation, and even understanding. Still, they have existed in Japan nearly as long as nature itself.

As an expression of humankind's inseparable interdependence with the universe, the principles described here form an aesthetic independent of a style or trend tied to a certain point in Japanese history. They actually mirror the perpetual character of nature. To comprehend harmony, artlessness, and impermanence is never-ending, much like the endless universe itself; and sincere understanding comes as we bring to light as well as reflect these states in ourselves.

Culture versus the Essence of the Way

It is widely recognized that the various Do (despite having been influenced by Chinese culture, art, and religion) originated in Japan. Because they are inextricably entwined with Japanese culture, an understanding of Japanese culture is needed to make more than superficial progress in their practice. This book was written to aid both writer and reader in arriving at this understanding.

Nevertheless, it is legitimate to ask to what degree the Ways and Japanese culture are separate, can be separated, and indeed if they should be separated. The evidence of neglect on the part of both Western and Japanese students of the Ways to deeply consider these questions makes such an inquiry even more important. In this book we are concerned with two entities: the different Japanese Ways and the Way itself. The Way means the Way of the universe, and so it clearly is not limited to a specific art. The Way is universal; the Ways are particular. Being both simple and complex, this distinction is sometimes overlooked. In a sense, it can and cannot be made. As the mind cannot truly be separated from the body, the Way and Ways cannot be separated. Still, the mind and body have different characteristics and modes of functioning; the mind has no form, the body has form, and so on. We can make distinctions and speak in terms of mental versus physical despite the fundamental oneness of the two. The Way of the universe and its outward expressions, the different Ways, are similarly inseparable but nonetheless distinguishable.

Most people who have practiced a Do seriously have, from

Kendo

The Way of the sword, a modern martial Way centering on the use of the Japanese sword and often practiced as a sport.

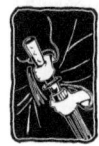

81

Kenjutsu

The art of the sword, a martial art based on the classical use of the Japanese sword.

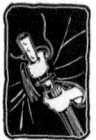

time to time, heard a Japanese teacher state that only a native Japanese practitioner of chado, shodo, budo, and others, can really understand the art. This sentiment, which seems to be less frequently voiced these days, is obviously infuriating to non-Japanese students of the Do. And while this may shock and further infuriate such individuals, I would agree with it—but only on one level.

The Ways are Japanese cultural arts. The Way is not. As Japanese cultural disciplines, the different Do are an outgrowth of Japanese art, history, religion, geography, government, and many other specific factors. And the reference is not simply to contemporary Japanese culture but includes everything that has come before. If we separate the Do from their cultural ground, they cease to exist, degenerating into nothing but a generic sort of art. While multiculturalism is a popular idea and a good thing in general, there is no value in reducing the art forms of other cultures to whatever an individual practitioner is comfortable with based on his own cultural preferences. This kind of homogenizing will only render the arts of other cultures bland and shallow.

The Americanizing of cuisines from other traditions provides a simple example. I like spicy food, and so I frequent Thai restaurants. I'm often disappointed, however, when I discover the food is bland and inauthentic. Querying owners, I'm usually informed that the cuisine has been "adjusted to American tastes." Perhaps, but it has also sometimes been rendered unrecognizable and tasteless. I'd hate to see this happen to the Japanese Do.

Since the Do are an outgrowth of centuries of Japanese cultural development, they can never be understood by Westerners in the manner that native Japanese understand them. Plainly, Westerners aren't Japanese, and we must arrive at our own comprehension of these arts. Whether our comprehension of these arts is problematic depends on whether it results in a homogenization, or "dumbing down," of these classical arts. Like tampering with a rare classic car to make it "look cool" or painting big numbers on an antique clock to make it easier to read, facile alterations to these arts would damage their integrity. And make no mistake, a number of the Do forms are very much "living antiques" that derive part of their value from their antiquity. I, and a number of other Western and Japanese devotees of the Do, would urge Westerners to leave them intact, and if this isn't palatable, to consider a different activity more suitable to their tastes, rather than destroying venerable cultural artifacts.

Despite some Japanese arts and Ways having survived for centuries, as living arts, they are fragile and depend for their survival on the people who teach them. If these people, Japanese or non-Japanese, lose the art's essence that is rooted in Japan, then a given art may be rendered unrecognizable within a generation or two.

What with the westernization and internationalization of Japan, and the transplantation of the Do onto foreign soil, this consideration becomes vital. How will the Do grow outside of Japan? This and other crucial questions need to be looked into, but they form a topic that is beyond the scope of this book. Nonetheless, regarding the successful transplantation of the Do, we need to consider the following ideas.

I now and then hear some American teachers of different Do speak of "not needing the Japanese at this point," or "being better than the Japanese at . . . [insert your favorite art]." I can only shake my head. Competition of this sort has no place in the Do, as Westerners and Japanese should have the same goal: the understanding, dissemination, and preservation of traditional Japanese cultural arts and Ways. For when the Japanese aspects of an art are lost, so too are the art's history and character. In such an event, a different name should be applied to the art. At the least, if we alter the nature of such arts, we should note this by indicating that we teach or practice American karate or *European-style*

Ki

Life energy, chi in Chinese, its meaning ranges in scope from one's spirit to the animating force behind the universe. See also ki-in.

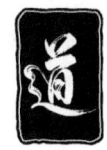

83

Ki-in

Rhythm of life energy. Describes a sensitivity to and harmony with ki on all levels. When the artist senses and unites with the rhythm of the ki of nature, the essence of the universe is expressed in art. A sustained rhythmic flow of ki and attentiveness in the execution of a work results in the union of body and mind and the creation of artwork that resonates with a life-affirming rhythm and dynamism even centuries after its creation.

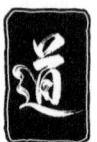

ikebana, instead of trading off time-honored Japanese traditions. The Do are, after all, *Japanese Ways*, as evidenced by their Japanese names.

But is that all they are? Decidedly not. If they were, I wouldn't have bothered to write this book. Because, although I enjoy participating in parts of Japanese culture, that wasn't my original motivation for getting involved in the Do that I study. And it isn't why I continue to practice them. My original motives had much more to do with the universal aspects of the different Do, aspects whose understanding allow us to cultivate attributes that are valued regardless of cultural orientation. These aspects relate to the Way as much as to the Ways (for the Way is ultimately the Way of the universe).

The Ways are Japanese, and Westerners cannot divorce these arts or themselves from Japanese teachers or culture without losing something significant. Yet just as the Japanese Do are Japanese, they're also expressions of a Way that transcends nationalities and political boundaries. Understanding this universal Way has *nothing* to do with where we were born. It is the Way of humanity, the Way of the universe, and its significance is boundless and timeless.

So, while we Westerners perhaps can't understand the Ways as the Japanese do, we can certainly grasp *the Way* itself. And between Japanese and Western students of the Do, this is a most important link. Although I have heard a few Japanese sensei state that "only we Japanese can understand a Do," *none* of my fairly large number of Japanese friends, seniors, and teachers (of several different Do) has ever made such a proclamation because of the ease with which it can be misunderstood. If your sensei makes this assertion, what he is saying might be true, but only on one level, and perhaps not the most important one at that. Such a claim also indicates that the person espousing it is focused primarily on the particular, cultural aspects of the Do, and such a teacher is perhaps not the best one for a student interested in the meditative, universal attributes of the Way.

Because of my long exposure to the Japanese arts, Ways, and culture, several of my teachers have urged me to serve as a sort of bridge between East and West, particularly in terms of the Do. Other teachers in Japan espouse the international proliferation of the Ways as a vehicle toward *sekai heiwa*, or "world peace." Thus the Ways have at their core both universal and particular qualities. The particular manifestation of the Ways is Japanese, but they are also human expressions of the very heart of the universe.

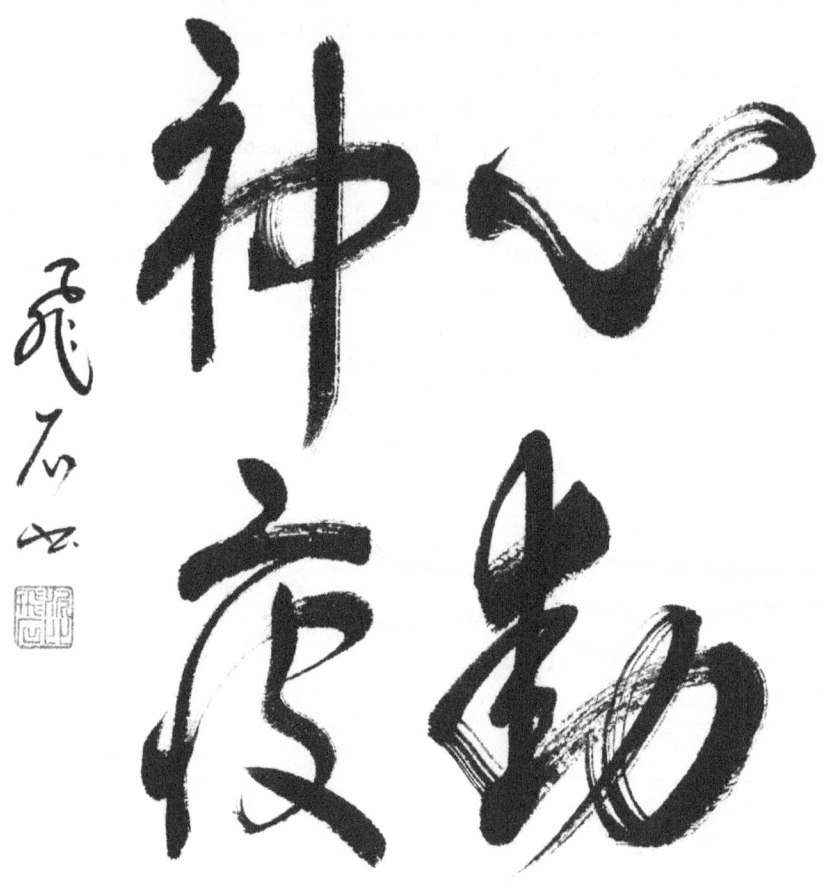

Kokoro ugokeba shin tsukareru.
"When the mind is agitated, the spirit grows fatigued."
CHIEI

This is from Chiei's 1,000-character *Sen-ji-mon*, a classic work that points to a sentiment found in all the Japanese arts and Ways: spiritual stability stems from fudoshin—"the immovable mind." Yet like the painted characters above, fudoshin is calm and unwavering, but infinitely dynamic and capable of instantaneous action. Effective Japanese calligraphy mirrors this oneness of movement and stillness.

Chapter 3

THE SPIRIT OF
THE WAY

The general public and beginning students of the Japanese arts often think that art comes from the body. They assume that the hand determines the skillful brush work of the calligrapher or the arm the expert use of the sword. Those long immersed in these arts know, however, that it is the mind that paints through the hands, and the mind that cuts, even more than the sword. In short, the brush and sword cannot move unless they do so first in the mind.

Despite this truth, training in the Japanese cultural arts is often directed toward the body, and it takes a wise teacher to help us train the mind so it can lead the body to produce art. It's also important to study how to see the mind via the body and its artistic expressions. In this vein, Japanese calligraphers often speak of brush writing as being "a picture of the mind."

Art Emanates Directly from the Mind

The following simple experiment provides an idea of the importance of the mind in action. Place your hands about six inches away from each other, with the palms facing as shown in Figure 8. Sit or stand, keeping your body upright but relaxed, and focus your eyes gently on your hands. The aim here is to move your palms together by the sheer force of your concentration.

First, create a mental picture of your palms coming together. Second, simply think

FIG. 8. Stand with your hands six inches apart and bring them together with the force of your will. Keep your eyes focused on the hands.

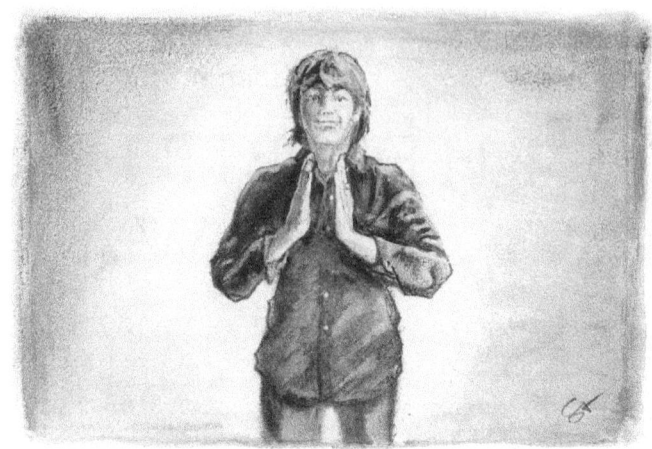

that your palms are already together, and hold that thought. Third, "talk to yourself," mentally directing your palms to touch. Each of these directions represents essentially the same thought process, but some people have more success with one approach than another.

The point is to use the strength of a concentrated mind to influence the body and to see how your body responds automatically to whatever thought is in the mind.

An "automatic response" is key to this exercise, and the experiment is to see if it is attainable. Don't make any tentative assumptions. Avoid deliberately bringing the palms together. Rather, just focus resolutely on one of the above thoughts or images, sustain this state of concentration, and see what happens. If close attention doesn't waver, and the body remains relaxed, many find that the hands move without any intentional effort. This effortless feeling is unlike the way many of us move our bodies, and it is one of the secrets to arriving in art at maximum effectiveness with minimum strain.

Japanese Ways as a Reflection of the Mind

When asked exactly how a Do form functions as a Way, as opposed to simply a mechanical skill, I frequently explain that the body reflects the mind, and so any art can function as a visible representation of our spiritual condition. The movement of the body in dance or martial arts, the sound of the flute, the lines of ink on paper—all these actions equate to the mind expressing itself through the body, and as such, they offer opportunities to see more fully into our true nature. It is on this level that they function as Ways.*

It is also true that a Do is nothing more than mechanical action if the mind is misused. To further examine how the Japanese cultural arts can function as a depiction of the mind, we'll look at a variety of experiments like the one just presented. Since the mind controls the body, the vigor of our concentration will be the determining element in these exercises.

Harmonizing the Mind and Body

The creation of art requires inspiration, a knowledge of our tools, and an effective technique for using those tools. The skillful expression of ourselves in art (or life), with maximum efficiency

---

* The mind leads the body's actions, and this isn't limited to Japanese Do. Not long ago I read about pianist Liu Chi Kung. In 1958, he placed second to Van Cliburn in a Tchaikovsky piano contest. Not long after, during the Chinese Cultural Revolution, he was imprisoned. He lived alone in his cell for seven years. When he was released, he almost immediately played a series of highly acclaimed concerts. The public was amazed that none of his virtuosity had been lost, despite seven years without a piano. When asked how he had retained such a high level of skill with no piano to practice on, he replied, "I practiced every day in my mind."

Kodo

The Way of incense. Brought to Japan in the sixth century by Buddhist monks, who used the aromas in purification rites, incense became entertainment for aristocrats two hundred years later. During the fourteenth century, samurai would aromatize their helmets and armor with incense for an aura of invulnerability. In the seventeenth and eighteenth centuries, incense appreciation spread to the upper and middle classes. Kodo has long been a wellspring of spiritual sustenance in Japan. Modern practitioners use incense to heighten the ambiance of home or office, to delight guests, to honor special occasions, to calm the mind after a difficult day, and to comfort nerves before retiring.

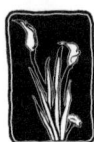

and minimum effort, also requires the most effective ways of using the mind and body; our minds and bodies are, in the end, the sole tools we really own in life. Using the mind and body together naturally, practicably, and harmoniously allows for freedom of action and self-expression and is the most effective technique for using these tools. When the tie between mind and body is weak, novices in any art can observe a skill demonstrated by an instructor, or in a book, comprehend it intellectually, yet still fail to physically respond in the correct manner.

Comprehending the mind-body relationship, founders of the different Ways seem to have envisioned their arts in part as a means to directly discover how to coordinate these two most basic tools. By uniting the mind and body in a specific art, we have the chance to do so in daily living as well. It is in fact only when the mind and body work as a unit that we arrive at self-harmony. By learning to focus the entire coordinated energy of our minds and bodies toward a task, we also bring the force of our total being to bear upon that activity, thus discovering latent abilities and talents. In the Ways, this full and consolidated human power is sometimes referred to as ki.

Ki

Many Japanese arts and especially Ways mention ki as an important aspect of their teachings. In some arts, ki and its relationship to unity of mind and body are also explored. However, this exploration has commonly occurred on a largely intuitive level, involving years of experimental practice. The late Nakamura Tempu Sensei, founder of the Shin-shin-toitsu-do Japanese yoga system and a Western-style doctor, used his medical and scientific training to evolve a way of consciously and rationally studying ki and mind-body coordination. His teachings echo those of the creators of a number of Do, including calligraphy, flower arrangement, and martial arts.

Nakamura Sensei viewed the mind as an invisible aspect of the body and the body as a visible aspect of the mind. He equated the mind and body to a stream, with the mind the upper part and the body the lower.

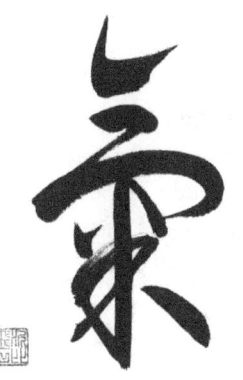

KI: *This interpretation of the character ki is brushed in the abstract and abbreviated sosho script—equivalent to cursive writing in English—and it means "life energy."*

Unhelpful or negative elements that enter the upper part flow to the lower part and thus affect the body and our well-being. Understanding this effect, all the Ways value positive thought patterns.

The use of the word "ki" in this book may be different from what you have read elsewhere; it is a deliberate attempt to linguistically point at something that, owing to its holistic nature, is beyond description and yet still wholly tangible in everyday existence. Looking at ki from a different perspective will help show what I mean.

Physicists explain that every natural phenomenon is made up of variable mixtures of energy and matter. Such combinations constantly disintegrate into their component parts and reintegrate to create fresh phenomena. Matter can be transformed into energy, energy into matter. Neither can be annihilated absolutely. The entirety of all matter and energy has remained unchanging since our universe came into existence, and thus energy and matter—the essence of heaven and earth—are everlasting. From this viewpoint the innumerable parts of life that result from this aggregation of matter and energy are also infinite and eternal.

In recent years, a sort of union of quantum physics and deep

Kohai

One's junior in school, place of employment, or a traditional art. See also sempai; tate shakai.

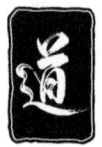

mysticism has frequently been touted in popular media. Conversations with actual scientists and physicists reveal, however, that some of the claims are based on a poor understanding, and not all such views are embraced by the majority of scientists. Nonetheless, speaking broadly on the basis of the nature of energy and matter as outlined above, I use ki to indicate an indestructible union of matter and energy, something that is both ever changing and constant. Ki describes the elementary essence of existence, which experiences continual integration, disintegration, and re-creation. Ki can be understood as the connective tissue of creation, and, more specifically, as the component that joins mind and body. It is nondualistic in nature and thus beyond description, but it is not beyond experiencing.

It is also not exclusively spiritual or nonphysical. Ki is no more spiritual than it is material. It is, however, all encompassing. The body is ki as much as the mind is, in that every cell in the body exhibits a metabolic process, is alive, and thus has life energy. It is a visible form of ki, whereas the mind is refined, invisible ki. Ki is made tangible in nature through its manifestations, the limitless actions of nature's infinite number of integral parts. The action of ki is visible also in the body.

Because such verbalizing can easily become abstract, the late Dr. Nakamura invented straightforward exercises to experiment with the relationship between the mind and body, the intrinsic power of mind-body coordination, and the manifested action of ki. Since most Japanese arts, in addition to Shin-shin-toitsu-do, value the positive cultivation of ki and the harmony of body and mind, many top instructors in other arts and Ways have pursued Nakamura Sensei's teachings, and some of these concepts and exercises have found their way into other disciplines, notably the martial arts (aikido in particular) and healing arts.

This chapter presents experiments derived from Nakamura

Sensei's exercises for consciously experiencing ki and mind-body coordination. You'll need a friend to help with these experiments; since they aren't practiced alone, they amount to not only a means of studying the relationship between mind and body but also a method of examining interpersonal relationships.

Koryu Bujutsu

*Ancient martial arts.
Refers to any of the
classical martial arts
used by Japan's feudal
warriors.*

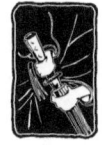

EXPERIMENT ONE

Sit in a kneeling position, with your legs tucked under you and your left big toe resting on top of your right one. Leave some space between your knees and keep an erect posture. This is called *seiza*—"correct, calm sitting"—and it is utilized almost universally in some form in most Japanese cultural arts. If you cannot comfortably sit in this position, you can perform this exercise while seated in a chair.

With your shoulders relaxed and your elbows down at your side, place your palms together, fingers pointing up. Have your partner grip your wrists and try to pull your hands apart. Tensing your arms, resist your partner's efforts. If both of you are of roughly equal strength, your hands will separate quickly. This represents the limits of your body's power and exemplifies the way most people try to exert their strength and typically deal with conflict. But don't take my word for this. By experimenting and observing yourself and others in life, find out if this statement is true.

Next, visualize ki flowing through both arms and uniting at the palms and projecting upward from the fingertips. Try thinking of two powerful rivers that merge in your palms. To help create this feeling of merging, press your palms together firmly so that you experience a clear connection, but still lightly enough that tension isn't present. Ask your partner to attempt to pull your hands apart again, using the same amount of force as before (for accurate

FIG. 9. Seiza with palms together. Your partner tries to pull your palms apart. Visualize ki flowing toward the palms.

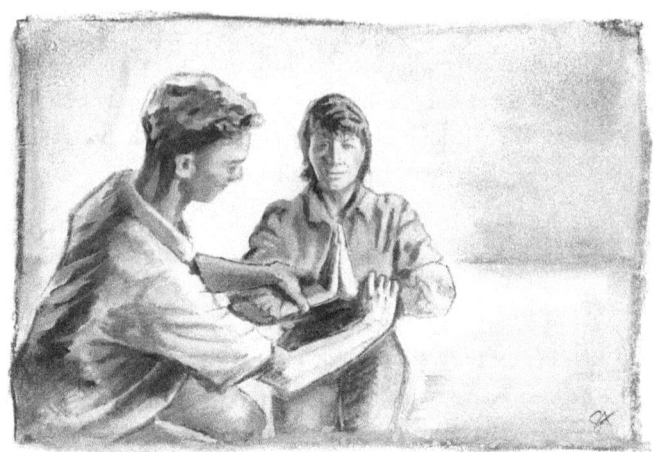

comparison). Keep the palms gently pressed together as explained, but don't add extra muscular exertion. Do not resist, do not give up. Do nothing and simply sustain the image of ki flowing into your palms and merging, as shown in Figure 9. It might take several repetitions, trying both approaches each time, to thoroughly understand the ramifications of this exercise. (This will be equally true of the experiments that follow.) Once you get the hang of it, you should notice a tangible difference between the contrasting states of body tension/resistance and nonresistance with the correct use of ki.

Even if your muscles are strong enough to keep your partner from separating your palms on the first attempt, how does it feel when you do this? In comparison with the second approach, much more tension and effort are usually required to keep the hands together. The correct and natural use of ki isn't supernatural, but it does allow us to arrive at maximum efficiency with minimum effort, a quality valued in all the Ways and most prominently espoused by Kano Jigoro Sensei, the creator of judo.

EXPERIMENT TWO

Kneel or sit in a chair. Visualize the movement of ki toward your palms and ask your friend to try to pull your hands apart. They should be immovable as before. Then, while your partner continues to try to separate your palms, suddenly think of reversing the flow of ki, away from your palms and back into your body. In most cases, coinciding with this rapid pulling in of ki, the hands separate. Yet, your partner is simply maintaining the same pressure. What has changed isn't your friend's amount of force, and no contrast is being made in this case between muscular tension and the relaxed use of ki. Rather, the contrast lies in the way in which the mind is used and in the movement of ki itself.

When ki manifests in human form, it is analogous to a flame. When the flame burns cleanly and strongly, it gives off a powerful outward projection of heat. As the flame begins to die out, its radiation of heat withdraws. When the flame dies, its outward projection of heat also ceases.

Tension and/or the negative use of the mind in living is referred to in Japanese as *ki ga nukeru*, "withdrawal of ki," and it results in a loss of mind and body unification. When the body is relaxed and the mind positive, ki flows outward dynamically from all parts of the body, and mind-body coordination is sustained. Experiment Two compares these two conditions.

EXPERIMENT THREE

Remaining in the same position, have your friend press down on your fingertips, as shown in Figure 10. First, focus your attention on where your partner's palm is touching your fingertips, thus stopping your mind and ki at this point. Your body and arms are not tense, but not limp. Have your partner press downward

Ma

Literally "space" or "interval." Refers to the physical and/or psychological space that exists between people and/or things. It constitutes a technical principle in many of the Japanese arts and Ways. In the martial Ways, for example ma (or ma-ai) refers to a proper combative distance; in visual arts such as shodo, it describes the appropriate space between strokes of a character and between individual characters.

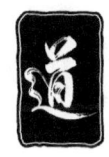

FIG. 10. Seiza with palms together. Your partner pushes down on your fingertips with his palm. Visualize ki flowing out of the fingers.

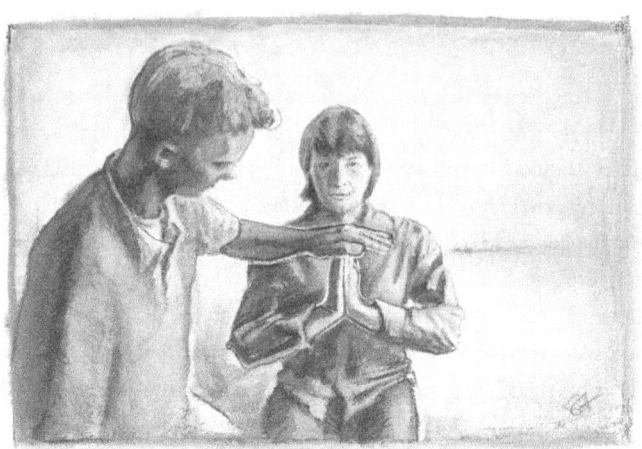

until your fingers buckle and/or your hands are forced down. How much power did it take to accomplish this action?

Now, keeping the same feeling in your body and arms, visualize ki flowing powerfully from your fingertips and up toward heaven. Aim for the sensation of it continuing forever to join with the infinite body of ki that is the universe, so that your flow of concentration remains unbroken. Once you obtain this feeling, have your partner press down on your fingertips as before, but this time don't stop ki at your friend's palm; imagine it passing through his or her palm, along with any other obstacles, and continuing infinitely. Even though your partner has used the same force as before, do you notice a difference in your personal power?

The positive use of ki requires not only a supple and calm posture but also a mind that doesn't become stuck on anything or at any point in time, as this serves only to stop the natural movement of ki. Life is constant change. The ki that animates the universe is likewise in constant motion. Living things are not static, and, as "living power," ki too is in continual motion—a movement that the Ways harmonize with rather than impede. This harmony with the ever-changing nature of existence is arrived at via nonattachment, a quality valued in all the Do. Exercise Three is the outward expression of nonattachment.

EXPERIMENT FOUR

Let's try something different. Seated as before, place your palms together. But this time, state aloud, in a strong and clear voice, "I cannot." Immediately following this, have your partner press down again on your fingertips. How much power does it take before your hands are forced downward?

Next, maintaining the same erect posture as before, with the identical feeling of being not tense and not limp, say aloud, "I can!" At this moment, your partner should apply downward pressure on your fingertips. Don't fight back, but don't give up. What happens?

Providing you believe what you're saying, a clear difference should be seen in your power in each case. The positive use of the mind, encouraged by positive verbal expressions, releases and enhances the movement of ki. Likewise, negative thoughts lead to psychological withdrawal, which parallels the withdrawal of ki in a negative state.

Although the mental imagery used in the preceding exercises can only be used consciously and at specific times in the Ways and in daily life, a positive mental state can be cultivated and sustained on an ongoing basis. This state, both positive and active, equals the dynamic outward movement of ki that exchanges with the ki of the universe. This movement and exchange of ki is infinite, eternal, and thus ultimately beyond description. Nevertheless, these exercises, because they help us to directly and personally experience something that can only be suggested, are valuable.

These exercises are not meant, however, to dazzle friends,

Misogi

Purification, a ritual associated with Shinto spiritual training. While saying prayers or chanting, devotees sometimes strip to loincloths and stand under a waterfall to cleanse the spirit.

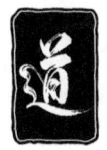

overmystify ki, or lend to the Japanese arts and Ways an inscrutable occultism: the natural universe is miraculous just as it is, and people's failure to recognize this is the origin of much dissatisfaction in the world. The exercises demonstrate that using the mind and body as a unit is more effective than focusing exclusively on muscular power. What's more, the linked use of the mind and body increases the efficiency of muscular action. These experiments can also show by example how mind, body, and nature are interconnected, and how "reaching out" with ki to harmonize with nature can cause results that resonate in material realities (the body, in this example). The exercises give us an occasion to experience a different mode of dealing with the world, a way that is at once harmonious and effective.

The discovery of new and meaningful principles must, however, be complemented by their expression in everyday life for them to have worth. These experiments with ki offer insights that lead the way to examining how to use our bodies naturally, maintain a positive attitude, and focus our minds, which will bring benefits not only in the Ways but also in life in general. Without these insights, the experiments are little more than party tricks.

Once we see the benefits of a positive attitude, concentration, and a natural, relaxed posture, it's necessary to train the mind and body in a methodical, disciplined fashion in order to realize these characteristics. And the classical Japanese Ways offer an opportunity to train ourselves in precisely this fashion.

Hara

Like ki, the concept of hara has a long tradition in Japan and is a prominent aspect of many Ways. In Japan, and to some degree in other Asian countries, the focus of mental energy in the hara, or "abdomen," has been viewed as a means of realizing a person's complete potential. The Japanese view of the hara as a human's vital center is not unlike the Western notion of the heart or brain. Although there are differences between East and West relating to this subject, there are similarities that make it possible for Westerners to grasp the idea of hara. For instance, we speak of "having butterflies" in the stomach, and the Japanese expression *hara ga tatsu*, "the hara is rising up," means to be enraged; thus the notion of the hara as being a place of strong emotion is shared by both traditions. *Hara ga nai hito* refers to a timid person, "a person with no hara," which is comparable to our adage that someone "has no guts."

By now it has likely become clear that focusing the mind in the moment increases mental force and enhances the ability to coordinate mind and body, and, in the tradition of Japan's classical Ways, the place to concentrate on to achieve harmony of mind and body is the lower abdomen—the hara. There are compelling reasons for this idea.

The weight of the upper body reaches its maximum point of density beneath the navel, and this area corresponds to the center of gravity and balance for the body. If we focus the mind on the front surface of the lower abdomen, about four finger widths under the belly button, we're joining the mind and body in the same place and at the same time. Since the body dwells only in the present moment, by calming the mind in the hara, we're bringing our mind into the present as well. We've connected the mind and body.

In Japanese arts, ki is concentrated in the hara as a means of not just coordinating the mind and body but also bringing about mind-body stability and the restoration of composure. Calming the mind in the lower abdomen can aid in everything from accomplishing better balance in sports to stabilizing the mind before

Mono no Aware

Aesthetic and spiritual concept describing a sentiment of pathos in response to an awareness of the fleeting nature of our relative world. Evokes a perception of beauty in the fragile, impermanent nature of life and suggests that genuine beauty depends on this very impermanence. Relates also to a harmoniousness with the constantly changing universe and with the universal cycles of creation and destruction.

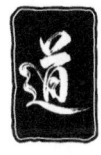

FIG. 11. Seiza with palms together. Your partner sits next to you and pushes your chest with his fingertips. Focus your mind on the hara.

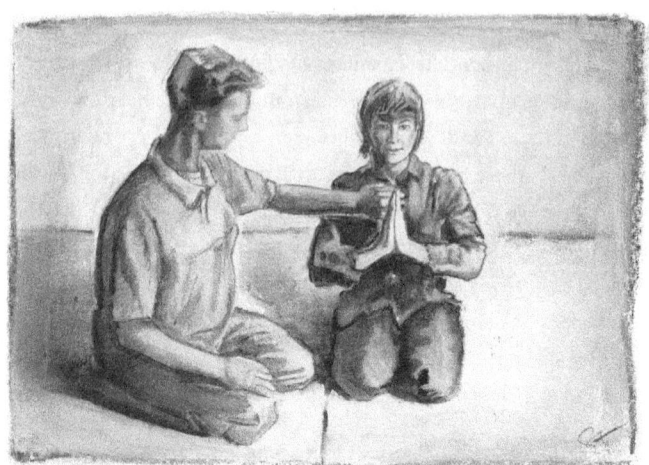

an important phone call. To see the legitimacy of this statement, judgment based on actual practice is necessary; only through personal experience is it possible to learn what hara is and how it relates to life. Following, then, are additional exercises, relating to the hara.

EXPERIMENT FIVE

Sit in the same seiza position as before, with your palms together. Sit up straight, aligning your forehead with your lower abdomen. Have your partner sit at your side, facing roughly the same direction you are, and place his or her fingertips of one hand on your chest (Figure 11). Your partner then pushes against your chest using a steady, gradual pressure that is parallel to the ground. Focus your attention on the hand pushing you, and try hard not to tip over. It usually doesn't take much force under such circumstances to upset your balance—mental and physical.

Now, put your mind on as small a point as you can imagine about four finger widths below your navel. Have your partner

apply the same amount of force as before as you allow the sensation of maintaining this natural center in the lower abdomen to
continue. Again, neither give up nor fight back; just center yourself and do nothing. After you arrive at a centered feeling, don't
force yourself to concentrate further. Just relax and let the feeling
remain. What happens?

You can try the same experiment with pressure applied to the
upper back, right between the shoulders. If the mind is calm and
stable in the hara, the body will feel virtually immovable, which is
a manifestation of fudoshin, "immovable mind," a concept I will
come back to shortly. The state of mind indicated by this experiment is one that notices both external and internal phenomena
but isn't upset by them. With this calmness of mind comes genuine relaxation, and when the above exercise is performed correctly,
you'll feel a sense of deep relaxation under pressure. This relaxed
state is vital for living a healthy, tension-free life. The exercise also
points out the fallacy of the common idea of relaxation being comfortable but weak. Relaxation is actually our most powerful condition, but it must be properly understood for this power to be
realized. And development of the hara can help us arrive at real
and correct relaxation.

EXPERIMENT SIX

Assume the same position as before or sit in a chair, but this time
let your lower back round and collapse. Sit heavily, resting your
weight on your heels, using a posture that looks "small," as if it's
collapsing in on itself (Figure 12). This amounts to a negative
relaxation that is all too common. In fact, for many people this is
relaxation. Ask your partner to push your chest as before. You'll
probably find yourself unable to avoid tipping over—even if you
concentrate the mind at the hara. In this posture, the weight of

FIG. 12. Seiza with palms together. Sit with your lower back rounded and slump. This is negative relaxation.

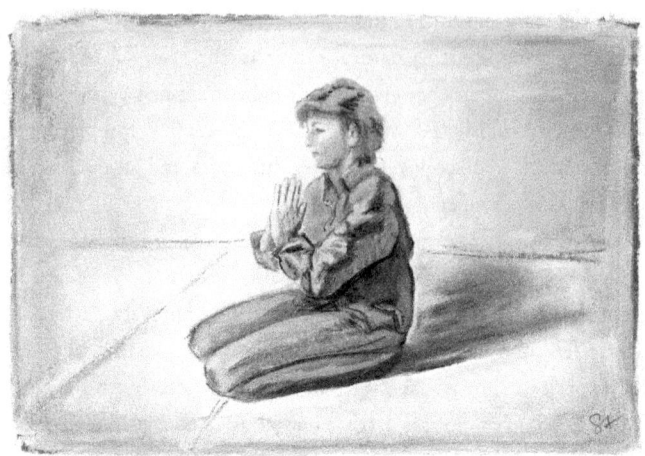

your upper body doesn't settle below the navel and on the front surface of the hara; rather, it shifts up and back inside the body toward the lower back. Focusing the mind below the navel in such a case isn't effective since the center of balance is now somewhere else. Centralization in the hara is as physical as it is mental, and a state of collapse does not equal genuine relaxation.

Next, lower your buttocks gently and lightly onto your heels or a chair, adopting a position that both looks and feels expansive. Keeping the small of your back straight, open your chest naturally. While relaxing and dropping your shoulders, focus your mind four finger widths below the belly button and allow your upper body weight to follow the mind down to that point (Figure 13). Now when your partner applies the same force as before to your chest and back, the difference is remarkable. Real, positive relaxation is connected to calming the mind in the lower abdomen, but it also relates to the maintenance of a correct and natural carriage, thus the emphasis on an upright, dignified posture in many of the Ways.

Finding correct posture, deep relaxation, calm composure,

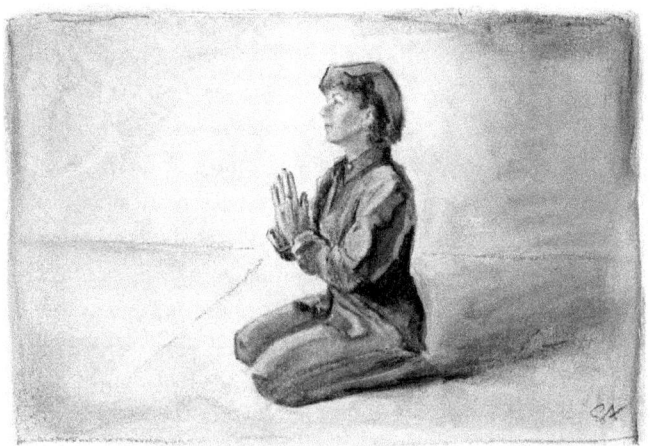

FIG. 13. Seiza with palms together. Sit with your lower back straight and with an expansive posture. This is positive relaxation.

and a more positive attitude, attributes needed for success in martial arts, healing arts, brush painting, and other Japanese Ways, is also important for living everyday life.

Ochitsuki

Ochitsuki, or "calmness," is universally valued in everything from tea ceremony to the game of go. Traditionally in the Ways, calmness of mind is often compared to a mirror: when the mind is still, it takes on the quality of a still pond, a mirrorlike condition that reflects life as it really is. And this mental composure has a physical expression.

Since the body reflects the mind, a stable body reveals a stable mind, and by the same token, a physical loss of balance indicates a mind that is not calm. The body is an object, albeit an animated object, and as such it is subject to certain natural laws—the law of gravity, for instance. Objects that are top-heavy are unstable. The currently popular Sport Utility Vehicles (SUV)

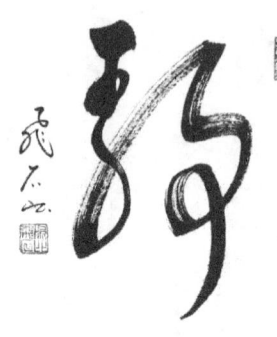

SHIZUKA: *"Peaceful stillness." In the varied Japanese Ways, a still and peaceful state of mind is valued. When the mind is calm and immovable— even in the midst of physical activity—then the body relaxes and each body part settles naturally into its proper position. Most traditional Japanese art forms simultaneously unearth, cultivate, and express this condition of dynamic serenity.*

are a good example of an object that is top-heavy and thus unstable, whereas the latest low-slung Porsche sports car exhibits a lower center of gravity and so greater stability. A mind that is calm induces the body to relax, allowing every body part to settle downward and into its proper and natural place. The hara is one such place, and settling down amounts to being more like the sports car than the SUV.

The following exercises will help demonstrate what this theory means.

EXPERIMENT SEVEN

Sit in seiza with the palms together. Lift the shoulders as shown in Figure 14. This amounts to drawing weight away from the hara and thus unsettling the body. Have your partner slowly lift your near elbow straight up toward the ceiling. Does it take much force to move it? Now, relax your shoulders and allow them to drop naturally. Have your friend lift the elbow again, using the same force as before (Figure 15). Which position is more stable?

Since the mind and body are one, instability in one represents instability in the other. If you go about your daily life with your shoulders raised, your mind likely reflects a similar state of agitation or unease.

EXPERIMENT EIGHT

Again in seiza with the palms together, have your friend sit

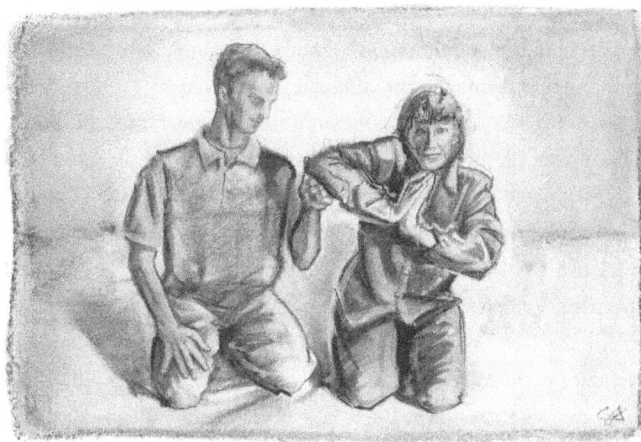

FIG. 14. Seiza with palms together. Lift your shoulders upward. Your partner can lit your elbow a couple inches with one hand because you are unsettled.

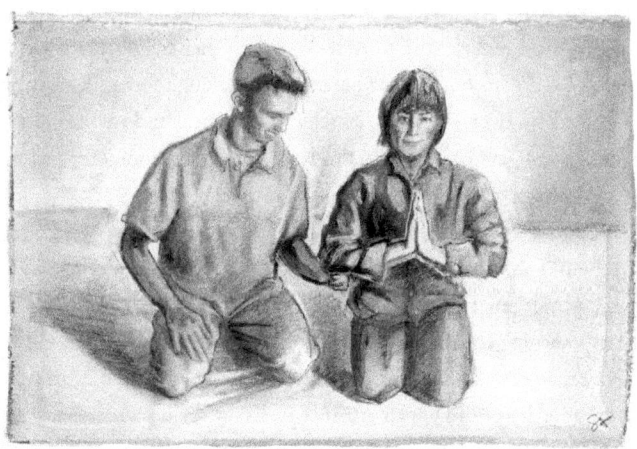

FIG. 15. Seiza with palms together. Keep your shoulders down. Your partner is unable to lift your elbow with one hand due to your settled weight.

next to you, facing the same direction as you. Focus your attention on the top of your head and relax into the posture previously described. Ask your partner to lift your near elbow straight up, using slow, steady pressure. Notice how little force it takes to move the elbow.

Then, visualize water dripping from your elbows and falling

Mu

Buddhist concept referring to "the void" or "nothingness," used in the Do, which are conceived of as particular expressions of the Way of the universe, to suggest the indescribable nature of the universe; used also in compound with other words to describe different mental states in the Ways. See also mui.

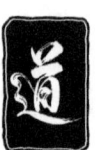

to the floor. While you sustain this image, relax and have your partner apply the same amount of power as before. In this case, the elbow should be much more difficult to lift. Why?

In the first instance, the upward movement of the mind caused a subtle unsettling effect in the body, making it more like the SUV. But in the second scenario, visualizing water falling downward created an internal settling of body weight that was more like the Porsche. Note that human beings jump—become unsettled—when they're surprised. And angry people often get red in the face owing to the upward movement of blood. Both examples point to the relationship between body and mind. Tension, unnaturalness of posture, lack of calmness—all these correlate to an upsetting effect on the body.

As we've seen, settling down isn't the same as sagging or collapsing. And locking the muscles, on the other hand, might keep the elbow down; but if your partner uses enough force, the entire body will tip over sideways. A relaxed (physical and mental) attitude is stronger than a tense one, and this relaxation comes from settling the posture. Calmness is dynamic, not dead.

These exercises bring an awareness of the effect of settling the body and concentrating the mind in the hara, and although some people might think that the cultivation of the hara involves always keeping the mind concentrated in the lower abdomen, common sense reveals that this is difficult to accomplish and unwise as an aim. I wouldn't want to ride in heavy traffic with someone whose mind was below the navel as opposed to on the road—even if they were driving a Porsche. The point of the previous experiments is to sense something beyond words, and to learn to identify when it is present and when it has been lost. Through ongoing training, the feeling of mind and body unity can be maintained as an unconscious habit.

I deliberately used the same posture for each experiment to

show how all these concepts are interrelated, and how each experiment ultimately produces the same feeling and result. It is that feeling that is important. It is beyond words, but not beyond our ability to experience. This experience is the essence of the Way.

Fudoshin

When real calmness arrives, the mind takes on an immovable characteristic known as fudoshin in many of Japan's Ways. Its physical expression is a posture that is so stable it may seem immovable as well—*fudotai*, the "unmoving body." (Review Experiment Five for an example of fudoshin/fudotai.)

Fudoshin doesn't mean a mind that *cannot* move, rather one undisturbed by the phenomena of the relative world, whether they are external or stem from the innermost recesses of the student of the Way. It's easy to misunderstand this point. Several years ago, I taught an elderly student named Charlie, who served in the American Navy during World War II. He was on a ship that had been bombed and was going down. Shortly after the initial explosion, the men rushed to abandon ship—all except one person, my student's friend, who was holding fast to a portion of the ship. Despite his shipmates' pleading, he was frozen like a statue, with a glassy-eyed expression. One of the sailors tried to pull him to safety, but he met with no success. Soon several men were pulling and tugging with all their might, but with no effect. In the end, Charlie was forced to bash this pillarlike sailor in the jaw, knocking him unconscious, before he could be moved. Charlie said to me, "That was some fudoshin, huh, Sensei?" Unfortunately, Charlie had confused being unable to move mentally, and therefore physically, with fudoshin. A deer frozen in the headlights of a car also exhibits this trancelike state, but it is not fudoshin.

Mui

Derived from the Chinese Taoist term wuwei. Refers to "doing nothing" and indicates a state of unaffected calmness in harmony with nature.

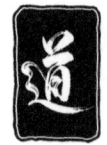

Arriving at mental and physical stability is altogether different. In this state, although the mind remains unperturbed by an emergency or traumatic situation, it is capable, because it is nonattached, of an instant reaction. Furthermore, although the body might be so settled and stable that it seems immovable, it is also capable of a quick reaction: the mind and body are calm and immovable when no need for action exists, and capable of immediate action when circumstances warrant a response.

This idea in turn ties to an old Asian maxim of the Ways: "motion in stillness, stillness in motion." When fudoshin is present, we are calm and physically stable even in motion, and at the same time, the mind is alert, aware, and intensely alive even in repose. Fudoshin describes a mind-body that is calm while in action, active while calm.

To acquire a real understanding of what this state is, actual experience is indispensable. And the Do provide situations in their practice that require fudoshin, thus giving us an opportunity to discover this quality for ourselves. Whether we're serving tea in chado or giving a demonstration of brush writing, we must concentrate. Yet if the mind becomes attached to one thought, we will be frozen like Charlie's buddy. Therefore, concentration, which makes possible effective functioning, is desirable, whereas attachment, which can lead to immobility, is not. Similarly, in odori or budo, our postures and movements must express calmness and stability, but they must also be capable of continuing motion. Since these arts require a psycho-physical state that is simultaneously immovable and capable of complete freedom of movement, there's less chance of misunderstanding the genuine nature of fudoshin than in an activity limited to seated meditation. Because the Do place us in situations requiring both immovableness and quick, flexible reaction, over a period of many years we also have many opportunities to discover the meaning of fudoshin.

Although the Ways embody meditative qualities, or at least a means for their realiza- tion, they are not akin to "stress management" classes that, in at least some instances, seek meth- ods to eliminate or avoid stress. Getting rid of stress is not the point here. Death, after all, is a stress-free condition, and happy occasions like births and wed-

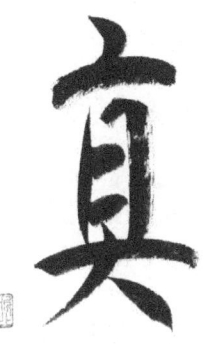

SHIN: *This interpretation of the character shin is brushed in the formal kaisho script—equivalent to printing in English— and it means "true reality." Participation in one of the classical Do forms can help us wake up to the true nature of reality and discover unclouded perception.*

dings are often stressful for the participants. So while the atmo- sphere in many Ways seems tranquil, it isn't a dead tranquillity; it's charged with ki. The tea ceremony, for instance, undeniably aims at a peaceful state, but ask any person who has seriously stud- ied chado in Japan if their practice was without stress. You will likely hear about an exceptional moment or two, where despite some difficult situation or having made a massive mistake, they entered into a condition akin to being in the eye of a hurricane: complete stillness in the midst of adversity and activity.

This stillness in the midst of action is different from the tranquillity pursued in other approaches. In college, I studied Hatha yoga under a wonderful teacher, from whom I learned a number of important things. We'd practice around lunchtime, and, being an exceptionally kind person, she went to lengths to create a peaceful sanctuary for us: dim light, burning candles, and the precursor to New Age music was playing in the background. During our concluding meditation, some students would even fall asleep. Most everyone enjoyed the practice, but a number of people mentioned that it was almost a shock to walk out into the brightly lit and noisy college hallways. More than one person wondered why, even after studying for some time, he or she was

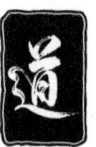

*A quality suggested by
such words as "mys-
terious," "extraordi-
nary," or "marvelous,"
it refers to a moment of
realized perfection that
is indescribable and
that occurs within the
process of—through
the practice of a
particular art—the
embodiment of the
Way.*

unable to sustain the tranquillity experienced in this womblike environment for the rest of the school day. The problem was that, although the atmosphere was nonstressful, the orientation per-haps subtly encouraged an avoidance of stress as opposed to its transcendence.

There's nothing wrong with creating a peaceful environ-ment to meditate in. The important point here is that the manner in which we approach practice determines what we get out of it, and what we do must relate to everyday realities. If meditation is a means of running away from stress or escaping from life, it's little different from a drug. Tranquillity is not a dead, negative relax-ation, and it isn't the absence of stress. What exactly is it then?

The Japanese Ways involve relatively everyday activities, and their practice is therefore alive and often not stress free. The goal, however, isn't the elimination of stress; it is the transcendence of stress and the transformation of our perception of stress: fudoshin. With fudoshin as the objective, teachers often deliberately place students in stressful conditions to give them a chance to examine the nature of the immovable mind more fully. From the martial arts teacher's rapidly approaching punch to the shodo professor's admonition that touching up or redrawing is not allowed—no matter how absorbent the paper or how many people are watch-ing—all the Do require an attitude that transforms stress from an enemy into an ally. It is an attitude of calm acceptance, a state of mind that views stress-filled situations not as moments to dread but as opportunities for self-knowledge, and such an attitude utter-ly transmutes the very concept of stress, giving rise to fudoshin.

Shisei

Just as the mind moves the body, our posture expresses our

mental state. When the mind is immovable, the body is exceedingly stable, and the posture appears natural and relaxed. *Shisei* describes this posture, but it also includes our mental carriage, which our physical state mirrors. Thus how we carry ourselves, physically and mentally, is of vital importance in many of the Do. Advanced sensei will frequently critique posture in painting, tea ceremony, Kabuki, or Noh drama. Perceptive students will realize this critique is also a comment on their mental state.

Because the Ways view the mind and body as one, their emphasis on posture is natural. Fudotai describes a body that is immovable. The bodily stability exhibited in the preceding experiments can be characterized as fudotai, an outward expression of the psychological stability that is fudoshin. Fudotai, like fudoshin, is a valued characteristic in the various Do (and isn't literally "immovable"; anyone's body can be displaced).

It is not necessarily the extent of immovability that is important; rather, fudotai is cultivated in relationship to fudoshin, and it is the fudoshin-fudotai connection that is truly valuable. This is true in martial arts, forms of Japanese dance, and other moving arts that require genuine balance in action.

The exercises introduced in this book are derived from the Japanese yoga of Nakamura Tempu Sensei, but since his death in the late 1960s they have been elaborated on and introduced into other Do by his top students like Tohei Koichi Sensei, Hirata Yoshihiko Sensei, and others. While not all teachers of the Ways will refer overtly to fudoshin and fudotai, or even to shisei (but will demonstrate these concepts in action), they are important in all of the Ways.

So let us briefly examine posture in the Do. Before proceeding, however, bear in mind that it isn't uncommon for interpretations of correct posture to vary between teachers and arts. Nonetheless, certain common points can be found, and although

Netsuke

Netsuke date back to the seventeenth century and are still carved as a craft today. Netsuke served both practical and artistic purposes. They were used when wearing a kimono to secure purses and were frequently used to hold tobacco pouches. See also inro.

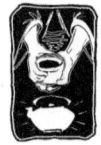

the following explanation might not match what everyone is doing in the Ways, it can serve as a useful starting point.

In general, all the Do aim for unity with nature and strive to manifest naturalness. This naturalness is often characterized as *shizentai*, or "natural posture." It does not necessarily refer to a specific stance (although it can) but points more toward a physical carriage that is natural and harmonious. Such a posture is in harmony with itself and nature: whether in repose or in motion, every part of the body functions to support every other part of the body. In particular, the hara, as the midsection of the body, unifies the action of the upper and lower halves of the body, which, in order to effect harmony, must work together.

In Western sports, for example, a baseball player rotates his waist as he swings the bat. To bat predominantly with the arms would diminish power by producing a disconnected movement and posture. Similarly, when a bowler steps forward to release the ball, she shifts her hara in the direction of the pins as she releases the ball. In both examples, the action of the hara allows the athlete to unite the force of the upper and lower halves of the body, bringing the force of the entire body into play. We've seen how focusing mental strength in the lower abdomen leads to a unification of mind and body, and since the body follows the mind, this focusing can also encourage us to move from the hara, as in these two examples.

In Experiment Six, we examined posture and its relationship to the hara. A brief review of the exercise might enhance your understanding of the discussion of shisei that follows. In particular, the illustrations are a valuable guide to a correct posture for the Japanese arts and Ways and to its usefulness in daily life for gaining better health, balance, coordination, and composure.

A natural, stable posture is relaxed, upright, and aligned. This posture is essential in everyday living, and it must be maintained in the Do. In the illustrations of people sitting in seiza, notice that they sit lightly on the heels, with the big toes crossed and some space between the knees. Although seiza is difficult, at first, for some people to adopt, it is effective for centering weight forward and down into the hara. Think of this point as a natural center in the lower abdomen that corresponds to your center of balance and gravity. When sitting in seiza or in a chair, sit lightly, almost as if your "bottom" were sore, and maintain a relaxed posture that looks "big." Avoid sagging. When standing or walking, it is important not to slump or raise the shoulders, or rest flat and heavily on your heels.

Many times during meditation or in practicing the Ways, and even in daily life, there is a tendency for the head to sag forward, while the neck collapses and bends, producing a "hump" at its base. The rest of the spine soon curves in on itself as well. You can correct this by concentrating on the hara and moving your head. Mentally release your muscles (along the neck and spine in particular). Visualizing your hara as a sort of anchor, direct the top of your head up and away from your hara, and then draw in your chin and bring your forehead back into alignment with your lower abdomen. Allow the spine and neck to lengthen until your posture is aligned. Envisioning the muscles along the spine growing longer and wider is an effective technique to bring this about. If you concentrate deeply and relax, the body will move naturally into the correct position. On the other hand, be careful not to force your body into an overly erect posture. By relaxing and using visualization, expand the chest and broaden the back and shoulders. The ears, shoulders, and pelvis should be squared and parallel to the floor.

In practicing sumi-e or shodo, students often sit in a chair, particularly in the West. If you sit in a chair, avoid sitting with your legs outstretched, as this causes your pelvis to roll backward and your lumbar region to curve outward in a slump. Sit with your

Nippon-to

The Japanese sword, popular symbol of the spirit of Japan and the soul of the samurai. Prized by fanciers worldwide, the Japanese sword is a tangible expression of Japanese history, customs, and aesthetics. From its appearance, aficionados can discern the contemporary style of combat, the tradition in which the smith worked, the aesthetic principles of its period, as well as the historical evolution of sword making in Japan.

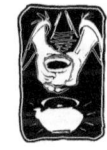

Niwa

A Japanese-style garden that aims at symbolizing a vast natural panorama in a limited area. Influenced by Zen and Shinto traditions, the niwa effects a naturalistic, asymmetrical beauty arrived at through a harmony of spatial arrangement.

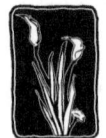

feet flat on the floor or tucked under the chair (almost as your legs tuck under your hips in seiza). This maintains your natural lumbar curve and shifts your weight toward the front surface of the lower abdomen, exactly where you want to center your weight and mind.

Regardless of the art being practiced or the particular position being used, relax your face and eyes and find the most comfortable posture within the context of the above instructions. This act of centering produces a particularly steady position. To sustain this free and relaxed condition of stability, avoid leaning in an unbalanced way, as the weight of the upper body must be in equilibrium at the hara.

The correct shisei is a posture that is unified, mind and body working together, upper and lower sections of the body aligned, and every body part working with every other part. This is the posture of unification, and it can be as beneficial in daily activities as it is in the Ways.

Do Chu no Sei and Hyoshi

Although we use the word "posture" to describe shisei, in the Ways posture is rarely static. Whether we practice tea ceremony, dance, or *raku* pottery, movement is involved. Thus, in the Ways of Japan, we experience shisei as a series of linked postures that form the essence of movement.

This emphasis on movement in the Do isn't surprising: the Ways have as their objective discovering the Way of the universe in the midst of activity. Do forms are, in fact, everyday actions—writing with a brush, preparing tea, arranging flowers—that have been "spiritualized" to become meditative disciplines. Although some Ways use seated meditation, the basic nature of meditation in the Do is dynamic, that is, "moving meditation."

For most of us, our lives are marked by activity, visual stimulation, and noise; we do not sit perfectly still with our eyes closed in silence. And yet sitting alone and perfectly still in a quiet, dimly lit room is precisely the sort of meditation many people engage in. That this form of meditation doesn't reflect what we do in our lives might explain the difficulty in transferring the meditative state into daily life.

It is indeed easier to unite mind and body while in repose; it is harder to sustain psycho-physical harmony in motion, and even more challenging to sustain this state of unification in relationship to others. Since many Ways involve activity, often in relationship to others (in the case of arts such as budo, chado, odori, music, and similar Ways), and because they're usually performed with the eyes open, they are practices of dynamic meditation that relate closely to life. They are also practices that can help us to translate the benefits of seated meditation into daily activity.

This quality of Do forms, active meditation, is pointed to in the phrase *do chu no sei* (sei, "calmness"; chu, "during"; and do, "movement"), which can be translated as "stillness in motion" or "calmness in the midst of action."

Another important term in relation to movement in the Ways is *hyoshi*. Hyoshi describes "timing" and "rhythm." In budo timing is critical. In jujutsu and aiki-jujutsu, there is a technique called *aiki nage*. Aiki—ai, "harmony," and ki, "life energy"— describes harmony with the life energy of the opponent and the universe; *nage* means "throw." (The term *kokyu nage*, "breath throw," is used by some aikido practitioners to describe this or similar techniques.) In one version of this technique, an attacker attempts to seize your wrist with both hands (Figure 16).

Moving the opponent into an unbalanced condition, which always precedes a throw, can be difficult once your wrist has been grasped, but beginners nevertheless attempt to struggle against the

FIG. 16. The attacker's objective is to hold the opponent's wrist with two hands. (Figs. 16–20 illustrate the concept of hyoshi, or timing and rhythm, in Japanese arts, using jujutsu as an example.)

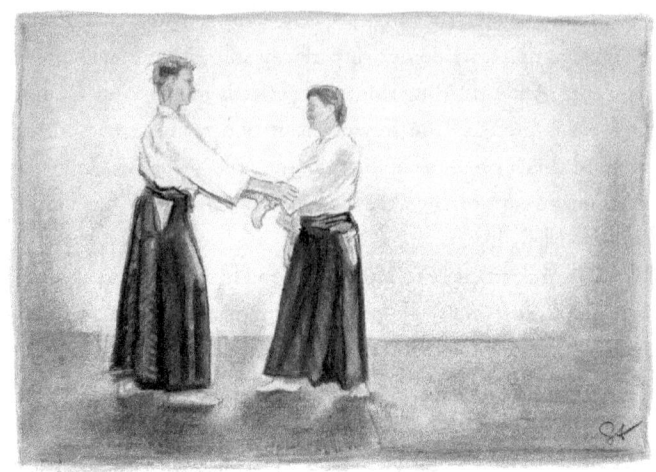

FIG. 17. The attacker is about to hold the opponent's wrist with two hands. He is leaning slightly and his hands are a couple of inches from the opponent's wrist. This is when the opponent should start to move—before he is held.

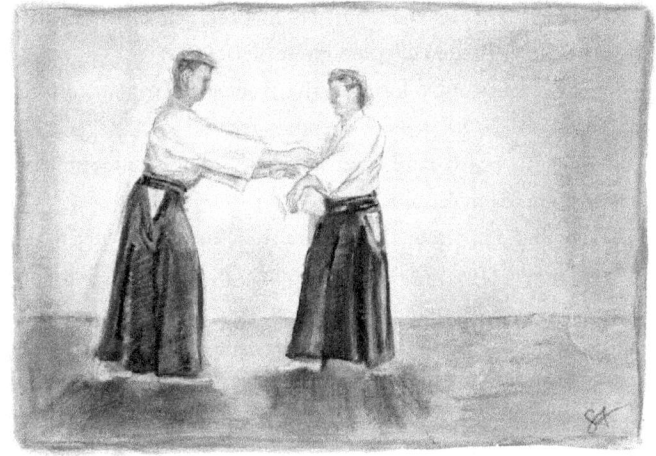

often superior physical strength and body weight of the other person. And although an individual might have a heavy body, there is no such thing as a heavy mind.

In budo, as in all the Ways, the mind moves the body, and the body's responses mirror the mind. Therefore, if you can draw

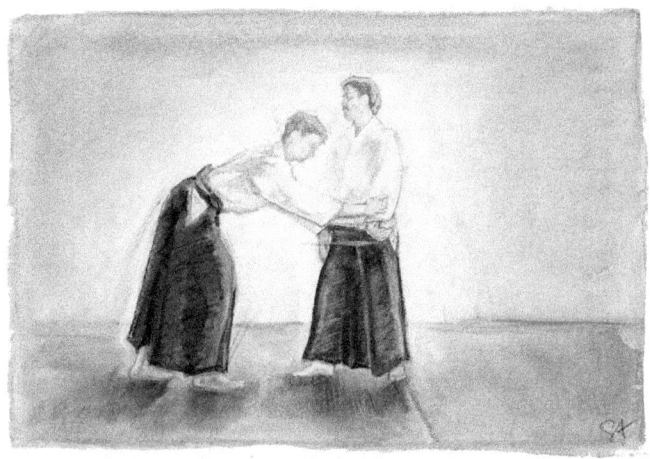

FIG. 18. The opponent has dropped his bent wrist to a point near his leg, leading the attacker into an unbalanced position. The attacker is unbalanced and holding the opponent's wrist with two hands at this point.

the attacker's mind in an advantageous direction, his body will follow.

The way to achieve this is to simply let your arm fall to your side when the opponent is just about to touch your wrist, rather than waiting until your wrist is already in your opponent's grip (Figure 17). Dropping the arm too soon will only cause an alert assailant to stop or pull back; too late, and your wrist is trapped and you are left to struggle against the entire weight and strength of the opponent's body. But if you move at the last second, smoothly and calmly, the attacker will follow the dropping arm into an unbalanced condition (Figure 18).

This just-so timing is what hyoshi refers to: at just the right moment, lead the opponent to believe your wrist is going to be where he expects, and then move it at the last second, but smoothly enough so that the attacker believes if he just reaches a little bit farther . . . he'll be able to grab it. He will, but in an unbalanced way. And he will not want to stay off balance for long. Anticipating his desire to rise, add power to his upward thrust, stay just a bit ahead, and lead the opponent upward with both arms (Figure

FIG. 19. The opponent turns and leads the attacker upward with both arms.

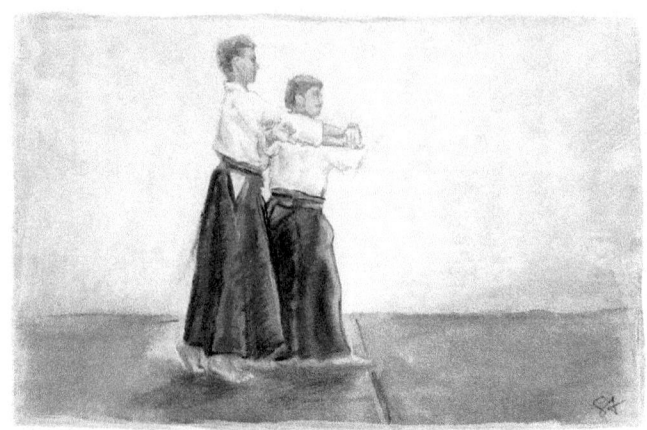

19). This causes his weight to be unsettled, since your added pow-er was unexpected, and the attacker's body "pops up" suddenly as a result. Next, because of this unsettling action, his weight will fall back down and onto the back of your wrist. At the moment the weight descends, drop your wrist and other arm out from under the attacker; the effect will be like pulling a chair out from under someone. A fairly spectacular fall is the result (Figure 20; the arms continue to drop further downward than can be seen here). All of this is accomplished through rhythm and timing.

The first action is dropping the arm and letting it swing back up. In relation to rhythm, this can be considered one beat. Next, you drop both arms for the throw, and that's the second beat. It should take no more than two seconds to complete this version of aiki nage, but novices often break the rhythm by creating three beats instead of two. That is, they drop the attacked wrist—hesi-tate—then raise both arms, and third, drop the arms again to throw.

But the throw isn't accomplished because the hyoshi was wrong. The first beat is down/up, not down and up. This sud-den down/up action makes advantageous use of the opponent's

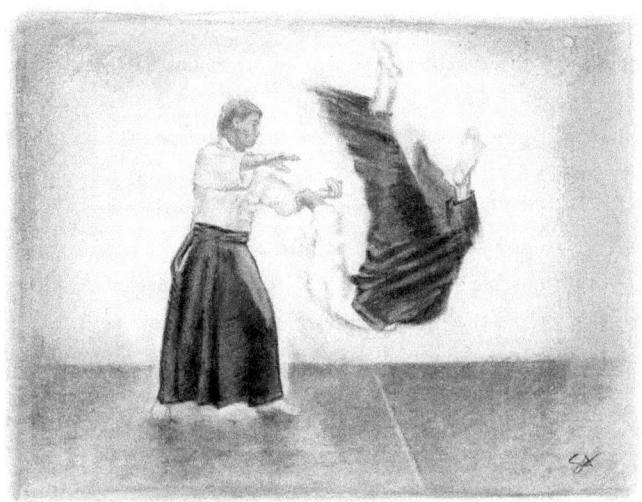

FIG. 20. The opponent drops his arms and throws the attacker with aiki nage.

psycho-physical reactions. A break in rhythm only inhibits those reactions. Hyoshi is critical.

Timing and rhythm are also important in the other Ways. Let's take a look at the visible rhythm in shodo.

Japanese characters, although sitting motionless on the paper, should nevertheless look like they're moving. This is an example of motion in stillness in shodo, an art that displays a visible rhythm in the manner that music evidences an audible rhythm. Such a rhythm can be achieved in shodo, and in other Ways like budo and chado, only by means of profound relaxation. Relaxation allows us to achieve calmness in action and action in calmness. Moreover, we're able to find and maintain rhythm only when we stay calm despite outward movement. Do chu no sei and hyoshi are interrelated, and they are essential for not impeding the flow of ki, and in turn the dynamic flow of the brush itself.

Relaxation is vital. Relaxation comes, however, only with naturalness. If we feel tension in any part of the body, or during any brush movement, it is necessary to find the source of the

Noh

The oldest form of Japanese theater, a dance-drama centering around heroic themes relating to gods, humans, madness, and demons and featuring a chorus of musicians and singers, masked principal actors, and highly stylized movement, costuming, and scenery.

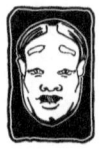

unnaturalness in our posture or way of moving. For example, the movement might be overextended, or we might be cramped by poor posture. A straightforward way to tell if a position or action is truly relaxed and natural is to pause at different points during the painting. Hold the position for thirty seconds and notice if you can "feel" the muscles in some part of your body. If there is a strong muscular sensation, it usually indicates the presence of tension.

No muscular sensation reveals that the muscles are properly relaxed and that the posture and movements are natural. We are unconscious of our bodies and selves, in a state, not of numbness or unawareness, but of serenity. This condition is the forgetting of self that occurs at a moment of peak performance in any activity, when we are aware of only the instant and the action of that instant. This is referred to as *muga ichi-nen*, or "no self, one thought." It is this state that allows shodo to transcend mere skillful brush writing.

In shodo, the brush is moved according to a definite rhythm. Rhythm both demonstrates and promotes coordination. All arts, including shodo, have a unique rhythm. Each character likewise has a particular cadence with which it is painted. Excellence results from finding and maintaining the correct rhythm. Breaks in rhythm register breaks in coordination of body and mind, and they usually happen when the flow of ki is broken during a lapse in mindfulness or a moment of tension.

Every character has a fixed number of strokes that must be brushed in a strictly defined order. The brush moves smoothly from one stroke to the next, flowing in an unconstrained and easy manner within each character. As the stream of life energy flows in a stable rhythm from one character to the next and from one line of characters to the next, a dynamic and yet balanced feeling results, and this lends the entire composition an appearance of unified rhythm.

To facilitate an unbroken rhythm and flow of ki, novices can count out loud as they make each brush stroke. Count each stroke like a beat in music, allowing about one second per beat. This is a simple way to get the feeling of unbroken rhythm in shodo. As students progress, they discover that the rhythm between (and during) certain strokes speeds up, and at other times slows down. Like a river, the fast and slow movements in shodo do not represent a break in rhythm so much as natural expressions of variation in a single, unified flow.

Every part of life has its own rhythm that must be found to be successful in a given activity. Sustaining rhythm also allows us to relax within what it is we're doing. Going against natural rhythm, in our work or personal relationships, only creates conflict. Nature has its own rhythm. To discover that rhythm, through any of the Japanese arts and Ways, is a fascinating, never-ending pursuit.

Kan

While the Ways consist of movements and trained techniques, the training method is based around *kan*. And when we become proficient in a Way, our movements and techniques are born of kan. Yet kan itself is elusive.

Kan can be translated as "intuitive perception," but the concept also includes the idea of "quickened insight"; it is the ability to perceive what is about to take place even before, for example, all the action has played out. In the Ways, kan refers to learning through direct experience, personal discovery, and intuition, and by means of the cultivation of heightened intuitive perception itself.

The cultivation of kan in a Do depends on the student's approach to its study and practice. As I've stressed, reading about

Ochitsuki

State of calmness universally valued in everything from tea ceremony to the game of go.

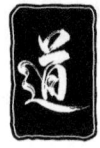

Odori

Style of dance usually associated with Kabu-ki drama but also practiced as an art in its own right. Mai is a dance form allied with Nob theater. These two forms, along with folk dancing, comprise the three main types of Japanese dance.

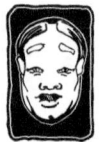

certain principles can be useful, but only through direct, actual experience does understanding occur. Effective teaching in the Do is like pointing a finger toward a desired end, and skilled teachers of a Do try to find the best methods of pointing students in the right direction, but in the end it is up to the student to see where the finger is pointing and travel the revealed path.

The Ways involve activity, and so their underlying principles can be discovered only by doing. This means hundreds or thousands of repetitions of basic exercises and techniques. Through such repeated practice—practice engaged in with full consciousness and not just mechanical repetition—beginners feel the principles their teacher has pointed to. It's important to keep in mind that a teacher points students toward an intuitive (as much as intellectual) understanding of a principle. Thus a shodo teacher will hold a student's hand from above so that the student can sense stroke pressure and rhythm, and the same shodo teacher, in response to a question about a character, will, rather than just verbally explaining the answer, repeatedly paint the character as the student observes. In budo, the martial arts teacher will "explain" an important throwing technique by repeatedly throwing the student using that specific technique, and the same budo sensei will allow himself to be thrown repeatedly to determine the effectiveness of the student's skills.

In teaching a variety of Ways for a number of years, it has been my experience that Americans, for example, often want to know what an art is all about without actually trying the art they're interested in. Certainly there are exceptions, but I've encountered many people who would like me to tell them what a given Way is, how it is practiced, and what the practice is like—all without actually stepping through the door of our dojo. Such an approach significantly limits what can be explained and certainly what can be understood of a Way.

By virtue of mindful rep-etition and practice, the pupil of a Way begins to intuitively feel the underlying, connecting principles, called *gensoku*, that the instructor has made refer-ence to. Over a period of years these gensoku are internalized. Again, this takes place not by means of mere thought, but by sensing and doing, over and over again. Once this process of embodying the gensoku takes hold, the novice disappears, and a real disciple of the Way emerges, a disciple who is able to vary and alter the fundamental techniques and forms of her art without violating the art's gensoku. In short, the disciple can now create *henka*, or personal variations, based on internalized principles.

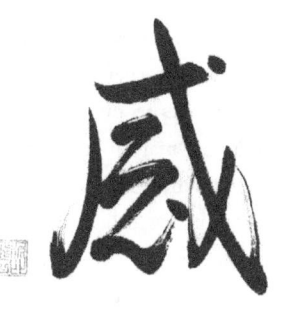

KAN: *"Intuitive perception." Brushed in the semicursive style of the renowned Chinese calligrapher Ogishi.*

In the course of a disciple's progress, he or she may reach a point in flower arrangement, for example, where flowers seem to arrange themselves. In budo, he may start to spontaneously create entirely new techniques appropriate to the combative situ-ation of the moment, while the shodo expert might, in response to a particular condition or event, intuitively alter a character in mid-brush stroke, only to create something more beautiful than intended. And so, we return to kan: an immediate perception of what is needed that is also invariably right but rarely prearranged.

Additionally, because in the Ways teachers instruct by example and demonstration as much as by direct explanation, and students learn by doing what they've been shown, longtime students develop a profound sensitivity to their teacher. This enhanced sensitivity to the ki of others is also an expression of kan.

123

Okuden

From oku, "inner," and den, "teachings," refers to the hidden or secret aspects of an art or its school. Used in conjunction with shoden (beginning) and chuden (intermediate) levels of instruction or competence, it indicates the advanced stages.

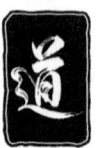

In any activity performed with other people, and certainly in Japanese music, dance, and the martial arts, sensitivity to the ki of others is necessary to sustain harmony. A musician who waits to hear what the others are playing will fall behind the beat. A dancer who hesitates to observe the other dancers has lost the rhythm. And in the martial arts, if you wait to see what kind of attack is being launched, by the time you figure it out, you've already been grabbed or hit. Still, a misjudgment can lead the musician to play the wrong note, the dancer to step at the wrong moment, and the martial artist to anticipate the wrong attack. The way out of these sorts of difficulties is, more than by use of the intellect, the development of kan. And, not surprisingly, direct, personal experience—*doing*—is needed to know kan.

Following is an exercise that will help you directly discover the nature of kan.

EXPERIMENT NINE

As with the previous exercises, you'll need a friend to help you with this. Either stand or sit in seiza and extend one arm in front of you with the palm up. Your partner lays his or her palm on top of yours (Figure 21), and your friend then begins to slowly move his or her hand up, down, sideways—in any direction. Your job is to stick to your partner's hand. The palms shouldn't separate, nor should you feel any collision between the two hands if, for example, your friend suddenly lowers his or her palm. The goal is harmony.

Reaching and sustaining such harmony can be difficult, particularly as the exercise progresses. Next, close your eyes gently, without creating tension. Your friend continues to move his or her hand, and now more than ever, you must truly *sense* where to follow. A still more challenging exercise is to extend both palms

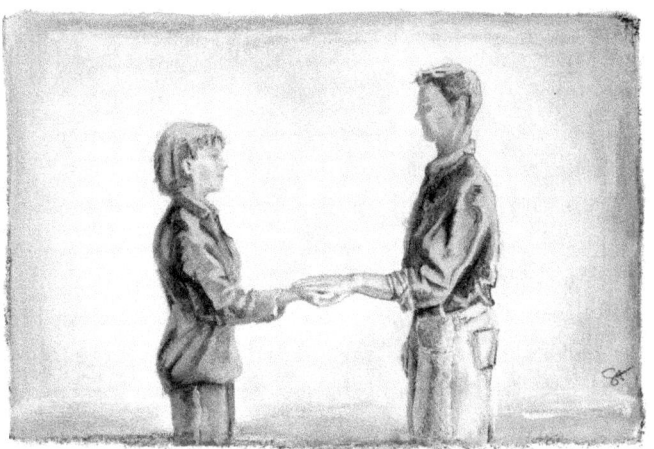

FIG. 21. An illustration of kan, or intuition. Stand with your palm touching your partner's palm. Your partner's palm is on top of your palm. Sense and follow the movement of your partner's hand and ki.

upward, eyes closed, and ask your partner to move both his or her hands simultaneously in any direction. Finally, he or she should move both hands quickly, then slowly, and with sudden stops— all without your palms separating or clashing.

This is a fun albeit formidable test of sensitivity to others and the ability to sustain harmony. The key to discovering harmony in action in this exercise, and in living, is kan. More concretely, waiting to see where your partner's hand goes or attempting to guess its course will most often be ineffective—but there is a solution to this exercise.

Before your partner moves, his or her mind (and thus ki) will flow in that direction first. For instance, if I'm going to pick up a glass, first I have the intention to do so, then my ki moves toward the glass, and finally the observable action occurs. The same can be said for any movement in life. The body doesn't move, act, or speak by itself, without mental activity.

If we calm the mind, we can pick up many subtle events taking place in our environment, including the movement of ki in the universe. By intuitively sensing where ki is going before the hand itself moves, and by acting as soon as we perceive this movement rather than waiting until we've seen the hand actually move, we can match our friend's actions. But this kind of sensitivity requires real calmness more than deliberately trying to sense something or attempting to read your partner's mind.

Frequently, students will think too much to arrive at kan. Deliberately thinking about where your friend's ki may or may not be going rarely works. Rather, notice what goes through your mind when you open a door or turn a page of this book. Obviously you have the intent to perform a particular action, but this intent is so quick as to be imperceptible under most circumstances, and the same can be said for the motion of ki preceding your partner's hand movement: by the time you finish trying to feel his or her movement of ki, the action has occurred.

The key is to calm the mind, and do nothing. Move only when you feel like moving. If the mind is truly calm, your feelings will accurately reflect where your friend's hand is about to go. Genuine calmness is the crucial ingredient in kan, along with repeated practice of activities that lead to the needed sensitivity. Calmness can be arrived at in a variety of ways, but a time-honored approach in the Japanese Do involves stilling the mind at a single spot below the navel. Still the mind as described in what follows and try the exercise again and compare the results of both attempts.

Sit or stand lightly, displaying an erect but relaxed posture that appears expansive and allows the body's weight and center of gravity to settle at a point in the lower abdomen. Allow the mind to focus on the natural center below the navel; in other words, focus the mind in the same spot where the weight has settled, which corresponds to your center of balance. Drop and relax the shoulders and upper body, as if dropping your weight into the lower abdomen, but without slumping or going limp. Once this calm, centered feeling has been attained, extend your upturned palm or palms, and perform the exercise as before, except this time simply move when you feel you should. The sensing of ki takes place naturally in this state of refined relaxation and composure.

A calm, composed mind can be compared to a perfectly still body of water. In this state, even the slightest breeze registers on the water's surface. If, on the other hand, the water is already turbulent, it takes a lot of wind before any change is noticeable on its surface.

Thus, when we calm the mind, even subtle changes in our environment register rapidly, including changes in the movement of ki, but if the mind is agitated, we fail to notice all but the biggest changes taking place around us, making our reactions slow or nonexistent. Notice that the water doesn't try to feel the breeze. Because its surface is calm, it responds naturally, and we can learn to do the same in this exercise and in our lives. Japanese arts and Ways give us a chance to study this in a structured environment.

We have to distinguish between the sensitivity mentioned here and the often spurious occult-type practices touted in some quarters. Certainly sensitivity to ki is involved in kan, but ki is all encompassing, as physical as it is mental. The mind and body are one, and the Ways are based on this fact. So, in Experiment Nine, we're not aiming at a psychic sixth sense that is separate from our physical senses of touch, hearing, and so on. To do so would simply engender a separation of mind and body, making sensitive and harmonious action impossible. Ki is everywhere and everything. Kan, in the Ways and in everyday life, requires a natural, holistic sensitivity to all aspects of ki, both physical and mental, visible and invisible.

Omote

Front or outside. Refers to what is visible, and in the context of human relations, relates to a "public face." With its counterpart, ura ("back," "inside," "hidden"), it speaks of a dualism in the arts of Japan and the visible-invisible, in-yo nature of the universe. See also ura.

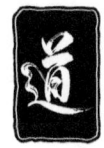

Ryu and Den

The Ways contain some concepts—kan, for example— that are relatively elusive and perhaps prone to diminishment or misunderstanding over the course of time. *Ryu* were developed to help preserve and pass down types of knowledge and related techniques. But before I discuss ryu directly, it might be useful to talk first about water.

Japanese culture has a long association with water. Of course the Japanese islands are surrounded by the sea, and fishing and the sea's bounty have always had a central place in Japanese life. Further, owing to Shintoism, the Japanese have a long connection with water in a spiritual sense. Shinto emphasizes purity, both of body and of spirit. "Ritual purification," or misogi, is a primary aspect of Shinto. Owing partly to Shinto's emphasis on cleanliness and partly to Japan's connection with the sea, many forms of misogi involve meditation under waterfalls, bathing in the ocean, and purification in icy rivers. And it isn't uncommon for these water-based austerities to take place in the dead of winter—a surefire way to drive just about any impurity out of you!

Thus, for geographical, historical, and religious reasons, aspects of Japanese consciousness are permeated with the element of water, and so are the Ways. And now we come to ryu. Ryu is a word relating to flow or currents in water. It is also used to describe the idea of transmitting inspiration and techniques from a Way's founder to succeeding generations. The same word also denotes a specific style, tradition, and system of art. Practitioners of classical martial arts will identify themselves as students of, for example, Tenshin Shoden Katori Shinto Ryu, or of Hontai Yoshin Ryu. A practitioner of flower arrangement might speak of being associated with Ohara Ryu, while another teaches Sogetsu Ryu.

Early in the development of the Japanese arts, trial and error revealed the best techniques in, for example, making pottery, wielding a sword, and manipulating a brush. In order to avoid reinventing the wheel, at some point in this ancient development, calligraphers, martial artists, flower arrangers, and others started to keep track of what worked. Frequently more than one approach would create a similar result, and different traditions of practice were thus born.

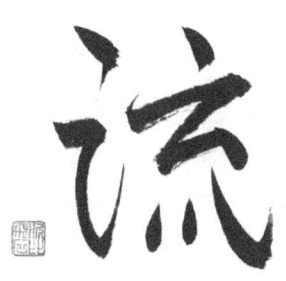

RYU: *Brushed in the antique gyosho script of the celebrated calligrapher Ogishi, ryu refers to a handed-down system of techniques. More than a mere style of a particular art form, a ryu is an unbroken living tradition that flows through the ages complete with multiple generations of head teachers and students. Practitioners of the various Ways often indicate that they are members of a particular ryu of flower arrangement, calligraphy, or other arts.*

For geographical and historical reasons, contact between people and places within Japan was limited, and this, too, encouraged the development of distinctive versions of the same art or Way in different parts of the country. Another important factor in the emergence of ryu is the heritage of ancestor veneration in Japan. If, for example, a person living long ago in the Aizu fiefdom (on the island of Honshu) originated, recorded, and taught a particularly effective version of a martial art, it would distincly differ from the same martial art as practiced in a different fiefdom located on the southern island of Kyushu. To emphasize its uniqueness, the leader of the particular fiefdom and/or the founder of the art would give it a name expressing its uniqueness. What is more, the founders of such ryu sometimes claimed to have received the teachings through a divine revelation, or, if not, they were revered as especially wise individuals. Combine this exalted view of the founder with students steeped in the veneration of ancestors, and you have fertile cultural ground for reverence of a founder, whose creation becomes a living entity passed from generation to generation. Such entities are called ryu and are widespread in all the Japanese arts and Ways.

129

Origami

"Paper folding." The art ranks with painting and sculpture and is associated with stylized traditions such as ceremonial etiquette and paper adornments attached to presents (noshi). In previous eras, paper was too costly to use for a hobby, so origami was resolutely established and restricted to ceremonial events. The oldest cases are male and female paper butterflies employed to adorn sake cups at marriage rituals.

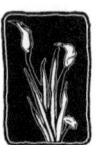

Regarding the development of ryu, Dave Lowry writes in *Michi Online*:

Partly because the mass production of literature is a historically recent development in Japan, and partly because a transmission of the Ways was considered to be too intricate and intimate to depend upon a textbook approach, the Ways were carefully codified and passed along personally from master to disciple. Eventually, this individualized method encouraged the formation of separate schools, or ryu, each with its own distinctive curriculum. A good example is found in kado, the Way of flower arranging. To the neophyte, two arrangements from the Ikenobo and Ohara schools of kado might seem quite similar. To the master, however, each is markedly different, reflective of the particular style of the school from which its creator came. The individual ryu also propagated their own preciously guarded "secret" techniques, which further serve to distinguish them. As with flower arranging, the secret itself might be as minor as a particular way of cutting flowers to retain their freshness longer. In the varying ryu of kendo, the Way of swordsmanship, the secrets often entail special tricks of body movement in attacking an opponent or luring him into a vulnerable position. Today, whether it be fencing or flower arranging, schools of the Ways are maintained by a continuum of headmasters and their loyal followers, each with its own teachings and traditions.[12]

That the ryu are living traditions means that a ryu ceases to exist when its exponents die out or when the skill level of its practitioners is lost. More than a collection of technical knowledge, a ryu truly is a living being that exists within the collective mind and body of its practitioners. As traditions that are alive, they cannot be maintained through only the written or spoken word but must *flow like water* from disciple to disciple, each of whom must feel and discover for him- or herself a particular tradition's true meaning.

In shodo, for example, it's common for the sensei to grasp the student's hand and literally paint using the pupil's limb and brush as an extension of the teacher. (Speaking as a teacher of calligraphy, this is much easier said than done!) When I studied a ryu of Japanese bodywork, my teacher would treat me and then have another student apply the same treatment to me. My job was to let my fellow student know if the treatment felt the same and, if not, identify how it differed from the sensei's. Then, my fellow student and I would switch roles. In other cases, my sensei would treat me and then have me apply the same treatment to him, again comparing the feeling of the therapy, the movement of ki, and the precise location of pressure. In this way, the quality and aliveness of the ryu are sustained and passed on.

I also mentioned *den* at the beginning of this section. Den means "transmission," a transmission that is essentially beyond words and one that lies at the heart of the ryu. Nevertheless, some ryu of tea ceremony, flower arrangement, and other arts have written records of their teachings that are handed down from generation to generation of the ryu's leaders and disciples. These recorded teachings, or *densho*, are often difficult to decipher for all but those immersed in the ryu, who have received the transmission "from mind to mind." Den can also refer to a particular tradition or teaching, and can thus have a meaning similar to ryu. For instance, teachings that are orally transmitted are called *kuden*, and esoteric traditions and methods are referred to as *hiden*. Although kuden and hiden can sometimes be found in books, their actual meaning can be discovered only through practice, a convention firmly anchored in the flow of generations of teachers and disciples.

Transmission of a ryu takes place in an intimate manner, and indeed it wasn't uncommon historically for teachers to have *uchi deshi*, live-in apprentices, who not only received formal lessons in a Way but also cared for the sensei by attending to household chores and other duties. With certain teachers, this tradition has continued unaltered into the twenty-first century.

The practice fulfilled, and fulfills, very real needs: immersion and intimacy. While I have never lived with any of my teachers, I have spent a fair amount of time with some of them outside the classroom or dojo setting. In some cases, I've served as an otomo for certain sensei. An otomo does everything from assisting with classes to carrying a teacher's luggage and making tea, and besides learning a great deal from the increased, intensified, and in-depth training such closeness afforded, I was surprised to discover that I also learned significant lessons from waking the sensei up in the morning and preparing the bath.

Such learning is not, however, unexpected when you realize that the arts and Ways are not only art forms but also Ways of living. By being close to a teacher, we have an opportunity to see the Way in action, to more directly experience what we are studying as a genuine Way of life. In one case, this took the form of my noticing how Kobara Ranseki Sensei, the headmaster of my ryu of calligraphy and painting, still practiced every day, even after over fifty years of training. Each morning he would rise at five and, after prayer, begin his practice. At the age of seventy, Kobara Sensei fell ill and was unable teach formal shodo classes for some time. Yet I understood that Sensei was still teaching a Way, and I stayed in touch with him during this period, noticing that he continued to practice despite his life-threatening illness. He told me that he had barely enough strength to lift a glass of water, but "the brush isn't that heavy, so I'd still like to practice." And he did practice, almost every day.

To some, this has little to do with painting, and this might be true in a narrow sense. But it has everything to do with the Way of calligraphy and the soul of Kobara Sensei's ryu. Sensei, his art-work, and his ryu all embody the same quiet, indomitable spirit.

Although living with a teacher might not be possible, it is important to attend classes and spend time with a teacher to the greatest extent possible; by doing so, you will understand that the Way transcends the techniques of a given art.

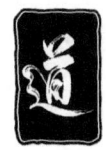

Reigi

"Techniques of respect." These are exemplified in bowing and other customs and attitudes in the Ways and Japanese culture aimed at self- and group harmony.

Seishin Tanren

Participation in a ryu represents a serious commitment since it is not aimed primarily at the acquisition of technical abilities, for example how to paint or how to arrange flowers. Knowledge of techniques can be handed down, but arriving at real skill in these techniques, no matter how effective the instruction, remains always an intensely personal matter. Despite slick sales pitches, encountered sometimes in Japan as well as in the West, no indi-vidual can simply *give* you skill. You must *find* it yourself.

Each time you find a new level of awareness and understand-ing, you are in fact learning the nature of the Way. Consequently, and despite common misperception, the practice of budo is not intended to teach students how to defeat an opponent (a gun would be more efficient), and there are quicker ways to make a good cup of tea than are found in chado. In the Ways, techniques and methods are a vehicle for *seishin tanren*.

Seishin means "spirit" and tanren means "forging." In the Ways, the spirit is forged in a manner not unlike that of a Japanese sword. *Nippon-to*, the sword of the samurai, is world famous for

133

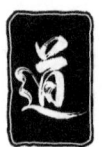
its incredible strength and amazing sharpness. The sword begins as a lump of iron that is heated, pounded, folded, and beaten into its correct shape. Through this repeated folding and hammering in the red-hot heat of the smith's forge, the Nippon-to emerges. It will eventually be plunged into icy water and tempered, assuming a form that is both beautiful and fearsome.

The sword stood for the soul of the samurai, who sought to shape his very spirit in its image: sharp, resilient, powerful, and pure. Considering the dominant place of the warrior class in Japanese history, it is not surprising that the samurai spirit still permeates Japanese culture, and its arts and Ways, even into the twenty-first century.

The forging of one's spirit is an idea common to all the Do, including the tea ceremony and calligraphy, and certainly the martial arts and Ways, which originally descended from the warrior class. Just as the proper forging of a fine sword demands intense heat and forceful pounding of the smith's hammer, a student of the Way must have his or her spirit purified, strengthened, and sharpened through the practice of the Do, which can seem overly severe until its purpose is understood.

Acquaintances often ask me about the various Do I practice, encouraging me to relate my experiences and explain what practice entails. Depending on the person, and to some degree my mood, I might describe how I regularly practice copying my shodo sensei's calligraphy, maybe even showing a sample of my efforts. They often wonder how many times I have copied a kanji character before achieving the desired result, only to be surprised that my copies don't number in the dozens but more likely in the hundreds. They're even more shocked when I explain that in a single session, I might copy a single stroke of a particular character more than a hundred times—without pause.

Other friends want to know why I go to our dojo on New

Year's Day, especially after a night of partying. I explain I go to practice meditation and breathing exercises with my students of Japanese yoga, which means sitting motionless in seiza in an unheated room for about an hour. These friends, both Japanese and American, who know what it's like to sit in seiza, sometimes grow pale at just the thought of an hour of such "torture."

I sometimes mention *kan geiko*, special training that takes place at the coldest time of the year. The form of kan geiko varies with the art and the teacher, but it is common in budo. In our martial art we go to a nearby beach to train continuously for around three hours. The seaside is cold in the winter, but no warm dress is allowed, just bare feet and a cotton uniform similar to what judo students wear. Once we're "warmed-up," we perform hundreds of throws and falls in the sand.

"Doesn't it hurt?" my friends ask. Yes, but only if you worry about it. "Doesn't sand get in your eyes?" You bet, and into just about every other bodily orifice! But, as severe as it might seem, it's easier than kan geiko undertaken in snow.

Why spend so much time perfecting a single brush stroke? Why not sleep in on New Year's Day? Why on earth would you want to roll around in cold sand or freezing snow just to learn self defense? Such questions inevitably follow.

Starting as a child, however, I was taught to think in terms of seishin tanren. And so, as I explain to my acquaintances, I'm not repeating a single brush movement merely to master a particular stroke. Real mastery of the brush requires self-mastery, and by perfecting my calligraphy, I have a chance to perfect myself—if I approach shodo in the right manner. And this is true of all the Do.

Such self-mastery undeniably demands a tremendous amount of repetition and hard work, but the discipline is something we build up to gradually. At the same time, remember that the mind controls the body, and the body is capable of far more

than we give it credit for, especially when it is motivated by a genuinely positive mental state. In the Do, a positive and indomitable
attitude is valued and cultivated; reaching it is the martial artist's
real motivation for training outdoors in the dead of winter. This is
what is meant by seishin tanren.

Finally, it's important to avoid the mistake of excess in the
other direction. The concept of seishin tanren has occasionally
been used as an excuse in the Japanese arts and Ways for everything from overzealous students, to charging exorbitant fees, to
the outright physical abuse of beginners. Returning to the sword
analogy, it must be noted that, during the forging process, the
sword is certainly exposed to high heat and forcefully beaten, but
too much heat or too much force will produce defects; and, during
the tempering, immersing the sword for too long or in water that
is too cold will likewise introduce defects. Forging a fine sword
requires heat and force, but also sensitivity and awareness, and,
in the same way, seishin tanren and the practice and study of the
Ways require balance and moderation. A student's spirit must be
forged but not broken.

Shugyo

If the Ways are vehicles for seishin tanren, it's because the
Ways aren't designed solely to provide instruction in a specific
activity such as arranging flowers or playing the shakuhachi flute.
All of the Ways, given their emphasis on seishin tanren, can be
thought of as forms of shugyo.

The term shugyo has quasi-religious overtones and means
roughly "austere practices." The sometimes lengthy meditation
periods found in Japanese yoga and the martial artist's special winter training are examples of shugyo within the Do forms. Shugyo is

an important, inseparable part of the Do, and it also offers something important to contemporary society.

For most of us, our modern, technological way of life has brought us far from the way our ancestors lived. Modern conveniences are a blessing and enable us to live life in comfort and safety. But in premodern times, humanity was necessarily in close connection to nature and inevitably forged toughness and a strong sense of self-reliance. As our lives have grown more comfortable, they have also come to lack a certain mental and physical strength and self-reliance.

The following story illustrates my point. Years ago I heard about a Japanese soldier who had been hiding for years in a remote part of the South Pacific, alone and unaware that World War II was over. Viewing nearby villagers as possible enemies, he always proved elusive when spotted, but he was eventually "captured" and returned to Japan. Once back in Japan, he became an immediate celebrity, and the media interviewed him on several occasions. During one of these interviews, the old man was asked if didn't feel he'd missed out on a lot living in the jungle with only wild animals as his companions. He surprised many by stating that he had gained a great deal from the experience and, contrarily, lost as much by returning to modern Japan.

After years of living in the wild, he discovered that his senses had become heightened, and he had developed a strong connection to his natural surroundings. He could smell the proximity of water and animals even at a distance, he could feel when rain or climatic changes were about to take place, and he could sense the presence of other people well before they were in view.

Back in Japan, however, he was rapidly losing most of these attributes, which in some ways he no longer needed. Moreover, he discovered that ringing phones, construction noise, honking horns, and all the other signs of modern technology frequently

Sabi

An aesthetic characterized by simplicity and austerity, rusticity, serene solitariness, the unevenness brought out in things through time's passage, the worn appearance of objects after long, loving handling but before old age completely destroys them; the feeling evoked by verdigris and patina, autumn, and twilight.

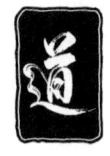

Samisen

Three-stringed instrument imported to Japan from China by way of Okinawa in the middle of the sixteenth century. Played by plucking using a large "pick."

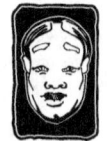

were stressful and upsetting to him. His improved medical care and new life in Japan brought him comfort and a welcome return to his homeland, but he had also lost something.

And so have many of us, often without realizing it. Our over-reliance on technological wonders has sometimes destroyed our sense of self-reliance. In the process, I think even our definition of fun has changed from that of our predecessors. In much of American society, for example, hard work is rarely seen as enjoyable. If it's hard, it can't be fun. If it's fun, it isn't work.

Maybe. But what about the great feeling of deep relaxation that sweeps over us like a warm blanket after a long, hard swim? What of the sense of accomplishment found in going beyond our imagined capabilities on a long, tough bike ride? If I were enclosed in a car instead of on my comparatively low-tech bicycle, I'd sweat less, but I'd also fail to see the wild rabbits that lope along beside me and miss the country smells of the rural road I cycle on late at night. Still, one of the most enjoyable things I do is go for a top-down, high-speed drive in an old sports car on a frosty springtime morning, wrapped in a heavy jacket, with the heater blasting and the smell of spring blossoms wafting through the cockpit of my roadster. Wouldn't it be easier to drive with the car top up or not ride a bicycle at all? Sure, but it wouldn't be as much fun.

Similarly, hard physical work outdoors in winter's cold or on a hot summer's day is no longer necessary for many of us, but chopping wood for heat on an icy morning or weeding a vegetable garden under a blazing sun gives us a greater appreciation for warmth and fresh, homegrown food and brings us closer to the natural world around us.

In short, making life too easy tends to take us out of touch with nature itself and our own natures. Of course, we don't want to, and perhaps cannot, eliminate technology in the twenty-first century, but we still need methods to train our minds and bodies, to preserve our link to the natural world. The Japanese arts and Ways can help do this, but only if they are practiced as shugyo.

Most of the Do are decidedly not high-tech. Chado students sit in seiza on relatively hard tatami mats in an old-fashioned tea room that is rarely climate controlled. In the winter, the first warmth they feel during the tea ceremony is when their lips are at long last allowed to touch the frothy green beverage. It might seem harsh, but it is in fact an exquisite experience, one that is markedly different from lounging about in a heated, vibrating massage chair while waiting for the microwave to signal that your instant tea is done.

Turning to budo, in *shochu geiko*, a special training session in summer, martial artists train their minds and bodies to the very limits of their endurance, and beyond, often finding new limits, all during the hottest time of the year. Needless to say, the hall in which this training is done is not air-conditioned.

Japanese gardeners spend many days each week in their niwa, rain or shine, winter and summer, hot and cold. Stooping to prune and cut, they often use methods and tools that are centuries old. Likewise, the late Nakamura Tempu Sensei encouraged his Japanese yoga students to exercise with him wearing only light shorts as a means of "strengthening the skin and training the body to be adaptable." They practiced indoors and out, winter and summer. *Koryu*, or "old style," swordsmanship is also often practiced outdoors in undesirable weather. And shodo students spend hours squatting on the floor in seiza, writing antique Japanese poems with an equally antiquated brush. Calling this low-tech is an understatement.

Such low-tech activities are, however, effective for connecting us to the world of wabi-sabi. They bring us back to something very elemental, even spiritual, in character. Within the Do, we connect with truths that are universal but that can easily be lost when life gets too easy or we become too insulated from the natural world. The Japanese Ways give us a means to sustain our innate relationship with nature and rediscover the kind of mental and physical resilience our ancestors possessed. And if we practice Do forms seriously, we don't need to hide out in a South Pacific jungle to achieve this state.

Although the especially intense training of shochu geiko and kan geiko is certainly a form of shugyo, one of my sensei offered a different interpretation related to these rigorous means of seishin tanren: "Shugyo is lifelong daily training in the Way." Compared to meditating under a freezing waterfall or practicing a martial art outdoors in suffocating heat, simply practicing every day over the course of a lifetime doesn't perhaps sound terribly difficult. Those who lightly dismiss daily lifelong practice as not too difficult have likely never studied a Do, and such a view perhaps explains the high drop-out rate among students of the Ways. It's one thing to begin to study a Japanese art, but it's another matter to practice vigorously. It is still another matter to continue to practice. Each day. For the rest of our lives. There are students of kado, chado, and other Ways, who practice extremely hard and rarely miss class—for awhile. The true challenge is to continue past a few months or even a few years of such earnest commitment.

Having discussed this phenomenon over the years with teachers of a wide variety of Do, the conclusion we all seem to have reached is that it is actually more arduous to practice a modest amount daily for a lifetime than it is to engage in severe, special shugyo a few times in your life. Certainly modest daily practice performed throughout life is much more beneficial than a few intense sessions.

Special periods of intensely challenging practice can amount to peak experiences that, though infrequent, can still have a lasting impact on one's life. Nevertheless, particular actions, engaged in as an ordinary part of daily life and repeated over a period of years, penetrate the subconscious, where real learning and understanding take place. After a lifetime of driving a car, for example, how easily could you forget to instinctively depress the clutch when shifting a manual transmission? Such is the value of repeated actions, engaged in as an ordinary part of daily life, over numerous years.

In some Japanese arts, students periodically undergo examinations in order to receive teaching certificates or advance in rank. Although many associate rank with the martial arts, flower arrangement, shodo, and other Do also have ranking schemes. If testing is required for certification, examinations are usually invitational, and the invitation is extended by the sensei. Over time, most students are invited to take such tests—but not all. Some students who are not invited complain that they are certain they could pass the examination if only their sensei would let them take it—and perhaps they could.

But that isn't the point: one teacher I know of tells students that the *real test* takes place each day when they come to train—or when they fail to come to practice. This real test continues during the practice session, when the sensei observes the students' attitudes—toward training, the instructor, their fellow pupils, and ultimately the Way itself. With teachers of this type—and they're common in traditionally practiced Ways—the greatest challenge isn't the examination but receiving the invitation to be examined, and this open door is rarely offered to students who practice irregularly or insincerely, no matter how talented they might be. Along the same lines, engaging in special austerities once a month or once a year is not as difficult, or meaningful, as simply practicing regularly, sincerely, and without giving up.

The discouragement and boredom that sometimes accompany routine practice can be met with the realization that the Ways

Seishin Tanren

Seishin, "spirit," and tanren, "forging," applies the analogy of the shaping and tempering of a Japanese sword to the forging of one's spirit through the practice of a Way.

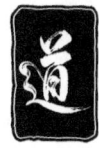

are most valuable when we're actually engaging in them. The advantages of training in a Do are found in the training process itself, not at some future point. Students of the Way discover the value of their practice in what it does for them as they drill each day and not in relation to some far-off goal. Truly, the Way exists in the present or not at all.

When we let go of training for a future goal, then discouragement isn't a factor. We become discouraged when we think we're not moving quickly enough toward an imagined objective. Doing our best in the moment, however, rarely produces such dissatisfaction. When we realize that we lose many of the benefits of an art if we cease to train in it, we have an added incentive to continue.

Perhaps you've heard someone state that they "know" karate, flower arrangement, or another Japanese art. This reveals a typical Western approach to the Ways that has nothing to do with shugyo. In the Do, having knowledge of a Way is of slight importance. Genuinely practicing a Way and arriving at a deep understanding of what ongoing training does for us over the course of our lives is what is most important. Likewise, to have studied a Way in the past, even rigorously, provides comparatively little benefit in the present. To *actively practice* flower arrangement or tea ceremony on a regular basis brings great spiritual and physical benefits. Our Way has become genuine shugyo, integrated with our daily life, and life itself has become shugyo.

Keiko

Regular *doing* with the full use of our mind and body is the key to successful shugyo, and in the Ways keiko, or "practice," is its basis.

In the West, we often speak in terms of having lessons or taking a class in some activity. Such expressions imply something momentary, that the goal is to absorb a set number of lessons and, once accomplished, the class comes to an end. The Do, in sharp contrast to this approach, are not ultimately a series of lessons, and the course has no end, as these disciplines represent a Way of life. Students come together to practice actions they have repeated hundreds of times in the past. New material isn't always introduced, and the teacher is sometimes virtually mute during the training session. Students don't meet with the sensei in order to receive the next lesson in a predetermined series, and the teacher doesn't always introduce the day's "lesson"; it is "found" by pupils in their ongoing repetition of basic patterns of exercise. Learning takes place, but it is frequently on a subconscious, intuitive level, and what is learned is often difficult to verbalize.

As mentioned, sometimes a neophyte will claim to "know" karate or shodo, and of course most use such expressions, not to mean they've fully mastered a given art, but simply that they have knowledge of the general parameters of their Way. In contrast, most Western and Japanese experts will simply say that they "practice" a particular Way, and "practice" is a common translation of keiko.

The term keiko is composed of two parts. The first refers to thinking or the act of reflection, and the second means "antiquity." Since most Ways make use of predetermined patterns of action, forms created at some point in the past and handed down, the ongoing repetition of these patterns involves, in a sense, reflecting on the past. Yet, in the endless repetition of ancient patterns, students discover, through personal experience of these patterns, something new. Take as an example the teacher of a science class, who commonly has students conduct experiments that have been assigned many times in past classes. Although the teacher could

Seiza

Literally, "correct sitting." Refers to sitting erect in a kneeling position with the legs tucked beneath the torso and the left big toe resting on top of the right one, with some space between the knees. It is a posture of resect used in the Japanese arts and Ways and for meditation.

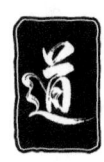

Sempai

One's senior in school, place of employment, or in a traditional art, where the term applies to someone with greater experience and expertise. See also kohai; tate shakai.

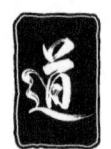

simply tell the students what the outcome will be, the students are made to conduct the experiments in order that they will see the results for themselves. Direct, personal, firsthand knowledge arrived at by actually *doing* has much more meaning than a mere intellectual grasp.

In the Ways, students strive for a union of body and mind. Practicing—keiko—established patterns of action, called kata, is not done only in order to master certain techniques but to know and come to embody the principles of the Ways.

Kata

If the Ways can be considered philosophies, then they are "philosophies" with a physical expression, or philosophies discovered through their physical expression. Chado, shodo, kado, and others can be thought of as Ways of art and life whose physical expression is keiko. But what constitutes keiko and why? Let us turn to kata, which are the means through which the Ways are practiced.

Kata means "form," in the sense of a prearranged form or formal pattern. In shodo, students strive to make exact copies of tehon, which are either books of classic calligraphy or samples of their sensei's brush writing. In sumi-e, every novice copies a specific painting and isn't allowed to progress to the next subject of study until the copy is exact. In the tea ceremony, chado disciples must work through a set series of rituals two centuries old, and in the martial Ways, practitioners endlessly repeat established combat sequences.

Yet even in Japan, there are those who claim that, in the martial arts, for example, fixed, predictable kata do not correspond to real-life combat. Similar comments could be made regarding the kata of many Japanese arts, not just budo. And these critics are correct in that the kata of any Do are artificial to the extent they are predetermined. They are incorrect, however, in supposing that practicing kata is inefficient and cannot lead to spontaneous action.

Continuing with our martial arts example, the key is to put aside combat and think in terms of education. Just as struggling with the "story problems" in arithmetic class and repeating over and over scales and "Mary Had a Little Lamb" during piano lessons gave us the rudiments of real-life problem solving and music making, and did so more effectively than if we had been thrown into real-life situations without this preparation, practicing kata in a martial art teaches fundamental principles that can be extrapolated to real life.

Occasionally there is the criticism that some martial arts kata don't feature realistic attacks and combat scenarios. The fallacy in this claim is the presumption that it's possible to predict the nature or form of a future attack. Will it be the bully in the schoolyard using the WWE armlock, or the mugger in the dark alley with the knife? The real deficiency is not in the use of kata in budo but in the practitioner's understanding of the methodology. Budo teachers aren't using kata to teach self-defense, and kata are not a collection of "self-defense tricks" to be memorized. Although many children, and adults too, come to the martial arts in search of secret tricks, and, sadly, many self-proclaimed experts will gladly sell these misguided people such tricks for a high price, there are no secret tricks. Having grown up practicing the Japanese martial arts and once undertaken a search for special techniques that would "really work," I can address this subject with some authority.

Kata are designed to teach principles more than techniques, principles that are universally applicable. These gensoku, fundamental principles, cannot, moreover, be learned intellectually.

Sennin

*Derived from the word
sen, in turn from the
Chinese word hsien,
describes the Japanese
Taoist equivalent to
a yogi. Also variously
translated as "Taoist
"immortals," "sages,"
or "mystics." See also
Sennin-do; Sennin
Ryoji.*

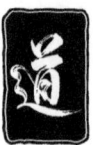

They must be learned by doing, which is the role of kata. Repetition of the kata gives us a chance to internalize these principles so that, eventually, we are capable of creating our own variations, or henka, and can thus effectively deal with new situations. In this manner, kan, or "intuitive perception," is cultivated, allowing us to eventually execute and create new or spontaneous techniques that are situation appropriate. This is crucial because we have no idea how we might be attacked; no matter what technique we drill repeatedly, we're still faced with adaptation. Ubiquitous principles can be adapted more broadly and universally than specific memorized techniques.

Another aspect of the rationale behind kata-oriented practice that is crucial relates to an esoteric quality. The founders of many art forms, from tea ceremony to odori, are at times said to have created their art through divine revelation. This kind of enlightenment and the sanctity with which such a tradition is preserved and passed on are by their very nature beyond verbal description. In the Ways, the means for communicating what is beyond words is again the kata, established forms that place the student in situations that require the development of certain attributes. While I can't get you to understand what calmness is simply by telling you what it is, I can place you repeatedly in a situation whose resolution requires the realization of calmness. The same can of course be said for other desired traits—coordination, concentration, and perseverance.

Kata are used and passed on from teacher to student because they have proved to be an effective means of discovering firsthand what is beyond verbal or written description.

Zanshin

As students of the Ways practice kata, they discover that stillness is as important as activity, not doing is equal to doing, and the moment following an action actually determines the success of the action itself, as well as the success of any following actions. This moment is called *zanshin*.

Zan means "lingering," "remaining," and suggests continuation, while shin is simply "mind." Zanshin can be seen in a sumi-e painter's continuing movement of the brush even after it has left the paper. It can be witnessed in a martial artist's freezing of movement after the execution of a final stroke of the sword or jujutsu throw—allowing the action to follow-through and the movement of ki to continue after the technique has been executed. But this pause is pregnant with potential . . . waiting to see if another action will occur or be needed.

Whether in fine art, martial art, or Kabuki drama, zanshin is present. It is a watchful stillness, a stillness that is gestating action. It is not the stillness of the graveyard but of the cat poised motionless before it pounces. There is in zanshin a unity of calm and action manifested in the form of physical presence.

Zanshin can also be observed in a Western context. The follow-through in a bowler's arm movement after the ball has been released and the continued movement of ki down the lane that takes the ball into the pins are examples. The follow-through in a batter's or golfer's swing is another. In all such examples, the instant following the action is as important as the action itself; it is where motion and stillness, doing and not doing merge into oneness.

It is interesting to note that we often fail in an action just at the moment before its completion, when we think we've got it, we have made it. In this instant of broken concentration, our awareness lapses, we fall out of the present moment, and we break our mind-body coordination.

Something I once witnessed at a judo tournament can serve as an example. In judo, a decisive throw garners a full point and thus victory. An imperfect throw, on the other hand, is worth a half point and means that the action continues. At this particular competition, I watched a teenager forcefully throw his opponent, which produced an accompanying roar from the spectators. Perhaps in the din he misheard the referee's assessment of the throw—or maybe he was just positive that he'd won; for whatever reason, he turned, raised his arms overhead, and acknowledged the crowd. Aside from displaying bad manners in traditional budo, the gesture was a very bad idea. The referee had declared the throw a half point, so the action had not yet stopped. The opponent rose from the mat, grabbed the "victor" in a stranglehold, and, falling backward, proceeded to squeeze his neck until he submitted (or fell unconscious; I can't remember which). As the crowd quieted down, I heard an elderly sensei from Japan sitting nearby comment, "Serves him right! Bad manners and no zanshin."

On a related note, my own judo sensei explained that a judoka, or "judo practitioner," doesn't begin things lightly: if he does start on a certain path, the judoka continues—to death, if need be—despite any obstacles, even if an alternate route must be discovered. And if the judoka dies on the path, his body will always fall in the direction he was going in. Zanshin indeed!

The power of zanshin is eloquently expressed in the arts of Japanese dance and drama. There is a momentary interlude following a gesture or movement during which the full impact, beauty, and drama is able to penetrate the hearts of the audience. The action isn't brought to a standstill, rather its effect is released to linger and reach deep into the witnesses of the performance. Imagine a massive temple bell, struck strongly. An immense, resonant note fades, but something remains, leaving the air charged with an almost electric sensation. . . .

Zanshin is not only the sustained concentration following an action but also an unbroken awareness of the moment and an indomitable spirit; it is the hallmark of all of the Ways, from aiki-do to shodo to odori.

Okuden

The kata used in the Ways have both visible and hidden elements. These hidden, or "secret," aspects of a kata or ryu are known as *okuden. Oku* means "inner," and *den* indicates a "tra-dition" or "teaching." Okuden have existed in the classical Japa-nese arts for a variety of historical reasons. Despite what is often assumed by overly romantic writers on this subject, aspects of this phenomenon have not always been especially esoteric or spiritual. In the 1970s, a friend told me of a man he knew in Japan who had just received okuden in the art of bonsai. (Okuden refers in some cases to a rank as well as the transmission of hidden knowl-edge.) After many years of practice and teaching bonsai, this man was finally initiated into his ryu's innermost principles—for only $10,000!

Why, I asked, would anyone pay such an amount? My friend replied that his acquaintance was quite serious about bonsai, but more, he was a bonsai teacher. And he ran a bonsai nursery. And this was Japan. Which meant, of course, that the acquisition of such knowledge—especially with the high rank attached to it—meant more students, more customers, and more money. It was an investment that would benefit both him and the *iemoto* ("lead-er") of his bonsai ryu, who received the substantial cash infusion.

Sennin-do

Designations used, along with Sen-do and Sen-jutsu, in arcane circles in Japan to indicate spiritual disciplines that trace their origins to esoteric Taoism.

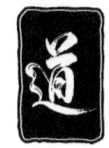

149

OKU: *Oku literally means "inner" or "interior," but when it is used in compound words like okuden, it suggests "hidden teachings." Okuden are the vital, yet not always readily apparent, esoteric principles that underlie Japanese art forms. In the various Do, what isn't always obvious is what frequently gives vitality and power to that which can be seen.*

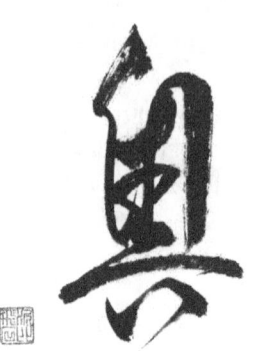

This is an extreme, relatively unusual example. Okuden is often transmitted freely, and teaching titles and ranks in the different ryu aren't invariably expensive. But again, there are exceptions.

Historically, transmitting the kata of a system but not all its inner principles served certain pragmatic purposes. In some cases, a teacher simply wanted to control who knew what. In other instances, the sensei was concerned about who would be ranked at a level where they could teach the more advanced curriculum—quality control at its most basic. In still other examples, an instructor simply might not have wanted too much competition from students who were as well versed as he was. Withholding secret techniques was a means of ensuring supremacy.

Granting that historical precedents and business concerns in Japan may have dictated this approach in the past, and even to some degree today, let's consider the more profound aspects of the okuden concept. In okuden is the implicit recognition that what you see is not all you get. According to in-yo cosmology, if an object has a front, it must have a back; correspondingly, if something can be seen, it must have an aspect that cannot be seen. In our increasingly materialistic high-tech world, with its sound bites, "15 minutes of fame," and a ten-easy-lesson approach to everything from fixing your car to fixing your marriage, it's easy to be persuaded that everything will reveal all aspects of itself instantly and with no personal effort. Because the Ways contain aspects that aren't readily apparent without serious observation, observation conducted by intense personal experience at that, even the simple understanding that okuden exist is a very important insight.

Suppose, for example, I want to explain to my new shodo student how to easily create *kasure*—an attractive effect that allows the white of the paper to show through the ink. I tell him that, as he touches the brush to his paper, he can press downward more strongly than usual, using a slight twist, and then abruptly decrease pressure as he continues the brush stroke to produce a beautiful dry-brush effect in midstroke. This effect causes the hairs to split, so I also explain how to turn the brush slightly on edge to cause the brush to veer off to the left and finish in a fine, smooth, well-defined point. Of course I could explain all this to the student immediately, but it is of little use to tell a new student how to do something that varies from the usual when he has not yet had sufficient experience to grasp what even the "usual" techniques are. Most beginners are struggling with how to hold the brush and make a straight line; asking them to attempt a special effect like kasure only adds unneeded complexity and hinders learning. Obviously a student can be given too much information.

In this sense, a teacher is not simply "withholding certain techniques" but is waiting until a student is advanced enough to be able to appreciate aspects of the art that would have been beyond reach at an earlier stage. Such a hidden point could be small changes in the way rudimentary techniques are performed, changes that might appear minute but that are significant.

Returning to the kasure example, when I do reveal this "secret teaching" at a later time, assuming the student hasn't already figured it out, it may seem to be a revelation and pupils might wonder why it was "held back." However, this misperception is simply the result of an incomplete understanding of okuden. For different cultural and historical reasons, this sort of misperception is not uncommon when Western students study with Japanese sensei,

Sennin Ryoji

Designation used in arcane circles in Japan to indicate healing arts that trace their origins to esoteric Taoism.

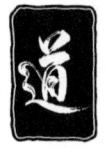

and one of my hopes in writing this book is to be able to contribute to the avoidance of such misperceptions.

Instruction in the arts and Ways is often divided into levels, *shoden*, *chuden*, and *okuden*—beginning, intermediate, and
advanced. Although some might assume that such levels of
instruction relate to degrees of hidden meaning, these stages are
as straightforward and logical as grade levels in school. They differ
from the comparison, however, in that they are not really hierarchical in scope: each level expresses different parts of a single entity—the Way.

Students at times misunderstand this and decline to enter
advanced training, claiming they're not ready, they haven't mastered the basics. Leaving aside the fact that mastery of any Way
is an impossibility, in many arts it is only when you learn the
advanced methods that you more fully grasp the fundamentals.
Advanced training illuminates aspects of the basics that couldn't
be seen before—their *okuden*. Thus the shoden-chuden-okuden
process in Do forms describes more a circle than a vertical line, so
that an understanding of the fundamentals leads to more advanced
methods that in turn refer back to the basics. A pupil's refusal to
move on to more advanced levels actually represents a refusal to
embrace the totality of practice, and this embrace of its totality is
crucial, as the Ways are not only nondualistic but also holistic.

Those are some of the basic points regarding okuden. The
concept is not always used by contemporary teachers of the
Do, even in Japan. And it is undeniably misused in some cases,
although many students report that the acquisition of such new
knowledge was meaningful. The important point is that the
essence of any Way lies in its fundamentals, and nothing in the
universe is truly hidden but is only waiting to be discovered. Serious, steadfast students often uncover okuden for themselves.

On the other side of this, deliberately holding back knowledge can be damaging for a teacher. Hoarding knowledge is ultimately destructive. The universe is infinite; the Way of the universe is infinite, as are the Do, which are particular expressions of the Way of the universe. We learn as long as we believe we have more to learn. Once we begin to store away a limited amount of knowledge, learning comes to a stop. We become like a glass filled to the brim, unable to receive any more. Even if we hang onto what we have, it becomes old, and we wouldn't want to drink a glass of "vintage water." If, on the other hand, we share what we have, we make room for something new.

Let us also consider the student's perspective. Most of us have an attraction toward hidden knowledge, because it seems easier to acquire something we don't have than to change ourselves (as well as our habitual behaviors that hold us back). Gathering knowledge is no different from buying houses, cars, and other items. An envious, greedy person will still be an envious, greedy person even in a million-dollar house or a fancy car. Anyone, within reason, can obtain knowledge. But the realization of wisdom, and the understanding of how to use knowledge, comes only through personal transformation. It has little to do with what we've accumulated, but instead, what we are.

New knowledge, new methods, and the like cannot produce realization. Understanding does not come from outside of us; it cannot be given or bought—not even in the form of okuden.

Omote and Ura

Okuden are present in the Do forms for two reasons: Japanese culture is based on the duality of a "public face" and "hidden face"; and the universe is composed of a similar visible-invisible duality (in-yo). Dualism in the cultural arts of Japan is sometimes

Sensei

Literally one who was "born before," an honorific appellation used after a person's family name to express respectful acknowledgment of his or her rank as teacher in a Japanese cultural art; it is never used when referring to oneself.

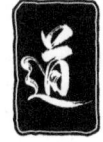

Shakuhachi

A bamboo, five-holed, recorder-like flute. The shakuhachi came to Japan from China and has long had certain associations with Buddhism. In some circles, perhaps owing to shakuhachi breath control paralleling meditative breathing exercises, playing the shakuhachi is seen as a form of musical meditation. Students of the flute, as in other traditional Ways, study under a sensei in a particular ryu or school.

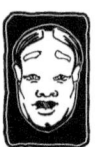

referred to as *omote* and *ura*. Omote means "front" or "outside," and ura means "back" or "inside." Omote is what we see; ura, which is just as important or maybe more so, is what is not immediately apparent.

As I've stated, advanced followers of ikebana are not practicing the art simply in order to learn to arrange flowers, devotees of the tea ceremony are not interested only in how to prepare tea, and martial artists are not studying primarily with the aim of self-defense. Subduing an opponent, making tea, and arranging flowers are the omote of budo, chado, and kado. The years of practice and thousands of dollars the study of these arts requires—a commitment of time and money that far exceeds what is necessary to attain a basic mastery of the techniques of these arts—are best understood in relation to the ura of these traditional Ways.

Because I teach a number of Ways, people often ask me to outline the benefits of practice. Long ago, I made a point of emphasizing that the outward forms of these disciplines are only a vehicle (omote) to help students arrive at the genuine goals of deeper concentration, relaxation, willpower, and calmness. These benefits, I explained, are the ura, the real reason for practicing. Over time, however, I realized that these cultivated traits are actually more the by-product of training and not the goal. If we make improved concentration our primary objective, we often miss the essentials of the omote that later lead to discovering this state. Even if we attain improved concentration, we might miss bringing together other vital character traits. The risk in making the by-product the goal is treating the ura as if it were the omote. Nevertheless, it is possible to point at the real meaning of practicing a Do, but not in ten minutes over the telephone. When I realized this, I wished for a book I could simply refer people to in order to help them see beyond the omote. So I wrote one.

Although this book isn't the only one that sheds light on

this important aspect of the arts and Ways, there is still a real need for such literature, especially in the West. In Asia, it tends to be understood that the essence of a Do is ultimately beyond description, and the outward forms of practice aren't the only reason for its study. As a result, students are more inclined to look for okuden, teachings that are not immediately apparent, and to wait for the ura to reveal itself. Because of cultural differences, and because Asian teachers are often disinclined to talk about what can only truly be felt through experience, the Western expression of the different Do sometimes has a distinctly omote flavor. Indeed, in many instances outside of Asia, the more popular Ways have become exceedingly superficial caricatures of their real forms.

However, since omote and ura are simply expressions of the nature of life, we can find omote-ura parallels in Western culture if we look for them. The average person only sees the omote of many things, and without training and intent observation the ura of even something as mundane as a beverage remains incomprehensible or even boring. If you have me sip a fine wine, as someone who doesn't drink, I'll probably just say it tastes like alcohol (omote). Give a wine aficionado the same taste, and he will likely elucidate a world of intoxicating wonders, filled with metaphor and subtle nuances (ura).

Omote and ura, seen and unseen, are telltale signs of the influence of Taoist yin-yang cosmology on a cornucopia of Japanese cultural forms. But more than this, omote and ura reveal the genuine nature of existence. We live in a relative world, made of dualities, and this world stems from a single universe that is absolute. Our relative world/the absolute universe, omote/ura, yin/yang, even heads and tails are part of the same coin that is life. It's not one, not two.

Myo and Yugen

Shibui, Shibumi

"Elegant." Shibui describes a quality of unaffected refinement, an unpretentious, timeless, rich quality, such as evoked in unpolished silver or gold, the hue of ashes or bran; shibumi suggests an image similar to the astringent taste of an unripe persimmon.

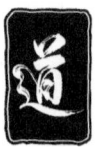

In performing the techniques of a Do, we absorb the Way, using a particular Do as a tool. In the process, we may experience a moment of perfection that is ultimately indescribable. To describe the indescribable, the Japanese arts and Ways use the word myo.

Myo indicates something "mysterious," "extraordinary," or "marvelous," but as usual in the Do forms, these words only hint at the actual meaning. Some books on Japanese culture and art mention that myo relates to *ki-in*, that is a "spiritual rhythm," or more literally, "the rhythm of ki." In short, ki-in describes a sensitivity to and harmony with ki on all levels. When an ikebana artist senses and unites with the rhythm of the ki of nature, she displays the very essence of the universe in art. If she perceives the rhythm and alternation of the ki of plants and blossoms—their growth, decline, and death, how they change in form and feeling with the seasons—then she can successfully arrange flowers. In her practice of kado, she liberates the spirit of all flowers, indeed the spirit of nature itself. In Japanese ink painting or calligraphy, when an artist can sustain the even, rhythmic flow of ki and attention in his craft, then a unity of mind and body results and so does art. In such a case, shodo becomes more than skillfully rendered lines on paper: the artwork displays a life-affirming rhythm and movement that reverberate ki-in and myo even centuries after its creation.

Ki-in, then, relates to the rhythm of ki on personal and impersonal levels. Every activity has its unique rhythm; even actions that we don't think of as rhythmic (such as the act of writing) have a rhythm to them that can't always be seen but that can be sensed. Part of this rhythm that relates to myo is what budo authority Karl Scott Sensei has termed "right place, right time, right frame of mind." When we sense and sustain the right and natural rhythm for a given activity, at the right place and at the right time, myo is the result.

Relating to and further elu-
cidating myo is the word yugen.
Yugen suggests something
"cloudy," "unfathomable." Yet
this cloudiness is not out and
out darkness but instead a state
beyond the limits of intellectu-
alization. But not beyond the
capacity of human experience.

Although   difficult   to
describe, yugen can be felt, just
as we can sense the blueness of the sky even when clouds obscure
it. Likewise, we shouldn't imagine that the unfathomable essence
of myo and yugen makes their experience less meaningful. The
ultimate nature of life and of the infinite universe itself is beyond
the intellect, but this doesn't make our feeling of wonder any less
meaningful.

It is in a state of mind and body unification, a state of self-
harmony and universal harmony, that all Do function at a high
level. When this condition expresses itself in art, it produces
actions and works that resonate a palpable movement or vibration:
ki-in. The effect and sensation produced transcend words and are,
in this sense, mysterious (myo). This state gives us a momentary
peek into the enigmatic world of yugen, which is a world that
encompasses the totality of existence, life on every level, mundane
and lofty. For serious students of the Way, this quality is sometimes experienced in actions that might seem commonplace. This
is to be expected, in that the Ways concern themselves with living our daily lives wholeheartedly more than with otherworldly
concerns.

Myo elevates simple acts of the tea ceremony, shodo, or
budo into bona fide art. It imparts a palpable aura to these arts

MYO: *Written in the
ancient gyosho script of the
famed Chinese calligrapher
Ogishi, myo hints at the
"miraculous." It suggest
actions or moments that
transcend mere technical
skill in painting, dance,
calligraphy, and other
traditional Japanese arts.*

157

when they are expertly performed that is noticeable but still indescribable. In the case of myo, it isn't what you do as much as how
you do it that's vital, or maybe what we do and how we do it are
equally important. But not everyone sees this, just as not everyone notices an indescribable cloud formation that's disappearing
as rapidly as it formed.

A few illustrations will help clarify the nature of myo and
yugen. In the 1980s, I participated in my first Kokusai Shodo-ten,
an international exhibition of calligraphic art sponsored by the
Kokusai Shodo Bunka Koryu Kyokai. My teacher is the vice-pres-
ident of the group, and he and I were to receive awards, so we met
up at the exhibition in Urayasu, near Tokyo.

Sensei suggested we have lunch with Ueno Chikushu Sensei,
the president of the Kokusai Shodo Bunka Koryu Kyokai. Ueno
Sensei was diabetic, very elderly, and rather frail. During lunch, I
suddenly realized that Ueno Sensei had been holding a heavy plate
for me to take. Despite toothpick-thin arms, his hand never wob-
bled. As we ate, I watched him use his chopsticks and hold his cup
of tea. I never detected the slightest shaking in his hands. When
I mentioned this observation to my teacher, Sensei shrugged and
said, "Lots of shodo practice." In this simple comment we find the
birthplace of myo.

Another example concerns my struggle to get a more powerful feeling in my calligraphy without sacrificing equanimity in the
characters. During one particular class, I saw Kobara Ranseki Sensei, my teacher, execute, without the slightest hesitation, a single,
decisive brush stroke that powerfully evoked myo in shodo. To a
casual onlooker it might have seemed to be nothing more than a
quick flick of the brush; but to me, someone who had many times
tried to produce this particular and powerful brush stroke, it was
much more. As Sensei conducted the lesson that day, he periodically made the stroke again under different circumstances. It was

always the same: resolutely powerful but completely composed, and invariably in the identical, correct spot—each and every time. More remarkable still was that he occasionally executed this action while talking to students, sometimes without even looking at the paper. I never asked Kobara Sensei about this striking ability because I knew what his response would be: "Lots of shodo practice." Ever hear the saying that the secret's in the little things? So is myo.

Mu

Just as the experience of myo eludes ready description, the essence of the absolute universe defies naming. In the Do, which are specific expressions of the Way of the universe, the word mu is used to suggest the nature of the universe. Relating but not limited to Buddhism, mu means "the void," "nothingness," with both cosmic and mundane nuances.

Mu is the unknown, but not an unknown outside human experience; as ever-changing and ultimately unknowable aspects of it, we ourselves belong to the unknown. And mu is a void, but the void isn't empty. Something that encompasses everything thus engulfs nothing, not one thing but all things. If I exist as part of everything, then the individual I dissolves into the totality of all things. "I don't exist" means everything exists. "Everything exists" means I exist. I am nothing; I am everything. I am the universe; the universe is myself.

Kenneth Yasuda, in *The Japanese Haiku*, explains:

> When one happens to see a beautiful sunset or a lovely flower, for instance, one is often so delighted that one merely stands still. This state of mind might be called

Shin-shin-toit-su-do

The Way of mind and body unification, a system of Japanese yoga and mind and body coordination techniques established by Nakamura Tempu Sensei in the early twentieth century; also called Shin-shin-toitsu-ho.

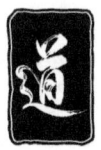

159

Shinto

"The Way of the gods." Shinto is an indigenous Japanese form of worship centered on a reverence for all aspects of nature, including one's ancestors. Central is the idea that all creations have their own kami, or "divine beings." Many kami are thought to have protective capacities. From Shinto, the Ways drew their emphasis on "purity" and purification well as a naturalistic emphasis in the form of practice, the style of the practice itself, and the aesthetics of the Do. Sabi ("rusticity") and wabi ("simplicity"), while inspired by Zen, have Shinto overtones. See also sabi; wabi.

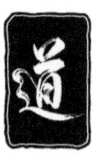

"ah-ness," for the beholder can only give one breath-long exclamation of delight: "Ah!" The object has seized him and he is aware only of the shapes, the colors, and the shadows. . . . there is here explicitly no time or place for reflections for judgements or for the observer's feelings.[13]

Nakamura Tempu Sensei conceived the same idea while living in the shadows of the Himalayas, and in his Shin-shin-toitsu-do system of Japanese yoga, he called it muga ichi-nen: "no self, one thought." Referring to Yasuda's example, the sunset is one thought, one experience, in which the experiencer and the experience merge. At that instant of union, there is no self-consciousness, which would pull the experiencer away from the experience itself; the moment of "ah-ness" can be fully experienced only when we cease to exist apart from the experience itself. This is muga.

In the Ways, the qualities that are cultivated, such as the faculty of concentration, in order to arrive at muga ichi-nen are as meaningful as the aim itself. In order to focus ki in an activity and reach muga ichi-nen, we must discover how to keep our mind free of distracting thoughts and outside stimuli; if the mind is arrested by a sound or thought, it can no longer be centered on making tea, arranging flowers, or playing the shakuhachi. Even using the mind to free itself is a distraction.

Imagine sitting in a crowded, noisy restaurant and suddenly noticing a fire break out in a building across from the restaurant. While you are concentrating on the fire you do not look at the people around you or listen to the sounds in the restaurant; they are a part of your awareness, but your focus is entirely on the fire. In the state of muga ichi-nen, exterior stimuli and internal thoughts are the passing people, and fire is the artistic activity—the one thought. We "watch" the moment, and "do nothing." In meditation, whatever thoughts or internal conflicts come up—*do nothing.* Don't try to force them to stop or change. And don't do nothing to still the mind, silence fears, or resolve conflicts—all of this is *doing something.* It leads to more struggling and hampers us from seeing the actual nature of thought and internal conflict. Genuine attention has no motive.

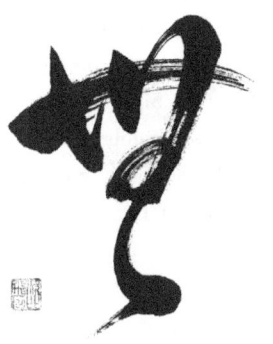

MU: *"The Void." Painted in the cursive sosho style of the renowned calligrapher Chici.*

Concentrated observation or listening doesn't involve effort. Effort distracts us from what is taking place in the instant. The effortless concentration that occurs when one is "lost" in rapt attention to a moving piece of music or compelling story, or the spectacle of a raging fire, is by its nature unforced.

This idea of effortlessness correlates to mui, which is a term believed to be borrowed from Taoism. Yoel Hoffman, in *Japanese Death Poems*, defines it as follows:

> Taoists define correct behavior as "non-action" (Ch., wu wei; Jp., mui), which does not mean "sit still and do nothing." Rather, it refers to action in which natural processes are not interfered with—actions as natural as the growth of sunflowers.[14]

The author rightly explains that sunflowers grow tall according to their nature; we don't need to pull up on them everyday to make this happen. In the case of seated meditation, mui does indeed mean to "sit still and do nothing," but the intent here is to illustrate that "doing nothing" doesn't necessarily mean, "don't do anything." It is in the nature of sunflowers to grow tall and no effort is required to make them do so.

Shizenteki

*Quality of "natural-
ness" and everence
for nature central to
Japanese art and tra-
ditional culture.*

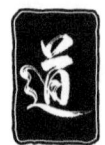

The concept of mu is not exclusively Taoist, and parallels
can also be found in Buddhism. There is a well-known sutra that
mentions form becoming empty and emptiness (ku) assuming
form. This emptiness is alternately characterized as ku or mu,
which have roughly the same meaning.

The notion of emptiness and form in this sutra has found
expression in the Ways. Ikebana, for example, is not only the
arrangement of flowers and branches but also the arrangement of
empty space. When I studied bonsai, I was told to prune and create enough space between the tree's branches so that a miniature
bird could fly through the bonsai. This attention to space, what
Western art refers to as negative space, is important in all the arts
and Ways, and in Japanese culture generally. Again, the experience of the meaningfulness of space is universally available.

We're often made aware of something by its very absence.
For example, I live at the entrance to a valley in a rural area. At the
right season, the sound of crickets fills the night air. Because the
sound is so ubiquitous, it's often unnoticed. Yet, when I ride my
bicycle in the valley late at night, my presence causes the trill of
the crickets to suddenly cease. And it is in this emptiness of sound
that I occasionally first hear the crickets' song.

In Japanese art, a harmonious balance between form and
emptiness, in-yo, yin-yang, is essential. Reality, as the Greek phi-
losopher Heraclitus observed, ultimately contains no opposites,
and in the Do we see a seamless joining of emptiness and substance that reflects life itself. A novice in a Japanese art has a free,
enthusiastic beginner's mind but little skill in technique. Later,
with the accumulation of knowledge and skill, self-consciousness
and a lack of spontaneity can arise. But if the student continues,
the underlying principles of the art are internalized and the practitioner returns to the beginner's mind. The expert, or meijin, began
in an unformed state, acquired form, then returned to a condition

of formlessness. No form to form to no form, as expressed in the Hannya Shingyo Sutra: *Shiki soku ze ku, ku soku ze shiki*, "From form to emptiness, and from emptiness to form."

Sen no Rikyu, founder of the tea ceremony as practiced today and greatly influenced by Zen, expresses the concept as follows:*

> *Keiko to wa*
> *Ichi yori narai*
> *Ju o shiri*
> *Ju yori kaeru*
> *Moto no sono ichi.*

> In your practice
> Start by learning one
> And continue until you understand ten.
> From ten you must return
> To the original one.

In the sixth century, the Indian sage Nagarjuna wrote of the Madhyamika sect of Buddhism and pointed to mu. Like most early Buddhists, he espoused the interdependence of all creations. If everything exists in relationship to everything else, for Nagarjuna, no one thing existed solely in and of itself. In other words, you, every other entity, and me are defined as distinct by comparison with that which we are not. And without the other, no such distinction can be made. We are everything. We are nothing.

Mu.

---

* Rikyu imbued cha no yu with a spiritual sensibility that had sometimes been previously lacking. Zen in particular is associated with use of the word "mu." *Mushin* ("no mind") and *munen* ("no thoughts") are terms common to Zen and the Ways.

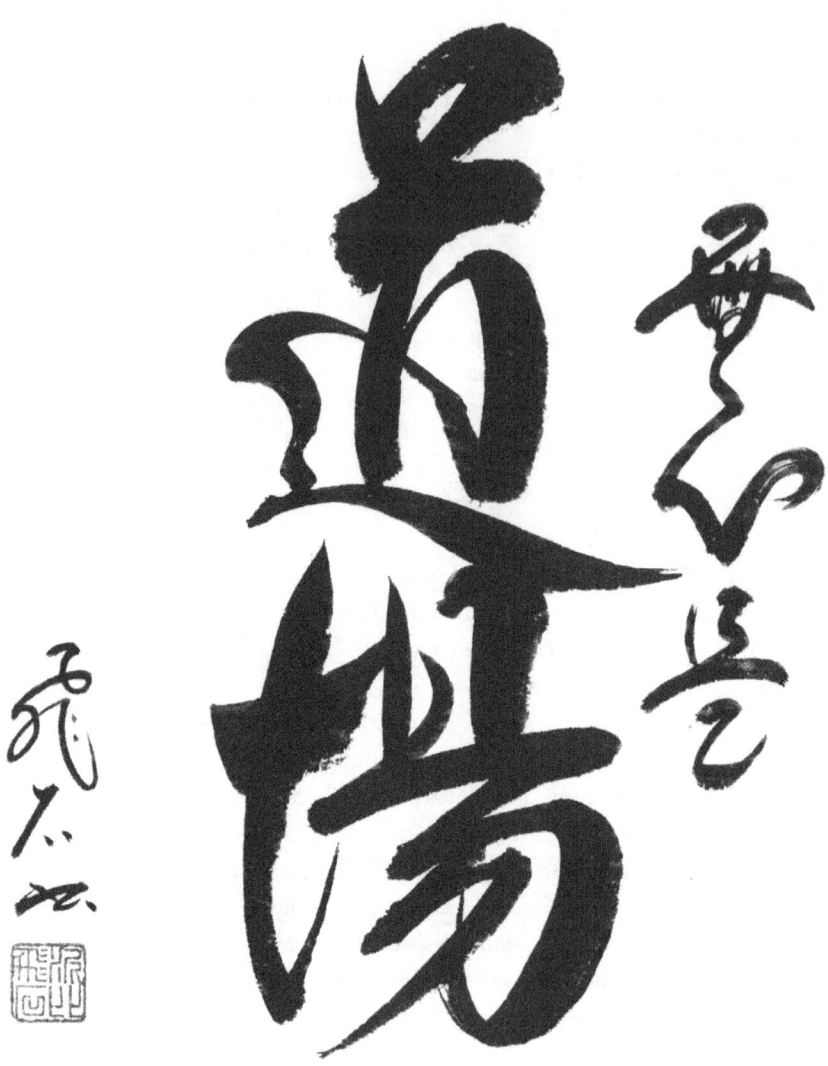

MUSHIN KORE DOJO: *"The empty mind is the true dojo."Mushin, meaning literally "no mind" or "empty mind," is easily misunderstood. It describes a state in which the mind is like a mirror: it reflects everything as it really is, but without clinging to any particular reflection. The mirror can do this due to its emptiness, yet the mirror isn't exactly empty—it always reflects something. A mind that is empty of conditioning, delusion, and attachments is free to reflect the actual Way of the universe. In doing so, the mind discovers the true dojo, or "place of the Way."*

Chapter 4

FOLLOWING
THE WAY

In writing this book, I've considered three types of readers: those who are studying a Do and understand it as a Way, those studying a Do but who don't understand it as a Way, and those who haven't studied a Do and aren't familiar with the practice of a Japanese art as a Way of life. In two of three cases, therefore, I'm writing for readers who haven't experienced the practice of a Japanese art as a spiritual path, and this chapter is aimed especially at this larger group of readers.

It might surprise you that someone could practice, and in too many cases actually teach, a Do form without realizing what it means to genuinely engage in it as a Way. Human beings frequently do things in a mechanical manner, unaware of what is taking place at the moment. Along with this tendency is the habit of making assumptions. It's common to assume that because we're practicing an art that ends in "Do" and our teacher is tossing off Asian-sounding platitudes that we are seriously investigating the nature of the Way. Assumptions, however, are based on the past, and reality is now and rarely matches our assumptions about it. We study the Ways to wake up to reality.

Because seeing reality for ourselves is potentially a scary business, many of us rely on the words and opinions of others to describe the nature of the universe and ourselves. The inclination to rely on what others say exists perhaps because we fear seeing things we would rather not see, which in turn could cause major upheavals in our lives. Real change involves stepping into the unknown, and the unknown can fill us with fear because we cling to a mistaken belief in an unchanging world.

Why we depend on what others say and fear seeing the true nature of the universe are important questions, but don't take my word for it. Ask the questions of yourself, find out if they are valid, and without assuming, look into what is taking place around you at this instant.

What is exists only in the moment. That is indisputable, as both the past and the future have no genuine existence except in our imaginations. Yet our minds are more often in the past or future than in the present. We worry about what we did or about what might happen down the road. We worry without realizing that worry itself only takes place in the past or future: the moment contains no time or space for worrying—only action. When you worry about something, is your mind in the present or is it in the past or future?

The Ways don't involve philosophical speculation but actually doing something, whether painting, serving tea, or engaging an opponent. And doing exists in the moment, as does the body, thus offering us a chance to explore unification of mind and body in the instant. It would be difficult to image a more valuable exploration.

It is obvious from the preceding that we cannot learn the Ways or discover the Way by reading about them. Nevertheless, books can point at universal truths. They can also inspire readers to take up the practice of a Do form. Perhaps most important, they can ask questions that cause us, writer and reader alike, to drop preconceived ideas about living, giving us, in that way, the opportunity to experience the beauty of existence as it really is.

So now you might be thinking about practicing a Do that has always fascinated you. You might go to the Yellow Pages or World Wide Web to find a suitable teacher and school. This might or might not be a useful method. Many genuine teachers are not in the Yellow Pages or on the Web. And in the Japanese Do, there are no teachers, only sensei. And sensei do not have schools or studios or gyms. And they don't have students, they have deshi, and deshi don't take classes. Confused? Let me explain.

Taking Classes versus Joining a Dojo

We live in a consumer-oriented world. It seems almost every-thing—and sometimes everyone—is for sale. When it comes to learning something, we expect to find a school, pay for classes, and get what we paid for. This works if you're taking a course in math. You pay for the finite series of classes, buy the textbook, listen to the teacher explain the material in the text, take the test, and you complete the course. You got what you paid for. But a dojo isn't a math class. The sensei cannot be bought. The course never ends. And the Way is not for sale.

I once had someone visit our dojo to observe group practice in one of the Do we study. He wanted to take only private lessons from me; however, the art he was interested in requires interaction with a variety of people if a person is to learn it well. I explained this and offered to teach him privately as long as he participated in some group instruction. He left promising to think about it.

I got a call from him a week later reiterating his desire for only private lessons. I also repeated my explanation, adding that, although I'd certainly bring in more money by teaching him pri-vately, I'd also be doing both of us a disservice. He offered even more money. I declined. At this juncture he grew incensed, unable to understand that money wasn't the issue. It might have been the first time he had been faced with something he couldn't buy— for any price. Isn't the customer always right? Perhaps. But a dojo isn't a convenience store. The Way is not for sale.

Similarly, I've had people visit who had made long-term

Shochu Geiko

Special summer train-ing during which martial artists (and practitioners of some other Do forms) train their minds and bod-ies to the limits of their endurance and beyond in order to find new limits. See also shugyo.

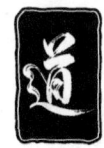

Shodo

The Way of calligraphy, an ancient art valued as a visual art form but also as a form of "moving meditation" and as a means to enhance concentration, willpower, and poise. The pictographic nature of Chinese characters lends shodo a quality in common with abstract art.

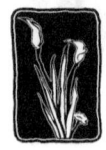

commitments to another sensei and another version of one of the Ways I practice. I usually encourage such people to honor their original commitment and continue with what they've started. For most, the additional time commitment alone would make sincere study at our dojo difficult. On more than one occasion, the person has been dumbstruck that I was sending them away: "But you're offering classes, and I'm prepared to sign up and give you my money." The Way is not for sale.

A sensei isn't selling the Way, and so he or she doesn't have customers. A dojo is not an enterprise designed to make money. It certainly can be run in a businesslike, professional manner, and in some cases it may be prosperous. The fundamental intent of a dojo, however, differs from a business or school.

"Dojo" is a term originally used for an area in a Buddhist temple employed for meditation. Do means "the Way," and jo means "place." The original Sanskrit term is *bodhimandala*, meaning "the place of enlightenment." The word for "school" in Japanese is *gakko*. Although many people assume that a dojo refers to a martial arts training hall, in fact dojo are not limited to budo. Not too far from our dojo, for example, is the world-renowned San Francisco Taiko Dojo. They practice the Way of the taiko drum, which is hardly a martial art.

A dojo, then, is an environment where firsthand experience and experimentation lead to deep understanding. The memorized data or theoretical understanding of a subject associated with a classroom setting are actually of a secondhand nature. What is secondhand is in effect borrowed; it isn't genuinely part of us since we haven't experienced it for ourselves. In the Ways, understanding comes from what we sense for ourselves by means of direct mind and body experience, and the place for this experience and understanding is the dojo.

Teachers versus Sensei

Sensei is a title of respect that is widely used in Japan. It means "teacher," but it connotes ideas not necessarily suggested by the Western notion of teacher. Because of a lack of knowledge of Japanese culture in general and the Ways in particular, misconceptions regarding the sensei as a concept and as an actual individual have crept into American and European understanding of the Do.

On the one hand, the sensei of the classical Ways are not equivalent to, for example, a high school teacher; the methods and place of instruction, for one thing, differ significantly. On the other hand, "sensei" shouldn't be taken to mean infallible master, cult leader, or Grand Pooh-Bah. Sensei is also not a designation reserved for teachers of ikebana, karate, or a particular Japanese art. In fact, doctors, lawyers, and certain other professionals receive the same designation. It's possible to suggest that a doctor, for example, is teaching the Way of medicine, but this understanding of teaching differs from that in the West.

Likewise, the assumption occasionally encountered in the United States that you can only have one sensei is patently false. Considering the broad usage of the term in Japan, this is obviously a Western myth. It is true that sensei will caution that trying to seriously follow several Do forms is frequently a mistake. Owing to the time needed to seriously study such arts, even practicing more than one is likely to be too much for busy people. Little is gained from studying too many Do; they are all aspects of a single universal Way. The point of practicing one Do is to follow the Do, not to acquire a diversity of technical knowledge or intellectual entertainment. Teachers in Japan also warn that having more than one sensei *for a specific art* can be a problem. Attempting, for example, to practice two systems of flower arrangement simultaneously can lead to confusion, not to mention serious conflicts

Shogi

Like the game go, shogi was brought to Japan from China centuries ago. Two participants play on a board made up of eighty-one squares. Somewhat similar to chess, the objective is to immobilize the other person's "king" and capture him. Each contestant has twenty pieces, which have eight distinct standings. Shogi offers a series of ranks (dan), and like go, is thought to cultivate concentration and mental power.

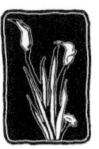

of interest. In this context, it is true that you can only have one sensei, but there are many sensei. So if you were to visit another teacher of flower arrangement, regardless of the system, and you failed to call him or her Sensei, you would be considered rude by that teacher and also by your own sensei.

Despite this, I've heard people in the United States refuse to call anyone Sensei other than their own teacher. Others sometimes even refuse to call their own teacher Sensei "until I'm sure I respect you enough to offer you that title." Beyond seeming bizarre to anyone who has studied a Way in Japan, these attitudes point to a misconception. Such people take their sensei and the title itself far too seriously. They are looking for a perfected being who will confer on them the Truth. This is fantasy. Skilled sensei of the Do point the way by passing on knowledge and creating an environment where students are able to arrive at a direct understanding through their own efforts and motivation.

At the other extreme, there are people who refuse to address their teacher as Sensei because "It's no big deal," "This is America," or because they simply can't be bothered. This attitude negates the distinctive relationship that exists in the Do between sensei and student. Although you might have little or no contact with your sensei outside the dojo, your relationship with him or her is not an impersonal one, "just business." Because of the spiritual and life-altering nature of the Ways, sincere study under an equally serious sensei produces a unique and close alliance. I've rarely socialized with some of my sensei, but, owing to the penetrating and long-term characteristics of our relationship, my sensei frequently know me better than some of my close friends do. My teachers might not know my favorite food, owing to a certain distance often needed in such relationships, but they have nonetheless plumbed the depths of my personality in a manner seldom encountered. (As sensei to my students, I have seen the counterpart to this.) If, therefore, I were to address my teachers by their first name, it would serve only to negate the special nature of the connection in the Ways between sensei and pupil. As significant, it would also reveal the superficiality of my intent. (This relationship isn't always paralleled in Japan between, for instance, a lawyer and his client, although the lawyer would be addressed as Sensei.)

As in life in general, a correct balance is needed in studying the Ways. Our sensei isn't a god, but we also don't have the kind of relationship with her or him that we have with our buddies or our sixth-grade teacher. This is because we are not classroom students; we are not taking classes or attending school, and we are not trying to simply acquire technical knowledge. We are interested in seeing and embracing the Way.

Students versus Deshi

A student who pays for a college or evening class is, in a sense, a consumer. In Japanese, *seito* is the term used to refer to this kind of student. A "student" of a Do form in Japanese is called a deshi, a word that is perhaps closer in meaning to the old Western concept of an apprentice. Since the Way is not for sale, and a dojo isn't merely a business, deshi don't actually take classes or pay tuition. (This is not to say that dojo don't charge a fee, they usually do, but the fee is more a donation to help sustain the operation of the dojo and support its sensei.)

Students *attend* a class and expect to be taught. Deshi *join* a dojo to discover and embrace a Way. Joining a dojo is closer to being adopted into a family than attending a class. Students seek information. Deshi make a commitment to undergoing transformation and gaining understanding. Students memorize facts;

Shoshin

"Beginner's mind." Believed to be derived from Zen, it describes a state of mind that always remains fresh, never bogged down by its own past. With shoshin, the student is able to look at each practice session in an art as if it were being experienced for the very first time.

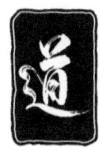

171

deshi learn through practice. To learn is to grow, and to grow is to change. Are we seeking actual growth, and thus change, or are we more interested in intellectual stimulation and/or the redecoration of what we already are? For the deshi, this is a key consideration.

When I first started to teach the Shin-shin-toitsu-do style of Japanese yoga, I noticed an interesting and ongoing occurrence. The principles of mind and body unification underlying this Way are universal, relating to a variety of people and subjects. Consequently, certain students would invariably enthuse that I was saying things they had always believed or introducing things they had always thought possible. Although such enthusiasm might seem harmless, it isn't always a good thing.

Some of these ardent participants dropped out as quickly as they had started, more quickly than many other people. I began to ask myself what might occur if I said something they haven't heard before, if they were challenged in what they believe or were required to consider real change. I discovered that such students are ardent if they feel I am confirming their beliefs or expectations and much less so when I surprise or challenge them. This phenomenon is not limited to my dojo.

Are we in fact looking for authentic growth, which is change, or just seeking confirmation of what we have already experienced? Do we seek escape from the prison cell of stagnation or only a redecoration of that cell?

If we have reoccurring problems, these problems repeat because we are carrying previous conditioning, and *what we were*, from the past into the present. This affects *what we are*. To break this cycle requires a break with the past, a break with the known and a leap into the unknown. The dojo, ourselves, the sensei all exist in the present. Clinging to the past in the form of beliefs, biases—conditioning of any kind—transforms the present into another version of our past. Certainly exposure to new, radically different ideas can forever change *what we think*, but the Ways continuously change *what we are*.

The Do or Tao is the Way of the universe, a Way that always exists in the present, changing and not changing, from moment to moment. Embracing the Way, then, invites freedom in continuous change and never-ending growth. Can such a Way be discovered by a mind that is conditioned by its own past and thus locked in a loop, a loop that it can modify but not escape? Freedom lies in adaptability to circumstances, and adaptability exists in a mind that embraces the ever-changing moment, a moment that has never existed before and that is by its very nature unknown, and thus filled with infinite possibilities.

Accumulated knowledge is not understanding. Humankind has accumulated knowledge from the past for generations. Although useful, it has not deeply transformed humanity: war, racism, and poverty still exist. Understanding is realized from moment to moment. The moment is eternal, existing beyond time. The Way is likewise eternal and transcendent.

Shugyo

Containing quasi-religious overtones, shugyo means roughly "austere practices." The Ways, with their emphasis on "spiritual forging," are themselves shugyo. The occasionally long meditation periods in Japanese yoga and the martial artist's special winter training are examples of shugyo in the Do. See also kan geiko; shochu geiko.

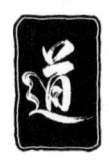

Reigi

What I have described in the preceding does not exist in the West or in Japan without exception. Some sensei see themselves as teachers with students and schools, and not all sensei describe their place of practice as a dojo and their students as deshi. Nonetheless, what I have described reveals the traditional approach to practice of the Ways, and an awareness of this approach will be of value to students who find themselves in traditional or more westernized settings. Certainly an idea of what can be expected in the more traditional dojo will lessen the likelihood of "culture shock."

173

Soji

Ritualistic cleaning of the training hall. From Shinto, the Ways drew their traditional emphasis on purity and various purification practices (misogi). Cleanliness and purity are closely connected. Whether you visit a martial arts dojo or a school of calligraphy in Japan, it's common to see students engaging in soji. Soji relates as much to the purification of the individual as it does to the tidiness of a practice area. See also misogi.

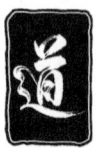

And culture shock is not too strong a term to use. Since many sensei are Japanese or are Westerners who have trained in Japan and know they are dealing with important Japanese cultural properties, you may wonder if, when you step into their dojo, you've suddenly entered a foreign environment. Even if your new sensei goes to lengths to make you feel at home or to explain her teachings in a manner understandable to Westerners and novices, don't assume that she is the same as a schoolteacher. Most sincere sensei are nice people, and Japanese culture is gracious toward new acquaintances. These impressions can lull you into thinking that your dojo isn't that different from your tennis club. If you've found an authentic dojo and a genuine sensei, this assumption couldn't be more wrong.

Like any culture, the dojo has its own means of functioning that may not be familiar or compatible to you. Indeed, because the culture of the dojo is not necessarily the same as that of modern Japan, even Japanese can suffer from a sort of culture shock. Yet among the valuable aspects of training in a Do is cultural exchange itself, and it's only clinging to what we're comfortable with that can make this experience a negative one. What's more, the different culture you're moving into isn't different simply because of its Japanese overtones. The greatest, most important, and yet most subtle difference lies in the culture of the Way itself, which doesn't always conform to current social norms.

In Japan generally and in the dojo in particular, the means of harmoniously interacting with a sensei and other deshi are called reigi, "techniques of respect." Reigi is often translated as "etiquette," but I feel this trivializes the concept.

Its most common expression is the traditional Japanese bow. Bowing and other behavioral aspects of reigi will be explored momentarily. For now, however, I'd like to stress that this explanation of reigi is my own; repeating what others have written is of little interest to me or the reader. My description of reigi is based on spiritual concepts I have defined in this book, and in that sense transcends culture. Of course other interpretations, from a historical or social point of view, are viable, but my orientation is primarily spiritual.

The Spirit of Reigi

All creatures originate from the universe and, in a spiritual sense, are manifestations of its creative impulse. We come from the same origins and return to the same state at death. In this view, we are linked with one another and all things in the universe. When life is viewed holistically, all people, plants, and animals deserve respect. To respect others means respecting ourselves, for we exist by the grace of nature and its vital ki. Ideally, reigi in the Ways, if not always in Japanese society, embodies techniques to demonstrate and explore respect—rei—for all things. Serious exploration of this respect could perhaps lead to a discovery of our oneness with the universe. (Although the phrase "oneness with the universe" has been so frequently used as to become a cliché, such an important human exploration is anything but cliché.)

It isn't uncommon in Japan to hear experts in the Ways state that "Such-and-such a Do begins and ends with rei." In the case of the tea ceremony, for example, one of the most influential Ways, respect for fellow participants and nature is considered paramount. Confirming this are the four essentials of chado: harmony, respect, purity, and tranquillity, which are in fact valued in most Ways.

Western students of the Do, however, sometimes think that reigi simply refers to bowing. Of course, rei does mean "bow," but it also means "respect," thus indicating a correlation between the two. More important, rei meaning both bow and respect demon-

175

strates a historical inclination to not divide the mind and body, thoughts and actions, in the Ways (if not in Japan in general). Bowing is, however, one of many physical expressions of reigi that is not more important than the attitude underlying it. In order to understand the essence of the Do and reigi, it is important to look deeply into their ultimate implications as well as their current expressions.

It might come as a surprise to know that such serious consideration of reigi and other aspects of the Ways does not invariably occur in Japan. For many Japanese a bow is a bow, and reigi amounts to a social custom. This sort of taking things for granted is perhaps not really unexpected; it's not unlike the way we in the West take the handshake and its implications for granted. How often is this gesture performed sincerely, mindfully? Japanese culture is no different in this sense. For this reason, a number of experienced Western (and in some cases Japanese) teachers of the Do believe that the Ways may make a leap in growth now that they have been transplanted in the West. Why? Because they're foreign to us, we don't take them for granted. This refers, of course, to earnest Western students of the Do who have tried to see beyond the external form of the Ways, their omote.

The martial Way of aikido is an example of this phenomenon. Several prominent aikido teachers in Japan and the United States have commented on how Westerners are more inclined to look into the spiritual side of what is widely touted as the most spiritual form of budo. In Japan, they complain, pupils often view it as a hobby, health-maintenance program, or social activity. And these days, more people are practicing aikido outside of Japan than in it. Likewise, tea ceremony practitioners, in both East and West, grumble about how chado has become nothing more than a "finishing school" for young Japanese women who want to be seen as cultured in order to improve their marriage prospects.

Before we pull a muscle from excessive back patting, it must be pointed out that, although this phenomenon certainly exists, many Westerners lack an understanding of how aikido, chado, and other Do function as Ways. Even fewer realize the manner in which reigi works as more than etiquette. Further, it's admittedly simplistic to think that because Japanese students don't sit around philosophizing about their art, as Westerners are sometimes overly inclined to do, it means they aren't serious about its spiritual side. Still, owing to our lack of familiarity with such Ways and customs, the potential for a renewed, reinvigorated examination of the Ways (and reigi) is possible. Whether this potential is realized is up to people like you and me.

Although it is certainly true that ultimately the deepest roots of the Do lie in the human heart, where there are no nationalities or borders, in order to understand the meaning of reigi and the Do more generally it is worthwhile exploring their Japanese cultural context.

The Tradition of Sempai-Kohai

To understand Japanese culture, we must grasp tate shakai, or "vertical (or class) society." Japanese society is based on a system Westerners might compare to the relationship between a parent and child. It defines relationships between employer and employee, teacher and student—indeed, virtually all relationships in Japan. Ideally, it's not so much a system of strict hierarchical relationships as one of mutual service, duty, patronage, and respect, alternating from one level to the other and back again.

According to this model, just as a child follows and respects a parent, Japanese adopt this same attitude toward, for example, a teacher, religious leader, and, to some degree, even an employer.

Suiseki

An art symbolizing natural phenomena, from countryside to the universe, using a stone a few inches to a foot and a half in dimension. Suiseki begins with the discovery and acquisition of stones in nature and consummates in a sensation of beauty as well as a spiritual connection between the collector and the stone. An ideal suiseki pleases the eye, yet kindles wonder as it duplicates a mountain in small scale. It can also function as a spiritual and reflective form, a stone allegory that helps us identify with and comprehend things of value.

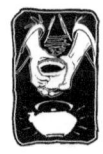

· 177 ·

Tachi-rei

*A "standing bow."
Bowing is a common
expression of respect
in the Ways and can
be a means of practic-
ing the coordination
of mind and body.
The manner in which
bowing is performed
will vary in depth and
duration—depending
on the social situation.
Deeper angles, held
longer, are considered
more formal and sig-
nificant. Za-rei, the
"seated bow" is also
more formal.*

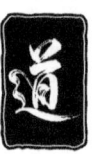

A primary example of this "parent-child" attitude is the tradition of sempai-kohai, or "senior-junior," which is found in traditional dojo and Japanese society generally. Sempai are individuals who have studied, trained, or worked for a longer period and have more experience than their juniors. A person who is employed ahead of you in a company, for instance, is your sempai and is treated accordingly. Many relationships within the dojo and in life can be described in terms of this relationship.

Westerners might have difficulty understanding this concept since relationships in Western societies are less hierarchical. But, rather than comparing one model to the other, it might be most useful to accept that the nature of relationships in Japanese and Western societies differs, and to recognize that, in this relative world, it is sometimes necessary to accept relationships according to such categories as senior and junior. In the absolute universe, every duality ultimately reduces to one. But we live in a relative world, where life is split into opposites. In recognizing our unity with the universe, we realize that dualities like sempai-kohai are actually complementary and form one harmonious whole.

In life and in the dojo, sempai should care for and respect their kohai while helping them to develop. Conversely, kohai should show support for their sempai while attending to their needs. This mutual relationship is upheld by reigi and embodies forms of etiquette such as bowing to seniors, cleaning, and main-taining the dojo, as well as possessing an attitude that accords with reigi. Although deference and respect are shown to everyone in the dojo and outside, students who are most senior and closest to the sensei often receive more elaborate displays of respect, just as planets closest to the sun receive the most sunlight.

This may be easier for Westerners to comprehend if they realize that kohai show respect to a certain sempai not merely in regard to the senior's present position but also for that person's *potential.* Behavioral researchers have observed that if our treatment of other people reflects what we would like them to become, there's an observable inclination for that to indeed happen. Therefore, if we encourage our seniors and sensei to excel by showing them our respect, they might grow into leaders we can genuinely admire. At the same time, of course, the sensei and sempai are expected to take a similar respectful approach in guiding the behavior of their kohai.

An additional correlation can be seen between the sempai-kohai relationship and the parent-child connection. Parents who constantly tell their children they will amount to nothing often produce individuals severely limited in their ability to develop, whereas the unconditional love and devotion of a child has in some cases influenced parents away from everything from crime to alcohol addiction.

Readers who have lived in Japan and seen the sempai-kohai system in action know that it doesn't always resemble a healthy parent-child relationship; frequent abuses by seniors take place in Japan, and mistreatment of kohai and deshi takes place even in the Ways. Nonetheless, any system, whether it's the sempai-kohai relationship, reigi in the Ways, or a form of government, is only as good as the people who participate in it. While the Way of the universe is one, the individual Do and their forms of relating and etiquette are human expressions of this Way, and as such, they are susceptible to human frailties.

The Sensei

The word "sensei" is made up of two parts that translate literally as "born" (sei) and "before" (sen). In practice, it is used as a designation of respect in reference to someone who, by vir-

Taiko

A Japanese drumming style. While taiko drums have been used for over 1,400 years, the style best known today began in the 1950s. Reputedly, one of the first uses of taiko was as a battlefield tool—to intimidate the enemy and to signal troops. Taiko were also used in the opening ceremonies of the Todaiji Buddhist temple in the eighth century, and they were incorporated into imperial court music as well. Taiko drums continue to find a place in religious observances, both Buddhist and Shinto. The modern-day taiko drum troupe, sometimes organized as a collective where the performers live under the same roof, is a relatively new development whose popularity has spread outside of Japan.

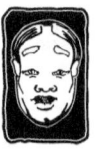

tue of greater experience and expertise in an art, for example, has attained a high level of mastery. The appellation is used in place of the ordinary honorific suffix -san, as in Yamamoto-san, which then becomes Yamamoto Sensei. One's sempai can be designated as a teacher, and in that case that individual is always addressed using Sensei. Furthermore, since a Do is a Way of life, sensei are normally called so even outside the dojo, and failing to do so is to practice the Way superficially, in isolation. Regular and correct use of Sensei is another important aspect of reigi.

At the same time, sensei and sempai must also observe correct reigi and take responsibility for helping their juniors and students. For this reason, exhausted sempai sometimes feel that their position of seniority is more a curse than a privilege. Correctly fulfilling the role of sempai means more than barking orders at those who are less experienced and demands giving serious attention to the growth and development of one's juniors, which is not an easy task.

Some students might wonder why the Do ask that they show respect for others through bowing, the use of titles, and other outward actions. They might believe that feeling a certain way toward another is sufficient, or that this attitude need not be visibly demonstrated. However, a student learns more effectively in an atmosphere that engenders respect for the teacher and the seniors. Reigi links the atmosphere of respect and those within that atmosphere, and in this way it brings an element of seriousness to the practice of the art that is beneficial. It encourages the sensei to be devoted to his students' welfare and students to show sincere respect to the sensei and the practice. This "vertical attitude" has proven effective for transmitting an ancient discipline from one generation to the next. In addition, the goal in pursuing a Way is a synchronization of mind and body: thoughts and actions should be one. Therefore, it is natural that students should bow and say

"Thank you, Sensei" to their teacher after receiving instruction. By physically showing gratitude at the moment it is felt and by expressing feelings aloud, students experience an integration of the mind and body, a harmony of belief and action. Over time, as they practice mind and body coordination in a given Way, this behavior and mind-body harmony carry over into their lives, which is indeed the ultimate aim of practicing a Way.

Self-discipline and Nyunanshin

Reigi can be considered forms of discipline. In fact, all Do are indeed disciplines and processes of strengthening ourselves spiritually and physically. But the nature of this "discipline" isn't necessarily what might be assumed. Discipline is not necessary to eat regularly, go to the bathroom, or step out of the way of a speeding truck because we clearly see the need for these actions. What if we just as clearly saw the necessity of the Way itself? This is an essential question for deshi of the Do. If we realize the value of what we're engaged in, that it relates to the very essence of living itself, discipline becomes unnecessary.

Assuming that our sensei is a sincere, competent, and compassionate person, why might we come to think of practice as overly demanding or difficult? Could it have to do with our failure to understand the real purpose and value of the training? I think this is often the case, and although we may understand this intellectually, genuine understanding comes through direct experience with the Way. So, if we participate in a Do, is our recognition of its purpose and value wholehearted or just conceptual? Many people might not even be able to tell the difference between the two. To rephrase the question, do we understand the Way in the manner that we know fire burns or that we need water to survive? This

Taoism

Taoism is based on the Chinese concept of the Tao, represented by a single written character that can mean a "road" or "path" or, in its spiritual context, the "Way." Taoism is known as Dokyo in Japan, and this same character is the "Do" used in the names of the Japanese Ways. Taoist teachings represent the outgrowth of a Chinese heritage of nature veneration and divination. The Tao was interpreted as the origin of all creations and the life power behind all action in nature. While both the Way and its power are beyond the limits of intellectual understanding, they can nevertheless be observed in the endless manifestations of nature, where they can foster a spiritual approach to being.

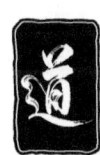

Tate Shakai

*"Vertical [or class]
society," comparable
to the relationship
between a parent
and child; it defines
relationships between
employer and
employee, teacher and
student—virtually all
relationships in Japan.
Ideally, it is not so
much a system of strict
hierarchical relation-
ships as it is one of
mutual service and
duty and patronage
and respect, alternat-
ing from one level to
the other and back
again. See also kobai;
sempai.*

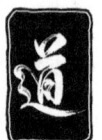

question is important for people who participate in the Ways of
Japan as spiritual paths. Because, with a profound recognition of its
purpose and value, the need for externally imposed discipline dissolves. All discipline becomes self-discipline, but there is no sense
of force; our manner of interacting with a Way is one of *choosing
to participate.* In sincerely making this choice, we naturally focus ki
on the completion of necessary tasks. To do less makes no sense.
And one of the valuable aspects of the Ways is the opportunity to
discover the true meaning of sincerity, in all aspects of living. To
be sincere is to live wholeheartedly.

Our sempai have more experience and have realized an
appreciation of the benefits inherent in following the Way, and,
because they care about us, they want us to realize these benefits.
As kohai, we in turn do our best to participate wholeheartedly.
We will then someday be able to repay the kindness of our sensei
in the form of our own teaching and contributions to the Way,
thereby forming a circle of harmony.

We have voluntarily chosen a Way. This entails certain
obligations, but they are obligations to us as much as to our sempai and sensei. If the obligations and their fulfillment are seen as a
problem, it lies in thinking of an obligation as a sacrifice, a sacrifice
we're making for some future, abstract gain. But the Way exists
now. Its benefits are realized in what we're doing right now. It
isn't something we do for the future, and its value is realized in the
moment and during the training itself. Without this understanding, practice becomes a "sacrifice" we make toward a future goal.
But the future might never come; the value of the Way exists in
this instant. A Do as a Way of life is of immense usefulness and is
worth following for its own sake.

In order to train effectively, we must be willing to change.
A fixed image of oneself or a strong ego can, however, obstruct a
willingness to change and grow. The Way lies in continual trans-

formation, and reigi helps us to transcend the ego and achieve a humble, open-minded state that makes real growth possible. This state is *nyunanshin*, or "pliable mind," and it is an essential component of all the Do. Just as stretching is less painful when we "relax into the stretch," so too is spiritual growth easier when we transcend the ego and open our mind. This is nyunanshin.

Nyunanshin requires harmony with the sensei, the training, and the dojo. It is to become one with the teacher, who at that point is free to go beyond superficial teaching. Such harmony and union come from a deep sensitivity to others, particularly our sensei. They come from first emptying yourself in order to become full. This emptying, which relates to reigi, is an ongoing, lifelong process. Through the discipline that comes from freely choosing to follow the Way and the pliant, open mind of nyunanshin, we discover the true meaning and value of the Ways as spiritual practice.

On and Giri

To further understand reigi, the Ways, and their cultural context, we must consider the concepts of *on* and *giri*. On refers to "obligations" people have to one another. This feeling of being obliged or owing honor or gratitude to someone can apply to anyone, but it is particularly important in relation to ancestors, parents, seniors, and teachers. Reigi is one means of expressing to them our appreciation.

Giri describes the debts incurred to one's *onjin*, or "benefactors." Giri can mean "code of personal responsibility," "loyalty," or "duty." Each dojo position has its own giri; indeed, this is an important tradition in the Japanese arts and Ways. In Japan, giri to acquaintances is repaid according to the value of the on received;

Temari

Decorative stitched balls usually given as a present. A thousand-year-old handicraft that has its roots in balls for children, temari produces an enchanting effect on observers. As a decorative focal point, the pattern is hypnotic. The theory is simple; the result refined. Stitches go in every direction—up and down, side to side, and diagonally—because of the random wrapped thread exterior of the ball. It's been said that if you can fold a paper ribbon into halves, fourths, and eighths, you can learn temari.

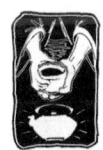

Tsuba

The hand guard fixed on a Japanese sword. It kept the hand from shifting up onto the cutting edge, offset the weight of the blade, made known the social status, philosophy, and tastes of its possessor, and safeguarded the hand from a rival's sword. Tsuba are still made from metals such as copper and its alloys (brass, bronze, and others) as well as silver, gold, iron, and other metals. Many have surface texturing, cutout openwork, or inlay/overlay of different metals. The style varies with time, locale, and the imaginativeness of the artisan. Tsuba are regarded as works of art and collected throughout the world.

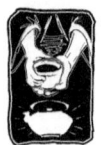

giri to nature, ancestors, parents, and sensei is sometimes understood as *gimu*, which refers to the sense that the duty and gratitude are ongoing. Recognizing on and giri sustains balance in nature and in relationships.

Giri is more than a codified means of preventing the shirking of unpleasant duties, though it occasionally degenerates to only that; it describes a sense of duty based on loyalty, which in turn is an outgrowth of compassion. In fact, compassion is the essence of loyalty. Both compassion and loyalty are a natural expression of the realization of humanity's interconnections and its unity with the universe. In this way, giri becomes something we embody and not just an idea we subscribe to.

Giri also offers, in the dojo and in life generally, a way to find the balance between individual self-determination and responding to group needs. This balance is essential, for we are not entirely self-sufficient and so must work with others, and yet we must realize our full potential alone if we are to truly benefit others. We are not one, not two.

Finally, giri is the mark of a sincere deshi. A good example of this kind of deshi is Yamaoka Tesshu, who lived during the mid-nineteenth century and was a master of meditation, calligraphy, and the sword. The tale is told that when Yamaoka was a young student he studied under a teacher in Edo noted for his great prowess. Not long after Yamaoka began his practice, however, his sensei met with a tragic death. Following the teacher's death came reports of a strange apparition lingering near his grave on stormy nights. One rainy, lightning-filled night, the teacher's brother was sent to determine the truth of these rumors. As he neared the grave, he noticed a figure on its knees in the mud and heard it saying, "I'm here, Sensei. Don't be afraid. I'll stay with you until the storm is over." That figure was Yamaoka.

Despite the master's prowess, he was afraid of lightning.

Yamaoka's giri transcended even the barrier of death, but, perhaps most important, he was able to accept his sensei's fears and weaknesses.

This is an important point. Western students tend toward extremes regarding their sensei—he or she is either godlike in infallibility or just one of the gang. Both are misperceptions. The bona fide sensei expresses the Way of the universe through a human form and a particular art, complete with all that being human entails.

In association with giri is the concept of *ninjo*. Ninjo means "human feelings," which take precedence over rules or profit. Teachers can change the rules affecting how a student is taught according to ninjo. My sensei often remind me that they teach "according to the student." What is appropriate for one student may not be for another.

Related to giri and ninjo is *tsukiai*, or "social debt." Students of the Ways traditionally showed tsukiai by providing their sensei with food, shelter, and whatever else was needed for the teacher's well-being. This is no longer common, having been replaced by a "tuition system" of sorts, but it is not unheard of or inappropriate.

Humility

The spirit of respect and service contained in concepts such as reigi and tsukiai underlies real learning in the Ways. True understanding comes from an immediate, unclouded perception of reality, and a learning mind is empty, empty of preconceived ideas about an art, its instruction, and acquisition. Such an unclouded, empty mind relates to humility.

Learning a Way takes time and sometimes requires a restructuring of lifestyle and habits. In order to make such changes and take the time needed to acquire skill, a student must have a cer-

Ukiyo-e

"Pictures of the floating world," a style of printmaking that started in the cosmopolitan culture of eighteenth-century Edo (Tokyo), when bureaucratic and military power was in the hands of the shogun and the nation was secluded from the world. Ukiyo-e related to the pleasures of theatres, restaurants, geisha, and courtesans in a bustling commercial atmosphere. Numerous ukiyo-e woodblock prints were in fact posters announcing theatre performances and brothels, or portraits of actors and teahouse girls. This more or less modern world of urban pleasures was also animated by the love of nature, and ukiyo-e artists like Hokusai had an influence on landscape painting worldwide.

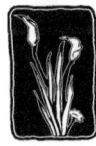

Ura

*Back or inside. Refers
to what is invisible,
not readily apparent,
and in the context
of human relations,
relates to a "hidden
face." With its coun-
terpart, omote (front,
outside, public), it
speaks of a dualism in
the arts of Japan and
the visible-invisible,
in-yo nature of the uni-
verse. See also omote.*

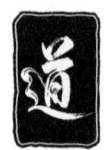

tain amount of perseverance. Many students, however, give up the Way too easily, believing that a lack of immediate growth indicates there is something wrong with the Way itself. A deshi with an attitude of humility realizes the fault is likely not with the training but with one's self. Through reigi, we can cultivate humility necessary for perseverance. Ultimately, however, understanding the Way is to enter into a state that transcends time, a state with no past and no future: *naka-ima*, the eternal now.

Remaining humble and persevering bring positive results. Bowing and other expressions of reigi relate not only to humbleness but also to respecting our seniors' differences and styles of teaching; different instructors teach differently, but each may still follow the Way. The unclouded, empty mind of humility recognizes this fact.

Just as one learns to be a good student, one learns to be a good instructor. These two roles are opposite sides of the same coin. The respect that kohai feel toward their sempai and sensei should be reflected in the way that sempai and sensei are aware of and respond to the needs of the kohai. In the Ways, we help those below us, while we respect those above us. Those who are kohai, if they continue, will become sempai and perhaps sensei. Sincere deshi, practicing with a qualified sensei, are rarely frozen in a single role but are simultaneously kohai, sempai, and sensei depending on the situation. They don't exist within a rigid and one-dimensional class structure. Like life, the Japanese arts and Ways are multidimensional.

Bowing and Seiza

Bowing is an expression of reigi in the classical Ways. It must not be done in a meek and inhibited manner. It is *not* a subservi-

186

ent act. A correct bow reflects the respect for all creation that lies at the heart of the Do, and it stems from a deep confidence in our essential unity. (This is valid despite the fact that it isn't always performed this way in Japan.) It should be done with great dignity, for only the truly confident can bow correctly. Western students of traditional Japanese arts who are afraid that bowing will make them weak and subservient are already weak. Their resistance is a reflection of what they bring to the study of the Way in the form of past biases, conditioning, and fear. And this sort of fear in the form of resistance is also evident outside the Do. How often is our reaction to certain situations based on fear, though hidden behind the guise of something else? This is a vital question for exponents of the Do, indeed for anyone. A mind caught in fear, and therefore in the past from which fear originates can delude itself in vast and intricate ways.

But the power of the Way takes us beyond illusions. Deshi manifest this power through caring and politeness. "Politeness"— only an approximate rendering of rei—is not simply taking pains to exhibit "good manners." Unfeigned reigi is instead the sincere and outward expression of compassion and respect. Forms of politeness and etiquette practiced in the Do echo a true harmony with the natural order. The attitude characterizing these forms is the same that has made the seemingly simple task of preparing tea into an art and spiritual discipline.

Since bowing is a common expression of reigi in the Ways, its correct execution must be considered. When properly performed, a bow can be a means of practicing the coordination of mind and body that is universally valued in the Do. Bowing is done from one of two positions: standing, *tachi-rei*, or seated, *za-rei*. Za-rei is more formal, and each Do may have slightly different customs relating to these two ways of bowing. The depth of the bow and the duration it is held will also vary depending on the

Wabi

An aesthetic ideal that strongly resists easy definition. In wabi art we find beauty with a feeling of austerity. Wabi is the recognition that beauty can be found informally, even in the depths of poverty. Objects of great refinement can often be constructed out of simple, inexpensive materials. A classical Japanese wooden house is an example of the unpolished appeal of wabi.

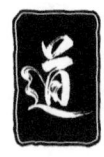

Waka

Classical Japanese
poetic form comprising
five lines of five, seven,
five, seven, and seven
syllables, respectively.
Waka themes center
on the poet's feelings
toward natural beauty
and human emotion.

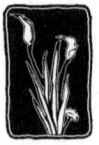

situation. A deeper, longer-held bow is more formal.* In essence, however, the bow doesn't vary much, and what follows is a general explication of tachi-rei and za-rei. The specifics can be discovered through discussions with sempai and careful observation. The following explanation is based on the arts I'm familiar with.

Tachi-rei starts with an erect stance in which the forehead and lower abdomen are aligned, a confident posture that "looks big." The heels are near each other, with the toes pointing outward at a forty-five-degree angle, which is more stable than placing the feet together. The mind and gaze are directed straight ahead.

Keeping the alignment between the forehead and abdomen, imagine that the hara is a hinge and bow forward. As you do, slide your fingertips along your thighs in coordination with the movement of your body. The bow stops when your fingertips reach the top of your kneecaps. (This is a good "all-purpose bow," but, depending on the situation, the bow may be deeper or more shallow.) Move from your hara, which means uniting the motion of your sliding hands with your body. Graceful, unified action that centers on the hara is the standard means of movement in everything from chado to budo. Our hara coordinates the upper and lower body in a way that allows us to gracefully manifest our full power in a number of activities, and bowing correctly is one means of training movement from the hara.

Some novices bend near their solar plexus and chest when they bow, thus rounding the back and destroying their aligned posture. Others bow while looking at the person receiving the bow, which bends the head backward and out of alignment. Not only does bowing in this way move the body in opposition to the eyes and mind but it is also viewed as being impolite and showing distrust.

---

* You can learn about the social and cultural aspects of bowing and reigi through a Way that focuses on the practice of traditional reigi: the Ogasawara Ryu. Check their Web site at http://www.ogasawara-ryu.com/.

Letting the head droop and thus exposing the back of the neck also shows a lack of coordination. It is effective to bow as if your head and hara were connected (Figure 22). Pause at the bottom of the bow, then rise, bringing the gaze up with the body. If the body rises while the gaze remains on the floor, it suggests that the body is ahead of the mind, since the mind follows the eyes and vice versa. And rising before the other person rises from her or his bow is impolite. When in doubt, move at the same time as the other person, which, since you're looking down, requires sensitivity to your environment and the ki of the other.

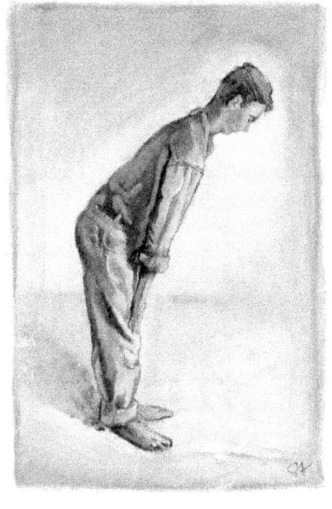

FIG. 22. Tachi-rei, a standing bow.

In sum, a correct bow involves the alignment of the forehead and hara as well as of the mind and body. Acting in harmony with the actions of others is also important. Bowing incorrectly, however, cultivates a habit of moving inefficiently while losing unity of mind and body. Thus, proper bowing cultivates the ability to move in a coordinated manner from the hara and harmony of mind and body, both of which are useful in the Ways and in life.

Za-rei is done while in seiza. Sit lightly on your heels with an erect posture. Men leave a space of about two or three fists between their knees; women need leave a gap roughly equal to one fist wide. Rest the hands gently at mid-thigh with the fingers pointed slightly inward and with space between the arms and body. Moving the gaze, mind, and body as one, bend from the hara as you slide your hands along your thighs and to the floor

189

FIG. 23. Za-rei, a seated bow.

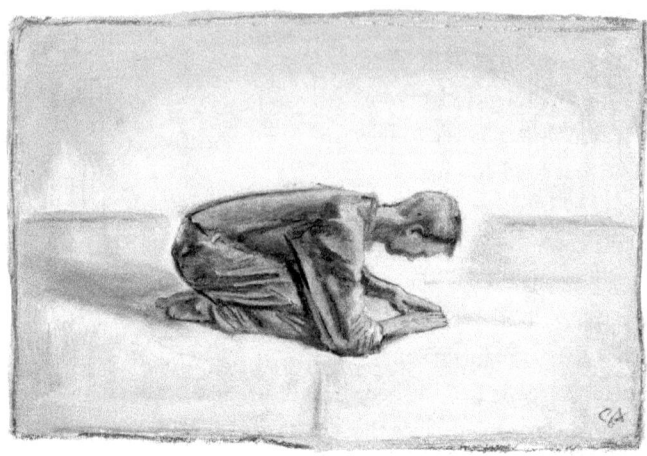

in front of you. Your hands touch the floor silently and lightly, with the fingers together and the thumb and index finger of each hand forming a triangle. Aside from being elegant, this focuses ki toward the person or place you're bowing to. The forehead is generally aligned with the hara, and it should be over your triangle, about two fists from the floor. The hips stay down and the back is fairly straight (Figure 23). This might seem simple, but bending from the hara while keeping the head, neck, back, and pelvis aligned without letting the buttocks rise much from the heels requires flexibility. Za-rei and tachi-rei cultivate and sustain excellent posture and flexibility, especially in the lower back and the pelvis.

Pause after lowering the head, then rise from your hara, sliding the hands in reverse along the floor and thighs while bringing the gaze and mind up with the body. Don't rest your palms heavily on the floor, and avoid pushing off the floor as you rise: move from the hara. Resting too much weight on the hands causes tension in the shoulders and produces a "top-heavy" condition that is unstable and that subtly alters your alignment.

Flexibility, excellent posture, sensitivity to others, unification of mind and body—these benefits of the art of bowing as an expression of reigi are available to people of any culture.

Understanding the meaning and functions of reigi is important for Western students of the arts and Ways. The reticence of Japanese teachers to explain about reigi and the consequent ignorance of their Western students can lead Western deshi to think of reigi as simply social customs and, in some cases, to resent this aspect of their practice. It is important that teachers offer explanations that at least give students an idea of the why or how of reigi and other elements of the Way. In that regard, I hope that this book will prove useful not just to novices but to their teachers, who have the task of translating the Way.

Inside a Dojo

To provide an idea of how a traditional dojo functions, I offer below a scenario based on my experiences with various sensei. While some of my teachers are conservative in approach, others are more westernized. How I relate to a sensei depends on the art, its traditions, and his or her interpretation of reigi. Although the specifics vary from sensei to sensei, the essence of the Way does not.

The sensei here is modeled after me and several of my teachers, and the "I" in the story is based on me, my students, and other deshi I've known. Because my dojo is traditional in atmosphere, the nature of training is exacting and conservative. Being exposed to this, however, is to your advantage: you'll rarely have problems in Japanese culture and arts from being "too polite," but you most likely will if you are impolite. The worst that can happen if you're too polite is that your sensei will tell you to lighten up, and this

Washi

Perhaps the thinnest, toughest, and most lasting of all handmade papers. It is also praised for its beautiful, delicate appearance and appreciated as high-level folk art. The secret of washi's durability lies in the natural material and the papermaking procedure. An unusual trait of washi papermaking is the application of bast fibers from three shrubs used as raw material. It's fabricated through a laborious and complicated process. Western-style paper is used throughout Japan, but traditional washi remains essential for specific artistic purposes and inseparable from Japanese culture. Its soft, durable attributes are unique, and its beauty has brought wide acknowledgment.

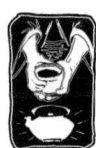

Yugen

Something cloudy or mysterious. Yet this "cloudiness" isn't out and out darkness but a state beyond the limits of thought . . . yet not beyond the capacity of human experience. We can feel yugen in great art as a kind of ineffable sensibility that resonates out from the work to captivate our moods and emotions. Each viewer and participant who has experienced yugen will identify it, but each person's experience of it is unique.

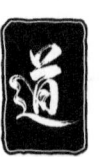

can be taken as a compliment. A rule of thumb in case of doubt or confusion is to watch your sempai's behavior, or, if you're still unsure, ask the sempai what to do. Avoid asking your sensei questions about reigi; this creates an awkward situation since such questions are often about how you should behave toward him or her. (But if you do get stuck, asking your sensei is unavoidable.)

It's Monday and I know I won't make it to practice on Tuesday. I leave a message on Sensei's answering machine to let him know not to expect me. This helps him anticipate who he'll be teaching Tuesday and, therefore, what to teach as well. Since I can't come to practice, I make a point of training on my own Tuesday evening.

It's Thursday, another practice day. I leave for the dojo a little early, allowing time so I don't have to worry about being late. Since I arrive early, I see Sensei pulling up in his Toyota. I greet him, open the car door, and help him carry a package to the dojo.

I get to the dojo door ahead of him and execute a standing bow as I enter. I greet the other deshi. I put the package down and hold the door open for Sensei. The practice area is covered with Japanese-style tatami mats, and so I remove my shoes before stepping on them. After placing my shoes in the designated spot, I step onto the mats and perform another standing bow toward the kamiza, a place of honor that houses the dojo shrine. I carry Sensei's package into the office, bowing again before I leave the practice area. Leaving Sensei, I visit the toilet to avoid having to go during class. Following this, I bow as I step into the practice area, and I join the other deshi, who are sitting in a line waiting for Sensei to start practice.

We sit in seiza. Everyone is silent. The deshi who arrived before me have cleaned the dojo. (The more things Sensei has to do, the less time he has to focus on what he's going to teach and the less time he has to teach it. Soji, cleaning the dojo, helps us as much as it does Sensei.) None of us speaks or moves as we calm and clear our minds to fully concentrate on the coming instruction.

Sensei walks to a spot in front of the kamiza. He sits in seiza, and we bow toward the kamiza en masse, paying respect to the spirit of the art we practice and to the generations of teachers who have paved the Way for us. Sensei turns. Still sitting in seiza, he and the deshi bow together.

He explains what will be practiced that evening. During his explanation, my legs grow tired, and I bow and sit cross-legged, sustaining an erect, alert posture. Every moment in the Ways is meditation.

The lecture is over, the instruction has been presented, and I sit in seiza again. We bow from seiza in acknowledgment of the instruction we have received. Standing up, we practice. Sensei notices me making a mistake and offers a correction. At his conclusion, I bow and say, "Thank you, Sensei." Nothing forced him to help me, and I'm grateful for the attention.

Not long thereafter, he claps his hands, signaling that he would like to move on. We form lines once again, sit in seiza, listen, and watch. Despite having visited the bathroom earlier, I need to go again. I raise my hand, indicate my need, and, with a quick bow, head off to the bathroom.

When I return, I see everyone is working in pairs. My sempai fills me in on what's going on. I find a person to practice with, and standing about six feet apart, we make a standing bow to each other. Our practice begins. After five minutes, we hear Sensei's clap, step apart, bow, and say to each other, "Thank you." This pattern continues throughout practice.

Later, while Sensei is presenting group instruction again, he asks me to assist him. I bow, rise from seiza, and move quickly

Zanshin

Zan means "lingering," "remaining," and connotes continuation, while shin is simply "mind." Refers to the moment following an action, seen, for example, in a sumi-e painter's continuing movement of the brush even after it has left the paper, or in a martial artist's freezing of movement after the execution of a final stroke of the sword or jujutsu throw; the "lingering" allows the movement of ki to continue. As students of the Ways practice, they discover that stillness is as important as activity, and not doing as essential as doing, and that the moment following an action determines the success of the action and the success of any that follow.

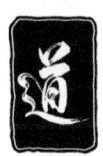

Za-rei

*A "seated bow."
Bowing is a common
expression of respect
in the Ways and can
be a means of practic-
ing the coordination
of mind and body.
The manner in which
bowing is performed
will vary in depth and
duration—depending
on the social situation.
Deeper angles, held
longer, are considered
more formal and sig-
nificant. Tachi-rei, the
"standing bow" is less
formal.*

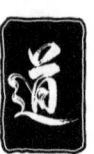

to help him with the point he's illustrating. During this demonstration, he begins to talk. I retreat a few feet and sit in seiza. I
rise again to help him with another point, and we're done. Before
returning to my place, I bow from where I'm standing and say,
"Thank you, Sensei." I'm ready for more practice . . . but first I
look around to see if any of my kohai appear lost and in need of a
more experienced person to work with.

At the end of practice, Sensei and the deshi sit again, facing
the kamiza. A seated bow is performed, Sensei turns, and we all
bow, saying, "Thank you, Sensei." Instruction is over. Sensei says
"Thank you" as well. It was hot, so I bring him water and ask
a question or two while I have his attention. I know better than
to assume someone else will take care of such things. Maybe they
will, maybe they won't. The dojo teaches us to take matters into
our own hands.

Later, Sensei prepares to leave, while the deshi make sure the
dojo lights are off, doors closed, etc. I help him with his jacket
and place his shoes where he can easily step into them. Opening
the door for him, the other deshi and I wish him good night. I
bow again toward the kamiza, and as I'm about to leave, I say
"Goodnight" to the remaining deshi. We always acknowledge
each other and extend our good-byes, because we realize that our
dojo must function harmoniously—and the deshi are the dojo.

From this example of practice in a dojo, you can see there is
much to remember and a great deal of bowing. But the bowing and
other forms of respect have a purpose beyond politeness and gratitude. Students have a lot to remember, and they can't, therefore,
absentmindedly blunder through practice. Ongoing awareness
is needed, and reigi helps students stay focused on what they're
doing and serves as a constant reminder of why they started practice to begin with. Reigi acts as an outward barometer of whether

or not we're awake during practice. It also helps us understand Japanese culture on more than a theoretical level, which allows us to comfortably interact with Japanese people or function in Japan. In short, reigi is cross-cultural education of a concrete nature.

The integral place of respect, gratitude, and compassion in the Do provides us a unique opportunity to truly consider their meaning and value. This opportunity is one of the functions of reigi. Reigi also allows us to demonstrate tangibly, with our whole mind and body, the essence of the heart. This wholeheartedness as an expression of reigi is called *kokoro ire* (*kokoro*, "mind/spirit/ heart"; *ire*, "to put in"). Kokoro ire in the Ways takes chado and kado, for example, beyond merely sipping tea and putting flowers on display. What reigi and its expressions cultivate, then, is constant awareness, cross-cultural understanding, respect, gratitude, and compassion, and these are qualities of value to anyone, regardless of cultural background.

An International Aesthetic of the Way

The arts and Ways of Japan are being studied and taught in many places outside Japan, and as a result they are continually evolving. Successfully transmitting a practice to a new culture, however, requires an intimate understanding of its native cultural context and also an understanding of the non-Japanese students of the art. Westerners, for example, thus have a responsibility to know deeply an art and its Japanese cultural home before attempting to alter or adapt that art in a new, Western setting. Japanese sensei, if they desire the integrity of their arts to be preserved in their transmission to Americans or Europeans, must make an attempt to understand Western students. From this mutual understanding a new international aesthetic can grow and develop.

Through the traditional Japanese arts and Ways, all of us have a chance to realize not only a unification of mind and body but also a unity of East and West, as well as a union of humanity with the Way of the universe. In this ultimate unification, the Do and the deshi become one, shining so brightly that all living things are illuminated.

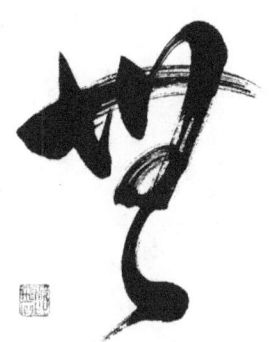

MU

FINDING A SENSEI

Having come this far, you are probably interested in proceeding further and are ready to search for a skilled instructor. This appendix offers assistance in finding a sensei and additional information about the Japanese arts and Ways.

The Sennin Foundation Center for Japanese Cultural Arts

Founded by me in 1981, the Sennin Foundation Center for Japanese Cultural Arts offers traditional instruction in a number of the Japanese Ways. Of primary importance to its students is the study of Shin-shin-toitsu-do, a form of Japanese yoga. If you are interested in practicing the mind-body exercises found in chapter 3 (as well as other aspects of Japanese yoga), please get in touch with us. Below you'll find contact information as well as an introduction to what we have to offer.

The Sennin Foundation Center
for Japanese Cultural Arts
1053 San Pablo Avenue
Albany, CA 94706

hedavey@aol.com
www.senninfoundation.com

JAPANESE YOGA

The main area of study at the Sennin Foundation Center is Shin-shin-toitsu-do. This art, inspired by the teachings of Nakamura Tempu Sensei, its founder, includes stretching exercises, seated meditation, moving meditation, breathing exercises, healing arts, and health improvement methods. The goal is the realization of one's full potential in everyday life through unification of mind and body.

In 1919, Nakamura Sensei, upon returning from studying yoga in India, began to share with others universal principles and exercises that could be adopted by all people regardless of age, sex, or cultural background. Nakamura Sensei placed importance on methods with observable and repeatable results and on principles and exercises that could withstand objective scrutiny.

He identified certain qualities that people need in order to meaningfully express themselves in life:

Tai-ryoku: "the power of the body," physical strength, health, and endurance

Tan-ryoku: "the power of courage"

Handan-ryoku: "the power of decision," good judgment

Danko-ryoku: "the power of determination," willpower for resolute and decisive action

Sei-ryoku: "the power of vitality," energy or life power for endurance and perseverance

No-ryoku: "the power of ability," the capacity for wide-ranging ability and dexterous action

Most important, Nakamura Sensei realized that the mind and body are our most fundamental tools, and in order to effectively express ourselves in life, we must use these tools naturally and in coordination with each other. It is this ability to effectively use and unite our minds and bodies that allows for freedom of action and skilled self-expression. Nakamura Sensei conceived a set of basic principles by which people could discover how to unite mind and body.

Using his background in Western medicine (he obtained a medical degree in the United States), Nakamura Tempu Sensei conducted biological research dealing with the nervous system and the unification of mind and body. The result was his Four Basic Principles to Unify Mind and Body. These are:

1. Use the mind positively.
2. Use the mind with full concentration.
3. Use the body obeying the laws of nature.
4. Train the body progressively, systematically, and regularly.

HEALING ARTS

Nakamura Sensei also taught self-healing and bodywork (*hitori ryoho* or self-massage). He emphasized *yuki*, which is the transference of life energy through a massagelike technique.

In life, it's important to throw 100 percent of ourselves into the moment at hand, and this positive mental state is called *ki no dashikata*, or "the projection of life energy." When our life energy freely exchanges with the life energy that pervades nature, we're in our happiest and healthiest state. We've all met exceptionally positive and animated individuals, people who project a "large presence." The intangible but unmistakable "big presence" such people project can be thought of as universal life energy, which is, as you now know, called ki in Japanese.

A relaxed body and positive mental state set this energy free, whereas physical tension and/or the negative use of the mind cause a withdrawal and loss of ki. Yuki functions in a way not dissimilar to a blood transfusion and "transfuses" this universal life energy. By studying methods of mind-body coordination and Shin-shin-toitsu-do meditation, it is possible to learn to transfer ki from the thumbs, fingertips, and palms to weakened parts of the body as a way of boosting the natural healing process. Students at the Sennin Foundation Center can receive instruction in this unique art of healing.

MARTIAL ARTS

The Sennin Foundation Center also has an aiki-jujutsu division. Jujutsu is Japan's oldest martial art. The warriors of ancient Japan used it for predominantly empty-handed combat. Aiki-jujutsu is a system that can be traced to the Aizu clan's Nisshinkan training hall in present-day Fukushima. It was taught in modern times by Saigo Tanomo Sensei (1829–1905), an Aizu clan elder adviser. Saigo Sensei taught aiki-jujutsu, formerly known as Aizu oshikiuchi, to Takeda Sokaku Sensei (1860–1943), disseminator of the famed Daito Ryu aiki-jujutsu system, who in turn taught Ueshiba Morihei Sensei (1883–1969), the founder of aikido.

My late father started studying jujutsu and Kodokan judo in 1926. After twenty years of training, he was stationed in Japan following World War II. While there he studied Saigo Ryu systems of aiki-jujutsu, jojutsu ("art of the four-foot stick"), bojutsu ("art of the six-foot staff"), hanbojutsu ("art of the three-foot stick"), tanbojutsu ("art of the fourteen-inch stick"), tessenjutsu ("art of the iron fan"), juttejutsu ("art of the forked metal truncheon"), sojutsu ("art of the spear"), and kenjutsu ("art of the sword"). He later became the first American to receive the advanced rank/title of Nihon Jujutsu Kyoshi from Japan's prestigious Kokusai Budoin, a worldwide martial arts federation established in Tokyo over fifty years ago. He was also a black belt in judo and aikido.

I began aiki-jujutsu at the age of five and studied judo and aikido. I've trained in Japan and the United States and have received the positions of U.S. Branch Director for the Kokusai Budoin and Councilor to the Kokusai Budoin World Headquarters.

I emphasize aiki-jujutsu as a noncompetitive art with roots in Japan's traditional past. Like aikido, aiki-jujutsu is based on aiki, or "union with ki." Aiki-jujutsu, however, contains a wider variety of unarmed and armed techniques than is found in most forms of aikido. These skills encompass throwing and pinning methods using all parts of the body, including the feet, plus close-distance and ground grappling, and a broad range of weapons.

Since aiki-jujutsu involves harmonizing with ki, it can transform the lives of its participants. This transformation does not take place only in the realm of dynamic self-protection. Owing to the unique characteristics of aiki-jujutsu, it is possible to experience enhanced calmness, relaxation, concentration, willpower, and physical fitness in daily living. Details of this martial art can be found in my book, *Unlocking the Secrets of Aiki-jujutsu.*

FINE ARTS

The Sennin Foundation Center also has a fine arts division that emphasizes the unification of mind and body by practicing traditional Japanese fine arts.

The Center's brush writing class stresses calligraphy, but it also includes ink painting and the study of haiku and waka poetry. Expanded attention, deeper relaxation, increased focus and resolve—students have a chance to achieve spiritual transformation through the classical art of calligraphy. Simple step-by-step exercises let beginners and non-artists alike work with brush and ink to reveal their mental and physical states through moving brush meditation.

Kanji, or Chinese characters, have transcended their utilitarian function and serve as a visually stirring fine art. Shodo allows the dynamic movement of the artist's spirit to become observable in the form of rich black ink. Many practitioners believe that the "visible rhythm" of Japanese calligraphy embodies a "picture of the mind," and calligraphers recognize that it discloses our spiritual state. This is summed up by the saying, *Kokoro tadashikereba sunawachi fude tadashii,* "If your mind is correct, the brush will be correct."

Since shodo is an art, it is not strictly necessary to be able to read Chinese characters or the phonetic scripts of *hiragana* and *katakana* to admire their dynamic beauty. Within Japanese calligraphy, we find essential elements that constitute all art: creativity, balance, rhythm, grace, and the beauty of line.

Finding a Sensei

Finding a suitable sensei is obviously paramount in achieving a successful, satisfying practice of a Way, and following are some ways that might be useful in locating a teacher:

- If a Japanese community center is nearby, check their classes.

- Sometimes colleges have classes in Japanese arts. Check their catalogs and especially night- and adult-school offerings.

- Many Buddhist churches and centers also present classes in Asian cultural arts. Look in the telephone directory for a Buddhist church.

- Try contacting the nearest Japanese consulate and asking for aid. Occasionally this can garner results.

- Talk to instructors of different Japanese arts; these sensei might be able to help you, even if they or their particular art is not what you're interested in.

- In general, get involved in the local Japanese community, as this will strengthen your awareness of all of the Japanese arts and can also open many doors.

Finding a capable teacher is rarely quick and easy. Some people have looked for several years before discovering the right sensei. Once a sensei has been found, be prepared to spend a considerable amount of time and labor in studying a specific Way. This might seem intimidating, but it is critical to realize that the effort and commitment to any Japanese art bring rewards in equal measure.

Using the World Wide Web

The Web offers a vast amount of data about an equally immense number of Japanese art forms. Unfortunately, it can also be the source of a large amount of misinformation. With that caveat in mind, undertaking a Web search can be useful. Try visiting the Web site *Michi Online: Journal of Japanese Cultural Arts*, which presents reliable resources relating to a large variety of Japanese arts and Ways. The site can be reached on the Internet at:

www.michionline.org.

A Final Word

A novice might ask if there isn't an easier way to start practicing a Japanese art or Way. Serious practitioners and teachers of any of the Ways are keenly aware of the tremendous benefits that come from the uncommon effort involved in their study. As a result, they're not always sympathetic to the novice's desire for a hasty, easy approach. A ten-easy-lesson approach to an art will bring only a very shallow understanding: meaningfulness demands serious effort.

Nonetheless, I can offer this bit of advice: be sincere, persevere, and keep your eyes, ears, and mind open. Once you find a sensei, be open-minded, maintain a good attitude, and attend class regularly. Both attitude and attendance are vital: attitude equals mind, and attendance equals body. Mind and body are of equal importance in the Ways. Attending every practice session but with a closed, resistant mind precludes learning; likewise, a sincere attitude but only sporadic attendance results in poor ability.

When I first started to study Japanese calligraphy, I had been practicing Japanese yoga and martial arts for most of my life, so I had some idea of what I needed to do to participate in a new Way. I didn't skip a single class for the initial five years. The first class I missed was when my art was being shown in Japan at the International Japanese Calligraphy Exhibition. I was in Urayasu to receive an award for my brush writing and was unable to attend practice. The second time was a few years later when my father passed away.

No matter how sincere the mind may be, if the body is unable to practice consistently under a competent sensei, progress will be slow. With the right attitude and regular attendance, a student is well on his or her Way.

NOTES & REFERENCES

1. Lao Tsu, *Tao Te Ching*, trans. Gia-Fu Feng and Jane English (New York: Vintage Books, 1972), p. 25.

2. Stephen Addis, ed., and Jane Carpenter, contrib., *Japanese Ghosts and Demons* (New York: George Braziller, 1985), p. 57.

3. Dave Lowry, "The Ways of Japan," *Michi Online: Journal of Japanese Cultural Arts* (Richmond, Calif.), Summer 1999, p. 6.

4. Michio Kushi, *The Book of Do-In: Exercise for Physical and Spiritual Development* (Tokyo: Japan Publications, 1979), p. 39.

5. E. J. Harrison, *The Fighting Spirit of Japan* (Woodstock, N.Y.: The Overlook Press, 1982), p. 155.

6. Daisetz T. Suzuki, *Zen and Japanese Culture* (Princeton, N.J.: Princeton University Press, 1970), p. 284.

7. Donald Richie, *The Donald Richie Reader: 50 Years of Writing on Japan*, ed. Arturo Silva (Berkeley, Calif.: Stone Bridge Press, 2001), p. 31.

8. Richie, *The Donald Richie Reader*, p. 31.

9. Soshitsu Sen XV, *Tea Life, Tea Mind* (New York and Tokyo: Weatherhill, 1979), p. 67.

10. Man-jan Cheng, *Lao-Tzu: "My Words Are Very Easy to Understand,"* trans. Tam C. Gibbs (Berkeley, Calif.: North Atlantic Books, 1981), p. 24.

11. Yanagi Soetsu, *The Unknown Craftsman* (Tokyo and New York: Kodansha International, 1989), p. 127.

12. Lowry, "The Ways of Japan," p. 6.

13. Kenneth Yasuda, *The Japanese Haiku* (Rutland, Vt., and Tokyo: Tuttle, 1957), pp. 30–31.

14. Yoel Hoffman, *Japanese Death Poems: Written by Zen Monks and Haiku Poets on the Verge of Death* (Rutland, Vt., and Tokyo: Tuttle, 1996), p. 68.

The following works helped in the writing of this book and may be of interest to readers.

Chamberlain, Basil Hall. *Japanese Things: Being Notes on Various Subjects Connected with Japan*. Boston: Tuttle, 1989.

de Garis, Frederic, and Atsuharu Sakai. *We Japanese*. London: Kegan Paul, 2001.

Draeger, Donn F. *Classical Budo*. Tokyo and New York: Weatherhill, 1996.

Furyu: The Online Budo Journal of Classical Japanese Martial Arts and Culture. http://www.furyu.com.

Leggett, Trevor. *A First Zen Reader*. Boston: 1980.

———. *Zen and the Ways*. Boston: Tuttle, 1987.

Lowry, Dave. *Autumn Lightning: Education of an American Samurai*. Boston: Shambhala, 2001.

———. *Moving Toward Stillness: Lessons in Daily Life from the Martial Ways of Japan*. Boston: Tuttle, 2000.

———. *Persimmon Wind: A Martial Artist's Journey in Japan*. Boston: Tuttle, 1998.

———. *Sword and Brush: The Spirit of the Martial Arts*. Boston: Shambhala, 1995.

Random, Michel. *Japan: Strategy of the Unseen*. Translated by Cyrian P. Blamires. Wellingborough, Northamptonshire, England: Crucible/Thorson's Publishing; New York: Sterling, 1987.

Slawson, David A. *Secret Teachings in the Art of Japanese Gardens*. Tokyo and New York: Kodansha International, 1991.

Brush Meditation

A Japanese Way to Mind & Body Harmony

H. E. Davey

Michi: Japanese Arts and Ways

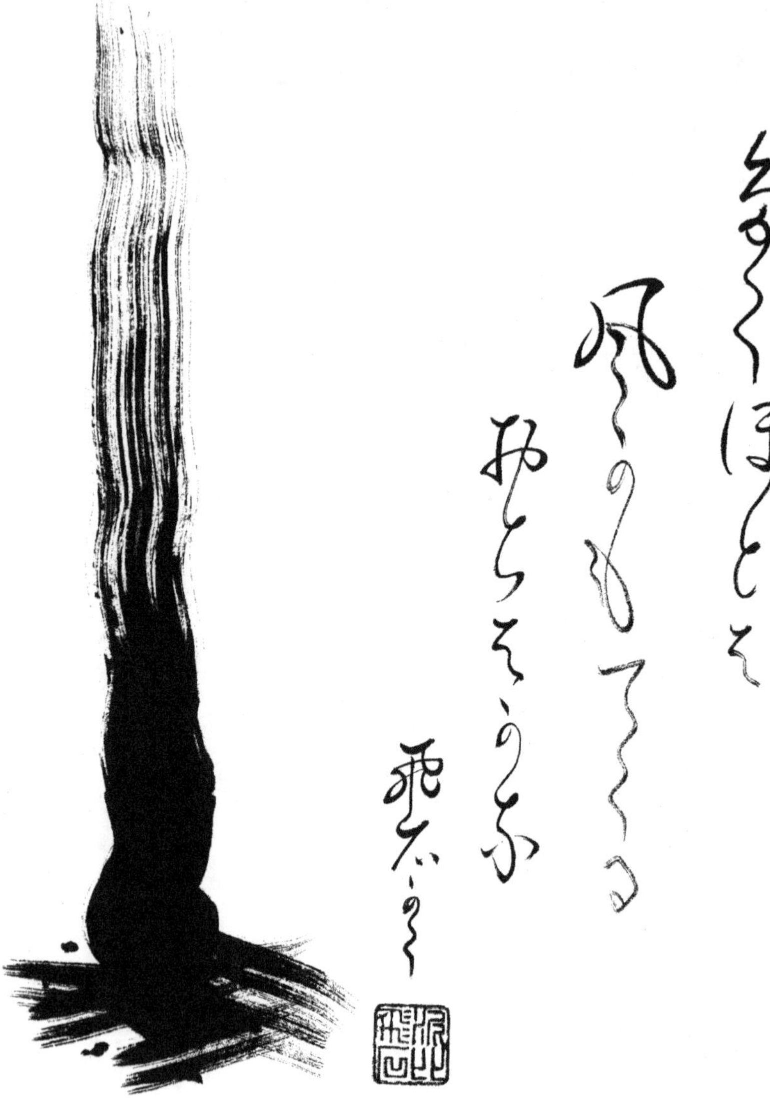

CONTENTS

PREFACE

We are witnessing the meeting of East and West. Through positive, nonbiased Eastern and Western cultural exchange, a new, more balanced, more enlightened global culture may result. While I explore calligraphic painting *(shodo)* as well as other Japanese cultural arts in *Brush Meditation*, and examine the meditative aspects of shodo and various Japanese arts, one of the main reasons I wrote this book is to let other Westerners know that it is possible, and meaningful, for non-Japanese to participate in traditional Japanese art forms.

At their deepest levels, the martial arts *(budo)*, tea ceremony *(cha-do)*, flower arrangement *(kado)*, calligraphy, and other Japanese arts are the same. Despite their obvious physical differences, these arts share a common set of aesthetics and, more importantly, they require the acquisition of identical positive character traits if you are to become successful in their performance.

Note that many of these arts end in the word *do*. "Do" means "the way," and it indicates that a given activity has transcended its utilitarian function, that this action has been elevated to the level of art, and that its proponents are teaching it as a way of life. A "do" form is an art that allows you to grasp the ultimate nature of the whole of life by examining yourself in great detail through a singular aspect of life: to grasp the universal through the particular.

Many artistic principles and important mental states are universal for the various Japanese "ways." One of the most significant and basic principles that these arts share is the concept of mind and body coordination. Few of us are required to use a brush in daily life, but most of us are interested in realizing our full potential and enhancing our mental state as well as our physical health. Because integrating the mind and body allows us to achieve these goals, the relationship between the mind and body, along with how to achieve a state of mind-body harmony, is one of the main themes of this book.

Some painters make statements to the effect that "if the mind is correct, the brush is correct." In Japanese swordsmanship, it is not uncommon to speak of a unity of mind, body, and sword. Likewise, in Zen meditation, students are encouraged to arrive at a state of mind and body coordination, a state of self-harmony. All of these assertions point to the necessity of integrating the mind and body in action. Mental and physical harmony is also vital for realizing our full potential in daily living, and it remains one of the central elements needed for mastery of any of the classical Japanese ways.

Yet, perhaps surprisingly, although I serve as Director of the Sennin Foundation Center for Japanese Cultural Arts, I'm not teaching and pursuing the above-mentioned art forms because of an overwhelming interest in Japanese culture. While I certainly am, of course, interested in Japan, my main intention in studying these arts is to examine the nature of the self, the universe, and life as a whole. This point is vital, as the miscellaneous "do" all indicate a "way" that transcends boundaries and limitations. It is in the end not a "Japanese way," but rather a human way and, ultimately, the way of the universe.

In *Brush Meditation*, shodo, or Japanese brush writing, will be used as a representative example of how the various "do" forms help us discover principles that relate universally to all aspects of living and that can enhance our lives. The book begins with a brief history of calligraphy and painting in Asia and explains why these arts hold relevance for the West. Following this is an explanation of mind-body unification in shodo and painting, as well as the basic techniques of controlling the brush. The aesthetics and principles that are universal for the Japanese cultural arts are also explored, along with their importance for cultivating calmness and concentration. Of course, a few introductory lessons in brush meditation, calligraphy, and painting are included so that you can work with the brush and begin to experience for yourself the mind-body connection. Sources for shodo and painting supplies are at the back of the book.

Shodo mastery takes years of practice, and formal instruction with a teacher, so your goal in using this book should primarily be one of exploration and discovery. Instead of worrying about the formally "correct" ways of drawing lines with a brush, for now you should concentrate on experiencing how movement, everyday life, and the spirit are inextricably linked.

I am not a master of any of the Japanese artistic disciplines. Still, in both the United States and Japan, I have had unique opportunities to study some of the Japanese arts that remain inaccessible to many people in the West. It is my wish to share with interested others a bit of what I have been able to absorb about these art forms. *Brush Meditation: A Japanese Way to Mind & Body Harmony* amounts to an act of personal study, self-examination, and analysis that I hope will also be relevant to other people interested in art, meditation, and Japanese culture.

ABOUT THE CALLIGRAPHY IN THIS BOOK

Compared to some methods of Japanese calligraphy, my teacher Kobara Ranseki's system of shodo follows the original Chinese version closely and is fairly conservative in approach. The inspiration for Kobara Sensei's methodology can be traced to his late teacher Fukuzawa Seiran Sensei as well as to the famed Chinese calligraphers Ogishi and Chiei. Mr. Kobara's artistic style features a precise execution of form. This is combined with characters that are dynamic, yet exceedingly smooth and elegant. Unlike the sharp corners and hard edges encountered in some forms of shodo, Kobara Ranseki Sensei's flowing system utilizes a natural and more rounded execution (similar to that found in Chiei's ancient calligraphy classic *Sen-Ji-Mon*). This relaxed, fluid, and graceful approach can even be detected in his *kaisho* (printed style) characters.

The calligraphy in this book reflects Kobara Sensei's influence. The large pieces scattered throughout have been provided to illustrate different styles of shodo and to serve as places to pause and reflect. I hope they will also inspire you to pursue formal instruction in brush writing.

ACKNOWLEDGMENTS

Brush Meditation: A Japanese Way to Mind & Body Harmony is dedicated to my teacher, Kobara Ranseki Sensei. Since 1985 Kobara Sensei has taught me the art of shodo. But more than this, he has served as a continual source of encouragement, communicated as much by his positive, kind, and gentle presence as through his direct words and actions. Kobara Sensei has been instrumental in showing me a way

of teaching and uplifting others that transcends verbal communication
. . . a rare art indeed.

As a child, I began to study Shin-shin-toitsu-do, a system of Japanese yoga based on the principles of mind and body integration, and this has been an invaluable aid in my understanding of shodo as well as Japanese ink painting. I would like to acknowledge my debt to my teachers of Shin-shin-toitsu-do, particularly Hashimoto Tetsuichi Sensei, who is a certified teacher with the Tempu-kai of Tokyo. While many founders of the Japanese arts mastered coordination of mind and body, Nakamura Tempu Sensei, originator of Shin-shin-toitsu-do, is an outstanding example of this mastery. After a number of years studying a wide diversity of spiritual disciplines, he achieved *satori* (realization) while living in the Himalayas. He returned to Japan from India in 1919, where he founded Shin-shin-toitsu-do: "the Way of Mind and Body Unification." Coinciding with this, he began to spontaneously produce works of calligraphic art in a unique and unprecedented style. Paintings, sculptures, and ceramic ware sprang from the same source of inspiration. According to Nakamura Sensei, this source was the essential unity of mind and body; if the mind could conceive or perceive something, the body could accurately create it—as long as no gap existed between the mind and body. This philosophy echoed sentiments held by the forefathers of most Japanese cultural arts, and it describes in a nutshell one of the primary aspects of personal development found in the Japanese art forms.

The idea of art as a tangible expression of mind has had great appeal to me for some time. The traditional belief in Japan is that one's personality is revealed in calligraphy. Leaders in any of the Japanese cultural disciplines were expected to be able to execute fine script. (When some of my teachers of various arts would visit, they would often offer their brush writing as gifts.) This fact, combined with a lifelong exposure to Japanese culture, my experiences in studying the arts of Japan, including Japanese yoga, and a wish to further my understanding of "the way" led me to pursue shodo and, ultimately, to write this book. Shin-shin-toitsu-do has greatly influenced the manner in which I teach shodo, and many of the concepts in this book are based on my experiences studying Japanese yoga.

I'd also like to acknowledge my mother, Elaine Davey, now over eighty years old, and my late father, Victor H. Davey, both of whom encouraged my childhood interest in art and music. What little artistic ability I possess is, at least partially, inherited from my dad, who was a talented watercolor painter and cartoonist.

Ann Harue Kameoka, my wife, helped with the editing and photography. She deserves a great deal of credit for putting up with my artist's temperament as well as for supporting my involvement in shodo and other Japanese cultural arts. Without her support and understanding, many of my accomplishments in these arts would have been much more difficult to attain.

Ohsaki Jun, my student of several years, posed for many of the illustrations. He was also helpful in checking my translation of Japanese texts and terms.

Finally, this book would not exist in its present form if my student Linda Shimoda had not introduced me to Stone Bridge Press. My thanks go out to Linda as well as to Peter Goodman and everyone at Stone Bridge Press.

H. E. DAVEY

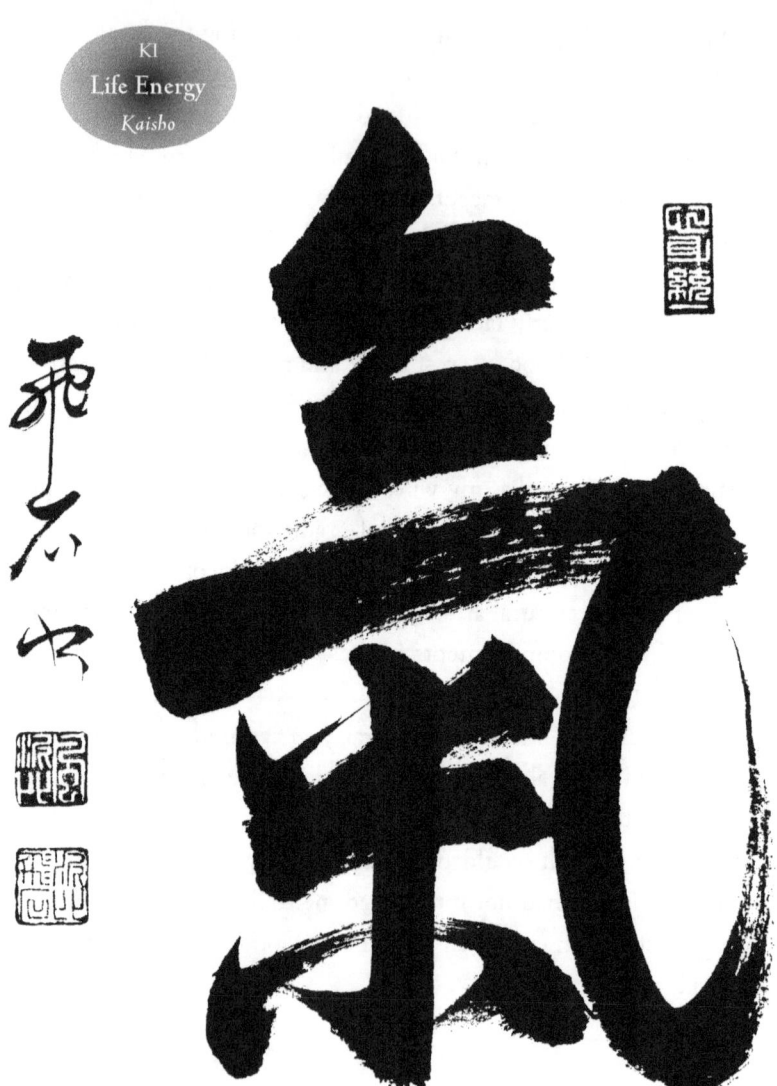

KI
Life Energy
Kaisho

Chapter 1

THE LANGUAGE
OF SHODO

Shodo, or the "way of calligraphy," has been one of the most highly respected arts in Japan for centuries. It is currently studied by an exceedingly large segment of Japanese society; everyone from executives to housewives seems to be involved in the practice of this ancient art. Surprisingly, shodo has received relatively little exposure in the West, but in recent years it is finally showing some signs of gaining recognition abroad.

The Origins of Shodo and Ink Painting

The Japanese written language is derived from ancient Chinese written symbols adopted by the Japanese around the fifth century. According to oral tradition, Chinese characters were born around 2700 B.C., the creation of an enigmatic man with four eyes called Tsangh-hsieh, who is said to have been captivated by the footprints of beasts and birds. The God of Heaven was believed to have been so moved by Tsangh-hsieh's ingenious bird-based characters that he made grain drop from the clouds as a symbol of his happiness with humankind.

Archaeologists have found uncomplicated drawings engraved on pieces of tortoiseshell and oracle bone dating from the Shang period in China (1766–1122 B.C.). These pictures on bone and shell were the archetypes of future Chinese characters. Ancient Chinese shamans would bore holes in the shells and/or bones, which were then placed in a sacred fire. The surfaces of these objects would crack and split, and the resulting fissures would be deciphered by the priests, who etched their impressions of the Voice of Heaven on the bone or shell in the form of simple sketches. (To this day, Chinese characters retain overtones of reverence and magic.) Eventually these pictographs were utilized for legal transactions, which were conducted via the exchange of etched strips of bamboo or wood. Later in China, these writings came into religious and official usage as bell inscriptions.

The Evolution of Script Styles

A nonstandardized system of script, known as *daiten,** or the "great seal script," developed from these bell inscriptions. Following this, a number of script systems were created by a variety of people and accepted by the government of the time for official use. During the Ch'in period (221–206 B.C.), Li Ssu altered the great seal script to make it simpler. His creation was called *shoten,* or the "small seal script." Shoten characters were uniform in size and widely taught in ancient schools as a means of attempting to tie together the many different lan-

---

* Here and elsewhere, in keeping with the convention of Japanese cultural arts, script styles and art forms that may have originated in China but that have been adopted by the Japanese are identified by their Japanese, not Chinese, names.

guages spoken across China. Also during the Ch'in period, China saw the introduction of silk surfaces for writing, ink sticks, and brushes. All of this made the characters easier still to write. Li Ssu is believed to have created only three thousand characters, but over ten thousand were being used by A.D. 200. About the same time, *korei* ("ancient scribe's script") was introduced by Ch'eng Mo. He straightened curved lines and made squares more circular. This made the symbols easier to draw and more pleasing to look at.

During the Han dynasty (206 B.C.–A.D. 220) the philosophy of Confucius became the official doctrine of China. During this same era, the Chinese invented paper, which allowed them to reproduce Confucian teachings by hand. Also during the Han dynasty *kan-reisho*, a variant of the scribe's script, was created, and it was from this that printed-style characters (*kaisho*) and semicursive-style writing (*gyosho*) were developed. Sosho, which is a fully cursive script, was not an even more abbreviated version of kaisho and gyosho, despite what is often believed. Sosho was, rather, an independent development of the cursive versions of the earlier seal script. (This is why there is not necessarily a strict correlation between the semicursive and cursive versions of the same character.)

Chinese Calligraphy in Japan

During the Asuka (A.D. 552–645) and Early Nara to Nara (A.D. 645–94) periods in Japan, many different elements of Chinese culture, including Chinese characters, came to this island nation. Initially the Japanese used the entire multitude of Chinese scripts, embracing quite a few of the Chinese readings while adding just as many of their own.

Eventually, characters were modified in Japan, and three new scripts were born: man'yo-gana, hiragana, and katakana.

During the fifth to tenth centuries in Japan, man'yo-gana (also called hentaigana) was developed as a sort of phonetic Japanese alphabet. That is, it did not make use of the actual meanings of the Chinese characters upon which it was based but used forms based on those characters to represent the syllables of the Japanese language. To arrive at a more standard written usage, sosho (cursive) man'yo-gana, which has many variants, was simplified and organized into the script known as hiragana. Hiragana is the primary phonetic script used in Japan today. Consisting of forty-six characters, its forms were finally standardized only in the past hundred years. Another phonetic script, the more angular katakana, was developed from kaisho using forms extracted from parts of Chinese characters. For more about hiragana and katakana, see pages 228–29.

Classical Japanese calligraphy should not be thought of as mere penmanship. Considering that Chinese characters began as simplified drawings, it is evident that no clear-cut dividing line can be found between drawing, ink painting, and calligraphy.

Hiragana and sosho man'yo-gana possess a soft, rounded appearance and were thought at the time to be more suitable for women. (In the eighth century, the famed poetry anthology *Man'yo-shu* was written by a woman using man'yo-gana.) The printed-style kaisho and semicursive gyosho were believed to be more suitable for men and were used for administrative and religious purposes during the same period. In China a distinction was never made between the writing of men and women. Modern Japan also no longer preserves this distinction.

Even though the spoken languages and cultures of Japan and China differ greatly, they share a common set of Asian characters. Note, however, that while these characters are used to form a system of written communication, classical Japanese calligraphy should not be thought of as mere penmanship. Considering that Chinese characters began as simplified drawings, it is evident that no clear-cut dividing line can be found between drawing, ink painting (*suiboku-e* or *sumi-e*), and calligraphy. In the Japanese language, the word sho (which is also pronounced *kaku*) can mean either "to write," "to draw," or "to paint." Likewise, the title *kakite* can be used to denote either a painter or a calligrapher. Even linguistically, a clear differentiation is not always made in Japan between painting and brush writing. To quote Yanagida Taiun Sensei, one of Japan's most well-respected artists and calligraphers:

> Sho (Japanese calligraphy) as we see it in Asia is an art that was created at the same time as and has developed along with the art of painting. But from the moment of creation, sho led a separate existence with abstract characters, as opposed to painting with specific images. Although the artistic value of each was the same until the present, these two media used absolutely different modes of expression. Sho has two functions: like the European alphabet it serves as a means of communication and like it is an expression of beauty. This led naturally to the development of expressing and drawing poetry and prose in an artistic manner. That is why in the East there is conviction about the aesthetic unity of painting and calligraphy. [1]

Shodo and ink painting cannot be separated from their historical and cultural matrix, which is why I've prefaced the painting exercises in this book with this historical section. Shodo is based on uncommonly elusive and elegant artistic skills, which are in turn based on technical and mental principles. While shodo's psychophysical concepts are universal in character, these principles developed from, and were affected by, their disseminators' modes of thinking, which were an immediate outgrowth of Japan's religions, arts, aesthetics, and history. (*Wabi*, *sabi*, and some of the more important Japanese aesthetic and philosophical ideals that influenced the development and style of shodo are explored later in this chapter.) Without at least some comprehension of Japan's historical and cultural matrix and some understanding of the esoteric principles that make up shodo, one's capacity to paint suffers.

Of course, shodo, at its deepest levels, goes beyond societal boundaries. Nevertheless, when avowing the art's unrestricted and universal aspects that transcend culture, you should not go to the opposite extreme of disregarding shodo's abundant elements that are an outgrowth of Japanese culture. Without these cultural characteristics that make up the structure of the art, your study is one-dimensional. A better approach is to observe that the most profound principles of shodo are universal—counterparts can be detected in many non-Japanese disciplines—while at the same time appreciating the ample Japanese components that give shodo its discernible framework.

I hope that this brief portrayal of shodo history will encourage you to more thoroughly explore the art's ties to Japan by practicing different Japanese cultural arts such as flower arrangement, Shin-shin-toitsu-do (Japanese yoga), and others—all of which have a much closer connection to shodo than you might think.

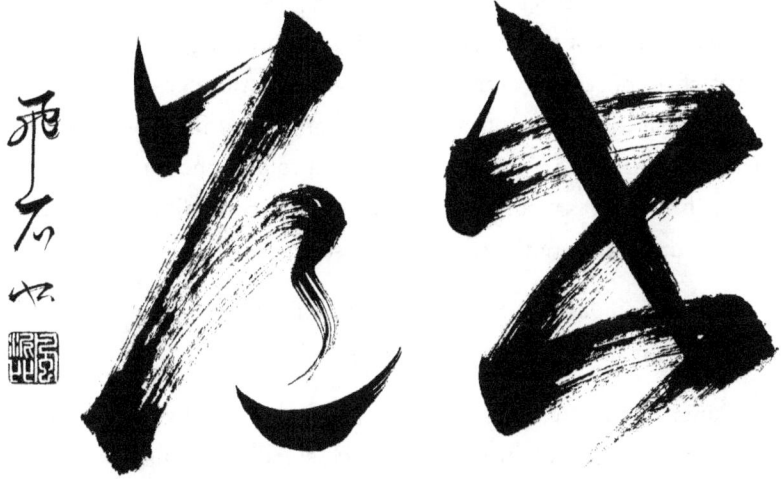

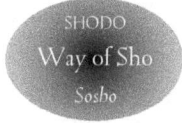

SHODO
Way of Sho
Sosho

Moving beyond Writing

The *kanji*, or written characters, used in both Japan and China have transcended their utilitarian function and collectively serve as a visually stirring piece of fine art. Shodo allows the dynamic movement of the artist's *ki* ("life energy" or "spirit") to become observable in the form of rich black ink. In great examples of shodo, you can sense both the rhythm of music as well as the smooth, elegant, and balanced construction of refined architecture. Many practitioners of this art feel that the visible rhythm of Japanese calligraphy ultimately embodies a "picture of the mind"—and accomplished calligraphers recognize that it actually discloses your spiritual state. This recognition is concisely summed up by the traditional Japanese saying:

Kokoro tadashikereba sunawachi fude tadashii.
If your mind is correct, the brush will be correct.

Some Japanese calligraphers and psychologists have written books on the examination of an individual's personality through calligraphy. Just as certain American and European companies have employed handwriting analysts to help them select the best individuals for executive posts, the Japanese for hundreds of years have expected their leaders in any field to display fine, composed script. (Recently this expectation has faded due to the advent of word processors.)

It is even said that health defects can be revealed in the appearance of *byohitsu*, or "sick strokes." This stems from the belief that brush strokes reveal the state of the body and subconscious mind—including its strengths and weaknesses—at the moment the brush is put to paper. People believed that the subconscious could be influenced in a

positive manner by studying and copying consummate examples of calligraphy by extraordinary individuals; by doing so you could cultivate a
strength of character akin to that of the artist being copied. Even today,
some of Japan's highest executives and politicians endeavor to develop the necessary traits for success by reproducing the artwork of an
emperor or famous religious leader.

Since shodo is considered an art form, you do not need to be able
to read Chinese characters, or the Japanese phonetic scripts of hiragana
or katakana, to admire its dynamic beauty. Within Japanese calligraphy, you find the essential elements that constitute all art: creativity,
balance, rhythm, grace, and the beauty of line. These aspects of shodo
can be recognized and appreciated by every culture.

Kanji and Kana

Most languages, including English, use a limited assemblage of
phonetic symbols to represent the sounds making up individual words
in written configuration. Japanese and Chinese, on the other hand,
use pictographs to represent words or concepts, as well as thousands
of ideographs, each of which has a particular meaning. This system
contains a vast number of symbols, thus adding tremendous variety to
Japanese calligraphy, and thereby producing a potentially infinite combination of expressions. Many kanji (Chinese characters) are literally
abstracted and abbreviated pictures (as opposed to letters) that can stir
emotion in the observer, as some paintings do, because of their depth
and diversity. Figure 1 shows the graphic evolution of the character for
"mountain" from its ancient "picture state" to the modern character.
Figure 2 shows the same elaboration of the symbol for "paintbrush."

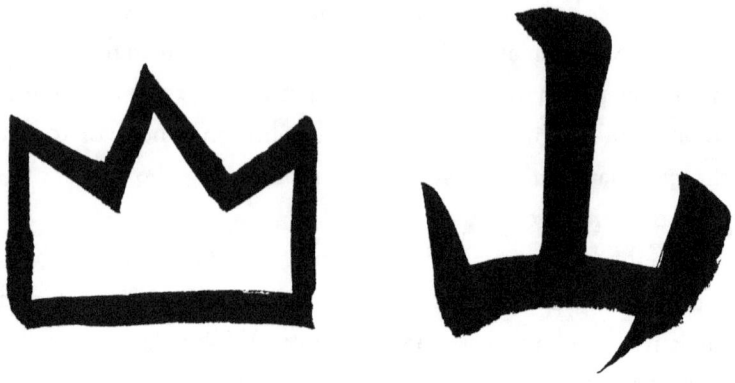

FIG. 1. The graphic evolution of the character for "mountain" from its ancient "picture state" to the modern character.

A hand holding a brush can easily be seen in the ancient character. To even the most casual observer, it should be clear that many characters are truly pictures, and for this reason the calligrapher paints or draws these characters as much as writes them.

Chinese characters can be divided into four categories: pictographs, ideographs, semantic composites, and phonetic-semantic composites. Pictographs started out as prehistoric images of natural phenomena and everyday objects. Ideographs are symbols, while pictographs amount to concrete signs. (For example, the ideograph for "above" was first written as a dot over a horizontal line.) When ideographs and pictographs were combined, semantic composites were formed by linking more than one existing character. (The semantic composite for "bright" is a fusion of the kanji for "sun" and the character for "moon." Both of these natural objects provide "bright" light.) A phonetic-semantic composite links a semantic element with a phonetic element; this sort of

226

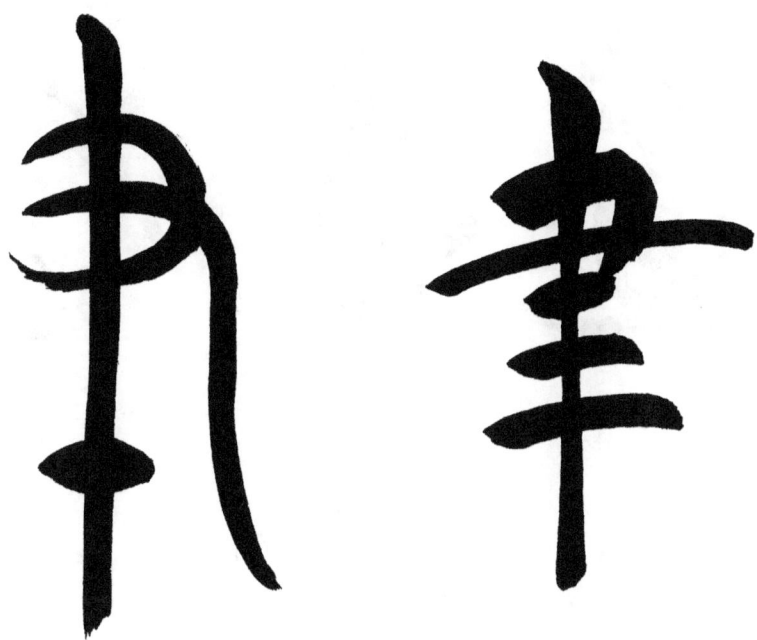

FIG. 2. The graphic evolution of the character for "paintbrush" from its ancient "picture state" to the modern character.

symbol will, therefore, take its actual meaning from one of its aspects and its pronunciation from another.

Each character can also be written in several different styles, which increases their creative potential. Kaisho (printed style), gyosho (semicursive style), and sosho (cursive style)—see page 219—are the most common variants. To illustrate these three basic scripts, the character do (also pronounced *michi*), which means "the way" in a spiritual sense, is presented in kaisho, gyosho, and sosho forms in Figures 3–5.

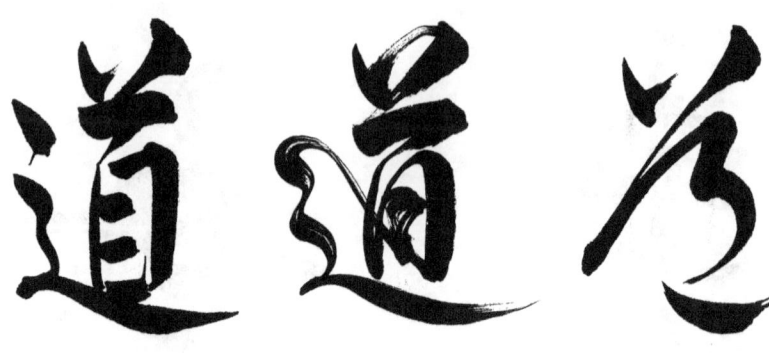

FIG. 3. The character *do* painted in kaisho (printed style).

FIG. 4. The character *do* painted in gyosho (semicursive style).

FIG. 5. The character *do* painted in sosho (cursive style).

Other more exotic methods, such as the aforementioned seal scripts and ancient scribe's script, exist as well.

As previously noted on pages 219–20, not too long after the Japanese adopted Chinese characters, around the sixth century A.D., they also originated two native systems of phonetic writing, hiragana and katakana. Both kana systems are syllabaries. That is, they are used to write all the sounds of the Japanese language. All modern Japanese texts are written in a mix of kanji and kana. In a Japanese newspaper, for instance, you will see a combination of kanji and hiragana with a sprinkling of katakana. (In principle, Japanese could be written with kana syllables alone—as many children's books are— but this would eliminate the meanings conveyed by the kanji and, because of the many Japanese homonyms, make the written text very hard to comprehend.)

Hiragana and katakana characters represent the same forty-six syl-

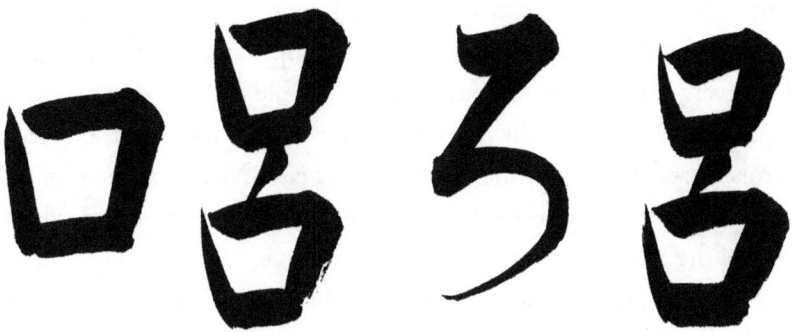

FIG. 6. The katakana version of the sylla-
ble *ro* is an extracted element of the character at right.

FIG. 7. The hiragana version of the syl-
lable *ro* is a simplified form of the character at right.

lables in Japanese texts, but they have different origins and are used in different ways.

Katakana characters are merely a single component of a kanji (Chinese character) that has sometimes been extracted or simplified. Katakana tend to be somewhat square and angular in appearance and are used for writing words borrowed into Japanese from foreign languages, for some scientific terms, and for emphasis. Figure 6 shows the katakana *ro* and the character from which it is derived.

Hiragana characters are an abbreviation and simplification of whole kanji forms and have a more rounded, flowing, and graceful demeanor than katakana. Hiragana is used to record grammatical inflections in adjectives, adverbs, and verbs and for words no longer written in kanji. Figure 7 illustrates the hiragana version of *ro* and its accompanying related kanji.

Since this book is designed primarily as an introduction to the cultural, artistic, and meditative aspects of Japanese calligraphy and painting, it does not include a complete list of kanji, katakana, and hiragana. However, any serious student of shodo should own a comprehensive Japanese dictionary, which should also explain the order of brush strokes used in each Japanese symbol. *The New Nelson Japanese-English Dictionary* (Tokyo and Boston: Tuttle Publishing, 1997), a revised edition of the classic work, is an excellent resource.

Few people are aware that many of the fundamental brush strokes in shodo are similar to or the same as the strokes employed in classical Asian ink painting. You use essentially the same sort of brush, ink stick, ink stone, and paper in both arts. Skilled calligraphers can produce simple yet quite respectable ink drawings merely by relying upon their experience in shodo, and the two related arts are not infrequently combined to form a single composition.

Universal Principles in Japanese Art

Certain philosophical and artistic ideals are universal and apply to all methods of Japanese art. From the martial arts to Japan's fine arts to the traditional tea ceremony, particular aesthetic codes are historically held in common. Shodo and sumi-e are no exception to this rule.

Among the most significant artistic ideas in Japan are the concepts of *wabi*, *sabi*, *shibumi*, and *shibui*. These aesthetic ideals, and others, have had a profound influence on the evolution of Japanese calligraphy. I believe that if you do not understand these aesthetic principles, no great appreciation of any Japanese cultural art, whether it be shodo or *shakuhachi* flute, is possible.

WABI AND SABI

"Wabi" actually means "poverty." This has no negative implications but hints at the innocent contentment that can be found when you listen to a gentle springtime rain tap-tapping on the roof of a simple cabin. Wabi is outside of intellectual complexity and all forms of self-importance and artificiality; it relates to the discovery of the simple truths of nature. Just as nature is asymmetrical, irregular, and imperfect, wabi is the flawlessness of natural imperfection. Asymmetrical balance is vital in shodo:

> Every time I teach, I explain that art is balance. This principle can be understood throughout the world.
> —Kobara Ranseki Sensei

Also important is the understanding of when to use light or dark versus heavy or light lines of ink. When writing *waka* (a form of poetry), the placement of every stanza, or line of characters, in relationship to every other line on the paper is crucial. All the lines must form a balanced and artistically correct design as a whole. Kobara Ranseki teaches that "unbalance of balance" is beautiful in Japanese art.

In a way, wabi is the elegance of artlessness and even ugliness. When this artless, imperfect beauty is coupled with a particular uncultured antiquity, or even the illusion of this aged attribute, Japanese artists employ the word "sabi" to describe it. "Sabi" is literally "solitude" or "lonesomeness," but in specific instances it can also suggest an effortless quality. (Like wabi, it is almost impossible to describe directly. It can only be truly found through bona fide instruction in one of Japan's cultural arts.) Sabi can be discovered while you sit alone in the peaceful silence of an old fishing town on an autumn nightfall or when you view a bright patch of green peeking through the snow in a mountain village.

A martial arts expert who throws his opponent with a single, almost imperceptible, effortless action is displaying sabi. (As opposed to achieving the same objective via numerous less efficient movements. The originator of judo, Kano Jigoro Sensei, expressed sabi through his principle of "maximum efficiency with minimum effort.") The same expert's humble, plain uniform, with a black belt worn all but white from age, declares a sort of beauty that cannot be detected in a Westernized gold lamé uniform and a new satin black belt. (Sometimes would-be American "experts," in an attempt to impress others with their depth of experience, will try to mimic this "worn" effect by scraping their belts with a wire brush. Unfortunately, this is simply silly, not sabi.) The natural beauty embodied by wabi and sabi can be seen in all Japanese arts, including calligraphy and painting.

Author Leonard Koren defines what he terms "the wabi-sabi universe" in the following way:[2]

Metaphysical Basis
* Things are either devolving toward, or evolving from nothingness

Spiritual Values
* Truth comes from the observation of nature
* "Greatness" exists in the inconspicuous and the overlooked details
* Beauty can be coaxed out of ugliness

State of Mind
- Acceptance of the inevitable
- Appreciation of the cosmic order

Moral Precepts
- Get rid of all that is unnecessary
- Focus on the intrinsic and ignore material hierarchy

Material Qualities
- The suggestion of natural process
- Irregular
- Intimate
- Unpretentious
- Earthy
- Murky
- Simple

SHIBUMI AND SHIBUI

Balanced imbalance, artlessness, solitariness, antiquity—all of this connects to wabi and sabi, which in turn have a connection with the terms "shibumi" (elegance) and "shibui" (elegant). "Shibumi" calls forth the image of something astringent in taste, while "shibui" suggests that which is unaffected or refined. In kado (flower arrangement, also known as *ikebana*), a shibumi flower arrangement evokes a feeling of coolness during a sizzling summer and warmth on a frosty day. That which is shibumi is quiet in refinement and soothing and satisfying to the heart in a manner that is not shaped exclusively by logic. It is the sentiment of "not too much," the use of aesthetic restraint in the finest sense.

Shibui indicates something that is not flashy (in color, for example), but ample in quality. Unpolished silver or gold and the color of ashes or bran can bring about a subdued yet elegant and serene shibui effect. The classical color scheme of a woman's kimono, a traditional martial artist's apparel of quilted gi (cotton uniform) and hakama (wide, skirtlike pants), the color layout of a Japanese guest room, the clothing and utensils in the tea ceremony—all evoke the attribute of shibui.

Zen has always placed emphasis on "Zen in daily life," or relating the meditative state to everyday activities. As a result, Zen monks have been expected to be able to display their enlightenment graphically through their brush writing.

Zen and Japanese Art

Zen is a school of Buddhism that was founded in the sixth century in India. Its founder is generally considered to be a monk named Bodhidharma (Daruma in Japanese). Shortly after founding Zen, he left for China around A.D. 520. There, according to oral tradition, Daruma sat facing a wall for nine years until he achieved enlightenment.

The term "Zen" comes from the Chinese word *Ch'an*, a derivation of the Sanskrit *Dhyana*. Zen was introduced into Japan from China by the monks Eisai (1141–1215) and Dogen (1200–1253). It was quickly embraced by Japan's military ruling class, and with its message of salvation through meditation it promptly made inroads into most aspects of Japanese life. Zen's emphasis on attainment of a state of oneness with the universe and being free from cerebral questioning influenced the entire Japanese cultural matrix, and many aesthetic qualities such as wabi, sabi, shibumi, and shibui can be said to have a historical correlation to Zen.

Due to its far-reaching historical influence in Japan, Zen has also affected most Japanese arts such as the tea ceremony, flower arrangement, and shodo. For some time in Japan, Zen priests (and the public as well) have believed that calligraphy can be thought of as a direct extension of the mind. Zen has always placed emphasis on "Zen in daily life," or relating the meditative state to everyday activities. As a result, Zen monks have been expected to be able to display their enlightenment graphically through their brush writing. Indeed, a number of them, such as Hakuin (1686–1769) of the Rinzai sect, were outstanding calligraphers/painters.

Zensho (Zen calligraphy) has been highly valued by the Japanese public despite the fact that while many Zen monks may be well trained in Zen, the depth of training has not always carried over into their artistic pursuits. (To put it bluntly, it is a mistake to think that all artwork produced by Zen priests is of a high caliber, even if it is confidently and spontaneously executed.)

Just like most other aspects of Japanese culture, Zen has naturally had an influence on Japanese brush writing, so there has been some borrowing of terminology. Zen first came into prominence in the West following World War II, when it was embraced by the beatnik generation. Along with this interest in Zen came an interest in Zen art, including calligraphy. As a result, Zen is intimately entangled with the history of shodo in America as well as in Japan. However, most schools of calligraphy do not identify themselves as Zensho, and while the calligraphy in *Brush Meditation* may be derived from a source of inspiration similar to the spirit of Zen, it is not Zensho. The same is true for the methods and techniques depicted in this book. Even though some over-lap of terminology and ideas may be present, this book does not deal with Zen Buddhism per se, although perhaps the material contained in these pages can be said to be imbued with Zen in a broad and generic sense.

Nonetheless, many schools of Zen make use of the ideas of ki and *hara*, which are also used in some schools of shodo.

Ki and Hara

While not exactly principles of art or design, the effective use of ki (life energy or spirit) and hara (abdominal centralization) can per-haps be considered part of the spiritual and technical aesthetics of all the Japanese arts. The terms have a long history in Japan, and they are a central component in traditional Japanese culture. Like so many aspects of the Japanese worldview, they are not always clearly defined, yet the ideas behind them are so much a part of the inherited Japanese consciousness that they have thoroughly permeated the language itself. For example, consider the word "ki." In an earlier publication of mine, *The Way of the Universe*, I wrote

> In Japanese, *byoki* means "sickness" and occurs when the spirit is weak. *Ki-chigai* is taken to mean "insanity," but it literally means "when Ki, or spirit, is wrong." *Ki ga kiku* directly means "when the spirit is sharply focused," but in everyday usage, it implies cleverness. *Ki ga chiisai*, or "when life energy grows small," is to be cowardly. *Jo Ki suru*, or "when the spirit is unsettled," is to be overly excit-

ed. *Ki o ushinau* literally translates as, "when life energy is lost," and means to be unconscious. The Japanese have traditionally maintained the great importance of using one's Ki, or spirit, correctly, and they have indicated how Ki influences every aspect of life.[3]

"Ki" can be used to describe everything from a feeling to a natural phenomenon (such as weather) to the ki of the universe itself, or God. In a way, it can be regarded as the basic building block of nature.*

"Hara" means "abdomen," and it refers to a natural center in the lower abdomen that is used as a point of concentration in various meditative disciplines and Japanese arts. In Japan, the term "hara" holds a similar and equal importance to ki:

> If someone is brave, the Japanese say *hara no hito*, or "person of hara." A coward is *hara ga nai hito*—"a person with no hara." Understanding is indicated by *hara ga oki*—"a large hara," while a closed mind is *hara ga chiisai*, or "a small hara." A clear conscience is called *hara ga kirei*—"a clean hara," and someone with *hara ga kuroi*, "a black hara," is unfaithful. To become calm is *hara o suete*, or "to settle the hara."[4]

The mere fact that these words are frequently used in Japanese society should not be taken to indicate that all citizens of modern Japan

---

* Both ki and hara will be discussed at greater length in the following chapters; this section serves only as a brief introduction to two concepts that have a long history in Japan and that have influenced the evolution of shodo.

possess a deep or innate understanding of ki and hara. Consciously or unconsciously, it is for this very reason that many people in Japan seek out instructors of classical arts, such as Japanese calligraphy, that involve the development of these concepts. Even in Japan, however, it is relatively rare to find a teacher who can efficiently communicate these ideas, provide a concrete means of developing them, and then show how they can be utilized to enhance one's everyday life.

Shodo and Other Japanese Arts

Because all the Japanese arts share the same aesthetics, shodo enhances the study of budo, kado, and other art forms. The same feeling of balance that is needed for "sculpting" a successful flower arrangement is likewise needed in Japanese brush writing, in which every character must display a dynamic balance. In odori (dance) and the martial arts, participants should also master a dynamic or moving balance that is comparable to the asymmetrical balance used in Japanese calligraphy.

The identical unity with nature that is stressed in flower arrangement is also emphasized in the martial ways of aikido and aiki-jujutsu, while shodo demands an incredibly strict attention to detail and brush form that is not unlike the formal precision cultivated by pupils of ikebana. Cha no yu (tea ceremony) is based on wa-kei-sei-jaku (accord-respect-purity-solitude), and Japanese calligraphy and flower arrangement both seek to embody similar qualities. The tea ceremony's philosophical equation amounts to a particular expression of wabi, sabi, shibumi, and shibui. These artistic, perhaps even spiritual, characteristics are universal for all Japanese art.

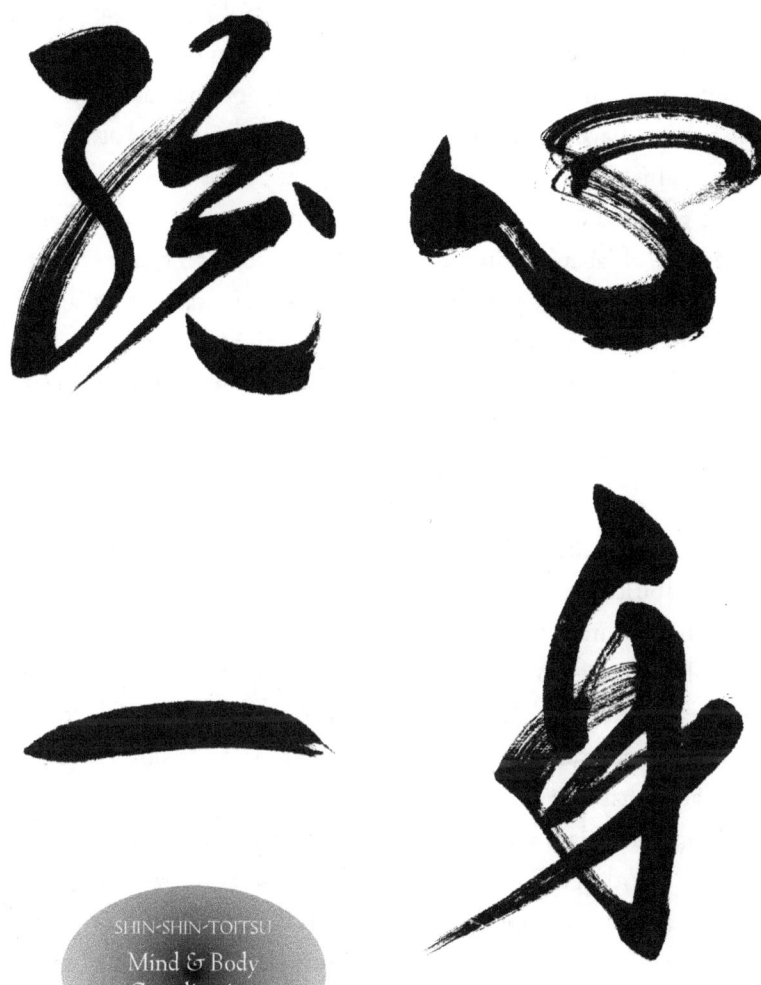

SHIN-SHIN-TOITSU
Mind & Body
Coordination
Gyosho

Shodo and sumi-e allow you to comprehend these qualities in such a way that their study can enhance the practice of different art forms. The opposite is true as well. Many Western students of various Japanese cultural arts frequently miss out on the importance of these ideas, and as a result have merely a pale copy of the genuine art that they are studying. This may be due to cultural differences, in some instances a language gap, and in other cases out-and-out ignorance. Nevertheless, studying one of Japan's cultural arts without a comprehension of these vital artistic principles is like trying to dine on the imitation food seen in front of Japanese restaurants. It may seem like the real thing, but it certainly doesn't taste like it, and the nutritional content is pretty meager.

The Universal in the Particular

Japan has traditionally excelled (due in part to the predominance of Zen) in spiritualizing comparatively ordinary activities such as brush writing, the preparation of tea, the military arts, and the arrangement of flowers. The goal is to perceive the whole of life through a particular enterprise or individual part of living. Master calligrapher, famed Zen adept, and founder of Muto-ryu swordsmanship Yamaoka Tesshu Sensei indicated that one of his main martial teachings was "the practice of unifying particulars and universals." He also wrote, in his *Notes on Kumitachi*: "Within these varied techniques there is deep meaning. Cast off subject and object, function as one; abandon self and others, form a single sword."[5] D. T. Suzuki, author of numerous books on Zen and Japanese art, likewise made reference to "the One in the Many and the Many in the One."

Consider a specific technique, or exercise to be copied, as a "particular." In shodo, for example, you do not copy a new character exclusively to learn to paint that symbol, and in sumi-e, you do not strive to make an accurate copy of bamboo or a bonfire solely to learn how to paint such individual pictures. Contained within a given lesson or particular technique is the essence of all techniques. You imitate and study a particular form to grasp the universal principles that allow the technique to work in the first place and that will finally enable you to transcend the form itself to discover the formless. In doing so, it is often possible to observe that these universal principles encompass something much greater than the individual art you are studying; they actually amount to vital lessons in living.

On an even more profound level, experts in flower arrangement speak of attaining a state in which they sense the inclinations and true characteristics of the flowers they will be arranging—a union with nature in which the particular (the artist) is united with the universal (nature). Martial artists, similarly, speak of a condition in which they become one with their opponent—or even multiple opponents—and eventually the universe itself. Perhaps then, the ultimate historical aesthetic running through all of the Japanese arts is a state of naturalness in which the distinction between individuals and nature dissolves into oneness.

Shodo and Personal Transformation in the West

Shodo's uniquely Japanese aesthetics and universal principles can not only serve to enhance the appreciation and understanding of other Japanese arts but can also have an impact on the way we engage in Western art. Shodo and other Japanese arts are steadily making inroads into Western culture precisely because of their universal aspects. Numerous Americans and Europeans are also drawn to shodo's universal spiritual message. For example, some Zen meditation experts, such as Omori Sogen Roshi and Terayama Katsujo Sensei, authors of *Zen and the Art of Calligraphy*, are enthusiastic supporters of shodo as a means of developing stronger powers of attention. Shodo is also valued as a method of cultivating the unification of mind and body in action. Several Zen educators have used shodo as a sort of "moving Zen."

Based on the number of teachers of other spiritual disciplines and Japanese arts found in shodo classes, it would seem that anyone would be able to utilize shodo as a mechanism for personal transformation, which could then be put to use in his or her specific art or calling. This has been one of the primary motivating factors for the gradual emergence of shodo in the West.

Contained within a given lesson or particular technique is the essence of all techniques. You imitate and study a particular form to grasp the universal principles that allow the technique to work in the first place and that will finally enable you to transcend the form itself to discover the formless.

Calligraphy teaches the artisan to realize a condition of comprehensive self-mastery. Western and Japanese practitioners of shodo cite expanded attention, improved peacefulness, stronger willpower, and deeper relaxation as just some of the advantages of their training. It is for this purpose that many devotees of shodo in Japan partake in calligraphy instruction in the first place. Classes are not taken exclusively to better your handwriting, as is regularly postulated; rather, Japanese students have come to actualize the personal gains that such a spiritual discipline has to offer and that, to many Westerners, make shodo so tantalizing.

SHODO AND ABSTRACT EXPRESSIONISM

As previously noted, Americans appear to have first come into contact with shodo and sumi-e following World War II. At that time, American artists were searching for something beyond the limitations of their own culture for motivation. Shodo inspired numerous abstract expressionist painters in the 1940s and 1950s, around the same time that avant-garde interest in Zen meditation was beginning to appear. Beat poetry was influenced by Zen and other forms of Buddhism, often as a reaction against materialism.

Abstract expressionist artists such as Franz Kline frequently chose to work in black and white, having been affected by monochromatic shodo and the minimalist aspects of Zen. In the 1990s, famed artists like Robert Motherwell, who has written of his lifelong interest in sho-do, and Cleve Gray are executing works that are reminiscent of Japanese calligraphy. Motherwell, in fact, produced a series of paintings entitled Shem the Pen Man in homage to an expert calligrapher. These paintings feature a calligraphic ideograph suspended in a plot of color.

John Graham, author of System and Dialects of Art, has stressed the importance of spontaneous gesture and écriture, a French word meaning "calligraphy." He suggested that individualized écriture should evoke innovation in a calligraphic fashion that made use of "accidents." Graham, in turn, discovered and influenced Jackson Pollack, Willem de Kooning, Lee Krasner, and David Smith—four of the greatest abstract expressionists, who all produced works that are reminiscent of Japanese calligraphy. Al Reinhardt, after breaking away from cubism in the early 1940s, also turned to shodo for inspiration.

Art critic Barbara Rose has written about Japanese calligraphic art:

Since calligraphy neither depicts shapes nor closes contours, but maintains a fluid, fluctuating open form into which space may flow, it represents a system of marking ideally suited to an art style like Abstract Expressionism that sought to marry painting with drawing, eliminating the dichotomy between the two that exists in Western art, even in Cubism. The reconciliation of opposites, the unification of dualism is of course another Oriental concept especially attractive to Abstract Expressionists.[6]

Japanese artists and calligraphers noticed what was taking place in the American art world of the forties and fifties and were in turn influenced by the abstract expressionist movement. In 1951, noted artist Hasegawa Saburo wrote of Franz Kline's work and the fashion in which Asian art was altering abstract expressionism. This and other such articles began to affect Japanese calligraphers and painters.

In light of all this, it is evident that contemporary shodo is actually a spontaneous creative gesture that has as much in common with abstract expressionism as it does with the conventional written word. I make this point because I have found that many Americans have an interest in abstract art but are somewhat intimidated by the apparent "foreignness" of shodo. Once I explain the parallels and historical links between abstract expressionism and shodo, however, they are more easily able to relate to Japanese calligraphy.

SHODO AS A UNIVERSAL METHOD FOR REVEALING THE SPIRIT

After I explain to newcomers how shodo can function as a means of self-realization and meditation, many people express a sincere interest in learning more about this art form. I believe that this is because in shodo (unlike many other pursuits) one's degree of mental power becomes clearly and instantaneously seeable. Shodo makes the immaterial palpable in the form of smooth and elegant monochromatic designs. A person's authentic character is laid open through the brush, which, though less efficient than the pencil, is a most potent device for discovering the smallest wavering of mind or body. The pliant strands of hair in the *fude*, or brush, give birth to radiant, natural symbols that surpass divisions in nationality. Given, then, the universal character of this ancient Japanese way of the brush, and because of its pragmatic advantages, it is fairly clear why this art has landed on the shores of twentieth-century Europe and North America. Shodo and Japanese ink painting have a definite place in modern Western art and personal transformation.

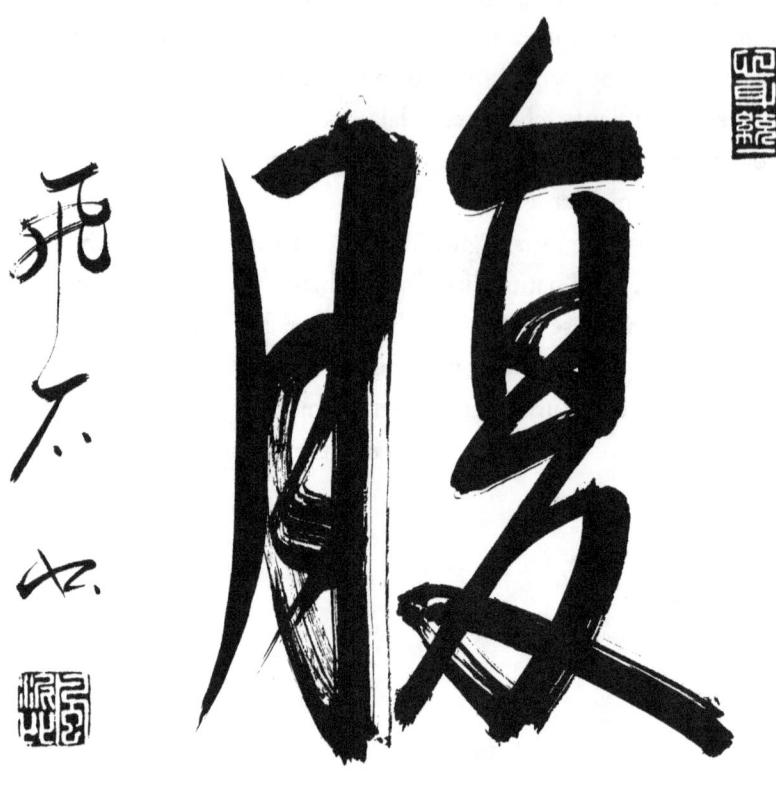

HARA
Abdominal
Centralization
Gyosho

Chapter 2

MIND & BODY CONNECTION

1. Use the mind in a positive way.

2. Use the mind with full concentration.

3. Use the body naturally.

4. Train the body gradually, systematically,
and continuously.

Standard shodo demands that the calligrapher brush every stroke perfectly; expert calligraphers and even beginners never go back to touch up any character or piece of artwork. Each movement of the brush must be performed with the full force of mind and body. There should be no faltering or indecisiveness.

In Japanese calligraphic art, as in living your life, you cannot go back, though in the beginning many novices lack the mental focus to paint the characters decisively. Every stroke must be delivered like the slice of a razor-sharp samurai sword, yet the brush must be handled in a serene manner. Gradually, the student's mental condition is altered

FIG. 8. A basic brush stroke, tapering to a fine point at the left.

through regular training. This transformation of consciousness can be carried over and applied to your daily life as well, even to academic and vocational pursuits.

Classical shodo demands (and develops) a complete union of mental and physical force. In spite of what most assume, it is surprisingly tough to make the mind and body work together as a unit. A seemingly uncomplicated feat, such as drawing a solid, straight line that tapers to a fine point, requires an unhesitating hand and mind. Figure 8 shows a

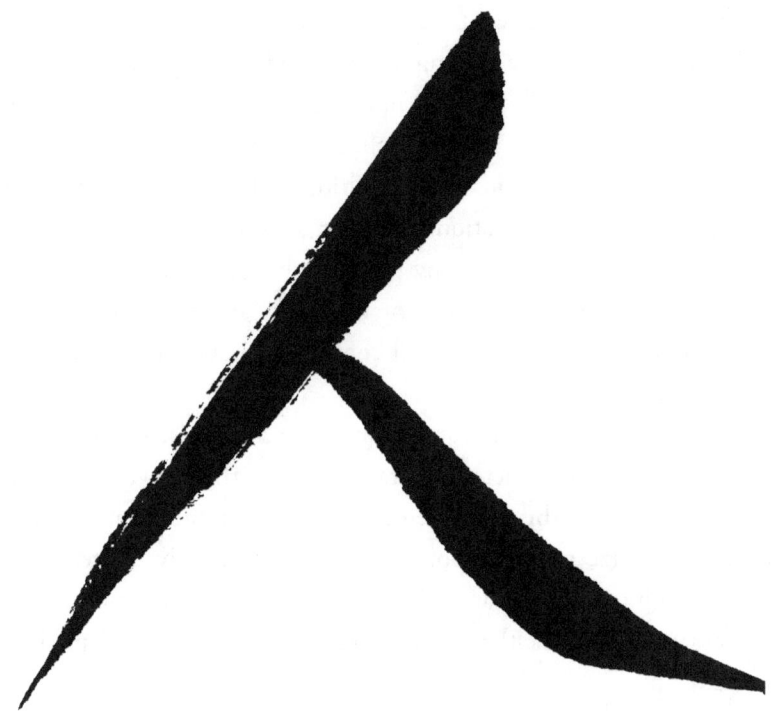

FIG. 9. The character *hito*.

basic brush stroke. Figure 9 shows the character hito, "human being."
Notice how the left side of *hito* uses the tapering brush stroke seen in
Figure 8.

Being capable of executing skillful brush strokes with genuine
dexterity and decisiveness is an amazing challenge and can be attained
only through the coordination of your mental and physical faculties.
(If you'd like to try your hand now, skip to Chapter 4, where materials
and basic brush strokes are introduced. After you've tried to reproduce

the character *hito* just a few times, I think you will appreciate just how challenging it is to make the mind, body, and brush work together in harmony.) A powerfully focused mind commands the brush, and the brush is allowed to act as a perfect reflection of your mental movement. All fine arts, crafts, music, and a multitude of different activities call for this attitude of coordination. However, shodo ideally represents one of the greatest levels of harmony between thought and action: it both serves as a mechanism for depicting this unity and supplies a path for cultivating it. Both psychophysical coordination and the lack of it are unveiled on one's paper.

To arrive at a condition in which the mind precisely controls the body, and the body reflects this state, requires the growth of earnest concentration. It is this improvement of concentration that is needed for you to realize your full potential in shodo or daily existence. To fully realize how to arrive at such a state of attention and unification, it is necessary to examine the actual characteristics of the mind and body in detail.

Use the Mind in a Positive Way

The mind moves and regulates every part of the body, with the body ultimately reflecting our mental condition. Some of this regulation is being exerted unconsciously by means of the autonomic nervous system, through which the mind and body remain unified at all times. It is necessary to realize this if you are to competently learn any activity, including shodo, because the mind can positively or negatively sway the innate mind-body connection. (When this relationship is unstable, you may witness a Japanese character being painted by a teacher and comprehend it intellectually, yet fail to physically copy it on paper in the correct form.) This chapter explores the correct use of the mind, and later the body, as it relates to masterful mental and physical coordination in art.

Positive and energetic use of the mind is one of the most crucial points in learning Japanese painting and calligraphy, for without it we seldom have the determination to effectively master any other aspects of these arts. Beginners should consider the ways in which a negative attitude can influence the body. (Psychosomatic illnesses are but one example of the debilitating effect our mind can have on our body.)

Conversely, to be positive and decisive in art, as well as in life, is not the same as being inflexible or hard-headed. A truly positive mind has confidence in positive outcomes for most incidents, and is consequently capable of being at ease and adaptable in response to all circumstances. A positive mind has no reason to be upset or to resist, because it can confidently deal with every circumstance. It is this powerful state of mind that many shodo authorities have outlined as *fudoshin*, or "immovable mind," which again does not suggest rigidity but a confident condition of mental stability.

EXPERIMENTS WITH THE POSITIVE USE OF THE MIND

A positive outlook is most freely achieved through a conscious and rational examination of the nature of our thought patterns. Take a moment to reflect on the real, immediate state of your mind. Is your mental state positive? If it is not, what are the actual roots of this negativity?

We have all met people who see themselves as positive yet who are not seen by others in that way. The mind, being invisible, is easiest

251

to view through an individual's expressions, actions, and posture. Japanese calligraphy, and indeed all forms of art, gives our bodies a means to make the invisible mind visible. For this same reason, psychologists will sometimes offer disturbed children crayons and paper to play with. By observing not only the drawings that are produced by these children but also the manner in which the sketches are created (confidently or hesitatingly, calmly or violently, and so on), the therapist can better understand the child's mental condition.

Hashimoto Tetsuichi Sensei, a top student of the late Nakamura Tempu Sensei, himself a leader in psychological development, wrote the following in his unpublished English interpretation of Nakamura Sensei's teachings:

> For example, if we say, "How hot it is today!" almost overwhelmed by the heat, then the attitude of our mind and our words are of a negative nature. But if we say, the degree of temperature is very high without being annoyed by the heat at all, then our attitude of mind and our words are not of a negative nature. This kind of differentiation we call self-examination or introspection, and on such introspection or self-examination, of course, we have to put our minds always in the state of positiveness, so that our words and deeds are also of a positive nature, making other persons feel at ease, happy and encouraged for the future.[7]

My Japanese yoga teacher, Hashimoto Sensei, has indicated that you must also consider the nature of your surroundings. Try putting this book down for a moment, and take a look around your house or apartment. Is it in order or disarray, immaculate or dingy? Your mind is affected by the words and behavior of others, by the appearance of your environment, and by a wide variety of elements. These elements amount to "suggestions" that we receive from our surroundings and cir- cumstances. Awareness of what is positive or negative or true or false in our environment, based on our understanding of the nature of reality (as opposed to how we were raised or our common cul-

Shodo ideally represents one of the greatest levels of harmony between thought and action: it both serves as a mechanism for depicting this unity and supplies a path for cultivating it.

tural beliefs, which may or may not be true), is vital for self-realization. Shodo, being a "way," has as its ultimate goal just such a state of self-realization. Again, shodo is not merely the act of manipulating a brush. Rather, the handling of the brush—as a specific and particular action— is primarily useful for helping us to discover broader truths that relate to every aspect of living. This book is an examination of these truths as they relate to daily life as well as shodo.

CREATING A POSITIVE ENVIRONMENT

By discovering the actual nature of our environment, we can attempt to restructure our surroundings so that our subconscious minds are affected in a positive manner. In Japan, a traditional callig-rapher's studio is usually neat and orderly. For the same reason, a classical martial arts training hall is always tidy, uncluttered, bright, organized, and natural in look, as these factors alter the manner in which one learns. Before attempting the exercises and examples out-lined later in this book, take a moment to clean up the area where your painting will occur. Reflect on what the appearance of your room or home says about you.

By being conscious of the influences we receive from our surroundings, we can endeavor to be unaffected by the negative expressions, acts, and gestures of others, and in this way we can keep our minds free from pessimistic thoughts. For this reason, pupils of shodo or any Japanese art are discouraged from making negative remarks such as "I can't paint that character." Such a statement not only weakens them but has a dispiriting effect on others practicing in the same setting. You must always consider the effects of your words and behavior upon the other students in your class. (None of the Japanese cultural arts can be learned in great detail without a teacher, or in isolation, and discovering more positive and effective ways of relating to others is just one of the numerous benefits of studying these art forms.) Talking to people in a depressing fashion not only can weaken them, but can sadden them, which in turn taints your own surroundings. This vicious cycle is in fact a recurrent cause of lack of harmony within a school of art, a household, or even within civilization as a whole.

In the Japanese cultural arts, the cultivation of wa (harmony) is considered to be fundamental. Without this personal state of harmony, because the body and brush reflect the mind, one's calligraphy will become rough and unbalanced. Yet, we are not separate from others and our environment. This discovery means we need to consider the nature of harmony on both personal and interpersonal levels. Without harmony, a school of art (or even a nation) cannot operate effectively. But harmony can, at least to some extent, be developed by considering the effects of using positive, hopeful words when speaking.

THE POSITIVE ATTITUDE OF THE BUSHI

As you paint, and even in daily living, to keep the mind in the present is to unite the mind and body. The act of focusing your attention on the moment is not merely a component of shodo but is a feature found in all the Japanese arts, especially the martial arts and ways, where this idea has an exceptional and long tradition.

Budo (the martial way) is ultimately derived from the old traditions of the *bushi*, the classical warriors of ancient Japan. For a bushi (or samurai, as he was also known), facing the possibility of death was a common consideration. The bushi's mortality was regularly compared to that of the Japanese cherry blossom, which flowers just briefly, shows off lively hue and beauty, and is then scattered by the breeze. A bushi's principal responsibilities and code of morality focused on the notion of giving his life in the service of his clan and feudal lord. Relating to this part of *giri* (obligation) was the awareness that he could be required to lay down his life, without hesitation, at a moment's warning. To deal with the severity of this situation, some warriors resolved to live every day as if it were their last. They subsequently learned how to experience life thoroughly, without doubt or remorse. The bushi's aim was not to merely exist, but to live a rich life.

For the bushi to be capable of sustaining a positive attitude in the face of conceivable immediate death, he had to learn not to be troubled by either the past or, particularly, the future. This detail is also critical for the modern student of shodo and/or ink painting. Essentially, if the mind remains in the present, it is impossible to worry. We tend to worry solely about an occurrence that *has* happened or that *may* take place in the future. The immediate moment holds no time or space for worry.

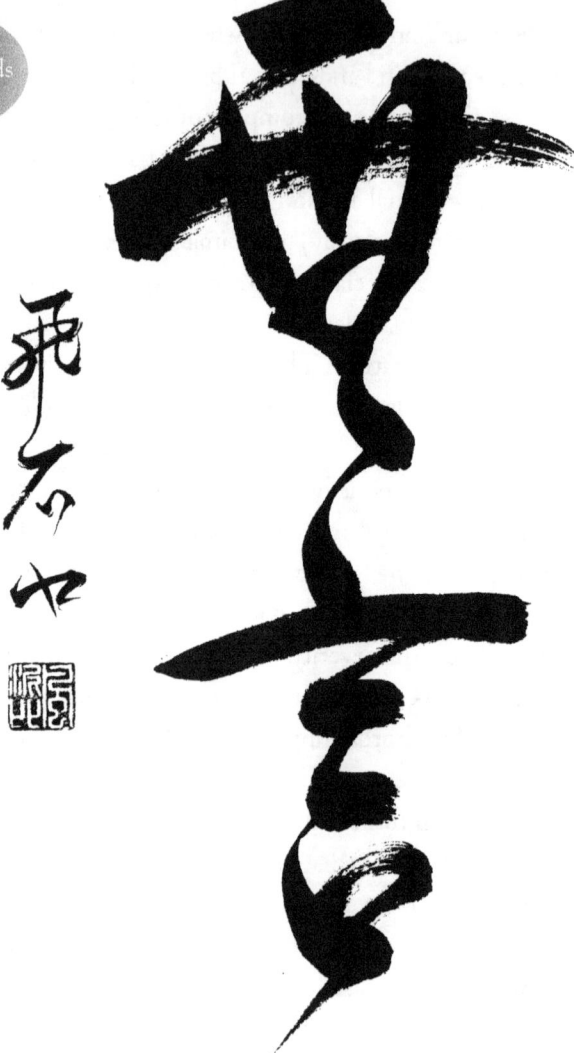

MUGON
Beyond Words
Sosho

One's past cannot be altered, and to become caught up in it is inefficient in terms of both time and effort. And by fearing for the future, we only drain ourselves, making us less capable of positively responding when the future is truly upon us. When worrying about a crisis that may or may not take place, we often end up experiencing the affair twice—once when imagining it and again when we actually undergo it.

Understanding the nature of keeping your mind in the present will make it possible to calmly face the paper you will paint on. (Because touching up is not allowed in shodo, fear is a very real possibility, especially when you are about to demonstrate the art in front of others.) When you rest effortlessly in the moment, no thoughts of past failures or future mishaps will be alive in your mind, and a genuinely positive mental state will come about. This is fudoshin, "immovable mind."

FOUR EXPERIMENTS TOWARD A POSITIVE MIND

To further your understanding of the power of a positive mind, try the following four experiments in your daily life. You may discover that they have a profound effect on how you function, and whether or not your mind and body are able to work as an effective unit. You may wish to work on just one of these experiments each day for four days.

1. Do you know what your mental state is from minute to minute? Why, and at what moment, does your state of mind change from positive to negative? This is an experiment in introspection or self-awareness.

2. What kinds of "suggestions" are you receiving from others and your environment? Are these influences positive or negative? Take note of each suggestion, remem-

bering that this is an experiment in the analysis of your surroundings.

3. From moment to moment, what is your attitude toward others? If it is not positive, observe yourself in relationship to others to discover where your negativity comes from and what effect it has on your environment.

4. Is your mind in the moment? When do you start to worry about the past or the future?

Self-examination under the above four circumstances can lead to a new, more positive way of using the mind. Taking note of the nature of negativity and seeing its source is an effective technique for unifying the body and mind and cultivating positive characteristics that are necessary for producing art. Never forget that it is the mind that moves the brush, and brush meditation reveals the character of the mind. When the mind is positive, the necessary unity of mind and body is preserved and you are able to display your full capacity. A negative mind will unconsciously retreat from the action presently taking place, which it consciously or subconsciously does not want to participate in. This causes a definite disconnection of mind and body, making one unfit to respond quickly to the ink's rapid interaction with the paper. In shodo, it is important to apply 100 percent of ourselves spiritually to what is taking place at the instant of painting. This positive mental condition is at times labeled *ki no dashikata* (the pouring forth of life energy).

KI AND THE POSITIVE USE OF THE MIND

We have all seen particularly positive and inspiring people, individuals who have a large presence. This invisible but tangible presence is ki, and it is a central part of shodo and Japanese art. (This same concept can be found in Japanese spiritual traditions and martial arts. For example, consider the martial disciplines of aikido and aiki-jujutsu. The expression *aiki* includes the symbol for ki, and it suggests an act of combining with the ki that pervades nature.) In *Japan: Strategy of the Unseen*, Michel Random defines ki as

> Energy. The manifestation of the vital inner energy that is to be found in every man, and which is none other than the original creative energy of the earth and the Universe. . . . Ki is thus the fundamental energy of being, beyond physical, chemical or natural phenomena. Attention, mental force is itself ki, and therefore it can be directed into every part of the body or turned outwards towards the external world.[8]

One of the easiest ways to release and focus your ki is by making use of positive visualization. In shodo, students can visualize ki flowing from their fingertips and through the brush as a means of connecting themselves spiritually with their brush. This results in a coordination of hand, brush, and mind, which in turn results in greater control of your brush movements. You can also think of drawing lines of ki on your paper, slightly preceding each brush movement, as a way of helping yourself to produce straight lines and balanced characters. The focused, concentrated use of the mind focuses your ki in a powerful manner.

All of the above methods of projecting and focusing ki help to facilitate the coordination of mind, body, and brush. They also have profound implications in daily life, which I hope you will experiment with and discover on your own. Many of these uses of visualization and ki, as well as simple means of actually testing the power of ki, will be explored later in this book. For now, try thinking of ki as a natural biological link between the mind and body. In this sense, your mind can be seen as a form of refined ki, while your body may be thought of as unrefined ki. In an even larger context, ki has been described as "the fundamental building block of the universe"—the one, indivisible element underlying all aspects of creation. The principal lesson to bear in mind is: ki amounts to the power that enlivens every living thing, and the positive operation of the mind liberates it while the negative use of the mind gives rise to *ki ga nukeru* (the withdrawal and the weakening of ki).

Use the Mind with Full Concentration

In shodo as well as the Japanese healing arts and martial arts, countless examples exist of phenomenal exploits and exhibitions of mental and physical expertise. These exhibitions are frequently thought to be examples of the force of ki. In many instances, however, these apparently superhuman capabilities can be attributed to the positive and concentrated strength of the mind applied in combination with the body's force. Therefore, it can be said that the effectiveness of one's ki, and the ability to make use of ki, is directly connected to an individual's aptitude for positive thought and close attention. Just as the assertive use of the mind unleashes the energetic force of ki, the focused use of the mind permits you to firmly influence and focus your ki. Like most other tendencies, attention is a state that must be cultivated. It is critical for shodo students to think about what sort of training will permit them to grasp the power of attention.

Quite a few activities, ranging from seated meditation to Japanese yoga (which I encourage my pupils to engage in), can be used to cultivate the strength of close attention. However, it is not only conceivable to attain exceptional concentration by engaging in everyday conduct, it is essential to do so.

EXPERIMENTING WITH THE POWER OF ATTENTION

When do you lose your concentration, and consequently give up your awareness of the moment? For most of us, it is when we are doing something habitual, such as putting on our socks. Try to recall which sock went on first this morning. Can you do it? As you learn to be aware of this type of break in attention, you will start to cultivate unclouded consciousness and pure attention in daily life as well as art. This exercise of unchanging awareness may lead you to a peerless state of mind that leaves no opportunities for slips of the brush.

Have you ever become so obsessed with the end result of an action that you failed to concentrate on the activity taking place at that moment? Take a moment to reflect on this. Many of us do it all the

In the Japanese cultural arts, the cultivation of wa (harmony) is considered to be fundamental. Without this personal state of harmony, because the body and brush reflect the mind, one's calligraphy will become rough and unbalanced.

time. In shodo, some beginners are so concerned about eventually creating a great work of art that they do not adequately concentrate on the real learning process occurring at the present moment, and drift off into a sort of fantasy world. When people are trying to finish an undertaking in haste, they are inclined to sacrifice concentration. This, however, does not mean that it is impractical to act promptly and still be able to pay attention. The point is that you should be certain that you are truly concentrating when in a rush.

Many folks also are disposed to turn off their concentration to do something that they assume to be boring. Beginning disciples of most Japanese arts (including shodo), for instance, grapple with the numerous repetitions of fundamental drills required by their teacher. They often grow bored, failing to recognize that the essence of these arts rests in their basics, which must be ceaselessly practiced if they are to become automatic responses. Their seniors generally have no difficulty training important brush strokes regularly, as they are steadily scrutinizing and refining detailed aspects of these proven fundamentals.

Whether or not you can pay attention is, at least to some extent, determined by whether or not you have a positive spirit. Even if nothing of appeal can be discovered in a particular activity, it is still possible to use that activity as an interesting experiment or practice to help your concentration. In fact, paying attention to those actions that you expect are of no worth is another technique for developing vigorous powers of attention. What you deem to be useless is, of course, relative. By actually paying attention to particular activities, you can often spot worth where you had imagined none was present. This is especially meaningful for beginners in shodo, who learn that this art is not based on short-term rewards, and that the genuine importance of many parts of practice becomes obvious only after quite a number of repetitions. Keep your mind centered on any bodily action or brush movement, even when it appears to be of slight benefit (understanding that no uncondi-

tional measure of value is likely). You may discover that this is an effective means of cultivating potent attention.

People who decline to recognize the significance of concentrating
will unwittingly cultivate the opposite tendency of not being able to pay
attention even when they need to. Any repeated mental or physical act,
whether positive or negative in character, starts to build up in the subconscious to form a habit. Plus, contemporary information in experimental psychology suggests that the more energetically and attentively
we use our minds, the less worn out we become, on both mental and
physical levels.

Bearing this in mind, it seems reasonable to adopt the samurai's
principle of executing every feat in life as if it were for the last time.
Using shodo and painting as a visible demonstration of your capabil-
ity to unrelentingly utilize the mind in a positive and focused way, it is
possible to vitally transform yourself. It becomes natural to throw 100
percent of yourself into every moment, pour ki into each instant of life,
become thoroughly alive, and truly live as opposed to only existing.

To further your understanding of the power of attention, try the
following four experiments in your daily life. You may wish to work on
just one of these experiments each day for four days:

> 1. How often do you fail to concentrate on that which
> you are familiar with? Try to notice the exact moment
> and activity that provokes this lapse in concentration.

> 2. Are you able to keep your mind on things you are try-
> ing to do in a hurry? Take note of when you become pre-
> occupied with the result of an action, and when you lose
> consciousness of the actual process you are engaging in.

3. How often do you disturb the flow of attention, and thus the flow of ki, by failing to concentrate on that which you think is not interesting? What happens if you actually pay attention fully during such an activity?

4. How often do you lose your awareness of the moment, and therefore your concentration, when you are forced to participate in something you feel is of little value?

People tend to lose their power of attention under the above four circumstances. Taking note of this tendency, seeing its origins, and being sure to focus the mind at these times is a supremely effective method for developing concentration. It is also an ideal way to unify the body and mind, invigorate your ki, and cultivate positive character traits that are absolutely vital for producing art. The above methods have a long tradition in Japanese yoga, and they are equally valuable to students of shodo.

Use the Body Naturally

We are born, exist, and die as an element of nature. This is fairly clear, but many men and women do not think about its real significance or how it connects directly to their lives. Merely being part of nature is no warranty that we will behave naturally. Plants or animals seldom conduct themselves in an unnatural fashion incompatible with their innate makeup. But human beings have free will and must make the decision not only to be part of nature, but to conscientiously heed the laws of nature. Being in harmony with nature vitalizes your ki, because ki amounts to the animating force of nature itself.

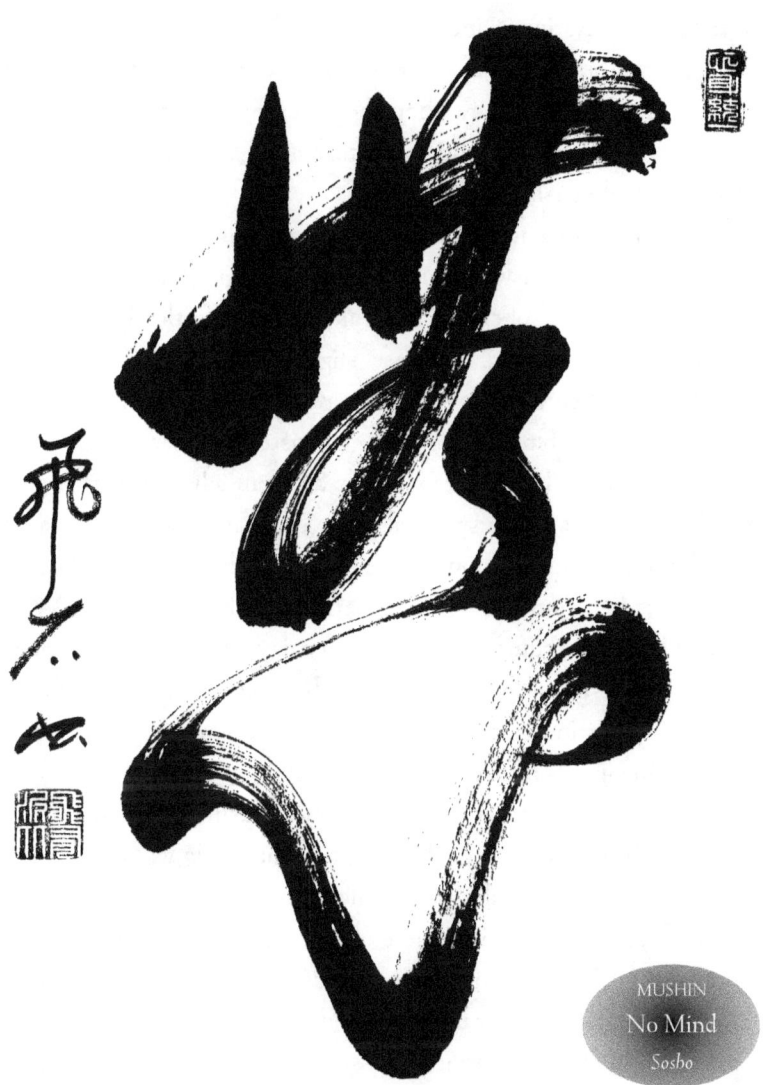

MUSHIN
No Mind
Sosho

To relax and pursue your genuine makeup is to be in agreement with nature. Relaxation is indispensable for learning shodo, and while various instructors of the Japanese fine arts acknowledge this, they are frequently at a loss as to how they should communicate it. Without a relaxed state, it is hard to realize balance, beauty, and power in Japanese ink painting and brush writing.

Shodo must extend to other aspects of living beyond moving a brush on paper. (Otherwise you are simply engaging in shuji, or hand-writing, not "the way of sho.") Even if you can effortlessly create one masterpiece after another, this has slight significance if your body breaks down. When a shodo student experiences stress-related illness-es such as elevated blood pressure or persistent headaches, it is clear that he or she has failed to obtain all the different advantages that come from pursuing the art as a spiritual path. Ultimately, the idea of art in shodo is comprehensive enough to encompass the study of relaxation and calmness in action as a way of experiencing the art of living. While few individuals are required to paint every day, many of us experience daily stress, and shodo (when it is correctly practiced as a form of medi-tation) can aid us in discovering the roots of nervousness and anxiety, as well as showing us how to resolve these problems.

If you do not discover how to stay cool during moments of pres-sure, it is doubtful that any of the methods you study will be fully real-ized. If you freeze mentally in a difficult predicament, you seize up bodily as well, and will be incapable of executing any competent action or brush stroke. Stressful moments arise as a matter of course in shodo and ink painting. The paper used for shodo can bleed easily if you pause too long. It can slip if too much pressure is applied to the brush, and because the brush hair is flexible you can never be absolutely certain which way it may twist or bend. To deal with uncertainty effectively and consistently produce art rather than pretty characters, you must understand the real nature of relaxation.

EXPERIMENTING WITH NATURALNESS AND RELAXATION

Try a simple experiment. Tense your arm as much as possible, and draw a circle rapidly in the air with your index finger. Do it over and over. Next, try relaxing your arm as much as possible, and draw the same rapid circle. For most of us, it is much easier to draw a quick, smooth, and dynamic circle in a state of relaxation.

Many people comprehend this, but few seem able to truly attain relaxation in activity. This is not because relaxation is unnatural or exceptionally complex. The dilemma stems from mistaken convictions and faulty habits (such as painting with the shoulders slightly lifted, which causes tense shoulders and headaches, instead of relaxing and allowing the shoulders to settle into their suitable spot naturally). Many either consciously or unconsciously believe that relaxation is comfortable but powerless. They think that relaxation does not permit a person to display noteworthy physical force. So, when they attempt to produce a particularly dynamic-looking character, they also frequently produce tension. This tension, in turn, creates something that, to the discerning eye, actually looks rough rather than dynamic. Some individuals have even come to believe that when they are relaxed they are not working seriously or giving their all.

Once this impression becomes part of your subconscious, it sways all of your conscious responses. In a pinch, or during a stressful moment while painting, you'll discover yourself unable to relax although you wish to. As you consciously teach yourself to relax and remain peace-

267

ful during troublesome moments in painting, you'll also cultivate the capacity to relax under pressure as a subconscious habit, which will influence your everyday life.

Understand that both positive and negative kinds of relaxation exist. For many of us, the difference between the two is not crystal clear. Clearing up the distinction between these two states has been spoken of in the Japanese fine arts, as well as martial arts, since antiquity. The *Tengu-geijutsu-ron*, composed in 1730, declares, "Weakness and softness are not the same. Rest and slackness again are not the same. Rest does not let go the living ki; slackness is near to dead ki."[9]

Positive relaxation suggests an energetic posture in which the mind and body are one. When the mind and body perform as a unit, we are in our most relaxed and serene condition, but we are likewise filled with energy. Negative relaxation is to relax without this structure of coordination. It is a form of physical and mental limpness, one that results in giving up vitality and alertness. Positive relaxation is filled with energy but does not contain unneeded tension.

In shodo, and in daily living, you want to grasp a posture and demeanor that is not tense or flaccid—an alive state that is poised between tension and limpness. Relaxation and collapse are not the same, and each causes opposite results in terms of mind-body oneness and the free flow of ki. As an experiment, try to notice in your daily life when you fall limp and when you grow tense. What is your state of mind at these times? When do you most often fall into these two conditions? By understanding the nature of tension—and its opposite, limpness—you can find the middle path of positive relaxation.

We often assume that the opposite of tension is relaxation, but is this true? By observing yourself in a state free from preconceived ideas, you may discover that the opposite of tension is collapse, and relaxation is a different state altogether … a state balanced between and transcending opposites, in which your ki flows freely with that of nature.

THE HARA

One of nature's foundations is the law of gravity. This uncomplicated fact, like many others, has the capacity to bring about deep transformations in the way you choose to act in life and in calligraphy.

Because everything in nature tends to settle or drop downward, if you wish to relax and cooperate with nature, you need to permit the weight of your body to settle downward in a natural and relaxed manner. A stable and hence calm object's center of gravity has inherently settled to a comparatively low spot, while a wobbly object has a higher center of gravity.

Even if nothing of appeal can be discovered in a particular activity, it is still possible to use that activity as an interesting experiment or practice to help your concentration. In fact, paying attention to those actions that you expect are of no worth is another technique for developing vigorous powers of attention.

If you take up a thoroughly upright, aligned position that does not sag or cause you to slouch, your upper body's weight descends to a point beneath the navel. This place equates to your bodily center of gravity and center of balance. In the Japanese fine arts, healing arts, and martial arts, it is ordinarily alluded to as your hara, an idea with a lengthy and elaborate practice in Japan. According to Michel Random:

> The hara designates the area of the lower stomach, situated below the navel. For the Japanese this area is the origi-

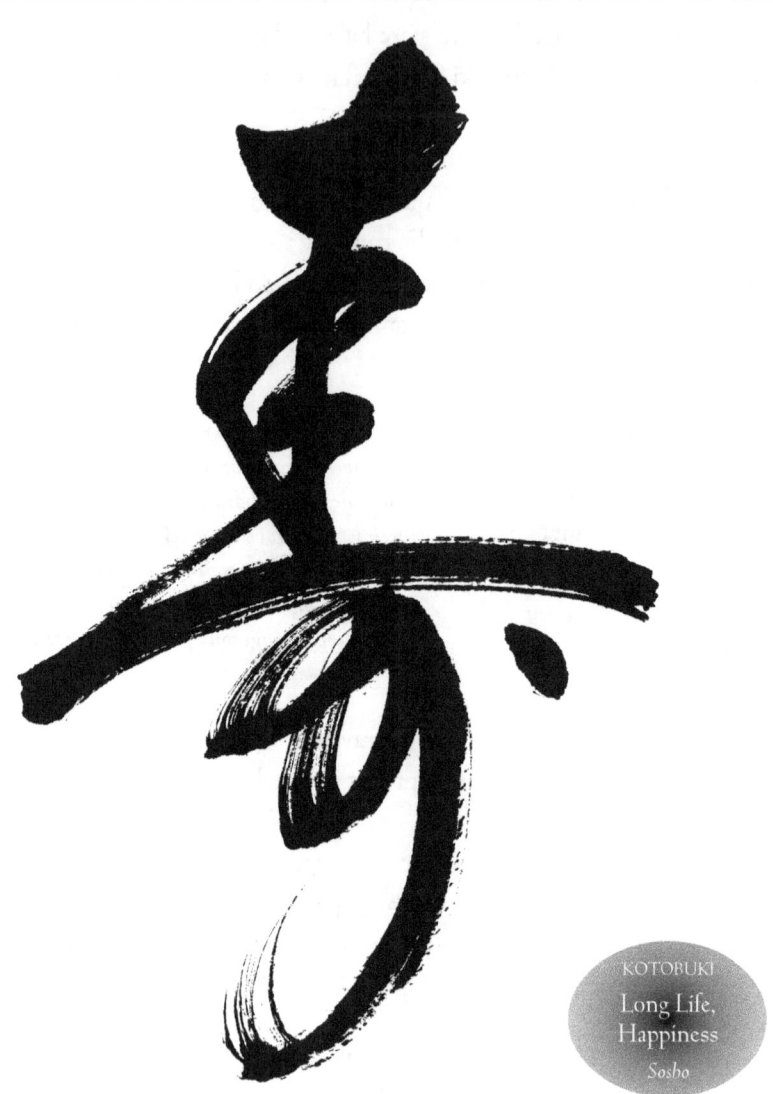

KOTOBUKI
Long Life,
Happiness
Sosho

nal centre of man, the centre of psychic gravity where the deep vital forces are concentrated. It is through the hara that a man communicates with the primordial unity of all things.[10]

Traditionally in Japan, people have supposed that if a person is going to exhibit his or her highest power, he or she must center all strength in the abdomen. On one level, this widespread idea is accurate. More specifically, however, you must concentrate the mind's energy and attention in the lower abdomen, or tanden. Still more specifically, an individual should focus his or her energy at a point, or natural center, in the tanden. This point is frequently thought to be three sun beneath the bellybutton. ("Sun" is a traditional Japanese measurement; three sun is about 3.6 inches. The correct point for a larger-bodied Westerner may be even lower below the navel.) If you embrace an upright, relaxed posture, your center of gravity falls to this place in the lower abdomen, which conforms to your center of balance. By paying close attention to this point, you can securely coordinate the mind and body, obtaining a positive kind of relaxation. This accord of mind and body, in turn, results in an especially steady posture and vigorous psychophysical state. (It is crucial to remember that in shodo, if your posture is unstable, the characters you paint will also be wobbly and off balance. Yet, the means of arriving at stability of posture is not always what you assume it to be.)

This relaxed posture is amazingly powerful, and it is stable to the point of being outwardly immovable. (An example of the power inherent in a posture centered in the hara can be found on page 291.) In this condition you are immediately capable of rapid response and flow-

271

ing brush movement. By regularly studying, via shodo, the distinctions between slackness, relaxation, and tension, you can impress these important differences upon the subconscious and in turn give birth to a vital or positive state of relaxation. In so doing, you can teach yourself to sustain a tranquil but vigorous condition in which you are equipped to confidently handle any emergency or stressful moment in painting.

By being mindful of your posture, you can cultivate a sort of usable relaxation, which, owing to its effective and vigorous constitution, can be put to use as well as preserved, even when you are under excessive pressure. Fundamentally, you need to sidestep a posture that is sagging and seems diminutive, collapsed, or withdrawn. You likewise want to avoid taking up a stiff posture when facing the paper to paint. Quick brush movement from such a position is troublesome. While you might be able to perform from a rigid posture given enough practice, and while an overly erect position has been advocated in certain shodo books, both are incompatible with free and spontaneous brush action.

When you use shodo to examine and expand your capacity to stay relaxed under strain, it becomes more than mere brush writing; it can be thought of as a moving meditation that permits you to cultivate genuine and unshakable composure. In shodo and in everyday life, serenity is strength.

Train the Body Gradually, Systematically, and Continuously

Shodo practice is a kind of physical activity, and it is necessary that training in this fine art be managed in a natural way. Without ease in training your body, you can rarely perform with maximum efficiency.

You can even sustain physical impairment, making ongoing practice difficult. Perhaps thinking of painting as a physical activity seems strange. But it is not uncommon for serious calligraphers to sit in one position for two or three hours at a time when giving lessons or working intently on a particular piece of art. If the body is held in a tense or unnatural way for an extended period of time, stiff shoulders and backaches are only two of the possible negative results. (Calligraphers and painters can fall prey to repetitive-stress-related problems such as tendinitis if the training of their body is not conducted in a natural, gradual, and regular manner.)

When poetry is painted on long sheets of paper, or if the artist is writing one large character using a big brush, the art of painting becomes even more physical in nature. Under such circumstances, we often squat over the paper, moving our bodies as we brush each stroke. In other cases, the calligrapher is standing but bending at a near ninety-degree angle and adjusting his or her bodily position as he or she paints. In shodo you paint with your whole body. If your artwork is produced on a small scale, your body movements are correspondingly small, but when you work on larger paintings, your physical actions grow in size. In Asia, it has traditionally been held that shodo and sumi-e experts enjoy exceptional health as well as longevity due to their cultivation of fine posture, calm and deep breathing, and physical flexibility.

In shodo, and in daily living, you want to grasp a posture and demeanor that is not tense or flaccid—an alive state that is poised between tension and limpness. Relaxation and collapse are not the same, and each causes opposite results in terms of mind-body oneness and the free flow of ki.

273

This state of improved health is only arrived at when you use your body naturally and train it continuously. Practicing irregularly does not produce results and allows the mind and body to fall out of condition. It is preferable to paint a modest amount on a continual basis than to practice a great deal from time to time.

Bear in mind that your body must be drilled in a gradual fashion to avoid future physical damage. How gradually an individual builds up to painting for longer periods is decided to a degree by that person's age and bodily state.

Your brain and body are in a perpetual state of change. The remarkable benefits of shodo training rest in a lifelong process of participation. If you discontinue your practice, no matter how long you have been painting or how skillful you are, both your soundness and competence will decline. Shodo training is helpful only as long as one is, in some manner, truly engaging in it.

Once in a while, students of the Japanese cultural arts question if the liberal amount of time they put into their training is worth what they are getting out of it. While this appears to be a sensible inquiry, it actually reveals a basic lack of comprehension about the Japanese arts, which is, sadly, not unusual. In essence, the time you put into the training of an art is what you are getting out of it. The process of practicing is what's actually helpful, not some future aim or outgrowth of practice. All of existence exists exclusively at this moment. The past and the future, in a way, dwell only in our thinking as self-constructed, artificial realities. In the classical Japanese arts, you must train to repose calmly in the instant, and in your timeless perception of the moment, you grasp a state transcending duality—a condition that is both everlasting and boundless.

Shodo training is the objective. Accordingly, to practice shodo with authentic awareness is also to realize the superior benefits of sho-do itself.

Through gradual, uninterrupted, and systematic shodo exercise, you can continue developing even as you grow old, because the art is essentially a never-ending meditation. Shodo is an art form that has existed for generations in Asia and still remains capable of vitally improving the lives of its followers for many generations to come.

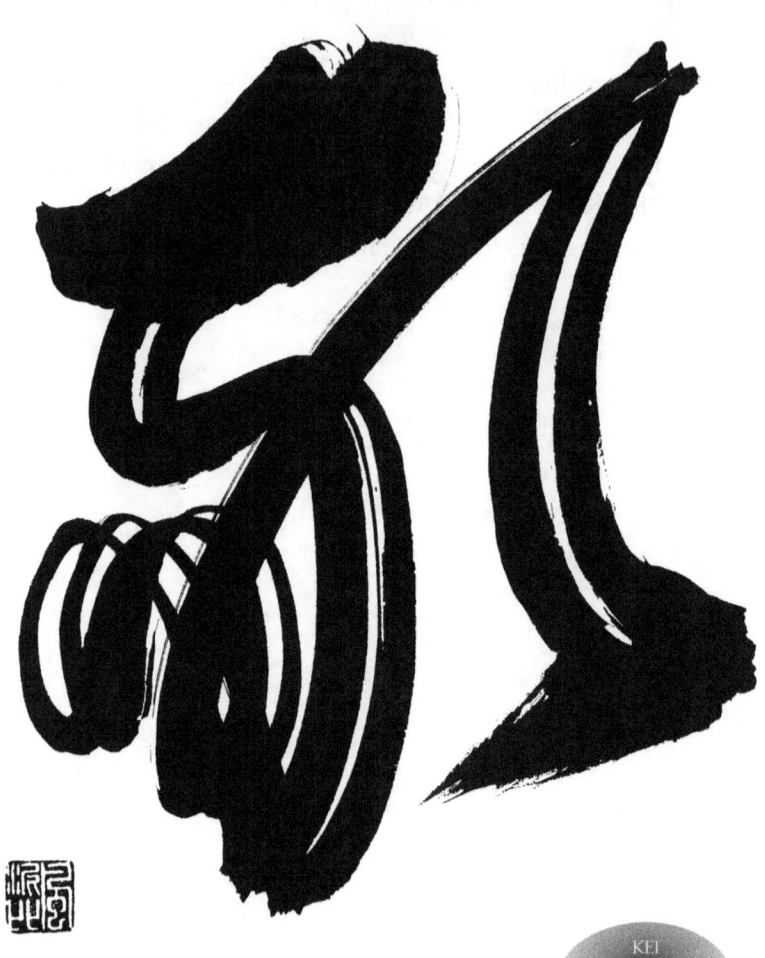

KEI
Respect
Sosho

Chapter 3

UNITING MIND, BODY & BRUSH

PRIMARY PRINCIPLES FOR BRUSH CONTROL AND MEDITATION

1. Grip the brush gently and focus your ki through the brush tip.

2. Before touching the paper, the tip of the brush must be calm.

3. Relax to let the brush move naturally and with rhythm.

4. The brush follows the movement of ki.

5. Do not cut off your stream of attention.

Obviously, the brush does not move by itself. Remember, it is the mind that moves the brush (or fude in Japanese), and any legitimate study of technique must be accompanied by a parallel investigation into your psychological state. Your brush is a kind of surrogate for your own degree of spiritual development. That is the fundamental premise of this book, and to the extent that you master the principles for brush control and meditation that follow, you are in a better position to broaden yourself spiritually. You will also have a far better chance of producing top-notch calligraphy.

Grip the Brush Gently and
Focus Your Ki through the Brush Tip

Physically speaking, shodo begins with the student's grip on the brush. Unless a suitable technique of gripping is mastered, no advancement is possible. Figure 10 and Figure 11 show the correct method of holding the brush. Examine the photos closely, as several important points are illustrated.

First, your elbow should not stick up or out to an excessive degree. This would only create an unsettling of the arm's weight as well as produce tension in the muscles of the arm and shoulder. This tension can cause your flow of ki to clog in the shoulders and not be effectively transmitted through the brush into the painting. This point is important, and various Japanese calligraphy authorities have made note of its significance. In *Zen and the Art of Calligraphy*, the Zen master Omori Sogen Roshi, referring to his calligraphy teacher, writes:

> The work of a Zen artist, on the other hand, is permeated by what Hakuin called the "overwhelming force of enlightened vision." That force is *kiai*. Ki, the energy of the cosmos, is always present but remains dormant if not cultivated. Kiai is to be full of ki; it is incorporated in the ink as *bokki*.
>
> Setsudo wrote that "bokki is not, as most people believe, the colour of the ink, and does not depend on the quality of the brush, ink, and paper. If one's ki is not extended into the work, the bokki is dead." The clarity of the bokki is not seen with the eyes, it is sensed with

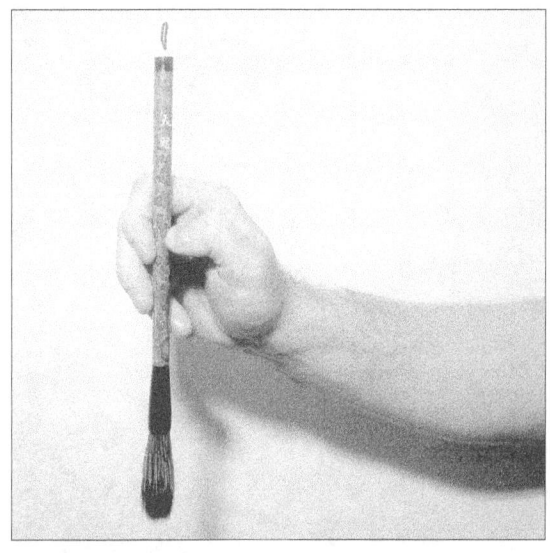

FIG. 10. Hold the brush stem perpendicular to the paper and bend the wrist slightly backward. The grip is supple but firm.

the hara, the physical and spiritual centre of one's body. Bokki reveals the calligrapher's inner light.[11]

At the same time, do not let your elbow sag or droop. As discussed on pages 267–69, positive relaxation is not the same as a state of collapse. When your elbow sags heavily toward the ground, it also tends to rub against the body and produces a cramped feeling that is expressed in your artwork. You should feel that your elbow is floating in a settled position a few inches from your body.

Next, notice that the brush stem is perpendicular to the paper. This can only be accomplished if your wrist is allowed to bend somewhat backward. If the top of your wrist bends upward, so that your palm turns in toward you, your elbow will also come out and your arm's weight will grow unsettled. Tension is created yet again.

279

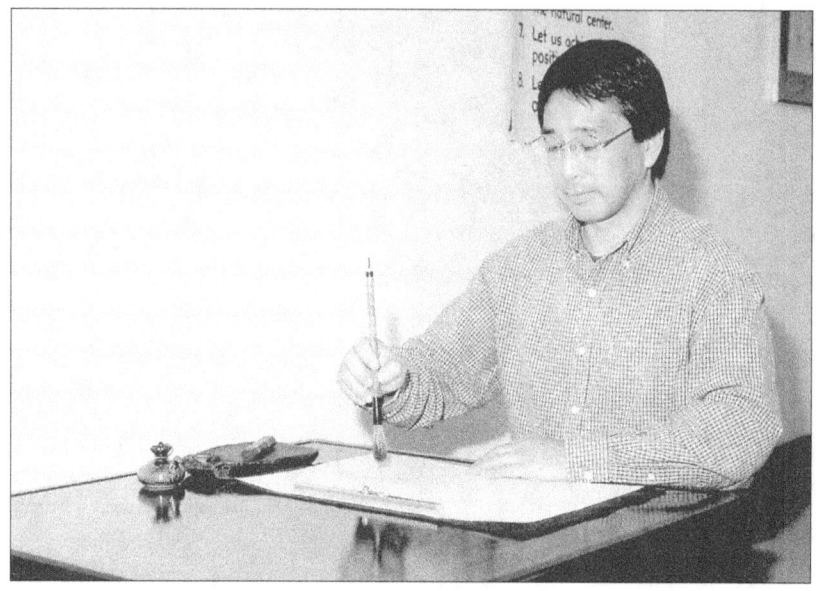

FIG. 11. Do not let your elbow stick out or droop but hold it in a state of "positive relaxation."

Some instructors have tried to abruptly pluck the brush from the student's hand as a means of testing the handhold.[12] An ink-covered hand would announce an incorrectly controlled fude. Squeezing tightly is not the solution, because this does not generate graceful, dynamic characters. Flaccidly gripping, on the other hand, results solely in a loss of brush control. It is imperative to find out how to grasp the brush in a manner that is neither tight nor slack, with a sort of "alive" handhold in which your ki is propelled from downward-pointing fingers through the fude, out of the tip, and into the paper. This supple but firm hold is vital and has been characterized as *ki de toru* (grasping with ki).

Following are four experiments that will help you learn not only how to hold the brush correctly, but also how to harmonize your mind and fude.

EXPERIMENT #1

Grip the center of the brush stem as illustrated in Figures 10 and 11. Ask a friend to grasp the top of the brush stem. Focus your mind on the place on the brush that your friend is holding. At this point, he or she, while holding the brush stem from above your grip, should start to slowly and gently lift upward. Note how much force is required to make the fude slip from your fingers or to cause your entire arm to come up (if your grip is not lost).

Now, holding the brush firmly but without tension, visualize a stream of ki flowing through the brush stem, through the bristles, into the paper, and continuing endlessly. The other person should try to gradually pull the brush stem upward again, slowly so as not to cause a loss of concentration, and using the same force as before. If your concentration and stream of ki are unbroken, the fude should be much more difficult to move, if it is not, in fact, immovable. (In this way, you become one with the brush, it will easily follow your mental commands, and accurate painting is much more readily accomplished.) This is an experiment, not a sort of competition, so it involves calmly comparing two different states, utilizing similar amounts of force.

EXPERIMENT #2

Next, try concentrating on the area of the brush stem that you are grasping, thus stopping the movement of ki in that spot. Your partner applies upward pressure as before. The brush will probably move. Follow that action by focusing ki through the brush, out of the tip, and

continuing infinitely. This time, the brush grip should remain undisturbed. In each case, your friend should gradually pull up on the brush
stem. Make sure that you do not shift your point of attention when
pressure is applied to the brush.

If concentration is maintained, and you do not tense up when your
friend pulls on the brush, the grip on the fude will be extremely solid.
This reveals a central point in shodo: if the mind becomes attached to
a particular thought or place, and the movement of ki freezes, mind
and brush coordination and control is lost. Kobara Ranseki Sensei emphasizes that your mind should not be stuck on the brush but
should instead be directed toward the brush strokes taking place on
your paper. In a special article written for the *Nihon Keizai* newspaper,
Kobara Sensei elucidated:

> I always explain when [my students] eat delicious food,
> at that moment, they become unconscious of the eat-
> ing utensils. Shodo is just the same as this. They must
> be unconscious of, and transcend the brush, thus act-
> ing spontaneously. To accomplish this, students must
> practice severely, every day, until they forget the brush,
> and make strokes freely. Calligraphers should not worry
> about gaining the teacher's admiration, or putting their
> art in exhibitions. They must forget the brush, and sim-
> ply practice in a state free from anxiety about results.[13]

EXPERIMENT #3

This experiment involves a more physical perspective with the flow
of ki. Take a look at Figure 10 and Figure 11 again, and notice that the

fingers gripping the brush are pointing downward, roughly perpendicular to the paper and in line with the movement of ki. This grip unifies
the mind and brush.

Hold the brush incorrectly, so that the fingertips point toward a
wall (parallel to the paper), but focus your mind on the tip of the brush
as before. Ask your friend to pull up as before. Most likely, the brush
will be moved despite your downward focus of attention. This clearly
shows that not only must ki be directed toward the paper, but your
fingertips must also be pointed in a similar direction. The mind and
body must function as one.

Now, imitating the photo (with your fingertips pointing downward) and directing ki from the brush tip, ask your friend to pull up
on the fude. If you are gripping correctly, the brush will be glued to
your hand. (Another central point when holding a fude is to make sure
that you grip with your fingertips, not your fingers or the sides of your
fingers. This is not to say that the sides of the fingers and knuckles are
not in contact with the brush stem, but that the main points of contact
are the fingertips.)

Before Touching the Paper, the Tip of the Brush Must Be Calm

With practice, unifying your ki with the brush and holding the
brush correctly become unconscious actions. For beginners, however,
briefly checking your grip and aligning your ki with the brush is a
necessary first action. Next, note if the tip of the fude is motionless or
shaking. A swaying brush not only makes it hard to paint stable characters, it reveals a rickety, nervous mental condition. Again, in shodo

the body reflects the mind. When your brush tip starts to tremble, this is often an indication of a break in composure and concentration and is an opportunity to lose control of the brush. By studying shodo, it becomes clear that in art, as in daily life, the mind and body are interconnected.

Suppose you notice that the tip of your fude is wobbling. One common reaction is to squeeze the brush more tightly, or in some way try to restrain its movement. Unfortunately, this usually only causes the brush tip to shake even more. Why? Imagine you are sitting in a pool of water. You notice that the water is not calm; you are surrounded by waves. One reaction is to take your hands and rub them across the surface of the water in an attempt to smooth out the waves. Obviously, trying to force the water to be calm will only make more waves. If you simply sit still, assuming no other external forces are at work, the waves will gradually diminish of their own accord. All water contains waves, but the closer you come to doing nothing, the more the size of the waves reduces.

If the mind becomes attached to a particular thought or place, and the movement of ki freezes, mind and brush coordination and control is lost.

Likewise, we all give off a brain-wave pattern, but some patterns are more calm than others. Your brush tip is a reflection of your brain waves, and the more you try to force it to be still, the more "waves" you create in your mind. (In a related example, many of us have figured out that if we deliberately try to fall asleep, our very desire to sleep will frequently keep us awake.)

Sometimes, even though you feel like you are doing nothing, your

284

brush tip and mind continue to shake. In such a case, to paraphrase Zen, you can try doing something that leads to doing nothing. Following is an exercise in calmness to help you understand this more fully.

EXPERIMENT #4

Hold the brush correctly above the paper. With your elbow down and in the proper position, move the brush repeatedly from left to right in an arc of about a foot. As you do this, focus your mind intently on the movement of the brush tip. Gradually make the size of the arc smaller and smaller. Keep your mind centered on the brush tip, and your brain-wave pattern will also grow smaller as well as calmer. In a short while, the movement will become so small that it is not outwardly discernible, but be sure to let the feeling of stillness that has just been generated continue infinitely.

If you are having trouble imagining what all of this should look like, tie a rock or relatively heavy object to a string. Start it swinging from side to side, then do nothing but hold your hand still. The object's arc will gradually become smaller and smaller, until it seems to be hanging motionless. You are doing something similar with your brush, except that you want to allow the sensation of endless reduction to continue within you. Once you get the hang of it, this trick should help you to calm the movement of your fude even when your projection of life energy through the brush has not been sufficient. This exercise is not only an effective means of stilling the brush and mind, but has the ultimate potential to lead you to a state of transcendence that is both endless and eternal.

Relax to Let the Brush Move
Naturally and with Rhythm

Shodo has a visible rhythm. Although the kanji (Chinese characters) are at rest on the paper, they must seem as though they are in motion. This is *dochu no sei* (stillness in motion), which is frequently alluded to in esoteric manuals of Japanese philosophy and religion. Its opposite is "motion in stillness." The harmony of these two conditions results in accomplished shodo.

Shodo is moving meditation, and as such it acknowledges that we are repeatedly in motion in daily activities. You must learn to remain calm and relaxed within action if you wish to translate the meditative state into your life. Shodo will help you discover exceptional levels of calmness in the midst of dynamic activity.

Before performing any action, including brush movements, it is important to center yourself in the lower abdomen. With a fully erect posture, relaxed but not limp, your upper body weight will reach its highest point of density in the hara. Concentrating on this spot is a helpful way to facilitate the settling and stabilizing of your body's weight and has a calming effect on the mind.

As you move the brush, you must maintain a posture that is relaxed, upright, and aligned. Figure 12 illustrates the correct posture for sitting in a chair. Figure 13 shows the proper position for sitting in seiza. (Seiza is a traditional Japanese way of sitting that is used for both meditation and painting. You sit lightly on the heels, with the big toes crossed on top of each other and some space between the knees. Although seiza is difficult at first, it is particularly effective for centering your weight forward and down into the lower abdomen. When

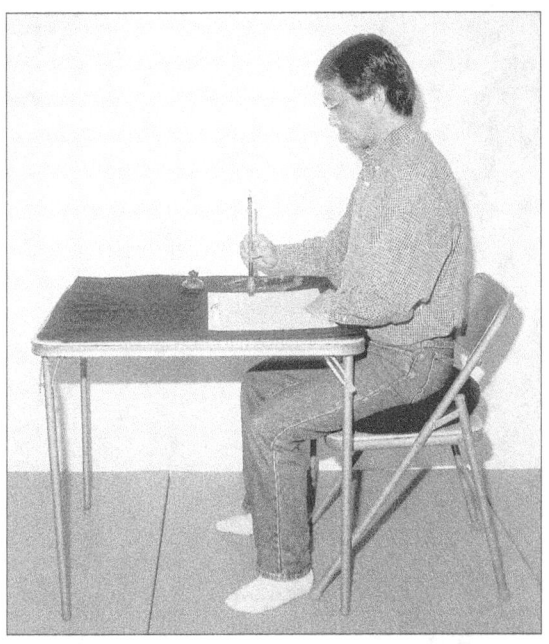

FIG. 12. The correct posture for sitting in a chair. Keep your feet flat on the floor or tucked under the chair so that you maintain a natural lumbar curve and shift the weight toward the front surface of the lower abdomen.

you're painting large pictures or calligraphic works, it is often advisable to stand. However, none of the painting exercises depicted in this book require standing.)

Several points are important if you are to take up a correct posture and paint freely. Do not slump or raise the shoulders, as illustrated in Figure 14. Sit down lightly, almost as if your bottom were sore, and maintain a posture that looks big, as discussed on page 269. Make sure that your table is not too high, as this can cause your shoulders to rise and tension to form.

Often when you're painting, you'll find that your head starts to sag forward while your neck collapses, bends, shortens, and produces a hump at its base. The rest of the spine soon curves in on itself as well.

287

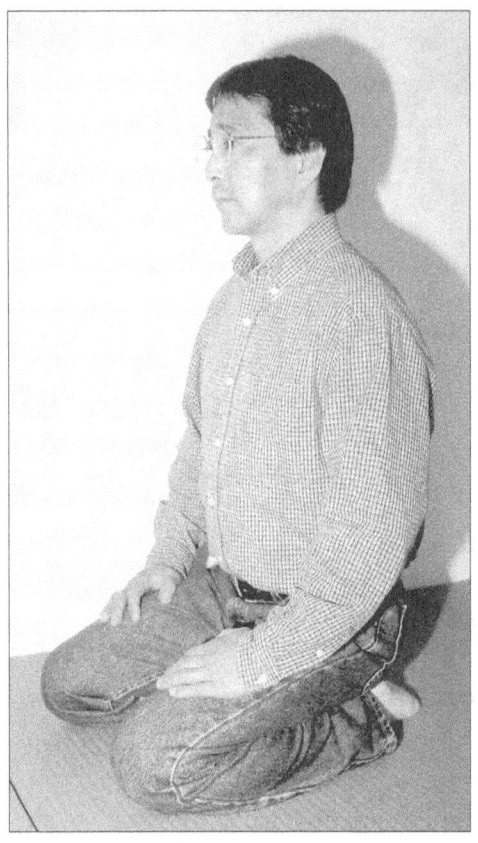

FIG. 13. The correct position for sitting in seiza. Seiza is effective for centering your weight forward and down into the lower abdomen.

You can alter this by centering yourself in the hara and by correcting your posture with the movement of your head. Mentally release your muscles, particularly along the neck and spine. Visualizing your hara as a sort of anchor, direct the top of your head up and away from your hara, then draw your chin and head back into alignment with your lower abdomen. Allow your spine and neck to lengthen until your posture is aligned. (Envisioning the muscles along the spine growing longer and

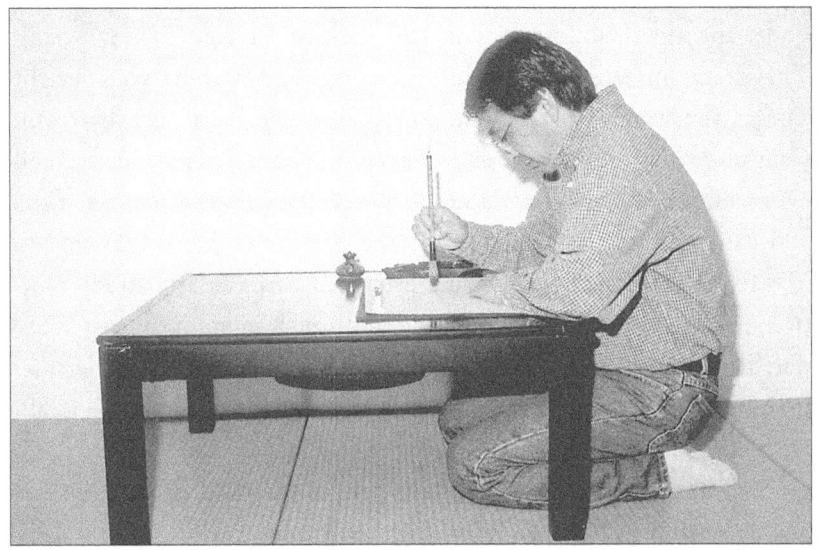

FIG. 14. This spine and shoulder posture is INCORRECT. Letting your head sag forward brings the neck and back out of proper alignment. To correct this, recenter the hara and adjust your posture by repositioning your head.

wider is an effective technique to use at this point.) If you concentrate deeply and relax, your body will move slowly into the correct position with little conscious effort on your part. But be careful not to force your body into an overly erect posture.

By relaxing and using visualization, you should also let your chest expand while your back and shoulders widen. In most cases, your ears, shoulders, and pelvis should be parallel to the floor, as is your table and paper. Your head, shoulders, and pelvis should not be twisted. Avoid sitting with legs outstretched, as this causes your pelvis to roll backward and your lumbar region to curve outward in a slump. When you're sitting in a chair, try to keep your feet flat on the floor or tucked under the chair (almost as your legs tuck under your hips in seiza). This maintains your natural lumbar curve, and it shifts your weight toward the front surface of the lower abdomen—exactly where you want to center your weight and mind in the hara. Relax your face and eyes, and find the most comfortable posture within the context of the above instructions.

Because this act of centering produces a particularly steady position, it frees you to move your hand and brush in an open, easy manner. To sustain this free and relaxed condition of stability, avoid leaning in an unbalanced way, as the upper body's weight must be in equilibrium at the hara.

All of the above postural points can be practiced in daily life and should result in a healthier, more tension-free life.

EXPERIMENT #5

This experiment will give you some idea of the power and stability of sitting with hara. In *Meditation Gut Enlightenment: The Way of Hara*, Haruo Yamaoka describes a means of testing the unique power of this natural center in the lower abdomen:

> Sit seiza (legs underneath). Fill your mind with thoughts and tense the muscles in your shoulders and neck. Next, have someone stand behind you, place his hands on both sides of your hip area, and push. He will be able to slide you across the floor very easily. If he should push around your shoulder area, you will fall over.
>
> Next, while you are in the same position, remove all tension from your shoulders and neck. Relax your arms.

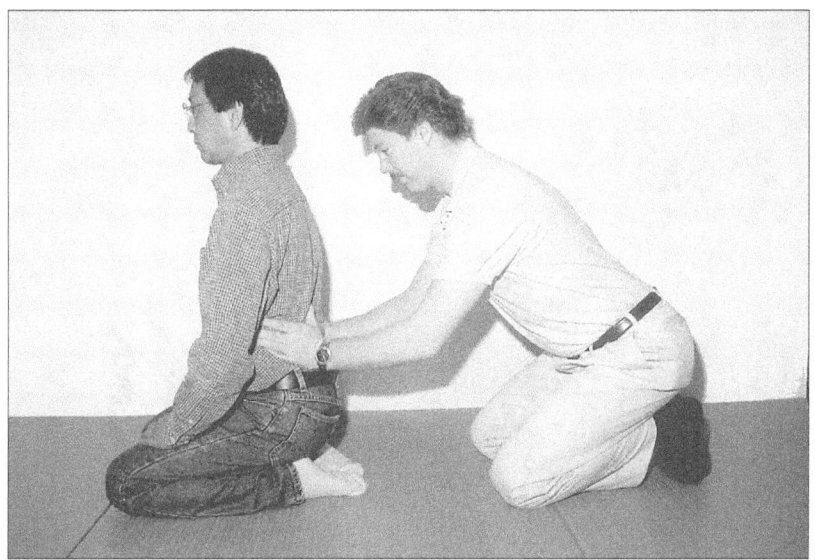

FIG. 15. Ask a partner to help you test your ability to stabilize the mind in the hara and realize a deeper sense of body-mind coordination.

In other words, relax the upper portion of your body. Focus on your hara. As you focus on your hara, your mind will become empty naturally. Ask your partner to push from behind as before. This time he will not be able to slide you across the floor. You will be firm, rigid, but relaxed. Most important, you will be in balance.[14]

Figure 15 shows what is being described here. Slowly and carefully try this experiment, as a means of grasping correct posture, learning more about stabilizing the mind in the hara, and understanding

POEM BY RIKYU

*Sosho kanji,
hentaigana, kana*

一をもり習ひしつくし
稽古とは

十よりかへるもとのその一

In your practice
Start by learning one
And continue until you understand ten.
From ten you must return
To the original one.

Keiko to wa
Ichi yori narai
Ju o shiri
Ju yori kaeru
Moto no sono ichi

the power derived from doing so. (Remember, in life and shodo the body mirrors the mind.) This is not only an experiment but a challenge to your ability to remain composed under pressure. You may have to practice for a while to achieve these results. Nonetheless, by performing these exercises with a partner in a gentle, noncompetitive style and freeing the mind from anxiety about results, you can realize a deeper sense of body-mind coordination.

In addition to being centered and focusing the mind at your hara, you also need to hit upon a kind of relaxed concentration. In *The Anatomy of Change*, Richard Heckler advises:

> It is important to remember that center is a state of being that is not confined to a certain posture or a constantly held image. . . . It is not that we have to find our center and then maintain it at all costs. Center is more a reference point to return to, so we can relate to our life situations in a complete way. . . . Sweeping through our bodily dimensions with the attention, to feel an overall balance, is the first step in touching the state of center. We line up our structure in order to touch that balance within. Being in balanced form opens the opportunity to feel oneself, and the dimension of feeling is directly related to center.[15]

Once you are centered in the hara, the body relaxes, and if that centering continues, the body remains relaxed. This is essential to avoid impeding the flow of ki, and in turn the dynamic flow of the brush itself. If you are to practice shodo as moving meditation, relaxation is vital. Relaxation, however, comes only with naturalness. If you feel tension in any part of your body during any brush movement, it is necessary to examine your posture and way of moving for unnaturalness. (The brush movement might be overextended or cramped by poor posture.)

THE FEEL AND RHYTHM OF RELAXATION

How can you tell, with any certainty, that a position or action is truly relaxed and natural? Try pausing at varying points in the painting process. Hold the position for thirty seconds or so, and notice if you can feel the muscles in any part of your body. If you detect a strong muscular sensation in any body part, what you are sensing is usually tension.

Muscles that are fully relaxed produce no powerful sensation, so you should be able to freeze at any time and in any position while painting and not feel your muscles. (If you cannot, you are moving in an unnatural manner, and it is vital to realize what kind of motion or posture is producing the tension and alter it.) When you create no sensation of tension, you are painting correctly. You become unconscious of your body and self. This, of course, is not numbness or a lack of awareness; it is a serene condition, so relaxed as not to be felt. At any moment of peak performance, in any activity, people tend to forget themselves. They are aware only of the instant and the action taking place. This is muga-ichi nen, (no self–one thought), and it is this mental state that allows shodo to transcend mere skillful writing.

You must learn to remain calm and relaxed within action if you wish to translate the meditative state into your life. Shodo will help you discover exceptional levels of calmness in the midst of dynamic activity.

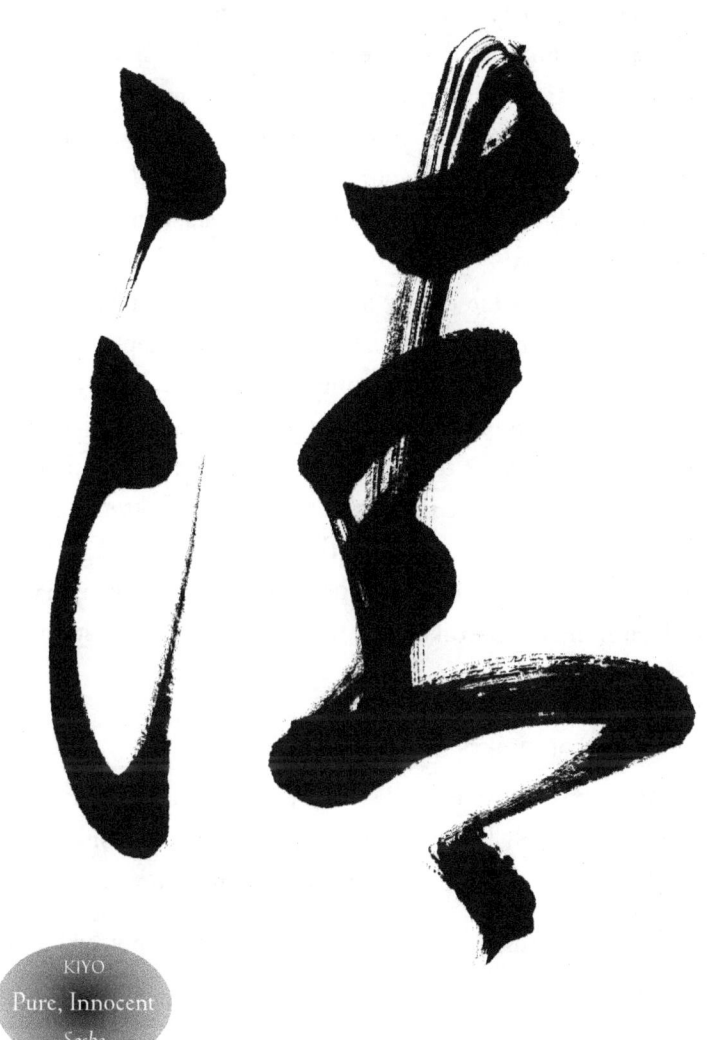

KIYO
Pure, Innocent
Sosho

As you continue to move the brush, maintain a constant cadence. Rhythm both indicates and promotes coordination, and all arts, including shodo and ink painting, have a unique rhythm. Each Japanese character has a particular cadence with which it is painted. Find the correct rhythm and maintain it to excel in painting. Breaks in rhythm reveal breaks in coordination of your body and mind. They usually happen when the flow of ki is broken during a lapse in mindfulness or a moment of tension.

The stream of life energy must continue in a stable rhythm from one character to the next until a line of words is completed. Your entire composition ought to sustain a unified appearance of rhythm. (Beginners should remember that lines of Japanese characters are traditionally written from right to left on a page, and in shodo characters are usually painted from the top of the paper to the bottom.) To produce this dynamic yet balanced feeling, the brush flows in an unconstrained and easy form within each character. Every kanji and kana has a predetermined number of strokes that must be brushed in a strictly defined order.

STROKE ORDERS FOR RHYTHMIC SHODO

While it is always possible to look up a kanji's correct stroke order in a Japanese-English kanji dictionary, the following simple rules are helpful for beginners trying to master rhythm in shodo:

1. The brush stroke order is from top to bottom of a kanji.

2. The brush stroke order is from left to right of a kanji.

3. When two or more brush strokes cross, horizontal strokes precede perpendicular ones (but there are some notable exceptions to this rule).

4. Paint the center component of a kanji first, then the left, followed by the right components.

5. If a perpendicular line runs through the center of the character, it is painted last.

6. Right-to-left diagonal brush strokes precede left-to-right diagonal strokes within a kanji.

These points should help in getting acquainted with the stroke order of Japanese phonetic symbols and Chinese characters, which is essential for a consistent rhythm. (Perhaps the most basic rule is to check a dictionary when in doubt.) Remember that within the framework of each character, the brush should move smoothly from one stroke to the next.

Once you start to practice the various compositions in this book, you will have a chance to work with rhythm in shodo. To help facilitate an unbroken rhythm and flow of ki, try counting out loud as you make each brush stroke. (In many cases throughout this book, you will find small numbers next to each brush stroke in a given kanji. These numbers indicate stroke order but can also be used to help master rhythm.) Try to count each stroke as you would a musical beat. Allow about one second per beat.

As you progress in shodo, you will discover that the rhythm between (and during) certain strokes will speed up but at other times

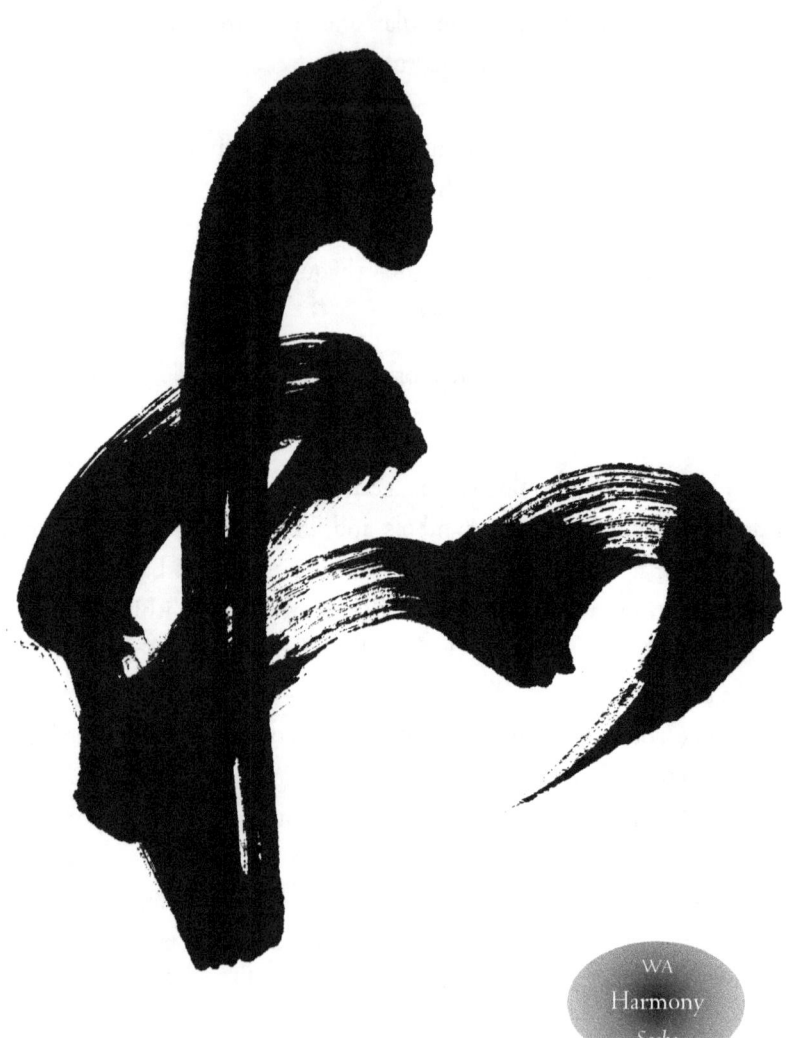

WA
Harmony
Sosho

will slow down. This is something that must be learned with a qualified teacher and through ongoing experience. While the rhythm of the strokes is rarely broken in shodo, you will not necessarily always paint at the same speed at varying points within a character. This is particularly true as you become more advanced in the art.

In a larger context, nature has its own rhythm. To discover that rhythm, through shodo and/or painting, is a fascinating and never-ending pursuit. Your highest objective in shodo, then, is to become one with the vibrant rhythm of nature and to let this pulsation flow out through the brush.

The Brush Follows the Movement of Ki

Your spirit controls your brush or, in everyday life, your body. For a split second, the student needs to powerfully concentrate on the character to be painted, and then without faltering move the brush in a relaxed fashion. In this way, the artist prevails mentally before even contacting the paper.

Practice seeing the image on paper before you move the brush. The instant you have a clear picture in your mind, apply the brush to the paper without the slightest delay. (While the mind moves first, it does not separate from the body but dynamically leads the brush into action.) The trick is to paint the character with your ki first, that is, mentally, and move the brush with the positive sensation of having already succeeded.

Central to this technique is developing sufficient concentration to first produce a clear mental image and then, decisively and with absolutely no hesitation, move the fude. In time, this becomes automatic, and an image is created in one second while the brush moves in the following second. A similar mental process can be used in most daily activities to harmonize the mind and body and, consequently, achieve greater results with less strain.

If you are a novice, try drawing the shape in the air over the paper two times while focusing the mind deeply on the action taking place. On the third repetition, paint the image. This is a more lengthy version of the same concept.

When ki dynamically leads the fude into action, a unity of mind, body, and brush is attained. This state of unity is both profound and all-encompassing, as writer Michel Random explains:

> Internal awareness, real efficiency, the accomplishment of every action, all require the union of body and mind. The energy which effects this union is called ki. It obeys the mind which can direct it, cause it to concentrate on one area, and make it flow.
>
> The meaning behind these words lies in a single fact, for ki, the fundamental energy of the universe (which connects and relates all things), is also the true body of things in the subtle sense. From there on, it can combine with breath and spirit and, in turn be the very emanation of breath and spirit.
>
> Ki is life itself. As long as ki exists, life continues. When the vital energy disappears, life ceases. The control of ki, therefore, represents control over life, health, harmony, and therefore energy.
>
> If ki gives at least a spiritual immortality, this is

because ki is the energy or original force which has been present ever since the creation of the universe and because this force is independent of time and space.

This concept explains why, as man is the emanation of universal nature, all consciousness stems from and returns to nature which is a common book for all of mankind.[16]

Do Not Cut Off Your Stream of Attention

Unless you preserve an uninterrupted flow of attention, the rhythm that gives your characters a dynamic demeanor will be shattered. Many people tend to cut off their stream of concentration at the culmination of an action. In calligraphy, this regularly takes place when an individual character or a line of words is completed. But in shodo, you must retain an uninterrupted flow of ki and close attention throughout the creative action.

This mental follow-through leads to an undisturbed state of peaceful awareness. Skilled painters' brush movements will often continue through the air, sometimes for a few inches, after the brush leaves the paper. In particular, when you're painting a stroke that tapers to a point at the end, you should not stop the brush abruptly after completing the action. Let the movement of ki continue by following through with the motion of the hand and mind as the brush is lifted from the paper. This is similar to the follow-through used in a skillful golf swing, or the batting of a talented baseball player.

The movement of ki continues even when contact with the paper is broken. This correlates not only to an act of mental and physical follow-through, but also to sustaining a flow from one character to the next. Although various characters are not visually linked by brush lines, they should always project a feeling of connection. This is known as ki-myaku (the unbroken pulse of ki).

In a broader sense, if you are to practice art as meditation, you need to retain your awareness of the present from the time you pick up your brush until the moment you cleanse it of ink. In the beginning, you may only maintain this heightened state of concentration for a few minutes. With practice, you'll realize that keeping attention rooted in the moment not only results in integration of mind and body but also amounts to entering into a condition beyond time. Because the act of trying is predicated upon your desire for some future result, it actually inter-feres with recognition of what is taking place in the instant. Perhaps the secret lies in uniting the mind and body and simply painting with a watchful attitude—an effortless state in which action occurs naturally. During pure observation of the instant, you may see what actually is, not what was or what you hope will be in the future, but the genuine nature of existence. If this observation is motivated by fear or the hope of reward, it is no longer pure.

At any moment of peak performance, in any activity, people tend to forget themselves. They are aware only of the instant and the action taking place. This is muga-ichi nen (no self—one thought), and it is this mental state that allows shodo to transcend mere skillful writing.

Learn to cultivate a condition of watchfulness without motive. In such a condition, you have an opportunity to see all things as they truly are, including your own thoughts. Is there, then, a separation between the mind that thinks and that which is thought of? Between the artist observing the process of creation and that which is observed? Between the artist who experiences and the experience itself?

It is my contention that, ultimately, no such distinctions exist. Reading about all of this has little value. Actually investigating pure attention, which contains no remnants of time but instead only what is —the absolute and eternal unity of all creations—this has tremendous significance.

FUDOSHIN

Immovable
Mind

Gyosho

Chapter 4

LESSONS
IN BRUSH
MEDITATION

While some books cover shodo techniques in detail, few books deal with the manner in which Japanese fine arts function as forms of spiritual realization. Because the meditative and aesthetic sides of shodo and ink painting are the main focus of this book, no attempt has been made to present an extensive series of technical lessons. Instead, this chapter offers a short series of exercises and compositions of varying degrees of complexity for you to experiment with. Although this chapter delves into the art of the Japanese brush, what is offered here will only be meaningful when studied as a visible expression of the principles of self-mastery that have been presented thus far. If you find it difficult to reproduce the compositions here, review the previous chapters with an eye toward more successfully integrating the meditative principles outlined with the technical material in this section.

If you want to begin serious study of any Japanese fine art, you need a competent teacher. Following this chapter is information about how to find an instructor and painting supplies.

Setting Up

Preparing to paint is neither time consuming nor expensive. You will need the following items to copy the compositions presented in this chapter:

> a medium-sized brush (chu-fude)
> a small brush (ko-fude)
> an ink stick (sumi) or liquid ink (bokuju)
> an ink stone (suzuri)
> paper (kami)
> a paperweight (bun-chin)

These are shown in Figure 16.

BRUSH

There is no standard regarding what constitutes a large, medium, or small brush in shodo. The medium-sized brush I recommend in this book has bristles about two inches in length, while the small brush's bristles are a little under one inch long. In general, buy the highest-quality brush you can afford. A bad brush only makes shodo more difficult for a novice.

INK STONE

Many different kinds of ink stones are also available. These can range in price from ten dollars to ten thousand dollars. The variable factor affecting the cost of the stone is the type of stone and its quality. Carving also has some impact on price, but not performance. Buy the most expensive stone you can find and/or afford. Try to get a natural,

FIG. 16. Tools for painting: medium brush, small brush, paper-weight (at top), inkstick, ink stone, and small water pitcher. An absorbent felt mat has been placed beneath the paper.

not artificial, stone if possible, as it will produce ink more easily and absorb the ink into itself less quickly.

INK STICK

An ink (sumi) stick, which looks like a dark, dull block of wood, produces the ink you will use to paint when rubbed with water on the upper surface of the ink stone. You get what you pay for. Some sticks produce slightly different shades of ink. This may be indicated on the package or stick itself, but it is often written in Japanese or Chinese, so ask the clerk if you are not able to read the package. Most sumi sticks do offer fairly similar degrees of darkness of ink, so you need not worry too much about this point. Chinese ink sticks tend to be harder than their Japanese counterparts and may thus require more grinding time. Liquid inks are also available.

PAPER

Paper is, like ink stones, quite variable in regard to price and quality, but finding variety is difficult outside of Asia. While even rough newsprint can be used effectively, try to find paper designed for sumi-e and shodo. Yasutomo and Company makes a good tablet of sumi-e paper, as well as acceptable liquid ink. The stores listed in the section beginning on page 341 are also worth contacting.

Your work can be mounted when it is finished. First, a backing paper is added to take out any wrinkles, and the work is then mounted to form a hanging scroll. This is an expensive process that is best left to a professional. As an alternative, you can purchase thick, stiff, pre-mounted pieces of paper called *shikishi* and *tanzaku*. (See Figure 17.) Both are fairly inexpensive. Shikishi are roughly eight inches wide and seven inches high, while tanzaku are usually just over two inches wide and one foot, two inches long. You can also buy commercially produced universal frames for these paper types because shikishi and tanzaku are uniformly sized.

OTHER MATERIALS

Serious calligraphers also often use a small brush rest (for when they are not holding an ink-covered brush); a water dropper, such as an eyedropper or small water pitcher (for adding water to the ink stone); and a felt mat (*shitajiki*) to absorb ink that may bleed through the paper. Of these last few items, the only one that is really needed is some sort of material to protect the surface of your table. For novices, several sheets of newspaper, placed under the painting/calligraphy paper, will suffice.

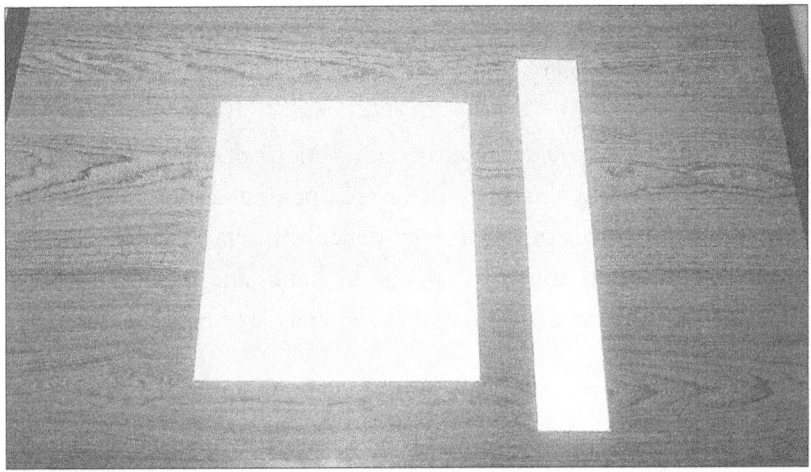

FIG. 17. Stiff, premounted paper for painting works intended for display. Shikishi paper is about 8 x 7 inches. Tanzaku paper is about 2 x 14 inches. Frames are available in both sizes.

Beginning to Paint

Arrange your paper squarely in front of you, on a level table that is not too high. You may want to sit on a cushion, as this is easier than trying to adjust the height of your table. If you own a low table, the *seiza* posture is recommended (see pages 286–87).

Control the top portion of the paper with your paperweight and the bottom section with your left hand. The work that is to be copied can be placed either above or to the left of your paper, and your ink stone rests off to the right side of the paper. Sumi-e and shodo paper often has a rough side and a smooth side. If the rough side is used, it is easier to produce a dry brush effect in which white paper shows through the ink (*kasure*), which is desirable in some cases. Kobara Ranseki Sensei feels that using the rough side of the paper is advisable for many students because it is less slippery, and consequently brush control is more easily maintained.

As you paint, you can adjust the positions of some of the items before you, especially the paper, but avoid tipping and tilting your paper at angles because this makes it more difficult to achieve balance in the artwork. Hold your brush in your right hand, and make a point of adopting a posture in which the mind and body are united.

GRINDING THE INK

Fill the receptacle portion of the ink stone with either liquid ink or, more traditionally, cool water. Fill it completely if you will be painting for some time, or just add a bit if you are only going to paint for a limited period. If you're using water, grasp your ink stick in your right hand, dip into the water reservoir in the stone, and draw some of the water onto the flat surface of the stone. Using moderate-sized oval motions, gently grind the end of your ink stick against the flat part of the stone's surface. In time, ink is produced, and the more you grind, the darker the ink will become. You do not need to always try to convert the water in the reservoir into ink. (This is possible, but time-consuming.) As the ink starts to run out, bring up some more water from the reservoir and grind a little more to make the color consistent. Ink color can be tested on another sheet of paper prior to painting.

USING THE BRUSH

A new brush needs to be soaked in water to remove the stiffening agent that holds the bristles together. Gently massaging the brush hair can speed up this process. Some authorities suggest that beginners leave this stiffening agent in the small brush because the small brush is used to paint fine lines.

Before covering the brush with ink, wet the bristles of the brush thoroughly and then gently squeeze the water out, forming a sharp tip with your fingers. (This helps hold the brush hairs together.) Using the tip of the brush, draw some ink onto the flat surface of the ink stone and wipe it over the entire surface of the brush hairs so that the bristles are completely covered with ink. It takes experience to learn how much ink to use in coating the brush. If you wish to produce a bleeding effect (*nijimi*), the brush is somewhat oversaturated with sumi. On the other hand, if you are aiming for the kasure dry-brush effect, you should use an undersaturated brush.

As you paint, the brush hairs may split, but they can always be formed back into a point by smoothing them against the flat ink stone surface. Be careful not to add too much additional ink while doing this.

When painting practice is finished, thoroughly clean your brush and ink stone using cool water and no soap. Squeeze the water from your brush and always form the hair back into a point. (Strangely, a fairly large number of people have arrived at the mistaken notion that the ink stone is never washed. This is false. Failing to wash your suzuri eventually ruins it and only helps to financially support ink stone manufacturers.)

To clean a brush from which the stiffening agent has not been removed, rinse it under water briefly and then wipe it repeatedly against a clean paper towel. Always wipe in the same direction by pulling the brush toward you, not by pushing the bristles away from you.

Exercise One: Controlling
Brush Pressure and Line Thickness

Hold the brush stem so that it is roughly perpendicular to the paper. Although the brush will tilt as you paint, the fundamental position of the stem is vertical. Control the thickness of line not by inclining the brush but by pressing down and raising up. Downward pressure will produce a thicker line, and lifting up to use the very tip of the bristles will produce a fine line.

Painting in a smooth, continuous fashion from left to right, try copying the line shown in Figure 18. You may require several attempts to produce a smooth transition from thickness to thinness and back again.

To control the thickness of line, you must be able to control your mind and body. The principles of mental and physical harmony that have been outlined in the preceding chapters contain many of the essential points for achieving such a state of mind-body mastery.

Exercise Two: The Three Essential Brush Strokes

Three brush strokes are introduced to novices studying Kobara Ranseki's system of shodo. They are utilized to learn daho (pressing method), nenpo (twisting method), and zoho (overlapping method). The following exercises do not necessarily represent the most common brush strokes found in shodo, but they will teach you the most about how to control your brush. Because the mind moves the brush, these exercises allow you to train your mind as well as your ability to coordinate the body and mind.

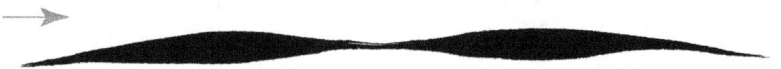

FIG. 18. Try painting a smooth transition, left to right, from thick to thin and back again.

DAHO

You study daho by learning to make a dot, as in Figure 19. Try copying this dot by pressing downward while holding the brush perpendicular to the paper. Your brush is lowered onto the paper at an angle, and downward pressure is applied to somewhat flatten the bristles. As you press down, draw the brush slightly toward the bottom of the paper and lift up as you draw the tip of the brush back to the center of your dot. A small semicircle is drawn, in conjunction with downward pressure, to form a dot.

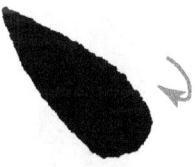

FIG. 19. Paint a dot to study daho, the pressing method. Press downward on the perpendicular brush and draw it slightly toward the bottom of the paper as you lift it up and bring the tip back to the center.

NENPO

In nenpo, you touch the paper using just the tip of the brush hairs and delicate downward pressure. (See Figure 20.) Twist the brush in the opposite direction as you continue to move it toward the bottom of the paper, and press down as in daho to form the rest of the brush stroke. (See Figure 21.) The brush starts off pointing to the upper right, twists downward to use the body of the bristles, lifts, and then the tip trails off slightly to the left. Nenpo is, more or less, daho with a gentle S-shaped curve. Although Figures 20 and 21 show nenpo in two stages, the stroke is drawn with one continuous movement of varying pressure.

FIG. 20. For nenpo, the twisting method, you begin by touching the paper using just the tip of the brush hairs and delicate downward pressure.

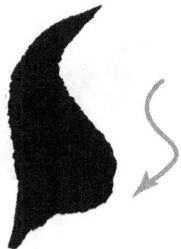

FIG. 21. Continue the nenpo stroke by twisting the brush in the opposite direction as you continue to move it toward the bottom of the paper; then press down as in daho to form the rest of the stroke.

ZOHO

To study zoho, begin by moving the tip of the brush lightly from right to left. (See Figure 22.). Then, go back over this thin line from left to right. (See Figure 23.) As you move the brush from left to right, apply gentle but gradually increasing pressure to thicken the line. At the end of the line, let the brush lift so that only the tip is touching again. Allow the pressure to trail off so that a fine point is formed at the end and the flow of ki continues to the right as your brush leaves the paper. Zoho involves a single continuous motion that flows briefly from right to left, and then from left to right.

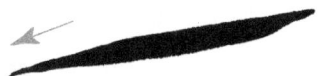

FIG. 22. To study zoho, the overlapping method, begin by moving the tip of the brush lightly from right to left.

FIG. 23. Then, to finish the zoho stroke, go back over the stroke in Figure 22 from left to right, increasing pressure to thicken the line in the center and then reducing pressure so that the a fine point is formed at the right. The flow of ki continues as your brush leaves the paper.

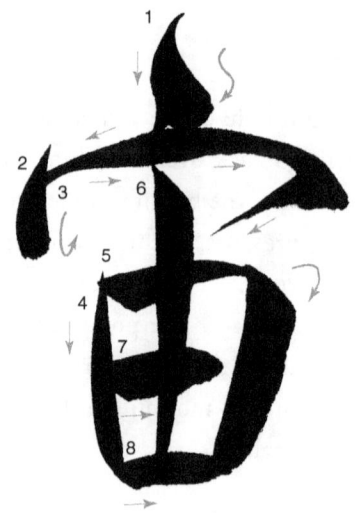

FIG. 24. Writing the top of the character character chu involves nenpo (at top), daho (the left stroke of the "roof"), and a modified zoho stroke that flicks back to the left (from the right edge of the "roof"). The remaining strokes are written with varying brush pressures to create a rhythmic range of thick and thin lines.

COMBINING THE THREE BASIC STROKES

Finally, you can try painting the character chu (heaven), which uses all three brush strokes to form the top component, or radi-cal. (See Figure 24.) Paint nenpo first, then daho on the left, followed by a horizontal variation of zoho that makes use of a returning flick of the brush from right to left. Then try the remaining strokes.

Exercise Three: Kaisho, Gyosho, and Sosho

The three most common script styles found in Japanese calligraphy are: kaisho (Figure 25), which is the equivalent of printing in English; gyosho (Figure 26), which is similar to semicursive writing; and sosho (Figure 27), which is equivalent to cursive English handwriting. Each illustration features the character kokoro, meaning "heart" or "soul," painted three different ways.

Each of these different scripts projects a different feeling, and each requires a unique state of mind. Studying kaisho, gyosho, and sosho allows you to understand and master divergent mental states. Try writing these three variants.

KAISHO

When using kaisho script, you will most clearly show the structure of the character. Note that the ends of certain strokes are tapered, and should have an almost organic appearance not unlike bamboo leaves and stems. Printed-style characters need a firm, but not stiff,

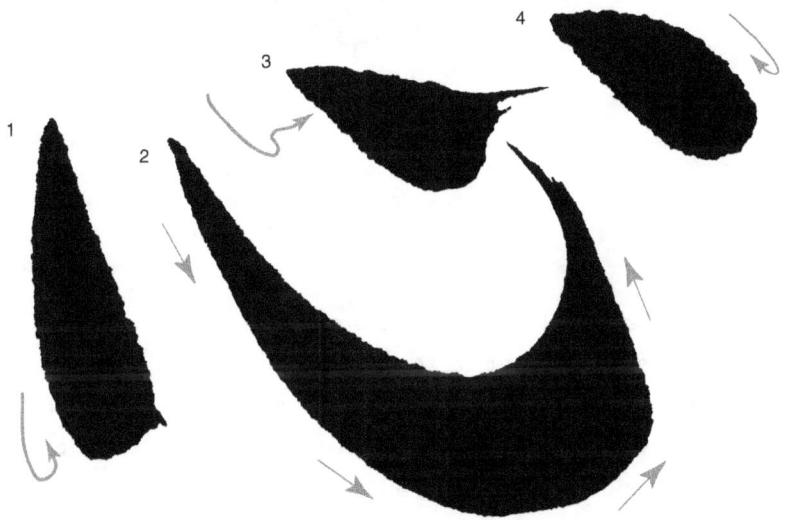

FIG. 25. *Kokoro* written in kaisho. This shows the clear structure of the character. Ends of strokes are tapered, and inside each stroke is a definite central line that represents the movement of the center of the brush bristles, effectively a line of ki.

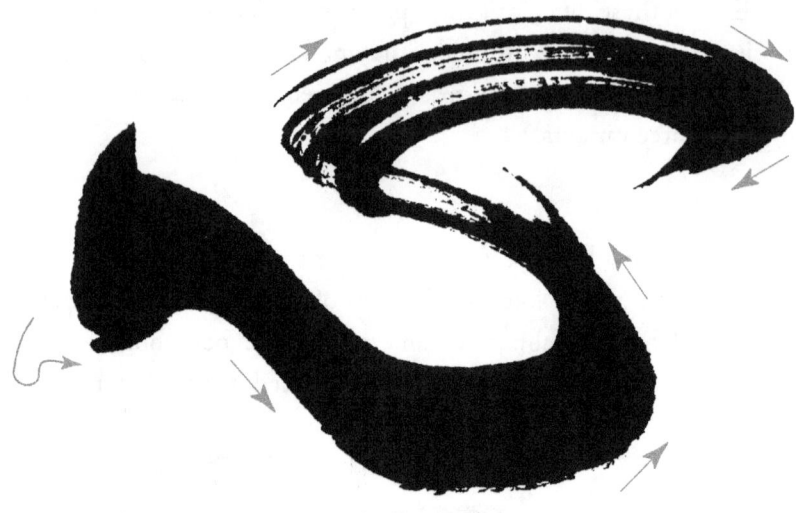

FIG. 26. *Kokoro* written in gyosho. This offers a strong sensation of visual rhythm made up of upward and downward pressure combined with thick and thin strokes. Gyosho rhythms are good for assessing mental tension and composure.

demeanor. Inside each brush stroke is a central line. This personifies the movement of the center of the bristles and it must be kept steady. It is actually more of a mental line—a line of ki. This ki line must be drawn decisively in your mind. Rigidly trying to hold the hand steady is not the answer because this will only create lifeless characters.

GYOSHO

While kaisho makes use of a superlative command of space, gyosho offers a strong sensation of visual rhythm. Rhythm is destroyed by tension, and semicursive-style characters will reveal when you are

318

tightening your body and losing composure. In gyosho, it is acceptable to run some strokes together, and although in this case the word "heart" is painted in one continuous stroke, rhythm is still present. It is a rhythm of upward and downward pressure combined with thickness and thinness of line.

SOSHO

Cursive-style characters are painted with an even greater sense of an unbroken flow of ki. They tend to be rather abstract, and most Japanese cannot read them unless they are studying shodo. Think of sosho

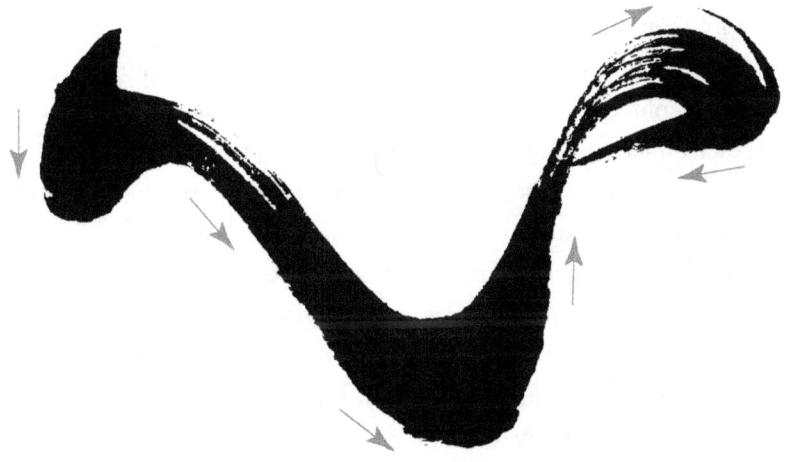

FIG. 27. *Kokoro* written in sosho. This cursive, more abstract style displays an unbroken sense of ki. It looks effortless but in fact is controlled by vigorous practice and a firm understanding of the character's underlying structure.

as being more abbreviated and quickly written than semicursive-style characters. While cursive style appears to exhibit an effortless quality, you should be careful not to totally lose the sense of structure that was developed in your study of printed-style symbols. For this reason, students learn kaisho before practicing cursive-style kanji. Sosho contains the structure of printed-style and the rhythm of semicursive characters, which are combined to create a script that flows like dynamically rushing water.

Composition One: The Enso

Originating in Zen, the enso at first glance may appear to be nothing more than a circle. (See Figure 28.) Yet when painted in a state of mind-body unification by a skilled artist, it is filled with ki and becomes a circle of infinity. The enso is not a Japanese character, but more a form of abstract art used to convey that which is beyond words.

Try painting an enso, circling from left to right, to get a visual representation of your mental and physical state at the moment.

While turning your wrist, press down strongly as in Figure 29. Note that in Figure 30 the wrist and arm have twisted the other way as the circle is formed, and pressure decreases to form a tapered point at the end. Your hand must not stop abruptly at this point but should gradually lift while the flow of ki continues through space in the same direction it was traveling. In other words, follow through mentally and physically.

Note that the enso began from a point of stillness, transformed itself into a dynamic, almost violent motion, and finally gathered all of its energy into a still and infinitely decreasing point at the end. The

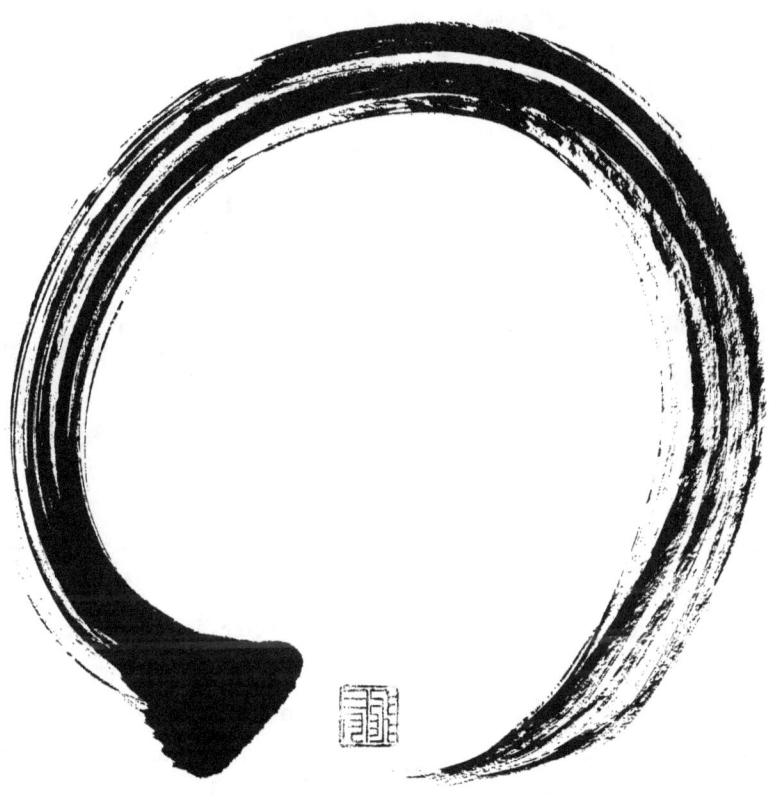

FIG. 28. Composition One. The enso, when painted in a state of mind-body unification, becomes a circle of infinity.

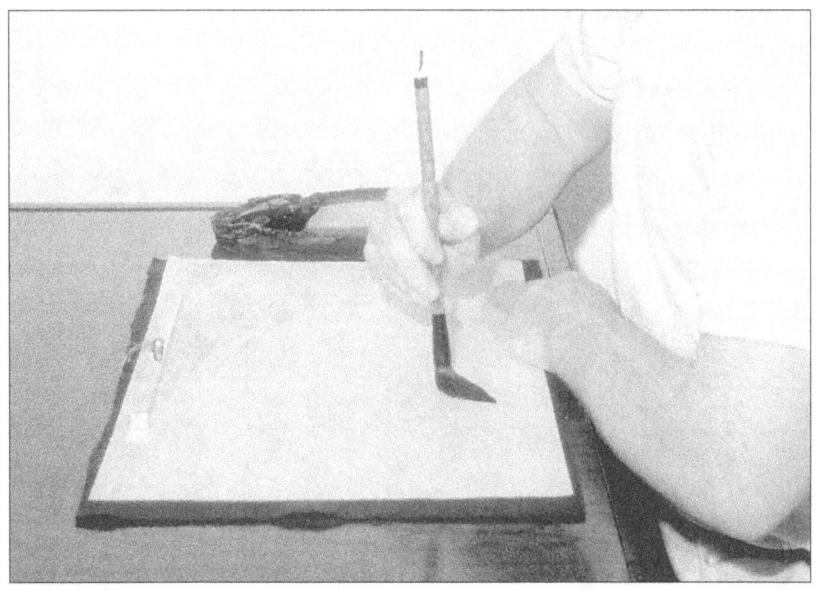

FIG. 29. To begin the enso, press down
strongly while turning your wrist.

enso expresses the essential oneness of opposites and acts as a depiction of the unity of all aspects of nature.

Your *inkan* (seal) that contains the characters for your name can
be placed in the space between the beginning and ending of your brush
stroke. Placement of the seal can have a dramatic effect on the balance
of your work, because it is the only spot of color in a monochromatic
field. Asian name seals and traditional red seal ink can be purchased
through the sources listed on pages 341–42.

Alternately, your name can be signed to the left of your work and
followed by the inkan.

Because your body reflects your mind, the painting of an enso is

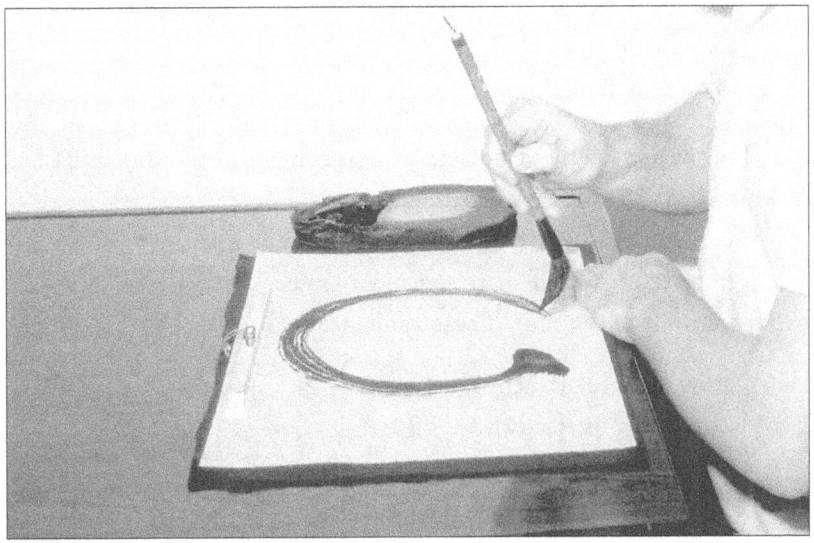

FIG. 30. To finish the enso, twist the wrist and arm the other way as the circle is formed; then decrease pressure to form a tapered point at the end.

an opportunity to see yourself more clearly by noticing the relationship between your attitude and the enso itself.

Composition Two: The Coin

Composition Two is an abstract painting of an Asian coin, complete with the square hole in the center. (See Figure 31.) At the celebrated Ryoanji Zen temple in Kyoto is an ancient well in the shape of this coin, with the water resting in the coin's square center. This image makes use of the famed Zen enso again, and the four characters on the coin read:

323

Ware tada taru o shiru.
The only thing I know is that I'm perfectly satisfied.

This design is unique and clever. It is composed of four kanji, each of which has an identical square component. These characters are read in a clockwise manner, following the motion of the enso. They are arranged so that they all share the square radical, which also serves as the center hole of the coin. These kanji are:

ware (I, oneself); see Figure 32
tada (only, perfectly); see Figure 33
taru (be satisfied); see Figure 34
shiru (to know); see Figure 35

Start by copying and practicing these characters before attempting to reproduce the complete painting.

Now, to try recreating this image, first paint an enso (Figure 36).

Next, paint the square center of the coin (Figure 37). It is also possible to write the entire kanji *ware* at this point, followed by the other three components.

Add the top of the first kanji (Figure 38), followed by the right side of the second character (Figure 39), then the bottom of the third symbol (Figure 40), and, finally, the left side of the fourth kanji (Figure 41). Your seal can be placed in the same spot as in Composition 1.

The kanji in the actual composition have strokes that are slightly more connected than in Figures 32–35, for a more dynamic feeling.

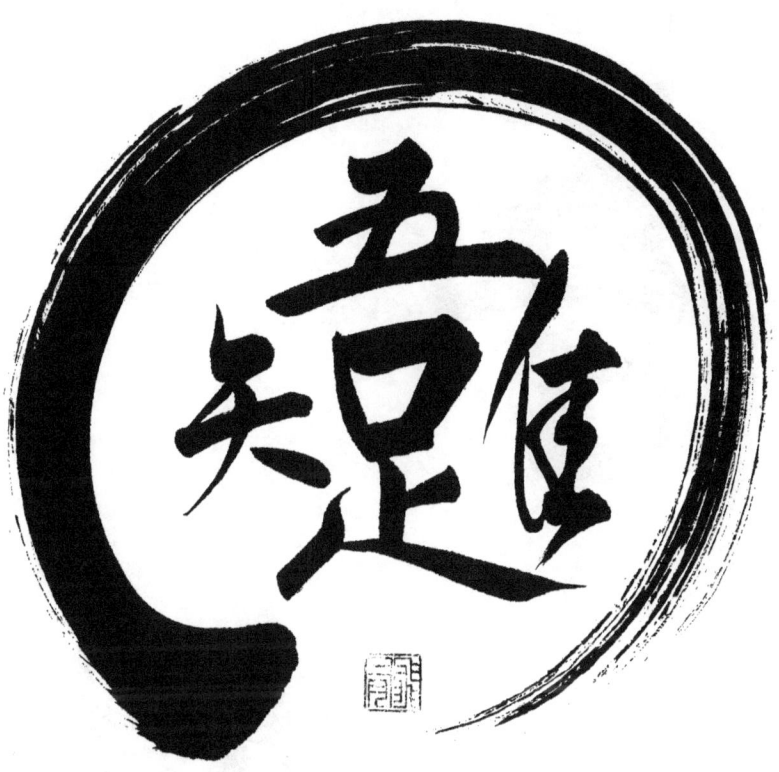

FIG. 31. Composition Two. Abstract painting of an Asian coin, complete with the square hole in the center that forms a part of the four characters arranged around it.

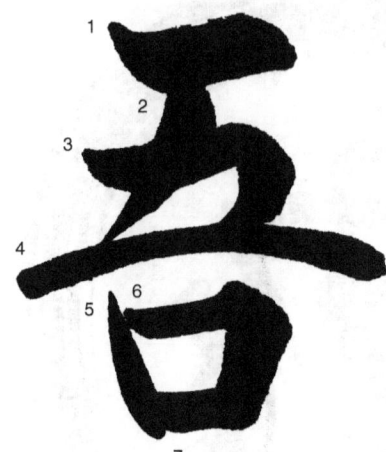

FIG. 32. *Ware* (I, oneself).

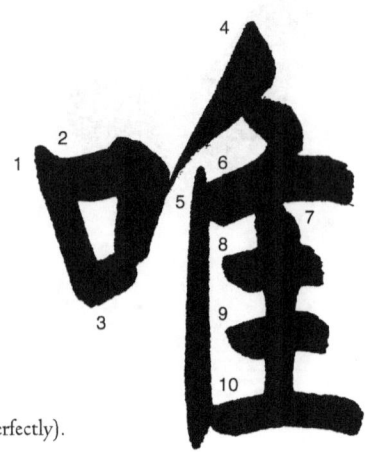

FIG. 33. *Tada* (only, perfectly).

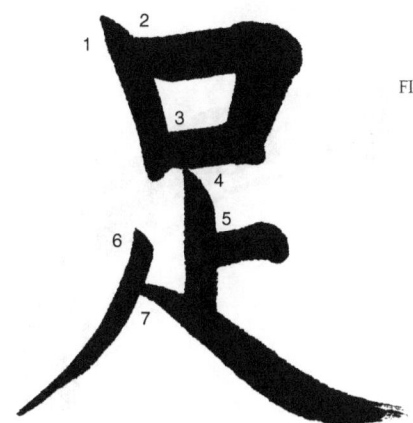

FIG. 34. Taru (be satisfied).

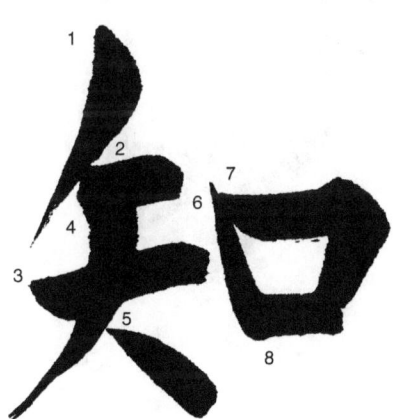

FIG. 35. *Shiru* (to know).

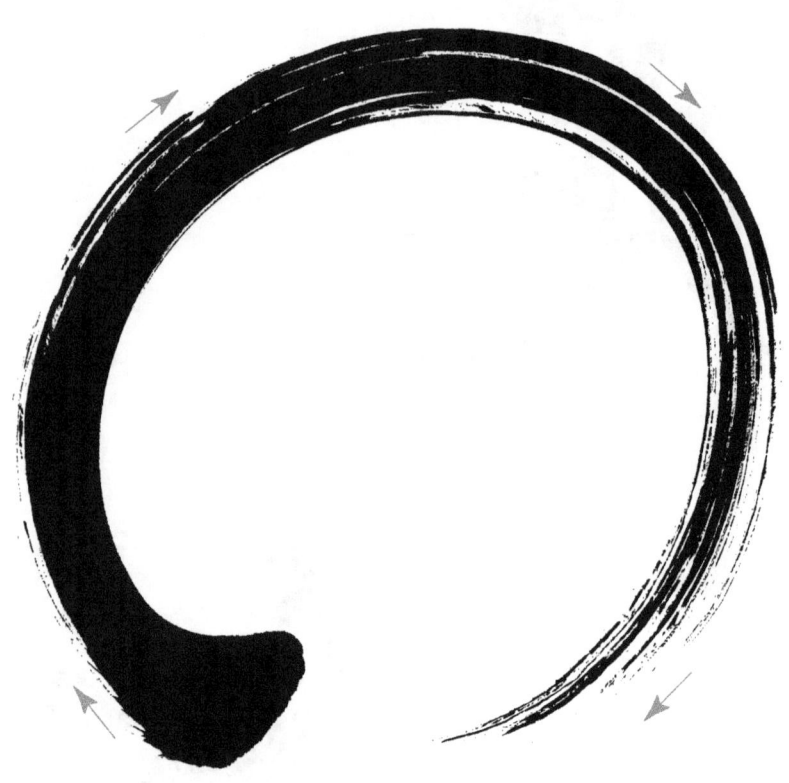

FIG. 36. To draw the coin, begin with an enso, as in Composition 1.

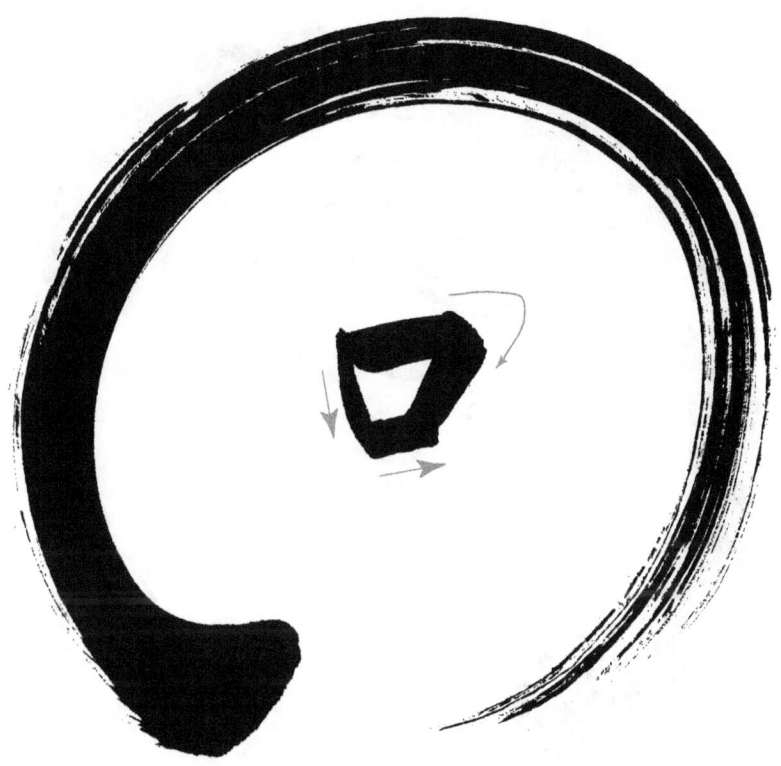

FIG. 37. Paint the square center of the coin.

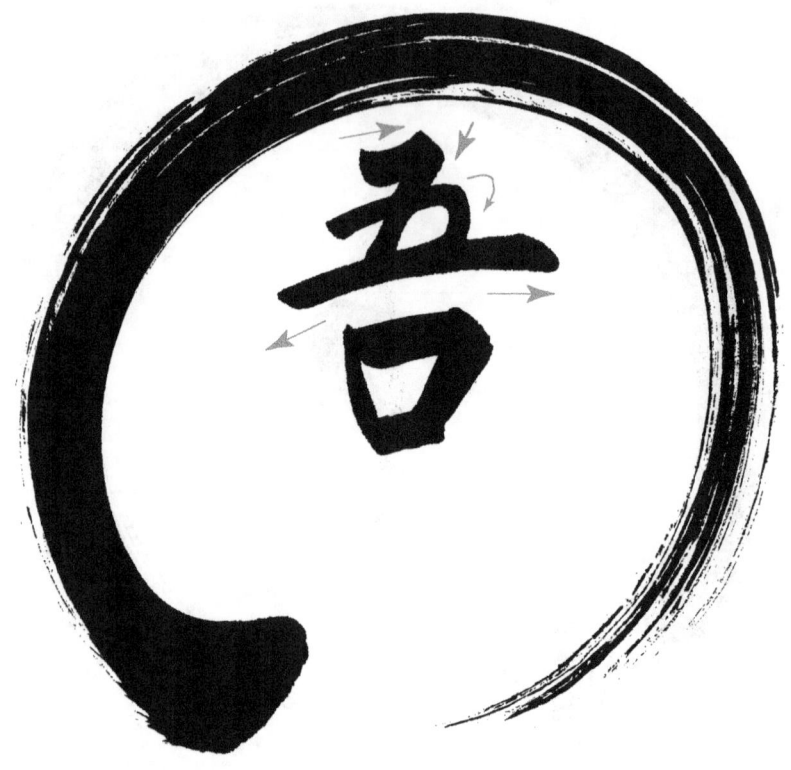

FIG. 38. Paint the top of the first kanji.

330

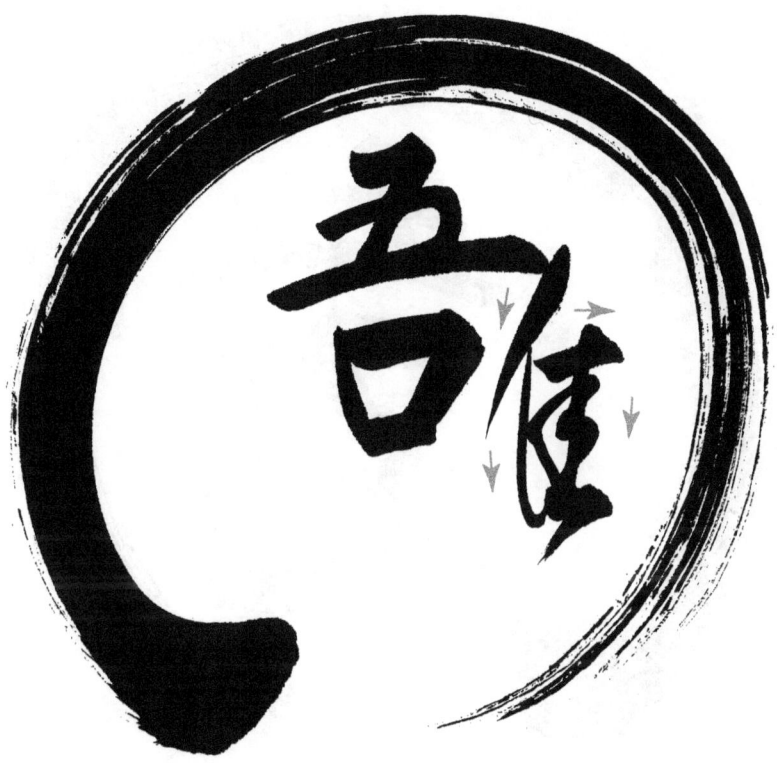

FIG. 39. Paint the right side of the second character. The
second component is written in one continuous stroke

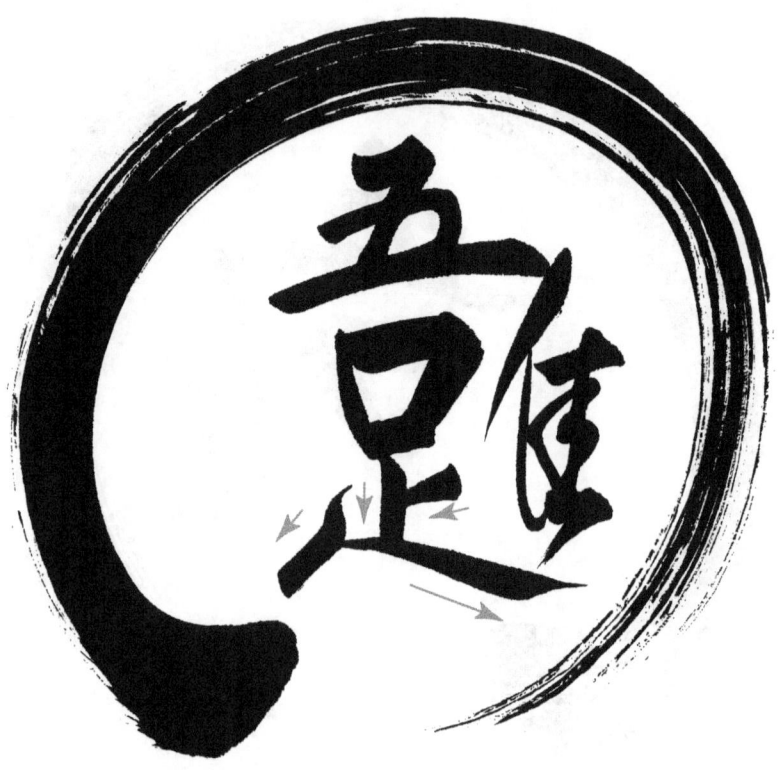

FIG. 40. Paint the bottom of the third symbol.

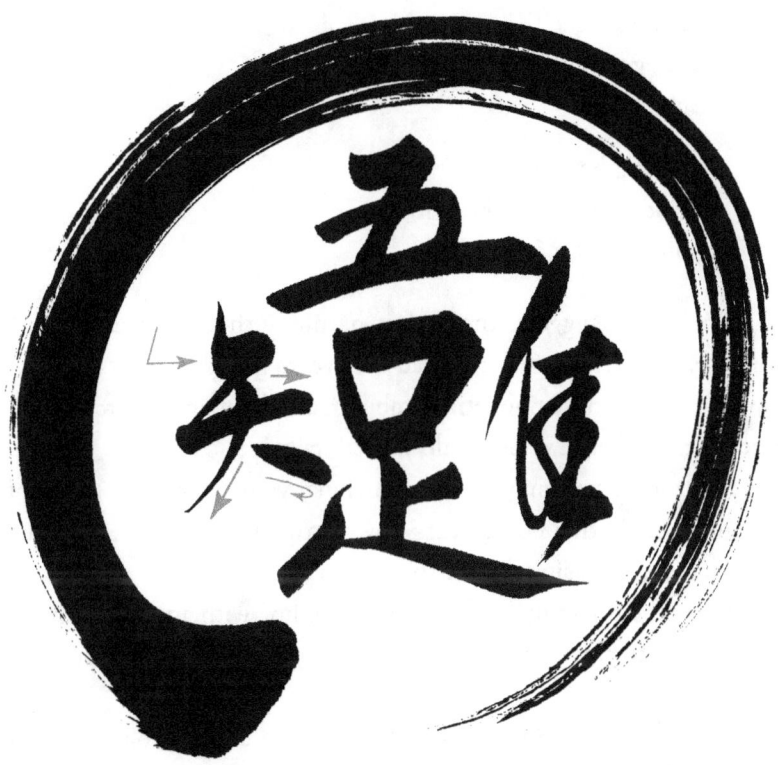

FIG. 41. Paint the left side of the fourth kanji.

Composition Three: A Bonfire and a Poem

Your final composition contains an abstract painting of a bonfire, logs, and scattered leaves, along with a haiku poem. The work in Figure 42 was painted by Ohsaki Jun, my student. The poem reads:

Taku hodo wa
Kaze ga motekuru
Ochiba kana.

Building bonfires
Wind currents are bringing
Falling leaves.

This haiku suggests the perfect harmony that pervades all of the universe. It is written in connected cursive-style and features the use of kanji, kana (Japanese phonetic symbols), and hentaigana (archaic Chinese characters used phonetically). See Figure 43.

Start off by painting the bonfire. Turn your wrist as in the photo in Figure 44. At this point, press down strongly, then twist the brush around and up, causing the brush hairs to separate.

Move the brush upward in a wavering line with an undulating up-down action to create smoke as in Figure 45. (Use a fairly dry brush for this effect.)

Now, making use of the split brush hairs, add the logs and burning debris by drawing wide left-to-right diagonal brush strokes. Form a point out of the bristles again and lightly dab the brush tip around the base of the bonfire, in a random pattern, to create leaves.

Last, using your small brush, write the haiku in smooth, contin-

334

FIG. 42. Composition Three. Abstract painting of a bonfire, logs, and scattered leaves, with a haiku poem. Painting by Ohsaki Jun.

335

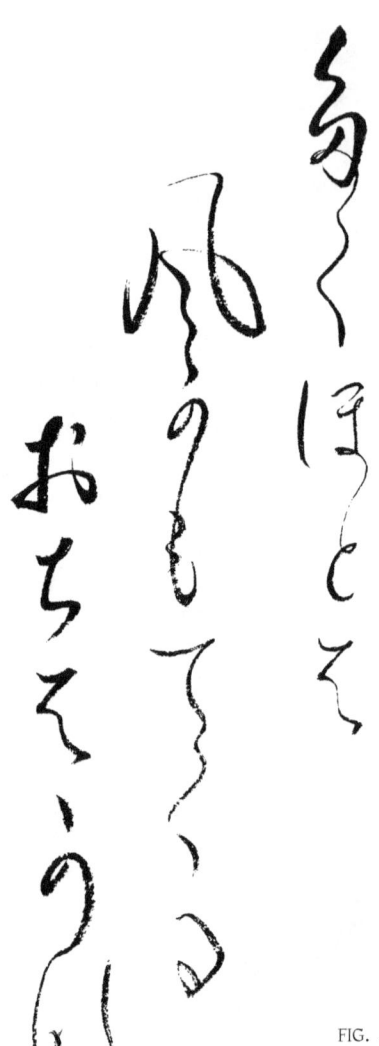

焚くほどは
風がもてくる
おちばかな

FIG. 43. Detail of the poem in FIG. 42: *Taku hodo wa / Kaze ga motekuru / Ochiba kana*. The poem is written in a mix of kanji, kana, and hentaigana. The same poem is also shown here in standard printed characters

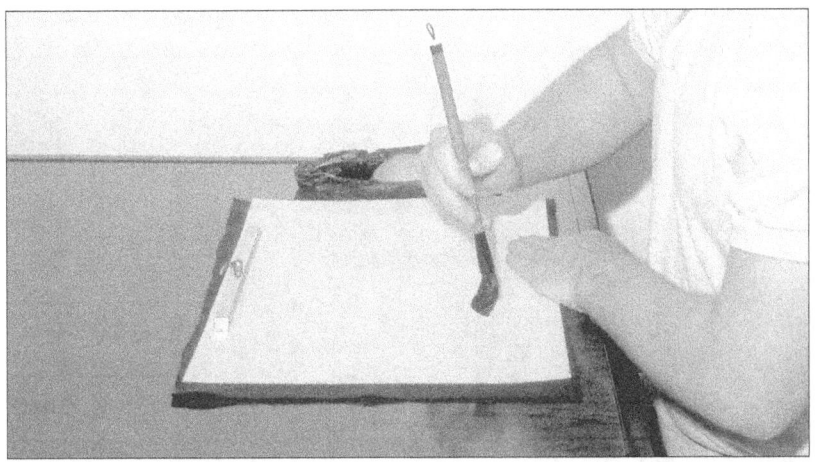

FIG. 44. Turn your wrist as shown to begin the bonfire stroke.

uous lines, moving from top to bottom and from right to left. Note in Figure 46 that the left hand (or wrist) can be used as a light support for the right wrist. Because it is easy for the hand to wobble when it's writing small characters, calligraphers often gently slide the right wrist along the back of the left hand or wrist as they paint down the paper.

Apply ink to the brush at the beginning of the first line of characters on the right. Let the ink gradually run out to create a lighter and drier second line.

Then, apply more ink for the third line, so that the first line is dark, the second line is light, and the third line is dark. This alternation of tone is known as *no-tan* (light-dark), and it is vital for creating a sense of variety and rhythm in your work.

Once the haiku is finished, your seal can be placed between the bonfire and the poem.

337

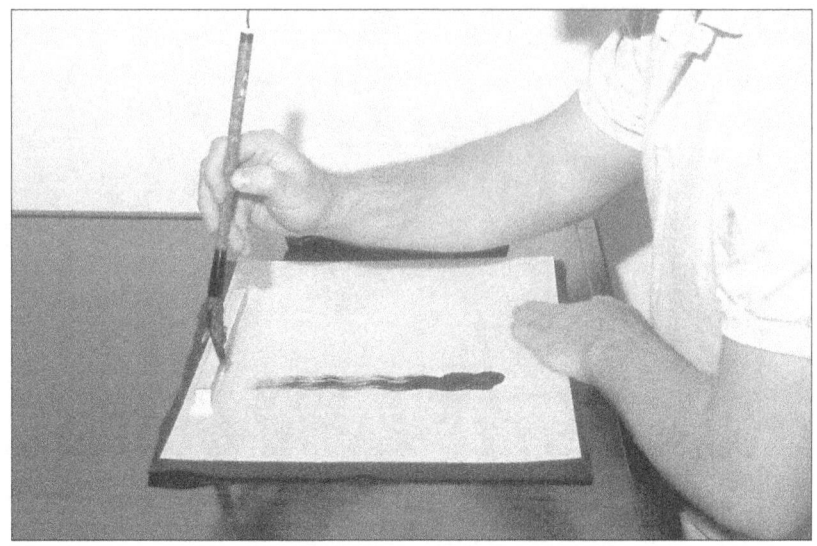

FIG. 45. Twist the brush around and up so that the brush hairs sep-arate. Move the brush upward in a wavering line to create smoke.

Painting kana with the small brush requires a different use of the mind and body than that required by a larger brush (although the principles of brush control are the same). Try to note how the use of the small brush relates to the larger brush. If you find this composition difficult, go back to the basic concepts of mind-body-brush unification that have already been outlined. These concepts do not change regardless of what you may be holding in your hand.

What Next?

Shodo has been used in this book primarily as a single representation of the Japanese "do" and as a means of exploring meditation

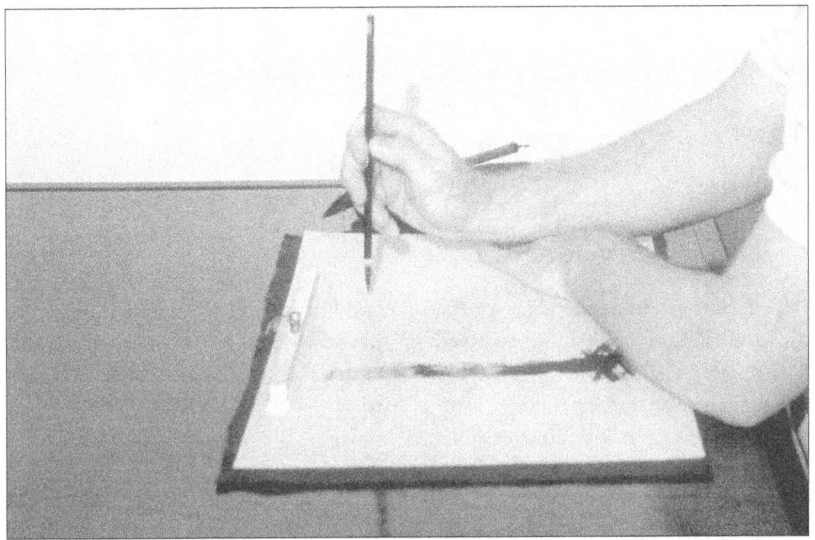

FIG. 46. When writing the haiku, use the left hand or wrist as a light support for your right wrist as you work.

in action. If you'd like to pursue shodo further, find yourself a good teacher (see the section beginning on page 340 for some advice on how to proceed). But even if you don't pursue formal shodo instruction, I hope *Brush Meditation* has given you a better understanding of Japanese cultural arts and how they can serve as meditative activities. The principles of harmony outlined in the preceding pages are more than just a means to success in shodo. They relate to the minds and bodies of people everywhere. You can thus use the topics outlined in this book to enhance many aspects of your daily life. I especially hope they will prompt you to look at the genuine characteristics of your self and its relationship to nature and, in this way, directly discover the true nature of your existence.

339

SOURCES FOR INSTRUCTION & SUPPLIES

All genuine understanding of the topics in this book must be arrived at through actual experience. This was the main reason for including a sampling of exercises and compositions for you to experiment with in Chapter 4. If, after reading this book and trying its exercises, you would like to proceed further, you may wish to find a qualified teacher. Or, you may need information on where to purchase art supplies like brushes, ink, ink stones, and paper. The following information should help.

How Do I Find an Instructor?

This, in many ways, is the most important question for any prospective student of the Japanese cultural arts. A competent teacher is indispensable, although some publications can serve as an introduction to a given art, offer material for contemplation, or function as an effective supplement to hands-on training.

I offer instruction in Japanese yoga

and fine arts. Please contact me if you have questions or comments about the material in this book. Write or email to:

The Sennin Foundation Center
for Japanese Cultural Arts
1053 San Pablo Avenue
Albany, CA 94706
HEDavey@aol.com

You can also find more information on the Sennin Foundation Web Site at:

www.senninfoundation.com

Another good resource is Michi Online: Journal of the Japanese Cultural Arts:

www.michionline.org

If you live outside of my immediate vicinity, a local instructor will be necessary. You'll probably have better luck finding a sumi-e teacher than a shodo teacher, but some instructors are competent in both arts. Here are some simple ways of locating a teacher:

- If a Japanese community center is nearby, try checking on their various classes. They may offer the kind of instruction mentioned in this text.

- Local colleges may have classes in Japanese calligraphy or painting.

- Many Buddhist churches and centers offer classes in Asian cultural arts. Look in the telephone directory for a nearby Buddhist church.

- Try contacting the nearest Japanese consulate and asking for assistance.

- If none of the above resources can point you to the kind of teacher you are looking for, try talking to instructors of other Japanese art forms such as judo or tea ceremony. These teachers may know of someone that can help you.

- In general, make a point of getting involved in the local Japanese-American community, as this will enhance your understanding of all the Japanese arts. It can also open many doors.

Finding a qualified teacher is never quick and easy. I looked for several years before discovering an exceptional instructor. Once you have a teacher, be prepared to spend a sizable amount of time and effort in studying. While this may seem a bit daunting to the beginner, it is vital to realize that the rewards are definitely equal to the energy expended.

Where Can I Buy Supplies?

The first place to check for shodo supplies is your nearest art supply store. Shodo and sumi-e both use the same sort of brush, paper, ink stone, and ink, so be sure to let the clerk know this. Bear in mind, however, that while you may get a good price at the local art supply shop, you will rarely find a good selection or tools of good quality.

For a fine selection of supplies of varying quality, the New Unique Company in San Francisco's Chinatown is excellent. Brushes, name seals, paper, and ink stones can all be purchased here. The owner sells equipment for Chinese calligraphy and painting, but most materials are the same as those used in Japan. Write or call for more information:

The New Unique Company
838 Grant Street
San Francisco, CA 94108
(415) 981-2036

The Kinokuniya Bookstores of America chain carries art supplies at some of its locations. (They are primarily booksellers and can help you

341

find additional written information about the Japanese fine arts.) They can sometimes offer suggestions about finding a teacher. Stores are located throughout the U.S. at:

Kinokuniya San Francisco
1581 Webster Street
San Francisco, CA 94115
(415) 567-7625

Kinokuniya San Jose
675 Saratoga Avenue
San Jose, CA 95129
(408)252-1300

Kinokuniya Los Angeles
123 Ellison S. Onizuka Street
Los Angeles, CA 90012
(213) 687-4447

Kinokuniya Costa Mesa
665 Paularino Avenue
Costa Mesa, CA 92626
(714) 434-9986

Kinokuniya Seattle
519 6th Avenue
Seattle, WA 98104
(206) 587-2477

Kinokuniya New York
10 West 49th Street
New York, NY 10020
(212) 765-7766

Kinokuniya New Jersey
595 River Road
Edgewater, NJ 07020
(201) 941-7580

Kinokuniya Portland
10500 SW Beaverton-Hillsdale Highway
Beaverton, OR 97005
(503) 641-6240

Other stores in North America that sell ink, brushes, and paper are:

Aiko's Art Materials
3347 North Clark Street
Chicago, IL 60657
(773) 404-5600

M. Flax
10852 Lindbrook Drive
Los Angeles, CA 90024
(310) 208-3529

Pearl Paint
308 Canal Street
New York, NY 10013
(800) 221-6845

Ichiyo Art Center
432 East Paces Ferry Road
Atlanta, GA 30305
(404) 233-1846

Five Eggs
213 West San Francisco Street
Santa Fe, NM 87501
(505) 986-3403

A wholesaler that can direct you to a store in your local area is:

Yasutomo and Company
490 Eccles Avenue
South San Francisco, CA 94080
(650) 737-8888

NOTES

1. Library of Congress and Yomiuri Shinbun, *Words in Motion: Modern Japanese Calligraphy* (Tokyo: Library of Congress and Yomiuri Shinbun, 1984), p. 44.

2. Leonard Koren, *Wabi-Sabi: for Artists, Designers, Poets & Philosophers* (Berkeley: Stone Bridge Press, 1994), pp. 40–41.

3. H. E. Davey, *The Way of the Universe* (Albany, Calif.: Sennin Organization, 1985), pp. 66–67.

4. Ibid., p. 80.

5. John Stevens, *The Sword of No-Sword: Life of the Master Warrior Tesshu* (Boulder, Colo.: Shambhala, 1984), p. 142.

6. Library of Congress and Yomiuri Shinbun, *Words in Motion*, p. 41.

7. Nakamura Tempu and Hashimoto Tetsuichi, *Ways for Unification of Mind and Body* (Tokyo: n.pub., n.d.), p. 7.

8. Michel Random, *Japan: Strategy of the Unseen* (Northamptonshire, England: Crucible, 1987), pp. 192–93.

9. Trevor P. Leggett, *Zen and the Ways* (London: Routledge and Kegan Paul, 1978), p. 197.

10. Random, *Japan*, p. 190.

11. Omori Sogen and Terayama Katsujo, *Zen and the Art of Calligraphy: The Essence of Sho* (London: Routledge and Kegan Paul, 1983), p. 10.

12. Trevor P. Leggett, *First Zen Reader* (Rutland, Vt., and Tokyo: Tuttle, 1960), p. 224.

13. Kobara Ranseki, *The Spirit of the Brush Favors No Nation*, trans. H. E. Davey (Tokyo: Nihon Keizai Shinbun, 1988).

14. Haruo Yamaoka, *Meditation Gut Enlightenment: The Way of Hara* (South San Francisco: Heian International, 1976), p. 69.

15. Richard Heckler, *The Anatomy of Change* (Boulder, Colo.: Shambhala, 1984), pp. 82–84.

16. Random, *Japan*, p. 190.

GLOSSARY

bokuju: liquid ink

budo: "the martial ways"

bun-chin: paperweight

chado: "the way of tea," tea ceremony

chu-fude: medium-sized brush

daho: "pressing method," a technique of manipulating the brush

do: "the way," used to describe a Japanese art that is practiced as a means of spiritual realization

enso: the painted ink circle of Zen

fude: brush

fudoshin: "immovable mind," a state of spiritual and physical stability

gyosho: semicursive-style script

hara: "abdomen," a natural center in the lower abdomen used as a point of concentration in various meditative disciplines and Japanese arts

hentaigana: also "man'yogana," an antiquated script that uses Chinese characters phonetically

hiragana: cursive Japanese syllabary

inkan: Japanese seal or stamp

kado: "the way of flowers," flower arrangement

kaisho: printed-style script

kana: Japanese syllabaries

kanji: Chinese characters

kasure: dry brush strokes

katakana: angular Japanese syllabary

ki: life energy

ko-fude: small brush

nenpo: "twisting method," a technique of manipulating the brush

nijimi: wet, bleeding brush strokes

no-tan: writing with alternatingly light and dark ink

sabi: elegant simplicity, an antique appearance

seiza: Japanese kneeling posture

sensei: teacher

shibui: elegant

shibumi: elegance

Shin-shin-toitsu-do: "the way of mind and body unification," a form of Japanese yoga

shitajiki: felt undercloth for absorbing ink

sumi: ink, ink stick

sumi-e: ink painting

suzuri: ink stone

wabi: unpretentious, simple refinement

zoho: "overlapping method," a technique of manipulating the brush

344

AFTERWORD

My Japanese and American friends often wonder how a Caucasian, with only mediocre Japanese speaking ability, came to teach Japanese calligraphy and painting. They may be equally mystified that I've written about a subject rooted in Japanese language and sometimes thought of, by Japanese and Westerners alike, as being impenetrable to non-Japanese.

Nothing could be further from the truth. The path leading to this book supports my assertion that it's possible for people of other cultures to achieve success in shodo or any Japanese "do" form. In 1926, my late father was among the first non-Japanese to study Japanese martial arts, earning black belts in more than one discipline. At five years old, I was practicing aiki-jujutsu with him. Later, I began Shin-shin-toitsu-do style Japanese yoga and Japanese healing arts. By 1981, I was the Director of the Sennin Foundation Center for Japanese Cultural Arts, which offers instruction in Japanese yoga, healing arts, shodo, and martial arts.

As a boy, I was encouraged to paint, and due to martial arts training, I was exposed to Japanese calligraphy. I was

an art major and sustained an interest in shodo and sumi-e, but to little avail. No teachers were accessible. In 1985, I met Kobara Ranseki Sensei, a master calligrapher/painter from Kyoto. Kobara Sensei, having received innumerable awards in shodo, including one from the Prime Minister of Japan, does not advertise for students. Because most of his pupils were from Japan, he taught in Japanese. Because he'd never attempted to instruct an American not fluent in Japanese, Mr. Kobara was none too sure about teaching me. Still, like a cliché from a bad movie, I kept coming back.

Since studying with Kobara Sensei, my Japanese has improved, and I've advanced in ranking and received various awards that substantiate shodo proficiency. I mention this only to support my assertion that it's indeed possible for people of other cultures to achieve success in shodo. Using shodo as an example, it's my intention to show the interrelationship between Japanese arts, as well as the way these skills, from flower arrangement to tea ceremony, can serve as meditations capable of enhancing the lives of everyone, regardless of nationality.

The Japanese Way of the Flower

IKEBANA AS MOVING MEDITATION

H. E. Davey

Ann Kameoka

Michi: Japanese Arts and Ways

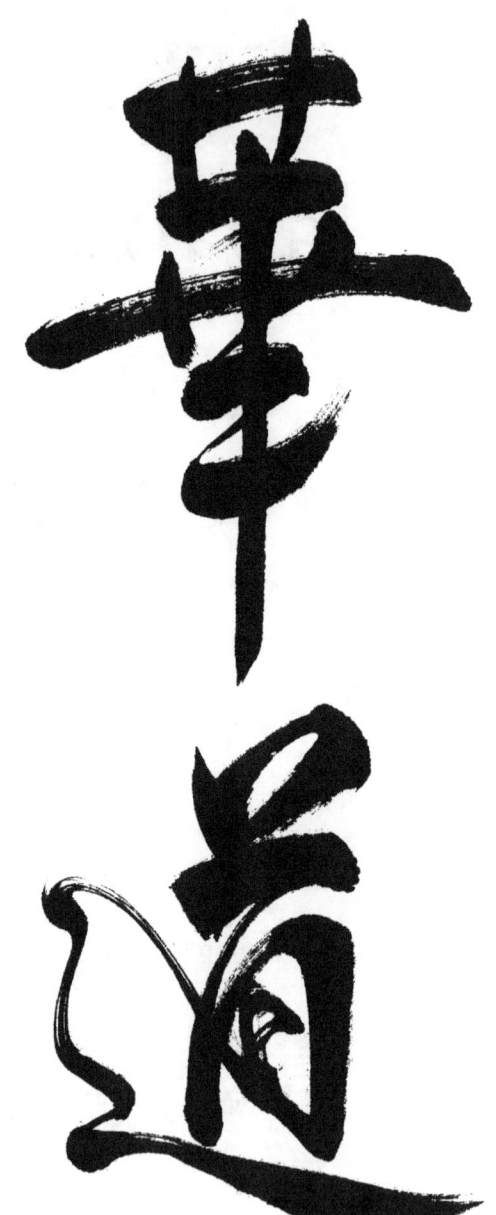

"Kado": The Way of the Flower
Calligraphy by H. E. Davey

CONTENTS

PREFACE

The Japanese art of flower arrangement is most frequently known in the West by the term *ikebana* (literally, "living flowers"). In this book, we favor the less-familiar word "kado" ("the Way of flowers") to emphasize that Japanese floral art is, more than simply the skill of arranging living flowers, actually a "Way," or path, of studying the essence of life itself.

Kado is one of numerous Japanese art forms—among them judo, *chado* (tea ceremony), and *shodo* (calligraphy)—with appellations ending in the character "do," meaning "the Way." While this use of "do" is prevalent in the Japanese language, how these various arts actually function as Ways is not always well understood, even in Japan.

Perhaps you've heard that flower arrangement and other related arts function as a Way of life, and that by practicing these skills you can transcend a specific art and grasp the art of living itself. While this statement is undoubtedly true, finding a teacher (or a book, for that matter) who can effectively explain exactly how the study of calligraphy, tea ceremony, or floral art can lead to spiritual realization is difficult. Even more unusual is discovering a source for genuine and effective exercises, relating to a given art, that are capable of bringing about personal transformation. To state the matter bluntly, while many books and teachers of various Do forms often pay lip service to the ideal of the Way producing spiritual evolution in its practitioners, they also often fail to offer direct explanations and methodologies to effectively help their students realize the Way. It is frequently (and incorrectly) assumed that the mere practice of making tea or manipulating flowers will somehow magically produce profound realizations. This is untrue and unfortunate.

It is untrue because it is the manner in which we approach the various Ways that determines what we will learn from them. Spiritual realization is not automatically guaranteed in any facet of life.

It is unfortunate because the deliberate, conscious practice of Japanese Do forms truly can result in the efficient cultivation of the human mind and body. Simply put, if we wish to use flower arrangement and other arts as meditative acts, we must completely investigate exactly how it is that these arts can lead to realization. Many people arrange flowers, make tea, or practice the martial arts without any sort of sudden insights into the nature of living. Any book dealing with Japanese art as meditation must first explain the manner in which a given art can serve as meditation and then outline exactly what kinds of principles and practices will allow its readers to directly experience that art as meditation.

The "Way of flowers," or kado, is a topic that has been the subject of numerous books in both Japanese and English. Few of these works, however, have explored the manner in which the art of arranging flowers goes beyond floral sculpture and enters into the realm of spirituality. Even fewer have offered techniques and effective methods of practice, which are needed if real personal growth is going to take place through this medium.

The Japanese Way of the Flower was written to answer that need. It is the second in a series of books written by H. E. Davey for Stone Bridge Press that will explore Japanese cultural arts as meditation. (The first, about Japanese calligraphy as meditation, is *Brush Meditation: A Japa-*

nese *Way to Mind & Body Harmony*.) Since the fundamental principles underlying all of the Ways are the same, we hope this work will introduce you to universal principles of personal transformation that relate to all of the Japanese arts, from painting and calligraphy to the martial arts. In this sense, we have used kado as a representative example of a Japanese "Way," and through this example we will introduce you to particular principles that are commonly valued in all of the Ways and that have a relationship with various parts of daily living.

Still, neither of us is a master of any Do form; in fact, the idea of mastering an art is anathema in all of the Japanese Ways. While we both have numerous years of experience in more than one of the Do forms—Ann Kameoka has teacher certification in Ikenobo-style floral art—we both remain lifelong students. We have no desire to function as gurus for the Japanese cultural arts, and we are not interested in doling out the "secrets" of the Japanese Ways to a group of followers.

This work is, then, a means for us to examine ourselves and our understanding of the Way more thoroughly. It has been a learning experience for us, and we hope our book contains ideas that will be of use to others as well.

The Japanese Way of the Flower begins with an in-depth analysis of the history of Japanese flower arrangement, followed by an examination of the relationship between the mind and body of the kado student. Coordination of mind and body is an important goal, or at least a valued quality, in most of the Japanese Do forms. Kado is no exception, but aside from the practice of arranging flowers, there are often no methods to directly cultivate mind and body harmony found in ikebana. We've therefore introduced exercises and meditations derived from Shin-shin-toitsu-do—a system of Japanese yoga—to help you grasp unification of mind and body in daily life as well as learn kado more easily.

Next, the book explains the actual methods of arranging flowers and greenery to form flowering sculpture. We investigate how the
meditative principles previously outlined connect to traditional Japanese
styles of floral arrangement, as well as how these concepts offer a process
for enhancing both your daily life and your flower arrangements.

At the back of the book is information about where to locate
supplies to create your own works of flowering sculpture, along with
information about how to find a qualified teacher of kado. The latter
is essential because it is impossible to fully master any of the Japanese
cultural arts solely through the use of a book. Nonetheless, we believe
that kado practitioners will find *The Japanese Way of the Flower* a useful
adjunct to direct training in this fine art. By experimenting with the
contents of this book, we also hope that both untrained and skilled
flower-arrangement enthusiasts will discover the vital relationship
between human beings and nature.

ABOUT THE ILLUSTRATIONS

The illustrations by Linda Shimoda of representative flower
arrangements have been adapted and modeled from the authors' collection of books, magazines, and other source material. H. E. Davey's
calligraphy of classical poetry is included to aid in an understanding of
Japanese aesthetics and to provide places to pause and reflect. All the
poems express typical Japanese sentiments toward flowers; their translations are not literal but are meant to approximate the meaning and
rhythm of the originals.

353

ACKNOWLEDGMENTS

This book, like all other aspects of life, is the outgrowth of the efforts of many people and generations. Kado has a lengthy history, and as a living art it is continuing to evolve. Ann Kameoka is a student of the Ikenobo system of flower arrangement, the oldest style of kado in Japan, and she would like to acknowledge the past leaders of Ikenobo as well as Ikenobo Sen'ei Sensei, the current leader of the school, and Fukuyama Suiho Sensei, her personal teacher. Special thanks to Shuji Ikeda for providing some of the vases that appear in the color photographs in this book.

H. E. Davey would like to acknowledge his students at the Sennin Foundation Center for Japanese Cultural Arts, who have all been instrumental in his personal growth over many years. He would also like to thank his wife Ann for her unwavering support. Without her, this book could not have been easily written.

Both of us are practitioners of the system of Japanese yoga known as Shin-shin-toitsu-do ("the Way of Mind and Body Unification"), and we would like to acknowledge our debt to our teachers and to Nakamura Tempu Sensei, founder of Shin-shin-toitsu-do. Several of the meditative exercises and many of the principles outlined in this work have been influenced by our study of Japanese yoga. Through our practice of Shin-shin-toitsu-do, we have come to realize more clearly the profound interrelationship between the various Japanese cultural arts and what the genuine principles connecting all of the Ways actually are.

This volume would not have come to completion without the help of the staff of Stone Bridge Press. We are indebted to Peter Goodman, Yurika Kimijima, Olivia Weber, Rick DeNoble, Max Tuefferd, and Hannah Weiss. We would also like to thank Linda Shimoda for her elegant illustrations.

Both of us also wish to acknowledge our parents: Noboru and Naomi, Victor and Elaine.

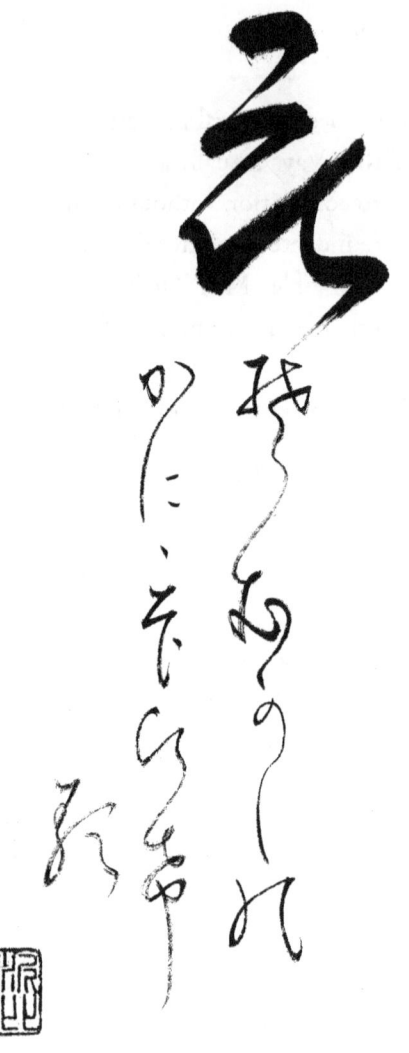

The spirit of the people
may have changed over the many years;
but in my hometown
the plum blossoms warmly greet me
with a scent I well recall.

KI NO TSURAYUKI FROM "HYAKUNIN ISSHU"

Hito wa isa
Kokoro mo shirazu
Furusato wa
Hana zo mukashi no
Ka ni nioi keru

Chapter 1

KADO: JAPANESE FLOWER ARRANGEMENT

Kado is one of Japan's oldest art forms. Many of you may wonder how kado differs from Western floral art. Even more of you may question why you would even want to spend years studying the Japanese art of arranging flowers when you could just grab a fist full of daisies and stuff 'em in a vase.

Issues of culture and art aside, the primary difference between Western flower arrangement and kado is the Do concept itself: that Japanese flower arrangement can function as a path that points toward realization. This is not to say that Western-style floral art can't be practiced as a "Do," or "Way of life." Indeed, any activity can become meditation and function as a Way. (In this sense, it isn't so much *what* you do, but *how* you do it that's meaningful.)

Still, kado has a long history as a Way, an important point that will be covered in this chapter. Even more vital is the simple fact that from

357

the moment it received the designation "kado," Japanese flower arrangement has directly strived for comprehension of the Way of the universe. And while critics might say kado has sometimes missed this target, this clear-cut statement of purpose, as well as the purpose itself, is what separates kado from the Western version of arranging flowers. In short, Western flower arranging does not have a history as a "Way."

Kado is said to have been born initially in China, where it became popular in connection with the decoration of Buddhist temples. When Buddhism came to Japan many centuries ago, flower arrangement came with it. Over time it evolved to become a Japanese spiritual path. In this sense, it is similar to other Japanese arts such as budo (the martial Way) and shodo (the Way of calligraphy) that have also evolved to become methods of personal growth. Today, however, it is no longer the exclusive specialty of the priesthood but is enjoyed by vast numbers of people throughout the world.

Searching for the Roots of Kado

Kado, according to some authorities, has been practiced for more than six hundred years. It is thought to have developed from Buddhist rituals involving the offering of flowers, which can be traced to the sixth-century introduction of Buddhism to Japan. Part of the worship involved the presentation of flowers on an altar in honor of the Buddha. In India, the birthplace of Buddhism, flowers were placed rather informally; sometimes only petals were strewn about. Nevertheless, by the tenth century, the Japanese were presenting their alms in containers. Altar offerings were the responsibility of temple priests, and by the middle of the fifteenth century, with the rise of classical styles of ikebana, kado was an art form independent of its religious origins, though it retained strong symbolic and spiritual aspects. Accordingly, the first teachers and students of the classical systems were priests and members of the nobility. Yet, in time, many different schools arose, styles changed, and kado came to be practiced by people from other levels of Japanese society.

Ikenobo, the oldest school of kado, stems from a priest of the Rokkakudo temple in Kyoto who was so expert in flower arrangement that other priests sought him out for training. Because he lived by the side of a pond (for which the Japanese word consists of the characters *ike* and *nobo*), this name was associated with the Rokkakudo priests who specialized in altar arrangements.

The Evolution of Schools of Flower Arrangement

Systems and styles evolved over generations, so that by the late fifteenth century, arrangements were common enough to be appreciated by ordinary people, not just the Japanese nobility and priests. This epoch marks the beginning of an art form/spiritual path with fixed rules and guidelines. At this time, texts recording these often secret principles and discoveries were written, the oldest of which is the *Sendensho*, a compilation covering the years from 1443 to 1536.

As time passed, kado became a major part of traditional festivals, and ikebana exhibitions were held regularly. Rules were prescribed, and materials had to be combined in specific ways. In these early forms a tall, upright, central stem had to be accompanied by two shorter stems; the three stems represented heaven, humanity, and earth. Specific Japanese names for these three elements differed, and continue to differ,

359

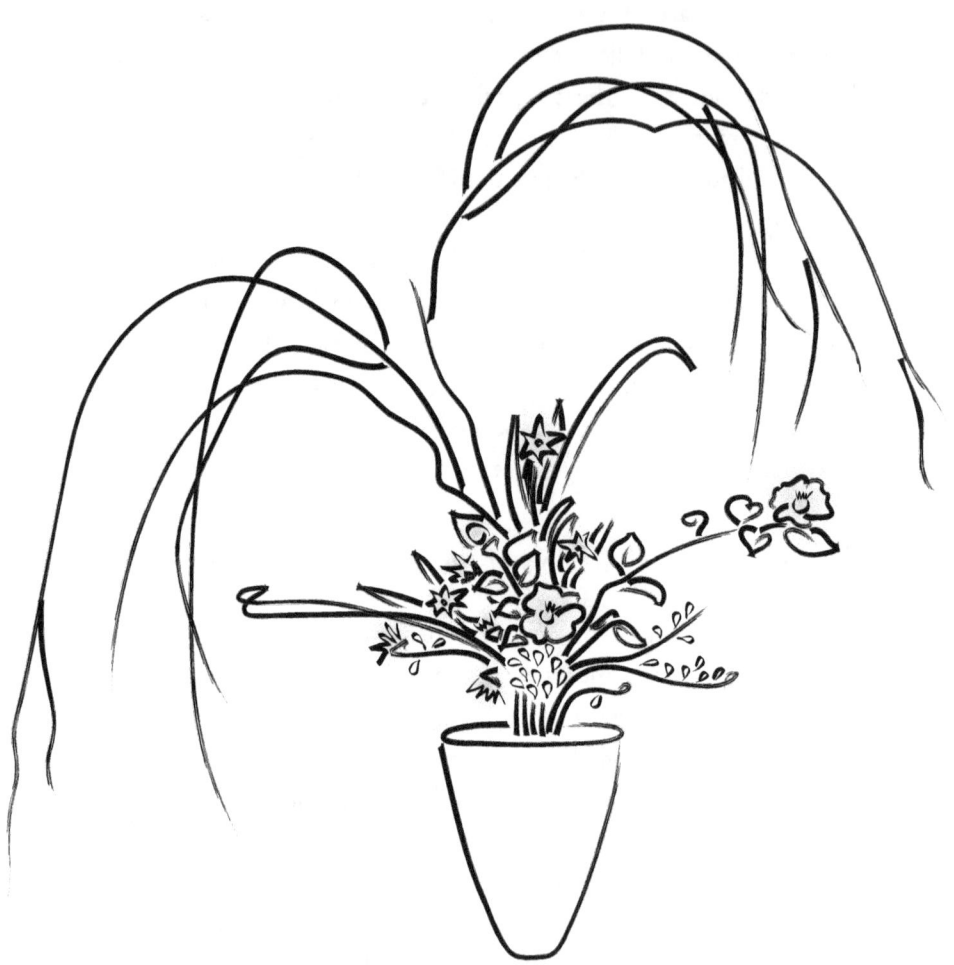

The rikka style originated in the fourteenth century and is one of the earliest forms of flower arrangement. The arrangement here uses weeping willow, narcissus, camellia, boxwood, young pine, Chinese hawthorn, and chrysanthemums to create a miniature landscape.

among kado systems. In 1545, the Ikenobo school, now well established, formulated the principles of *rikka* arrangements by naming the seven main branches used in that method.

THE EMERGENCE OF RIKKA

As far back as the birth of the Tokugawa shogunate (1603), various distinct schools were developing as the practice of flower arranging became more widespread. Just as in the martial arts, each system has its own unique traditions and areas of particular importance.

Some schools stressed the rikka, or formal "standing" style—the original type of early floral art. Rikka features very tall arrangements that seem to point toward heaven. The style first appeared in the sixth century in floral groupings on both sides of the altars found in Buddhist temples. Tall and broad, to harmonize with the lofty temple buildings, rikka was designed to function almost like a miniature physical universe, representing a landscape with mountains, streams, and lowlands. It towered high above bronze vases that were borrowed, along with other religious ornaments, from China. The tips of the branches and flowers pointed toward heaven in an expression of religious devotion.

Rikka arrangements evolved to grow wider and less rigid in appearance, though no less intricate in scope, and they continued to be the primary form of Buddhist floral art in castles, palaces, and temples until the establishment of the Kamakura government in the twelfth century. All rikka arrangements were an evolution of a particular kind of flowering sculpture of Shumisen, the holy Buddhist mountain that symbolized the universe.

Central to all truly classical versions of rikka, then and now, is a five- or six-foot pine tree representing the beauty of the Japanese landscape (pines can be found everywhere in Japan, from the beaches and on up into the mountainous regions). It is usually placed in the center of the vase. Cedars, cypresses, and bamboo are also commonly put to use in rikka. Rocks and stones in the miniature rikka cosmos are represented by pine branches; rivers and streams by white chrysanthemums; sunlight, shady areas, and various seasonal colors are symbolized through the use of plant settings arranged in the right spot.

THE BIRTH OF NATURALISTIC ARRANGEMENT

During the Momoyama period (1568–1600), many magnificent castles were constructed. During the same period, noblemen and royal retainers were creating large decorative rikka pieces, because the rikka style was considered a most appropriate decoration for those castles. (These days, the rikka style is often reserved for more formal occasions or ceremonies. It is also used for festivals and is certainly no longer the exclusive preserve of the Buddhist priesthood. In some circles rikka is seen as being somewhat old-fashioned, while traditionalists strive to preserve its unique characteristics.)

The style used during the Momoyama period was, in general, notable for its flamboyance. During this same period the tea ceremony made its appearance, as a counterpoint to the prevailing extravagant style— the tea ceremony's emphasis on rustic simplicity (wabi/sabi) contrasted sharply with Momoyama embellishment. (The terms "wabi" and "sabi" are explained in detail in Chapter 3.) Tea ceremony enthusiasts developed an unadorned complementary style called chabana, or "tea flowers."

By 1600, the religious significance of ikebana had diminished, and as a result floral arrangement gradually became a lay art. In the Edo period (early seventeenth to mid-nineteenth centuries), the simplicity of chabana helped create the *nageire*, or "thrown-in," style. It was this less-structured design that led to the development of *seika*, or *shoka* style, as it is called in the Ikenobo school. This style is characterized by a tight bundle of stems that form a triangular, three-branched, asymmetrical structure. Shoka is somewhat similar to rikka except that it has fewer floral elements and rules. It originated in the mid-eighteenth century. This form is now considered classic, and schools that teach it are counted among the "classical schools."

The more formal schools created the *ten-chi-jin* (heaven-earth-humanity), also known as *shin-soe-tai*, principle that all kado systems now follow. In essence, one of the goals of kado is to arrange the floral sprays in such a way that they represent heaven, earth, and humanity. For example, in some systems, if just one plant is used, the primary portion that shoots upward represents heaven. A twig on the right might then be bent sideways to symbolize human beings, while the bottom branch or twig on the left would be ever so slightly bent so that it points upward to represent earth. It is also possible to embody the ten-chi-jin principle by making use of three different plants or branches: bamboo can be used to evoke ten, plum blossom can depict chi, and pine can symbolize jin. These two different versions of the ten-chi-jin principle are sometimes referred to as *in* and *yo* arrangements. In this case, in represents the female aspect of nature and yo can be thought of as the male form. In and yo (*yin* and *yang* in Chinese) symbolize a dualism which creates the complementary but opposite aspects of nature that ultimately form the one harmonious whole that is the universe.

The three fundamental ten-chi-jin sprays depict the harmonious balance that should exist between human beings and the universe.

Arranging flowers according to the ten-chi-jin principle requires strict adherence to aesthetic form, and this in turn serves as a method of spiritual refinement.

The Emergence of the Ryu

New ryu ("schools" or "handed-down traditions") also began to appear, most derived from the original Ikenobo tradition. Each had its individual interpretation of shoka. The first school of kado, Ikenobo, pointed the base of the stems directly down, using a komi (forked stick) to hold them in place.

Other systems developed unique variations, which can be seen in their approach to shoka. The Ko Ryu school, for example, placed the komi at an angle, and the ends of the stems were cut at a slant and propped against the side of the vessel. The Enshu school exaggerated the curves of the branches by cutting slits in them, bending them, and inserting triangular plugs into the slits so that the branches held the desired curve.

Three ryu predominate at the present time: Ikenobo, Ohara, and Sogetsu. But several million people in Japan participate in over twenty well-recognized kado schools. Ikenobo, Sogetsu Ryu, Misho Ryu, Saga Ryu, Ohara Ryu, Kyofu Ryu, Ko Ryu, Enshu Ryu, Nakayama Bumpo-kai, and Adachi-shiki are a few of the most well-known versions of flower arrangement in Japan. More than two thousand different schools of ikebana are registered with the Japanese Ministry of Education. A detailed discussion of the various systems of kado is beyond the scope of this book. Because the Ikenobo system is the one we are most familiar with, the arrangements in this book reflect that tradition.

From Form Proceed to the Formless

Like all Japanese arts, kado requires that one start with the strict observation of, and adherence to, traditional and formal techniques. Through the study of these formalized arrangements one ultimately encounters the transcendent form of the universe itself—the void—spoken of in Musashi's *Go Rin no Sho* as well as countless other Asian martial and religious texts. Yet kado's formal techniques vary from the traditionalists, who favor a natural arrangement of living flowers, to the schools developed after World War II, which employ artificial materials such as plastic, metal, and glass to give the sensation of life through the effervescence of form.

The three fundamental ten-chi-jin sprays depict the harmonious balance that should exist between human beings and the universe. Arranging flowers according to the ten-chi-jin principle requires strict adherence to aesthetic form, and this in turn serves as a method of spiritual refinement.

Every system has its own methods, but all schools of ikebana involve deliberate ways of cutting and caring for flowers. All make use of the ten-chi-jin concept, and usually an odd number of branches or stalks are applied to create an asymmetrical balance that more successfully imitates nature and that is favored in Japanese aesthetics. Five, seven, and nine stems are often used, in keeping with the Buddhist concept of "becoming"—continuing to travel on the path to enlightenment as opposed to having arrived at a state of perfection, the latter of which could be implied by even numbers.

Traditional and modern styles all make use of flowers for the purpose of interior decoration, on both a personal and commercial basis (in the Japanese home, flower arrangements are often placed in an alcove called the *tokonoma*). But ikebana is not limited to the use of flowers. It also makes liberal use of shrubs and trees such as maple, bamboo, pine, and willow. In kado, the word *hana* ("flower") is used very broadly.

Kado & Western-Style Flower Arrangement

Just as Japanese homes, historically speaking, differ from dwellings in the West, so too does ikebana vary from Western-style floral art. While a large number of elements make kado distinct and internationally popular as floral art, the following differences are probably most noticeable.

Kado's origins lie in Buddhism and have a spiritual basis, so it is not purely decorative in scope. As previously noted, in the sixth century large floral arrangements began to appear on both sides of the altars in Japanese Buddhist temples; this trend continued through subsequent centuries. Voluminous rikka arrangements stood tall and rigid from elaborate bronze containers, religious artifacts brought to Japan from Buddhist temples in China. Both tree and flowering grass material were combined to create a religious offering. Intricate and elaborate rikka arrangements gradually softened in appearance over time through the addition of greater width and the suggestion of movement through flowing lines within the arrangement. Rikka arrangements were the dominant form of arrangement in both temples and palaces until the Kamakura period, in the twelfth century.

As noted earlier, the tall rikka design originated in the desire to suggest Shumisen, the sacred mountain and symbol of the universe

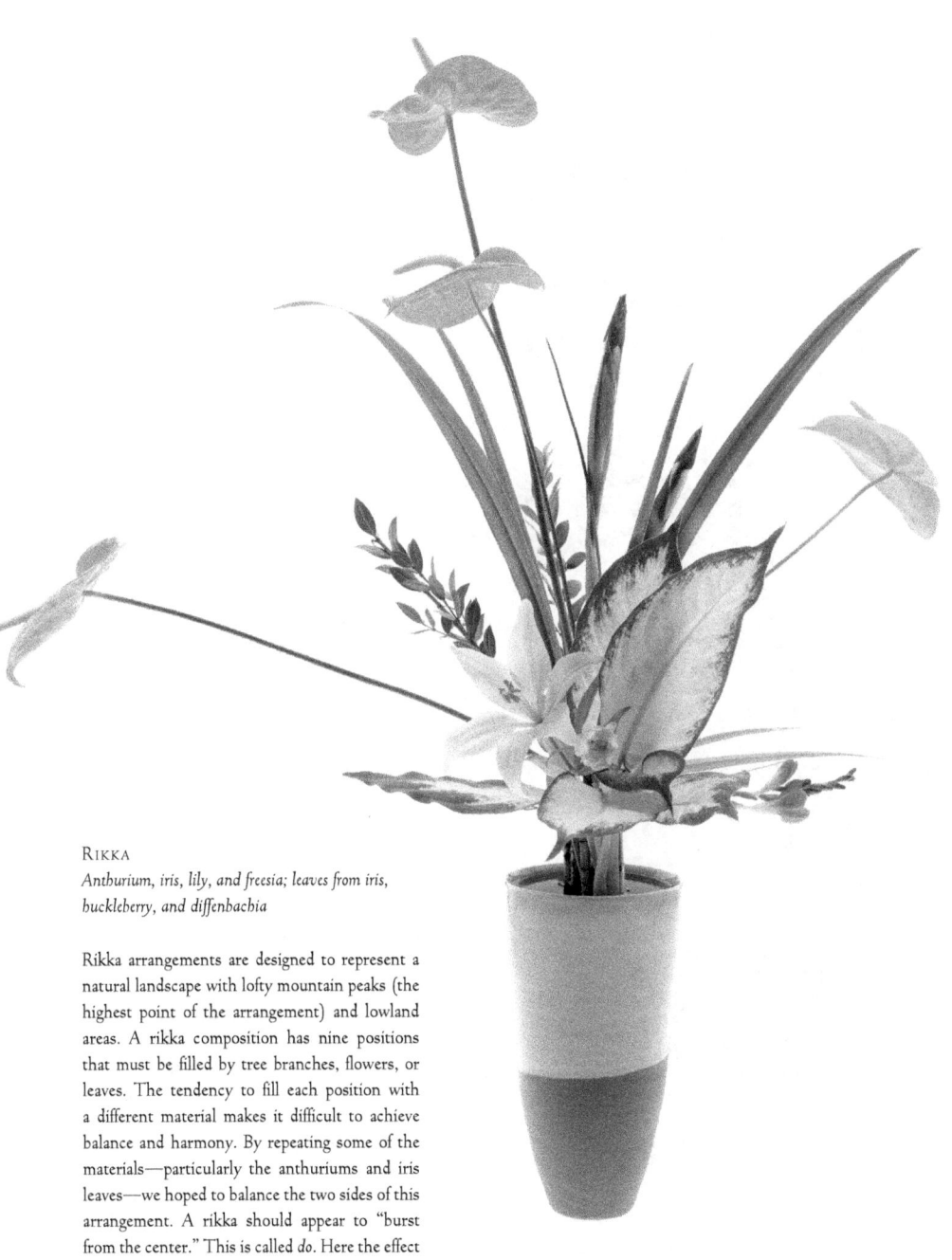

RIKKA

*Anthurium, iris, lily, and freesia; leaves from iris,
huckleberry, and diffenbachia*

Rikka arrangements are designed to represent a
natural landscape with lofty mountain peaks (the
highest point of the arrangement) and lowland
areas. A rikka composition has nine positions
that must be filled by tree branches, flowers, or
leaves. The tendency to fill each position with
a different material makes it difficult to achieve
balance and harmony. By repeating some of the
materials—particularly the anthuriums and iris
leaves—we hoped to balance the two sides of this
arrangement. A rikka should appear to "burst
from the center." This is called *do*. Here the effect
is created by yellow lilies and diffenbachia leaves.

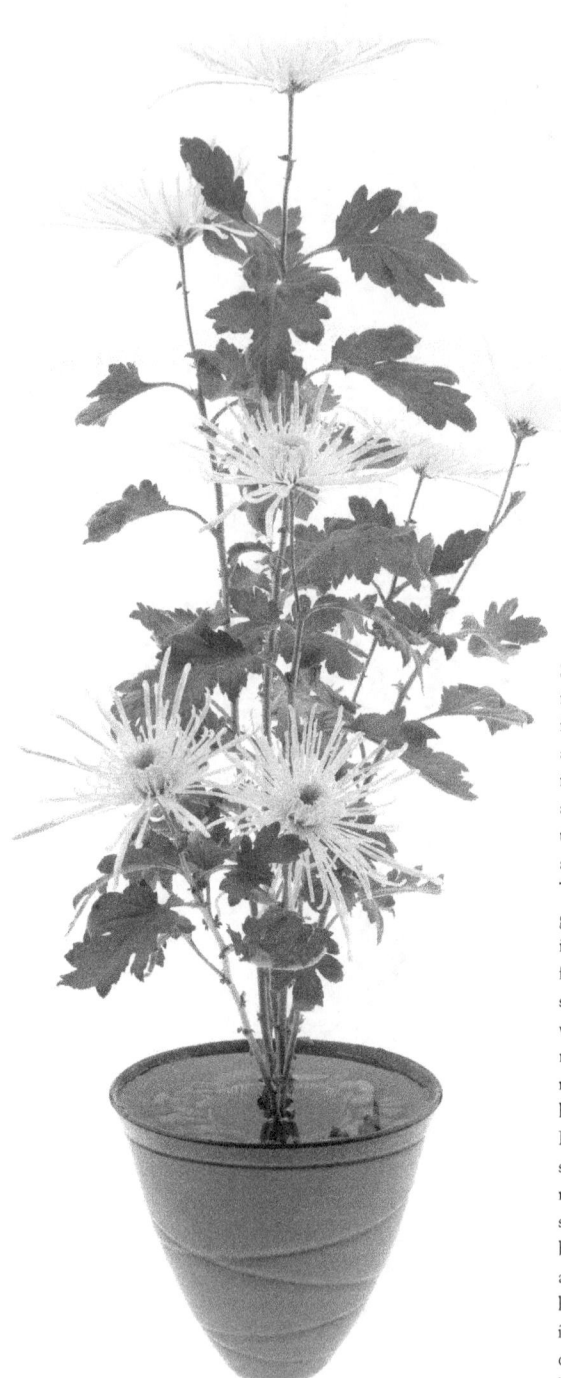

SHOKA SHOFUTAI ISSHUIKE
Spider chrysanthemums

Since only spider chrysanthemums are used in this traditional shoka-style arrangement, it is considered an *isshuike* or "one-material" arrangement. Japanese flower arrangement has its origins in Buddhism, and most classical arrangements incorporate an odd number of stems that symbolize a progression toward completion and perfection through spiritual enlightenment. The seven stems used here are divided into three groups—shin, soe, and tai. The first three stems in the foreground are considered the tai group, followed by the shin group and, in the back, the soe group. Each flower group is associated with varying degrees of visual strength and symbolic meaning. Shin has the most visual strength and represents the human being positioned between heaven (soe) and earth (tai). Through its Buddhist origins, shin can also be thought of as symbolically representing the present, while soe represents the past and tai the future. Each shoka shofutai arrangement expresses the Buddhist belief in the dualistic nature of the world: heaven and earth, light and dark, left and right, high and low. Shoka shofutai is thus a spiritual universe in miniature, blending together the duality of opposites in a desire for transcendence. You can learn to make this arrangement in Chapter Four.

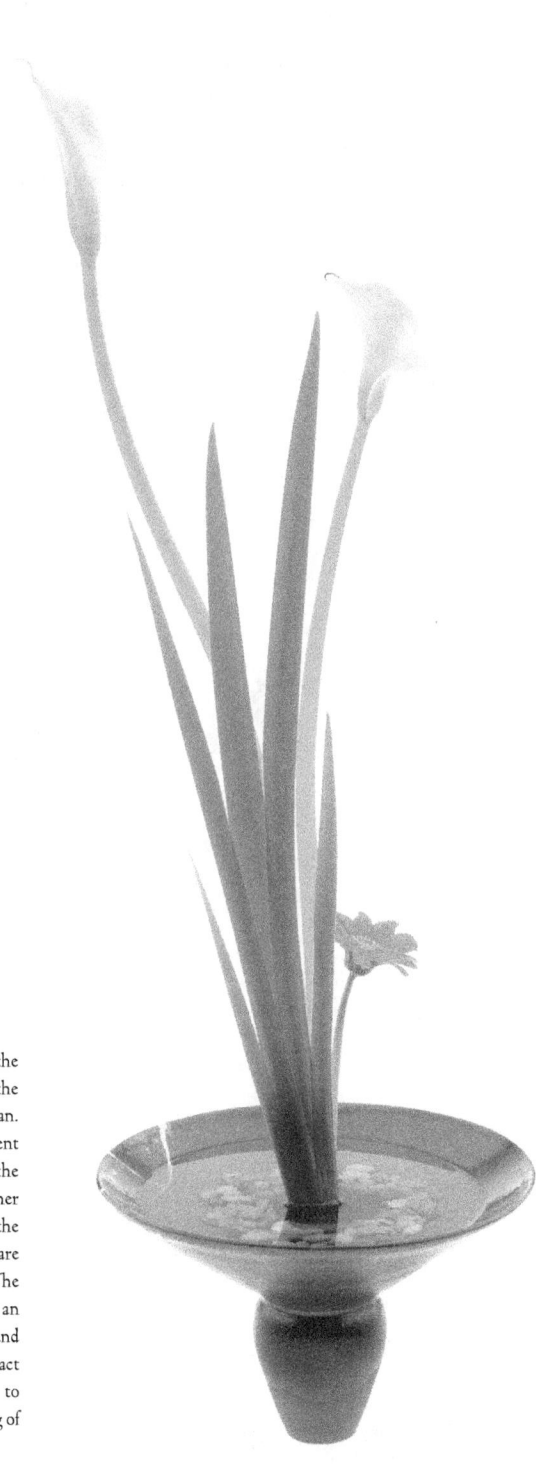

SHOKA SHIMPUTAI
Calla lilies, iris leaves, and gerbera daisy

The shoka shimputai style was developed in the late 1970s by Ikenobo Sen'ei, headmaster of the Ikenobo school of flower arrangement in Japan. Shoka shimputai typically uses three different materials of varying visual strength—shu (the strongest), yo, and ashirai—brought together to contrast and complement each other. In the arrangement here, the tall, curving calla lilies are shu by virtue of their height, shape, and color. The red orange gerbera daisy serves as yo, providing an interesting counterpoint in height, texture, and color. The iris leaves in front of the calla lilies act as ashirai and offer another striking contrast to the calla lily and gerbera daisy, giving the feeling of naturalness through its softer green tones.

FREESTYLE: "ARRIVAL OF SPRING"
Gerbera daisy, freesia, lemon leaf, bear grass

Here, a very commonly shaped vase demonstrates how even simple containers can be used to create a freestyle arrangement. The form of the vase suggests an armless body, with the gerbera daisy serving as a head and face. The bright yellow color of the daisy suggests a smiling, sunny disposition and is further accented by the spot of red from the freesia. The lemon leaf and bear grass provide lightness and movement in contrast to the solid earth tones of the vase, while the green colors offer cool relief. Since most freestyle arrangements play off a simple theme, this arrangement might be called *Happy Face* or even *Here Comes the Sun*. You can learn to make this arrangement in Chapter Four.

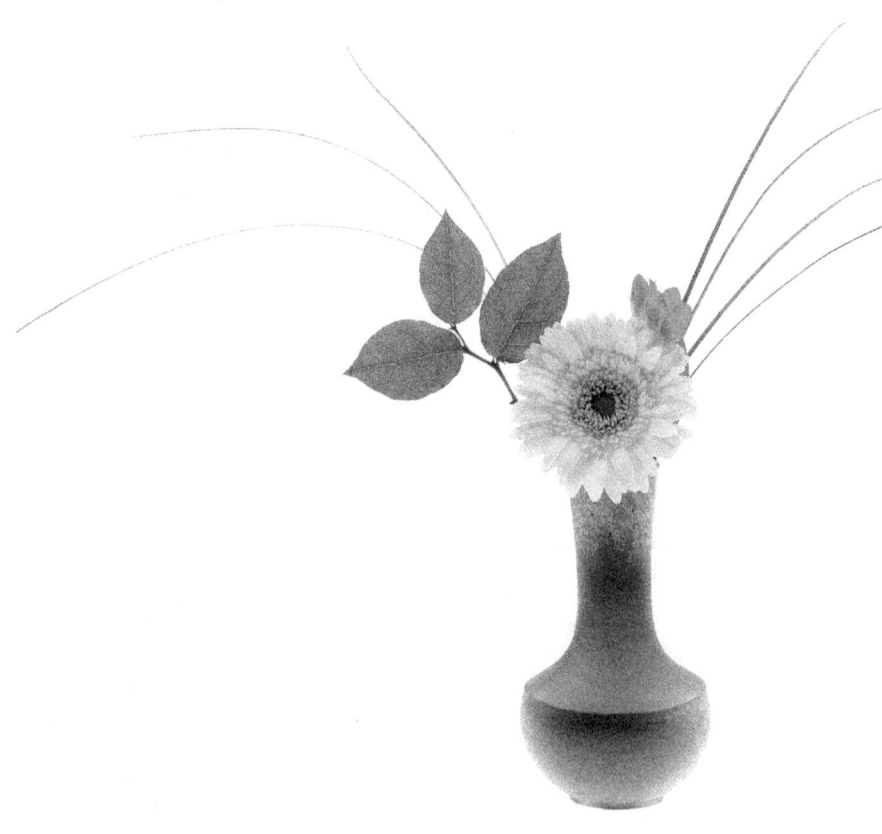

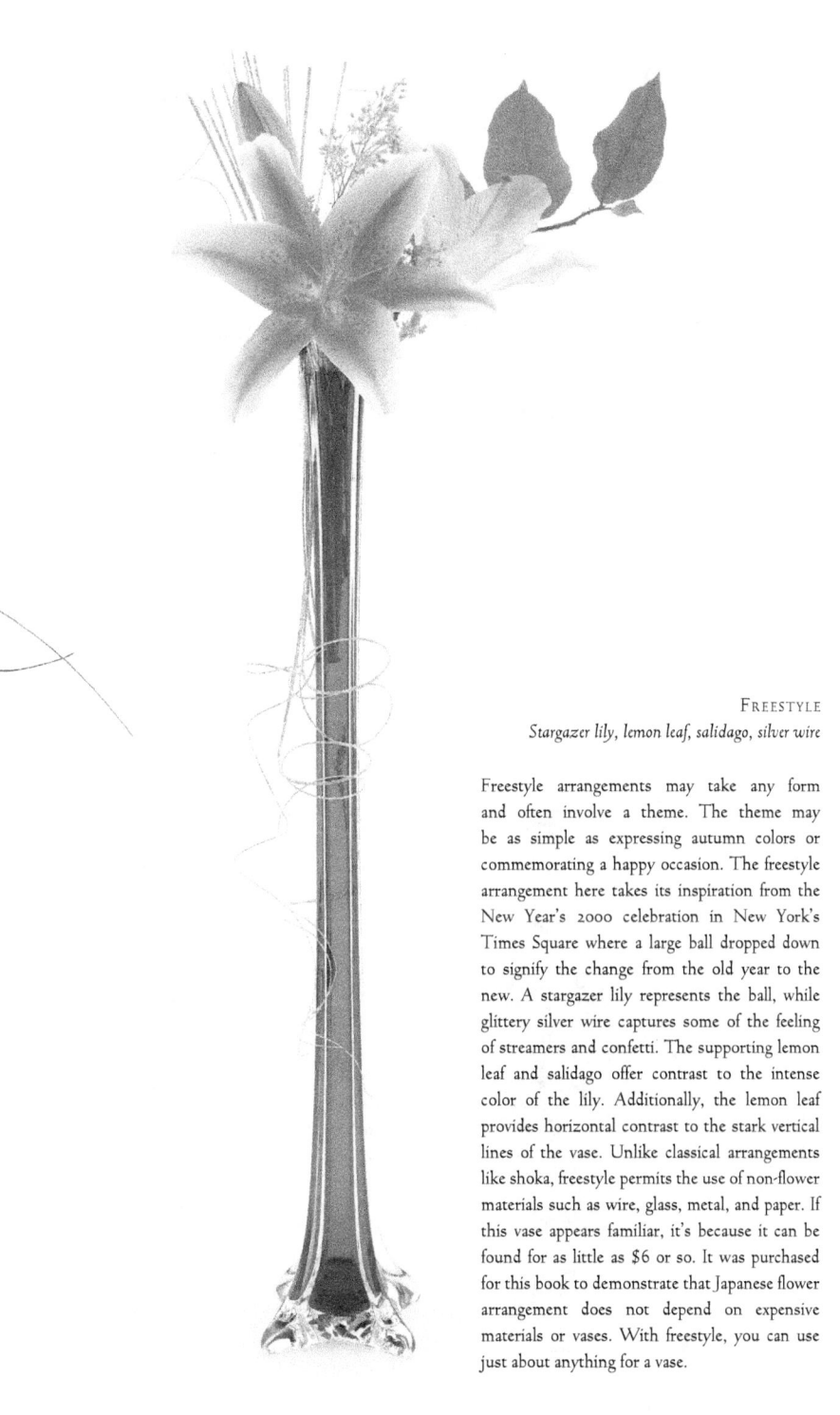

FREESTYLE
Stargazer lily, lemon leaf, salidago, silver wire

Freestyle arrangements may take any form and often involve a theme. The theme may be as simple as expressing autumn colors or commemorating a happy occasion. The freestyle arrangement here takes its inspiration from the New Year's 2000 celebration in New York's Times Square where a large ball dropped down to signify the change from the old year to the new. A stargazer lily represents the ball, while glittery silver wire captures some of the feeling of streamers and confetti. The supporting lemon leaf and salidago offer contrast to the intense color of the lily. Additionally, the lemon leaf provides horizontal contrast to the stark vertical lines of the vase. Unlike classical arrangements like shoka, freestyle permits the use of non-flower materials such as wire, glass, metal, and paper. If this vase appears familiar, it's because it can be found for as little as $6 or so. It was purchased for this book to demonstrate that Japanese flower arrangement does not depend on expensive materials or vases. With freestyle, you can use just about anything for a vase.

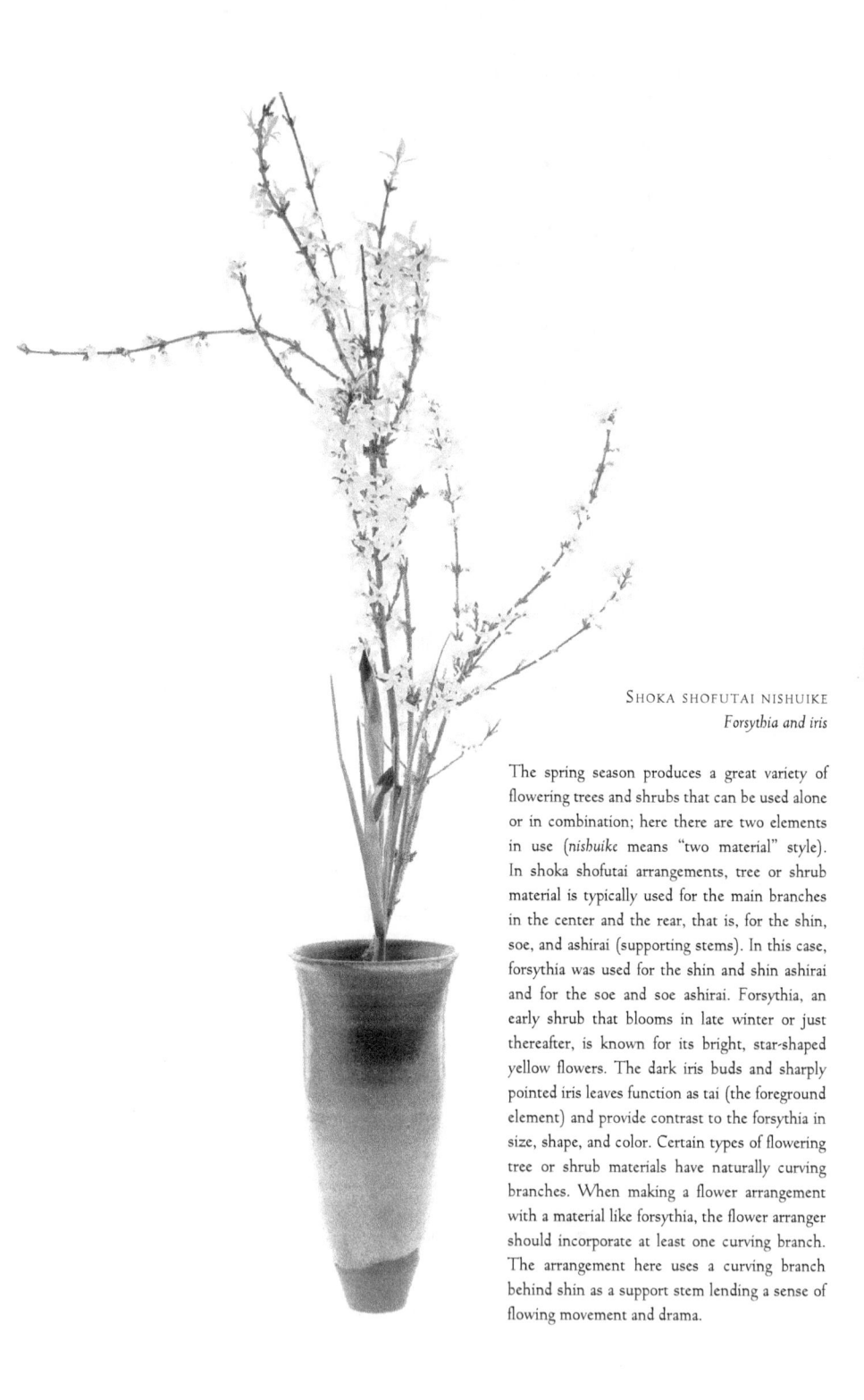

SHOKA SHOFUTAI NISHUIKE
Forsythia and iris

The spring season produces a great variety of flowering trees and shrubs that can be used alone or in combination; here there are two elements in use (*nishuike* means "two material" style). In shoka shofutai arrangements, tree or shrub material is typically used for the main branches in the center and the rear, that is, for the shin, soe, and ashirai (supporting stems). In this case, forsythia was used for the shin and shin ashirai and for the soe and soe ashirai. Forsythia, an early shrub that blooms in late winter or just thereafter, is known for its bright, star-shaped yellow flowers. The dark iris buds and sharply pointed iris leaves function as tai (the foreground element) and provide contrast to the forsythia in size, shape, and color. Certain types of flowering tree or shrub materials have naturally curving branches. When making a flower arrangement with a material like forsythia, the flower arranger should incorporate at least one curving branch. The arrangement here uses a curving branch behind shin as a support stem lending a sense of flowing movement and drama.

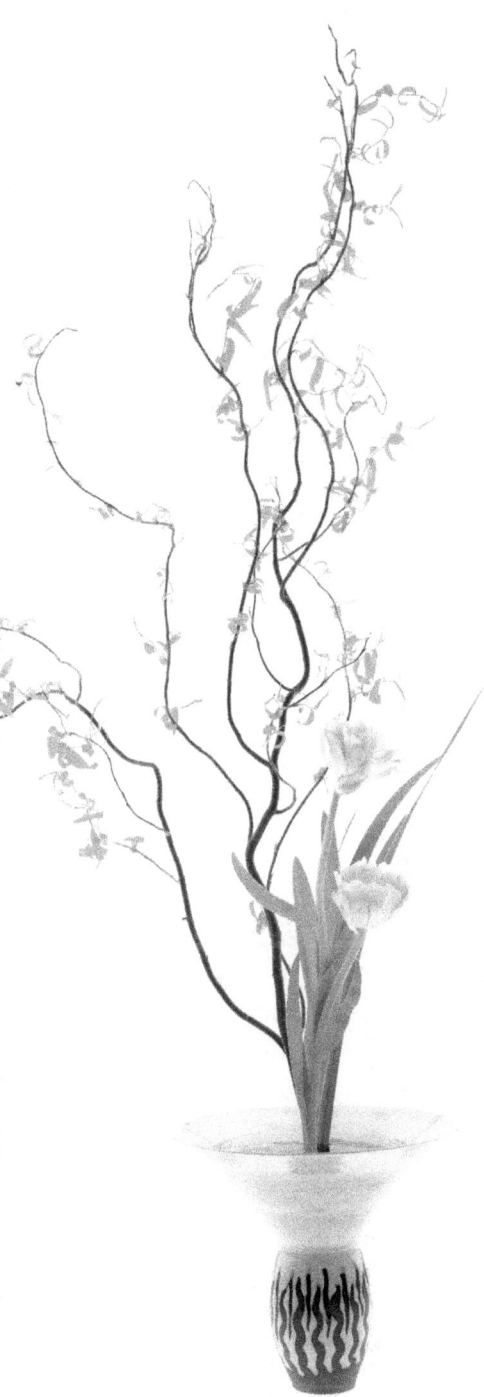

SHOKA SHOFUTAI SANSHUIKE
Curly willow, angelique tulips, iris leaves

This shoka shofutai arrangement is considered *sanshuike* since it combines three different flower materials. These three—curly willow, tulips, and iris leaves—harmonize well thanks to their common green color. Sanshuike arrangements may also combine very different materials in color, shape, and texture. One of the flower arranger's challenges is to use very different materials and at the same time create contrast and harmony. The artist can also take advantage of a plant's tendency to produce varied and eye-catching shapes as part of its natural growth pattern. An example of such a plant is the curly willow, with its numerous large and small branches that combine naturally to create the main shin stem and a supporting shin ashirai stem to the rear. Normally, a separate stem would have to be added to support shin, but in this case, just through some light shaping, only one stem was needed. A separate curly willow stem was added to the rear to fill the soe position. Angelique tulips are used for tai, the foreground element. (In most shoka arrangements, tai consists of three stems—tai shin, tai tani, and tai saki. But when using certain flower materials, such as tulips, traditionally only two stems are included due to the size of their flowers and leaves in proportion to the composition as a whole.) Since much of the visual strength of this arrangement is on the left side, the green iris leaf was placed to the right to provide balance. Its upward and outward movement helps balance the arrangement from side to side.

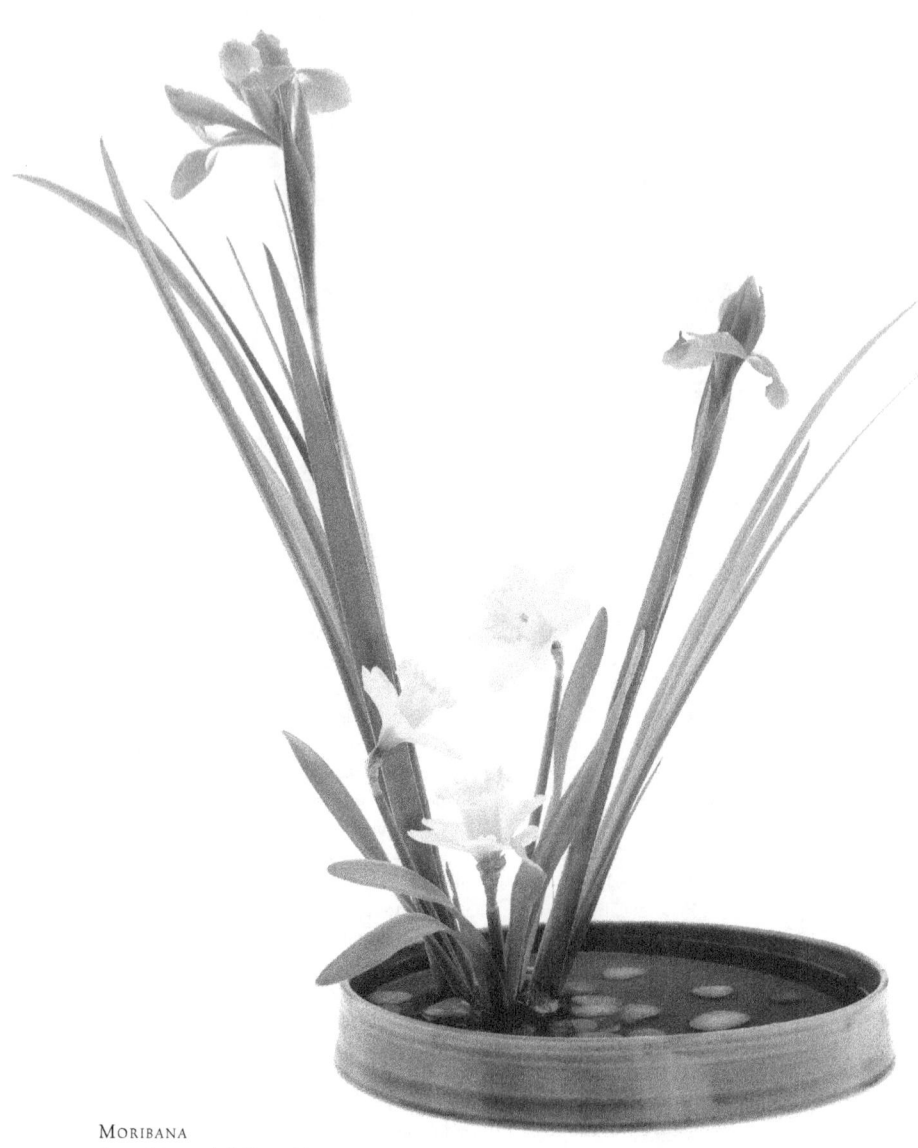

MORIBANA
Iris with leaves, daffodils with leaves

This moribana arrangement creates a naturalistic scene suggesting flowers near the edge of a pond. The two iris stems and the daffodil group form a three-dimensional triangular shape common to the moribana style. A second triangle is created by the daffodil group in the foreground. The emphasis on the triangular shape is to communicate depth, a key visual element (one, unfortunately, that is difficult to see in photographs). Moribana, like most flower arrangements, should not be constructed in only one plane so as to create a flat appearance. To add to the suggestion of depth, this arrangement makes use of both the iris and daffodil leaves for visual support; the iris leaves soften the appearance of the straight iris stems and enhance the naturalistic quality that moribana arrangements are known for. You can learn to make this arrangement in Chapter Four.

in Buddhist culture; rikka was also known as "a little garden within a house" since its form captures the idea of a miniature landscape. The original rikka material typically utilized pine branches at the top of the arrangement to symbolize lofty peaks, followed by other tree and flowering grass material to represent lower hills, waterfalls, lowlands, and the movement of rivers to the sea. Each of the branches and leaves in early forms of rikka also often represented individual prayers or requests to Shinto gods. (Shinto and Buddhism merged early in Japanese religious life; it was, and still is, common for Japanese to embrace both forms of worship.)

Modern rikka and other forms of Japanese flower arrangements continue today to incorporate Buddhist values, although in a very generic and nonsectarian way. As you study kado, you'll probably be profoundly impressed, like many others before you, with the spiritual depth of its theory. If you pause to reflect on what this ancient theory means to Western people, you'll have a chance to see the world in numerous new and significant ways.

Another important concept is the idea—discussed earlier—of the oneness, or the unity of opposites, known as in and yo. Classical arrangements are often divided on the left and right sides with designations as to whether they are the in or yo sides, with in representing the darker element and yo representing the lighter element. The merger of these opposite elements, or forces, as a miniature physical and spiritual universe is best depicted in shoka arrangements, where the main stem representing human beings stands between two subordinate stems symbolizing heaven and earth and all opposite forces. In a way, kado suggests that each of us is linked to, and suspended between, heaven and earth . . . more than mere animals but less than gods. Kado's rich symbolism holds a great appeal for many people and prompts them to consider their place in the universe.

The selection of material for each of the three basic shoka positions also suggests the Buddhist idea of the past, present, and future merging into a state of oneness, or a condition beyond time. For example, in the position known as shin, which represents humanity, the material should symbolize the present moment, so the flower should be either half open or recently open. The position for heaven, known as soe and located behind shin, should be a strong, fully open flower, slightly older than shin, that symbolizes the past. The front position ahead of shin, known as *tai*, should be a bud that symbolizes the future.

Working with concepts such as these requires a consideration of the nature of time and its meaning in our lives. Bringing the mind into the moment and observing ourselves in the moment is the essence of meditation—it allows us to enter into a state with no past and no future. In this everlasting moment, we find no birth, no death, no time, and no fear. This book offers forms of meditation based on this idea and discusses how the meditative state correlates to the "Way of flowers."

With its spiritual influences from both Buddhism and the native Shinto religion, which worships nature, the art of Japanese flower arranging has historically sought to recreate the natural landscape through not just flowering material but also the incorporation of trees, shrubs, leaves, and stems. In many arrangements, flowers serve as supporting players as an accent for color, shape, and texture while the main actors are the branches, stems, and leaves that serve as the focal point and anchor the arrangement. The Western taste for large, bright

376

arrangements with as many flowers and colors as possible is in sharp contrast to the historical use of flowers in Japan.

In keeping with an appreciation for nature, Japanese flower arrangements incorporate grass and tree materials that are associated with the seasons:

- In spring, for instance, quince, peach, and cherry blossom are commonly used, their bendable branches formed into strong curving lines to represent the powerful life force (ki) of spring.

- In the summer, flowers such as cosmos, larkspur, dahlias, canna, and Japanese anemone, as well as decorative grasses such as pampas grass, come into bloom and create full and spreading arrangements that often suggest the movement of the wind through a field of summer flowers.

- The fall season will always include tree material with fall colors, including Japanese maple, the snowball or viburnum shrub, and other trees or shrubs with brightly colored fall leaves.

- Winter arrangements will often use traditional winter material such as nandina, bamboo, and pine, accented with seasonal flowers such as chrysanthemum, rose, and camellia.

The Japanese love for naturalness in flower arrangements incorporates the idea of demonstrating and enhancing the natural growth tendencies of the chosen plants. For example, in the shoka style of ikebana, special arrangements exist for flowers such as the calla lily, agapanthus, amaryllis, daylily, and many others to represent the growth pattern of the flowers and leaves. These arrangements especially use a great many leaves, often with only two flowers to artistically recreate the natural growing tendencies of these flowers.

The appreciation of line is characteristic in all Asian art, and is true in the sensibility in kado that favors beautiful, flowing lines over the Western taste for mass, complexity, and color. This appreciation is manifested in flower arrangement through a balanced variety of moving lines similar in feeling to the linear beauty expressed in the brush-strokes of Japanese minimalist ink painting.

Kado strives for a balance of opposites, favoring asymmetrical beauty over symmetrical arrangements. . . . Following rules on proportion and placement, the lines and triangles create a pleasing and unique balance that, once again, more effectively mirrors the natural world where perfect symmetry is the exception rather than the rule.

In terms of form, unlike many Western arrangements that strive for perfect symmetry, kado strives for a balance of opposites, favoring asymmetrical beauty over symmetrical arrangements. This dynamic balance is created through the positioning of moving lines or stems that fall into many triangular or pyramidal shapes. Following rules on proportion and placement, the lines and triangles create a pleasing and unique balance that, once again, more effectively mirrors the natural world where perfect symmetry is the exception rather than the rule.

More and more people in both the East and West, particularly in metropolitan areas, are searching for a way to rediscover their innate connection with nature. Kado presents a time-honored means of doing just that.

As you might imagine, these are only a few ways in which Japanese floral art differs from its Western counterpart. This is not to suggest that one art is better or worse than the other, but ikebana has its own unique technical principles and aesthetics that have caused the art to spread throughout the world.

Kado & Other Japanese Arts

Since all of the Japanese arts share the same aesthetics, ikebana enhances the study of budo, shodo, and other Japanese art forms. (This is one more reason why you can benefit from studying Japanese flower arrangement—its concepts tie into other Japanese arts, making it easier for you to learn them, and its principles relate to daily life as well.) The same sense of balance that is needed for "sculpting" a successful flower arrangement is also vital in Japanese brush writing, in which each character must exhibit a dynamic balance. In *odori* (dance) and the martial arts, participants must also master a dynamic or moving balance that is equal to the asymmetrical balance used in kado.

The same unity with nature that is stressed in kado is also emphasized in martial arts such as aikido and *aiki-jujutsu*. Shodo requires an incredibly exacting attention to detail and brush form that is also not unlike the formal precision cultivated by students of ikebana. *Cha no yu* (the tea ceremony) is based on *wa-kei-sei-jaku* (accord-respect-purity-solitude), and flower arrangement involves the harmony of heaven, earth, and humanity. These aesthetic, perhaps even spiritual, qualities are universal for all Japanese art.

In short, ikebana can allow you to realize these qualities in such a way that its practice can enhance the study of dissimilar Japanese art forms. Of course, the reverse is true as well. Unfortunately, many students of various Japanese cultural arts in the West often miss out on the importance of these spiritual and aesthetic concepts and as a result practice only a pale imitation of the real art that they are studying. This may be due to cultural differences, in some cases a language gap, and in other instances outright ignorance. Studying one of Japan's cultural arts without a grasp of these important artistic principles is like trying to eat the imitation sushi seen in front of Japanese sushi bars. It may look like the genuine article, but it sure doesn't taste like real sushi, and its nutritional value is pretty low.

The Universal in the Particular

Japan has traditionally excelled (due in part to the influence of Zen) in "spiritualizing" relatively ordinary activities such as the preparation of tea, the military arts, and the arrangement of flowers. One's ultimate goal in these Do forms is to understand the whole of life through a particular endeavor or singular aspect of living.

Master calligrapher and Muto Ryu swordsmanship founder Yamaoka Tesshu Sensei felt that the primary principle of both arts was "the practice of unifying particulars and universals." He wrote in his *Notes on Kumitachi*:

> Within these varied techniques there is deep meaning.
> Cast off subject and object, function as one; abandon self
> and others, form a single sword.[1]

Zen authority D. T. Suzuki likewise made reference to "the One in the Many and the Many in the One." In kado, one finally observes a flower in a state of such heightened awareness that no distinction exists between the observer and the observed. And in that instant, one realizes the essence of existence in a single petal poised between life and death.

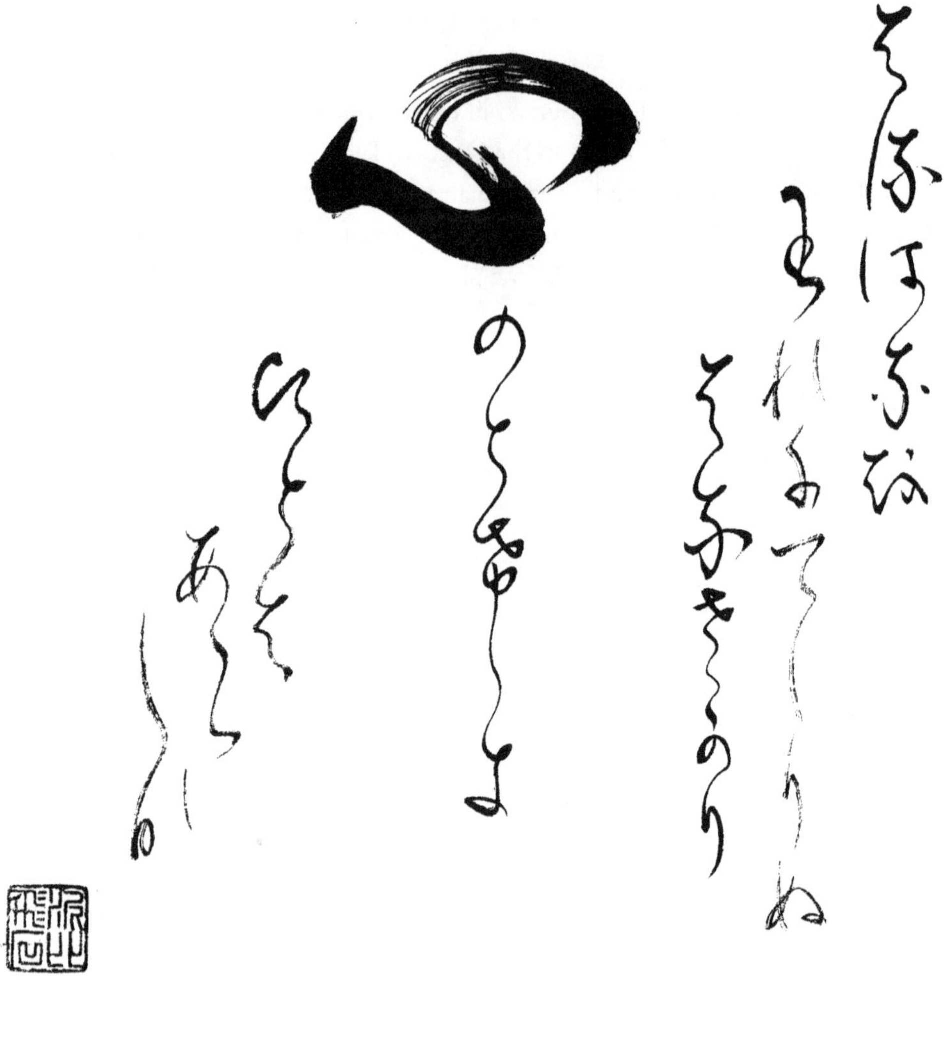

The flowers of spring,
that I have known so deeply,
are now in full bloom.
I'm one with them and wonder
if others know this feeling too.
TADAMINE

Haru hana o
ware nite shirinu
hanazakari
kokoro nodokeki
hito wa arajina

Chapter 2

UNIFYING MIND, BODY & NATURE

Even the most casual observer of kado will realize the art's deep-seated and remarkable connection with nature. This much is obvious, but what is not self-evident is how to achieve a profound awareness of our inherited unity with nature. What effect such a state of harmony can have in the course of our daily lives is also not immediately clear. Since this topic amounts to oneness with the universe (known as *satori*, or "enlightenment"), it should come as no surprise that neither of us claims to be able to teach others how to achieve this condition. That would be as silly as someone else professing to be able eat and digest your food for you.

As many of our parents are fond of noting, certain things you just have to do for yourself. Seeing into our true nature and that of the universe, despite what we sometimes read and what we might sometimes wish, is one of those things that must be discovered firsthand. Second-hand knowledge (for example, reading about someone else's experiences and/or conclusions) is not effective for "direct seeing into one's true nature," as one Zen-inspired writer described satori. While second-hand reading about the past experiences of others is sufficient for learning something such as math, directly and truly seeing ourselves, nature, and our relationship with nature requires the immediate observation of the moment. To see nature and ourselves without error, just as we really are, is to discover the truth about ourselves and our relationship with nature. Our minds, our bodies—the universe itself—actually exist solely at this second.

At what other place and time could we and nature exist? Our past is merely a memory—and a rather subjective one at that—while the future does not yet exist, and our thoughts regarding it are only possible predictions of unfolding events based on past experiences. (Since the future is by definition ultimately unknown, any sort of thought we might have about it is made of mental images from our past. We simply have no other sort of images for the mind to create or extrapolate with . . . unless we observe the unfiltered experience of reality that directly fills the senses in the present. Then the mind rests in the instant, in a moment beyond time.)

Reading or listening to the experiences of others is not the experience itself. It is a description of someone else's past or someone's beliefs that are based on their previous experiences. It is not your experience. It is not even your past. And, as "anti-guru" Jiddhu Krishnamurti was fond of stating, "the description is not the described."

Don't take our word for it. Letting go of all thoughts about the past or future, actually *see* a flower. (Instead of just *glancing* at the flower, with a mind that believes it has seen the flower in some form before, in the past.) Bringing your mind into the moment, find out if any ultimate separation exists between you and that flower. Holding it in your

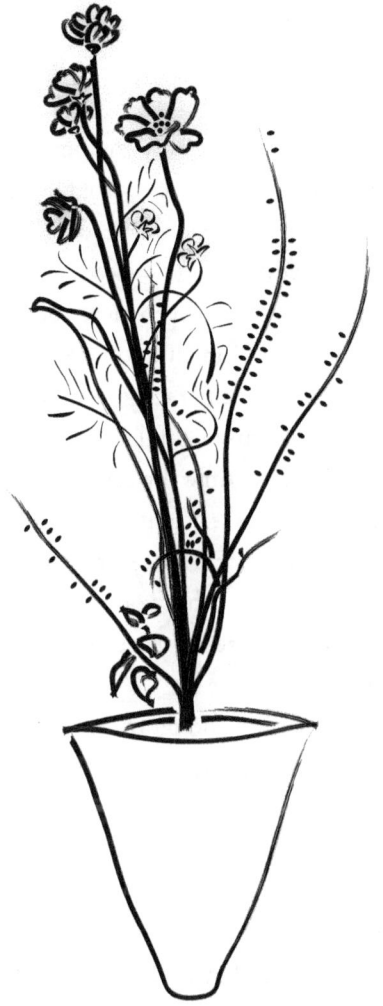

The shoka shimputai style often expresses a seasonal theme. In this composition, cosmos, polygonium, and bletilla leaf combine to suggest the transition
from summer to fall.

hand, find out if there is any absolute division between the mind that perceives the flower and the body that grasps it, or between you and nature.

This act of seeing, which actually encompasses all the senses, involves dropping the past and future—dropping all attachments so that the movement of the mind does not become stuck at any point in time. To practice art as meditation, you need to preserve your awareness of the present. This act has been described in many ways, in many different arts and forms of meditation, including Japanese brush writing. In shodo, or Japanese calligraphy, a number of teachers have described this same state and raised similar questions to be considered. For example, in shodo, from the time the artist picks up the brush until the moment she cleanses it of ink, attention is sustained. In the beginning, this enhanced state of concentration may only be maintained for a few minutes due to the very fact that you are *trying* to sustain it. The instant you say, "This is the present," that moment has already passed and you are in the past.

Keeping attention rooted in the moment not only results in unity of mind and body but allows the artist to enter into a condition beyond time. Because the act of trying is based upon our desire for some future result, it actually interferes with recognition of what is taking place in the instant.

Perhaps the secret lies in joining the mind and body and simply performing kado with a watchful attitude—an effortless state in which action occurs naturally. During pure observation of the instant, you may see what actually *is*, not what *was*, or what you hope *will* be. If this observation is motivated by fear or the hope of reward, it is no longer pure. It is a condition of vigilance without motive. In this condition, you have a chance to see all things as they truly are, including your own thoughts.

Is there, then, a separation between the mind that thinks and that which is thought of? Between the artist observing the course of creation and that which is observed? Between the artist who experiences and the experience itself?

Reading about all of this has little value in relation to actually investigating pure attention. Direct, personal experience is needed for understanding any of the Japanese Ways. It is something that can be pointed at but not given.

We mention this not only to point to a particular state of mind, but also to show the relationships between various Japanese Do forms. More importantly, we hope to reveal in *The Japanese Way of the Flower*, and in other works in this series, how the principles underlying the Ways are actually different aspects of one all-encompassing Way. As such, they are capable of universally relating to our daily lives, regard-less of our age, sex, or culture.

Unity with Nature

Written and oral descriptions can effectively point to that which is extraordinary, just as a finger can point to the moon or a mirror can reflect the magnificence of nature. Still, it is up to the spectator to look for himself at what the finger is pointing at. If he cannot see the moon, then through his effort a method must be invented. (The person point-ing at the moon may be able to see it quite clearly from her angle. You, however, may need to look from another angle or even buy a pair of bin-oculars.) Of course, the image of nature seen in a mirror is only a reflection. While it may prompt you to observe nature, it is not nature. Think of this book as a finger pointing at a Way that can lead to oneness with nature, and as a reflection of two people who are engaged in an ongoing examination of the Way. Use the book as a tool and make use of the detailed explanations of kado techniques and principles, but realize this book is only a description and a reflection. Then, with your whole mind and body, directly see and discover the truths of nature yourself.

Bringing your mind into the moment, find out if any ultimate separation exists between you and that flower. Holding it in your hand, find out if there is any absolute division between the mind that perceives the flower and the body that grasps it, or between you and nature.

In many of the Ways, we start by observing some aspect of nature. In budo (the martial arts), for example, we observe the opponent so intently that we come to know his very mind. This leads ultimately to a state of unity with the opponent—a state in which we control the attacker as we might control our own hands and feet. In fact, some budo teachers continually stress that you must spiritually join with the opponent and even mentally put yourself in his place. Yet the opponent is part of nature. Thus a number of experts have stated that the essence of budo lies in combining with and respecting the laws of nature.

Likewise, kado truly commences with our observation of flowers and plants in nature. (Many beginners, and even some teachers, miss this vital first step and rush into the actual arranging of materials.) For this reason, it is not uncommon for traditional instructors to urge pupils to grow their own plants and flowers—as a means of observing nature. Because kado aims at a creative (but still natural) artistic expression, unity with nature is essential.

While novices struggle to arrange even familiar flowers, visiting professors from Japan will sometimes be required to work with plants native to the host country that they are not always well acquainted with. Despite this, their arrangements are often skillfully executed.

In the same vein, a martial arts expert cannot always demonstrate with his or her students. When new pupils enroll, or during a public seminar, budo teachers will often be forced to execute their techniques on people they have never met. A *shihan*, or high-level teacher, will nevertheless correctly connect with and effortlessly defeat a new opponent without prior observation and usually without injuring the other person. Beginners, in contrast, frequently cannot control opponents they practice with on a weekly basis. This is not simply a matter of superior technique, since a particular technique cannot be forced on a flower or an opponent. Also, more than superior experience is involved, because these situations require interaction with aspects of nature that are unfamiliar. While top-notch technique and lengthy experience are certainly helpful, performing at a world-class level in any of the Ways requires more than a union with specific, well-known parts of nature: it requires unity with the essence of nature itself. In Japan, the universal essence that pervades all of the nature is called ki.

Ki & Oneness with Nature

Ki has been described in a variety of ways by an equally wide variety of teachers and writers. For the purposes of this book, we think of ki as the fundamental building block of nature, the connective tissue of the absolute universe—that universal stuff from which all things emerge, exist as, and return to. Just as the sum total of cells in your body is ultimately inseparable from your body, we can only draw an artificial distinction between the ki that connects all creations in nature and nature itself.

Unfortunately, discussions of ki are often cloaked in supernatural tones, and some writers have indicated that ki is invisible. This depends on one's point of view. Certainly it is difficult to see the movement of ki as an entity that is separate and distinct from the various and endless different aspects of nature. We probably wouldn't say, for instance, that we just saw some ki chasing Dick and Jane across the front yard. Yet this way of looking at the universe is based on a relative worldview—a dualistic way of seeing the world. Without a doubt, relativity and duality exist. If everything is one and that's all there is to it, then why does it hurt so much when you close your car door on a finger? Clearly, enough of a separation and distinction exist for the door to mangle your finger.

A nondualistic worldview does not necessarily deny the relative world but instead sees the absolute unity of nature that underlies all relative distinctions. In this case, a flower is ki, and when the wind causes the flower to sway, it is ki blowing. You are ki observing the movement of ki in nature, which is ki in and of itself. The wind blowing the flower, the shifting flower, the mind that perceives and moves with the wind and flower—all of these are outward reflections of different elements of ki, or of the totality of nature. Ki, then, is not occultlike, invisible, or intangible, but is instead all-encompassing.

Ki's true widespread and down-to-earth character is reflected in the Japanese language itself, which uses this everyday expression in a seemingly endless number of ordinary compound words and phrases, just a few of which are listed here:

tenki = weather, literally "the ki of heaven"

kiryu = air current, literally "flow of ki"

kikyu = air balloon, literally "ball of ki"

kitai = gas or vapor, literally "body of ki"

kikai = atmosphere, literally "ocean of ki"

kidosha = diesel train, literally "ki movement vehicle"

kichigai = insanity, literally "when ki is wrong"

kichigai mizu = alcoholic beverage, literally "when ki is wrong water"

kichigai-bana = a flower blooming out of season, literally "when ki is wrong flower"

denki = electric light, literally "lightning ki" or "electric ki"

byoki = illness, literally "sick ki"

genki = vitality, literally "origin [or source] of ki"

ki ga yowai = to be a coward, literally "ki is weak"

ki ga nai = to have no interest, literally "to have no ki"

ki ga nukeru = to lose hope, literally "ki is withdrawn" or "ki is missing"

ki ga tatsu = to be angry, literally "ki is rising up"

ki ga mijikai = to be short-tempered, literally "ki is short"

kiryoku = willpower, literally "ki power"

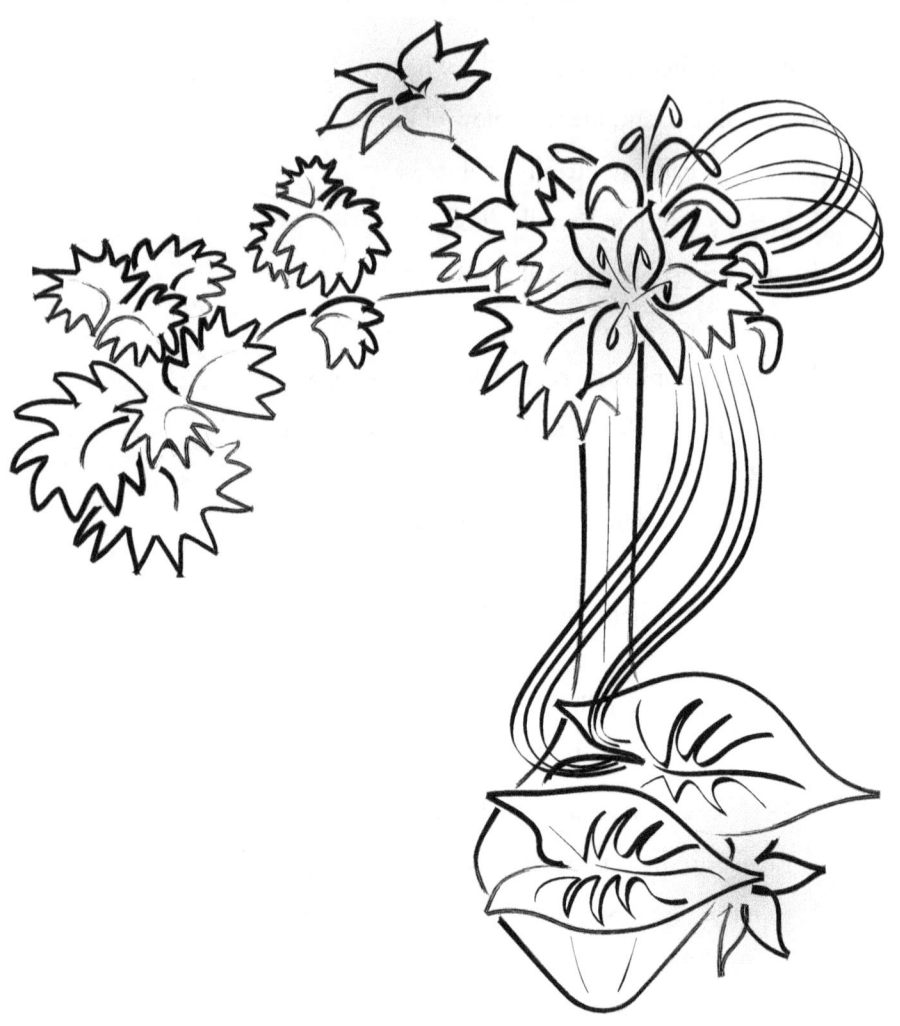

Jiyuka, or "freestyle flowers," is the most contemporary of the kado forms. The composition here uses maple, lily, clematis, caladium, and decorative wire. Wire is sometimes used in freestyle compositions as a contrasting non-floral element. Here it provides an interesting dynamic sweep.

Orenai Te: An Experiment with Ki

The late Nakamura Tempu Sensei, founder of the Shin-shin-toit-su-do system of Japanese yoga, taught extensively about ki and its rela-tionship to the unification of mind and body. His teachings, in many ways, echo those of the founders of a number of the Japanese Do forms, including kado. We've included some of Nakamura Sensei's exercises of mind and body unification in this book because we think they're use-ful for illustrating certain intangible concepts relating to kado.

Nakamura Tempu Sensei viewed the mind as a portion of the body that could not be seen and the body as the part of the mind that was vis-ible. He also frequently compared the mind and body to a river in which the mind was equal to the upper portion of the river and the body was equivalent to the lower part. If we drop garbage in the upper section, it will eventually flow downstream to the lower part of the river. Likewise, whatever thoughts are in the mind will, in the end, affect the body and one's physical health.

Ki can be seen as not only the connective tissue of nature but also as the linking element between mind and body. Just as ki is visible in nature through its reflections, that is, the endless actions of nature's infinite number of component parts, so too is the action of ki visible as a reflection on the body. Still, all of this discussion of ki can easily become nothing more than empty theory. Nakamura Sensei devised a pragmatic exercise, *orenai te*, to allow students to experiment with the fundamental relationship between the mind and body, the inborn pow-er of mind-body coordination, and the reflected movement of ki. "Ore-nai" means that something cannot be bent or broken, while "te" refers to your hand or arm.

Since most of the Japanese cultural arts, including kado, value the positive cultivation of ki as well as the integration of body and mind, respected teachers of various other arts appeared in Nakamura Tempu Sensei's classes. As a result, this exercise has found its way into a number of popular disciplines, especially the martial arts (aiki-do in particular) and healing arts. (It has also, in some cases, been taught with otherworldly overtones that were not found in Nakamura Sensei's original no-nonsense presentation.) Kado requires sensitivity to the ki that links flowers, plants, and human beings, so this exer-cise can offer flower-arrangement enthusiasts a number of valuable insights as well.

You'll need a friend to try orenai te with. Extend one arm about shoulder height, parallel to the ground. Clench your fist tightly and stiffen your arm in an attempt to make it unbending. Ask your partner to grasp your wrist and the bend of your elbow with both hands. He or she should then try to slowly collapse your arm by pushing your wrist back toward your shoulder, while the other hand presses down into the bend of your elbow. Try to keep your arm stiff, and focus your atten-tion on where your friend is touching your arm. Unless your partner is quite a bit physically weaker than you are, the muscular force of two arms will overcome the resistance of one arm easily.

Next, try a different approach. Relax your arm, open your hand, and leave a natural bend in your elbow, but make sure you do not fall totally limp. Then, imagine a stream of ki flowing through your arm, out of your extended fingertips, through whatever is in front of you, and continuing infinitely. (Many people use an image of light being projected.) At some point, rather rapidly, you'll no longer be able to mentally follow the image of ki, as it will reach a point that is too far

394

away to conceive of intellectually. At that time, do nothing and let the feeling of ki flowing continue on its own.

Have your friend slowly, so as to not disturb your concentration, bend your arm using precisely the same amount of effort as before. Providing your flow of attention is unbroken and your body remains relaxed, your arm should be largely unaffected by your partner's pressure. Remember that this is a comparative—not a competitive—exercise. Using equal force both times is needed for accurate comparison. You can also investigate letting your whole body sag limply, while your partner tries to collapse your arm. You'll probably find this to be as ineffective as tensing your body in response to his or her pressure.

Make a point of trying orenai te with an interested and cooperative friend, and follow these guidelines:

1. Pressure can be applied to the arm most easily by using two hands—one gripping the inner elbow and one grasping the wrist.

2. Apply pressure slowly, calmly, and with full awareness on the part of both participants.

3. Try dealing with the force in the following ways:
   • using muscular tension and resistance,
   • using limpness and resignation, and
   • using a combination of physical suppleness and the potent image of a line of ki that continues into the universe indefinitely.

With regard to the third step, the first approach amounts to setting up a barrier of resistance between you and nature. (Remember that your friend is just as much a part of nature as the flowers that you will later learn to arrange.) The second approach is equal to withdrawing psychologically from nature. The final approach involves an act of unification that is amazingly powerful. In this state of unification, you neither fight back nor withdraw. Instead, you allow your ki to connect with the ki in nature in such a way that it continues eternally to join with the never-ending process of change and movement that is the universe. At the same time, your mind is moving in the identical direction that your fingers are pointing toward; as a result, the mind and body are harmoniously connected in the same place at the same time.

You'll need to link your mind and body when learning to copy the basic flower arrangements in this book. If your mind correctly sees our illustrations but your body is incapable of demonstrating the coordination to effectively sculpt the flowers, no immediate success is possible. In other words, if there is a gap between the mind and body there will also be a discrepancy between your thoughts and your actions. When your ki flows freely, your mind and body are harmonized and your hands will accurately recreate what your mind sees.

Use of ki in orenai te functions on two levels: mental and physical. Both are equally important, and since mind and body are interrelated it is equally difficult to establish where the mind ends and the body begins. Tension only weakens the body, because your muscles are actually fighting against each other. Limpness is also inefficient in that your muscles and various body parts are disconnected from each other. Either state amounts to the withdrawal of ki (*ki ga nukeru*) in particular and a lack of personal harmony in general.

Focusing your attention on your partner's hands that are gripping your arm traps your mind, and thus your ki, at those points. Converse-ly, guiding your attention in the same direction that your fingertips are pointing in releases your ki. Holding your posture and arm in a supple, but not slack, condition also puts your body in a state in which it can best respond to your mind. Learning to transfer the psycho-physical lessons discovered through experimenting with orenai te is important for success in copying flower arrangements and for using kado as a ver-sion of moving meditation.

You can also try another orenai te experiment by extending your arm again in a relaxed (but not droopy) manner. First, visualize an out-ward movement of ki that continues infinitely to join with the ki of nature. Your arm will probably be as unbending as before. Then, while your friend continues to try to push your wrist back to your shoulder, suddenly think of sucking your ki back into your arm. At the instant many people think of pulling in their ki (withdrawing psychologically from nature), their arm immediately collapses. The partner only needs to sustain his or her bending effort.

In this case, your friend's force is the same, and this time no contrast takes place between a tense arm versus a relaxed arm. The change is in the movement of the mind and ki. (Like the wind, this movement is not readily visible. But just as the wind gives signs of its presence via the fluttering of leaves and the bending of trees, ki movement is reflected

Because the act of trying is based upon our desire for some future result, it actually interferes with recognition of what is taking place in the instant. Perhaps the secret lies in joining the mind and body and simply performing kado with a watchful attitude.

397

in the body. It is also reflected in the body's artistic expressions such as painting, handwriting, and flower arranging.) Yet, this activity of ki is not actually dependent on a visualized image; in fact, such an image will eventually be an obstacle. Obviously, we cannot effectively function throughout the day holding onto a particular mental picture. The mind needs to be free to focus upon action that is taking place in the moment. It is therefore vital that you learn to let the visualized image fade as it moves too far away to imagine, while sustaining the flow of ki and the state of mind-body coordination. As this mental picture is dropped, only pure attention remains—an attention that does not divide the ki of the experimenter from the ki of nature.

Despite what some books have claimed, orenai te is nothing mysterious; it is not literally "unbendable," and it in no way transcends the physical laws of nature. No occultlike force is involved; a change definitely takes place in the manner in which the muscles function when orenai te is correctly executed, which makes the arm surprisingly difficult to bend. By focusing the mind in the direction you are facing (the same direction your fingertips are pointing in), you are able to utilize the coordinated force of your mind and body. Quite simply, using the mind and body as a unit is more powerful than focusing solely on one's muscular strength. What's more, this integrated use of the mind and body actually enhances your muscular power. Simple as that.

This experiment illustrates how mind, body, and nature are interrelated, and how "reaching out" with your ki to harmonize with nature can produce results that are reflected on physical reality (the body, in this case). Orenai te not only gives you a chance to encounter a different way of dealing with the world—a way that is simultaneously harmonious and powerful—it offers a tangible means of experiencing a unification of mind, body, and nature. Kado has as its ultimate goal just such a state of unity, so this exercise can perhaps give flower-arrangement aficionados an alternate way of experiencing a mental and physical state that truly lies at the heart of their Way.

Further, orenai te is one means of cultivating several important qualities that are universally valued in the Japanese cultural arts, and usually in all aspects of daily living as well. To begin with, the exercise makes use of positive and dynamic imagery to promote a similarly positive physical state. You've probably heard of psychosomatic illnesses and the profound effect the mind can have on the body, but not everyone has had the opportunity to directly experiment with this effect. Orenai te offers just such an opportunity. It also gives you a chance to test the power of concentration. Clearly, it's pretty easy to lose concentration or confidence if a large person aggressively attempts to collapse your arm—especially if this were to take place in front of others. With the loss of concentration, or when the mind no longer believes it can perform orenai te, your arm will crumple. But with sustained practice of the Ways, it is possible to enhance your ability to positively concentrate the mind, even in the midst of activity (such as arranging flowers), or when the pressure is on.

On a physical level, the arm must be neither tense nor limp, and the same holds true for your overall physical posture. A collapsed, diminutive carriage or an overly upright, tense position are both equally ineffective in terms of performing orenai te successfully. They're also debilitating in daily life, and unfortunately many of us seem to waver eternally between moments of excessive tension and exhausted collapse. What we're often unsure of is how to use our bodies naturally in a state of functional relaxation. Again, orenai te gives you a chance to experi-

399

ment with the most natural and efficient use of your body (within the context of a given exercise). This is essential in kado, where some large and complex arrangements can take two hours to complete. A kado practitioner cannot effectively perform in a state of mental and physical limpness. Yet sustaining a tense condition for a couple of hours is rough on your health and your flower arrangements. What's needed is a kind of positive relaxation—a condition that is natural and comfortable but still functional.

Cultivating the mind and body in a gradual, rational, and continuous way; making positive and vigorous use of the mind; bringing the mind into the moment, with full attention; and all while using the body naturally—these points relate to orenai te, but even more, they equal a practical action plan aiming at mind-body harmony in flower arrangement and life.

Just as in science, however, discovering certain new and important principles is not enough. If these principles never find their way into common usage to enhance society as a whole, they have little value to the average person. Likewise, experimenting with orenai te is just that—an experiment. If we fail to research how to use our bodies naturally, sustain a positive attitude, and focus the mind, we also fail to derive much real-world benefit from orenai te in kado or anywhere else. It becomes nothing more than a party trick that has little relevance to kado or daily living.

Once we see the beneficial effects of positivity, concentration, and a natural, relaxed posture, it is essential to train the mind and body in a well-organized, gradual, and ongoing manner to embody these attributes. And kado, along with the other Japanese Ways, presents you with an opportunity to train yourself in exactly this fashion. This is only an opportunity. It is up to each of us not only to open the door when opportunity knocks but also to step through it and continue walking. Cultivating the mind and body in a gradual, rational, and continuous way; making positive and vigorous use of the mind; bringing the mind into the moment, with full attention; and all while using the body naturally—these points relate to orenai te, but even more, they equal a practical action plan aiming at mind-body harmony in flower arrangement and life.

Harmonizing the Mind & Body

Unity of mind, body, and nature is essential for creating high-level flower arrangements. Certainly, anyone can learn the techniques and styles of arranging flowers in a Japanese manner if all they're interested in is copying and memorizing. Genuine kado is much more than a copy of classical forms (that are, in turn, a copy of nature), because simply creating a duplicate of nature is not art. It is also not especially impressive; the real thing is vastly more majestic and moving. Flowering sculpture takes place when the unity of the artist's ki and vision combines with the ki of nature to give birth to something magical and heartfelt. This special quality goes beyond words but is still obvious to the average person. It only happens when the artist's creative vision merges with nature; this blending of ki enables kado to go past the mere arrangement of flowers to become art.

Flowers are arranged by hand. Unless the mind's movement is translated by your body into a precise reflection of your mental vision, art can never be effectively created. At least one aspect of any art is the skillful expression of our creativity, which can obviously only occur when the mind and body are working together in harmony. Since this

401

book is concerned with more than shaping cute arrangements of flowers, we need to consider the creation of art. Two elements are essential for the artistic process: combining human creativity and the forces of nature, and sustaining a coordinated mind and body.

Shodo (Japanese calligraphy), like kado, offers you a great chance to analyze the nature of mind-body coordination. Most shodo students find that being capable of executing skillful brush strokes with genuine skill and decisiveness is a remarkable challenge that can only be accomplished through the coordination of mental and physical faculties. This condition of psycho-physical integration is present when a powerfully focused mind leads the brush and the brush is allowed to perform as a perfect representation of your mental movement. All fine arts, crafts, music, and a variety of different activities call for this attitude of coordination. However, shodo, like kado, ideally represents one of the greatest levels of harmony between thought and action; it serves as a tool for depicting this harmony as well as providing a path for cultivating it. Both psychological coordination and the lack of it are exposed on one's paper. Just as striking your thumb with a hammer implies a lack of coordination in daily life, poorly shaped strokes and wavering lines show flawed coordination in calligraphy. To arrive at a condition in which the mind perfectly controls the body and the body reflects that state requires the growth of deep concentration. This development of concentration is needed for you to realize your full potential in shodo, kado, or daily life. To fully understand how to arrive at such a state of attention and unification, it is necessary to examine the actual nature of the mind and body in detail.

The mind commands the body, with the body ultimately reflecting our mental condition. It is necessary to recognize this if you are

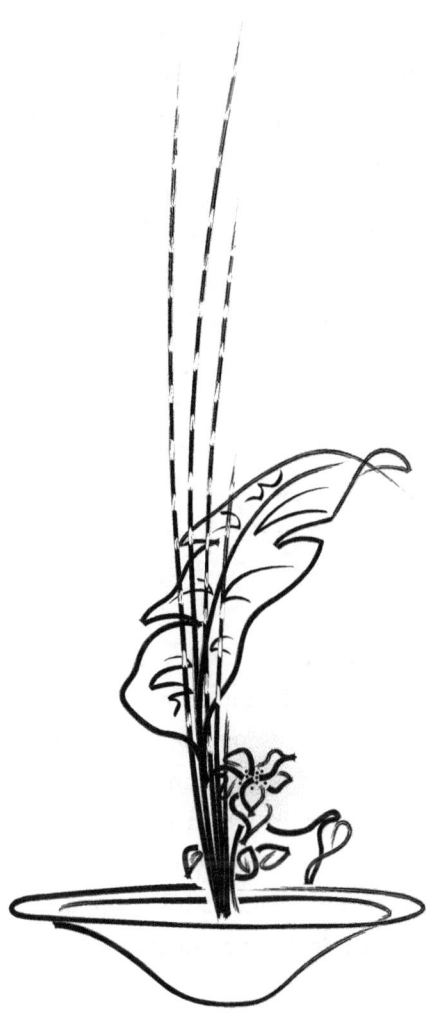

This shoka shimputai composition features bulrush, Japanese banana leaf, and lily. A shimputai arrangement has two parts, primary and secondary. The secondary element is chosen as a "response" to the primary material to express the artist's feelings.

to learn any activity, including shodo or kado, competently, because the mind can positively or negatively influence the innate mind-body connection. When this relationship is unstable, you may see a Japanese character and comprehend it intellectually, yet fail to physically copy it on paper in the correct form. The same is true for the arrangement of flowers, the study of Japanese martial arts, and a vast variety of other activities. Simply put, you may know what you want to accomplish, but your hands may not be able to shape the flowers to accurately reflect what you have in mind. One of the purposes of this book is to introduce you to principles that are truly universal in scope and that are therefore capable of enhancing every part of your life. In this sense, we are using the ancient art of flower arrangement as a representative example of the Japanese Ways as a whole and as a means to study the nature of existence itself.

Because this book is only an introduction to a vast and subtle art, we have certain limitations when it comes to presenting fully detailed explanations of the principles of mind and body harmony. Fundamentally, the mind must be in a positive and vigorous state. It must also be in an attentive condition in which it is fully concentrated in the present. At the same time, the body must be relaxed, with a posture that is not stiff but not limp. And both the mind and body should be used in a natural manner (this being in essence what this entire book is about).

Orenai te was discussed earlier as an illustration of this concept. Now we will present two more methods of studying unification of body and mind: *muga ichi-nen ho* (a meditation that makes use of a flower or external point of focus) and *anjo daza ho* (a meditation that begins by focusing on the sound of a bell). Be sure to notice the main points that are discussed in each of these exercises. In particular, note the points that overlap, as these repeated themes are most important for unity of mind and body in kado and daily living and are needed for effectively practicing the flower arrangements that will come later. Of equal importance, these forms of meditation give you an opportunity to discover and cultivate your innate coordination of mind and body through direct experience. Enhanced calmness, concentration, willpower, and physical health are just a few of the benefits of these methods of meditation. Study them well, as the same state of mind is required to sustain concentration, along with coordination of hand and mind, while arranging flowers.

Muga Ichi-nen Ho Meditation

This meditation has the unique benefit that it can be practiced pretty much anywhere and at any time. A mental state similar to muga ichi-nen ho is also necessary while arranging flowers, and practice of this meditation can help you become successful in kado as well as transfer the beneficial insights from kado into everyday existence.

Muga means "no self," but is perhaps more readily understood as "no self-consciousness." *Ichi-nen* is simply "one thought," while *ho* is a "method" or "exercise." Be aware, however, that understanding how words are defined is not the same as grasping the state of mind that is being pointed at. Actual practice produces genuine, firsthand experience that defines itself.

Muga ichi-nen ho can be practiced under most circumstances, but it is common to use the *seiza* sitting position (Figure 1) and/or a full or half lotus position similar to the seated postures in Zen and yoga

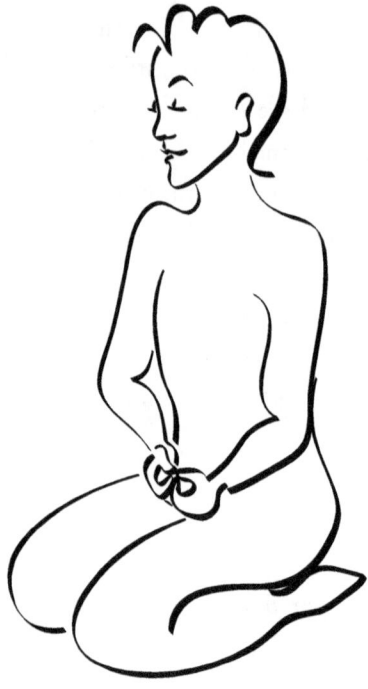

FIG. 1. The *seiza* sitting position is commonly used when practicing muga ichinen-ho.

(although it is easier to maintain the correct alignment of the spine in seiza). You can also sit upright in a firm chair (Figure 2). More important than the specific position you sit in is the posture that you sustain while sitting. It must be an erect but relaxed position—a posture in which every body part responds to gravity and naturally settles into its proper place.

Try imitating the drawings, and be sure to keep in mind the following points, as they are important for mind-body unification in kado and meditation. All of the following steps can be practiced in daily life and should result in a healthier, more tension-free life.

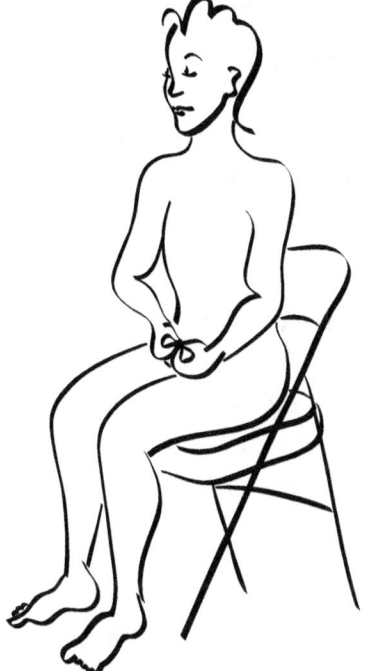

FIG. 2. Muga ichi-nen ho can also be practiced sitting upright in a chair.

1. During meditation, maintain a posture that is relaxed, upright, and aligned.

2. In seiza, sit lightly on the heels, with the big toes crossed on top of each other and some space between the knees. Although seiza is difficult to adopt at first for some people, it is effective for centering your weight forward and down into the lower abdomen, or hara. Balancing one's posture at the hara and focusing the mind in the same place has a long tradition in Japanese arts and forms of meditation. Your hara can be thought of as the spot

where your upper body's weight naturally settles and reaches its highest point of concentration and density. It is easiest to work with a point on the front surface of the abdomen, about four finger widths below the navel. Think of this point as a natural center in the lower abdomen that corresponds to your center of balance and center of gravity.

3. Do not slump (this causes body weight to shift backward and away from your hara) or raise the shoulders (this unsettles and lifts your body upward and away from your hara). Sit down lightly, almost as if your bottom were sore, and maintain a relaxed posture that looks "big."

4. Many times during meditation, and even in daily life, the head starts to sag forward, while the neck collapses, bends, and begins to round off at its base. The rest of the spine soon curves in on itself as well. You can alter this by concentrating on the hara and by correcting your posture with the movement of your head. Mentally release your muscles (along the neck and spine in particular). Visualizing your hara as a sort of anchor, direct the top of your head up and away from your hara and then draw in your chin and bring your forehead back into alignment with your lower abdomen. Allow the spine and neck to straighten until your posture is aligned. (Envisioning the muscles along the spine growing longer and wider is an effective technique to use at this point.) If you concentrate deeply and relax, your body will move slowly into

the correct position with little conscious effort on your part. On the other hand, be careful not to force your body into an overly erect posture.

5. By relaxing and using visualization, you should also let your chest expand while your back and shoulders widen. In most cases, the ears, shoulders, and pelvis should be parallel to the floor; be careful not to twist your head, shoulders, or pelvis.

6. If you sit in a chair, avoid sitting with legs outstretched, as this causes your pelvis to roll backward and your lumbar region to curve outward in a slump. Instead, try to sit with your feet flat on the floor or tucked under the chair (almost as your legs tuck under your hips in seiza). This maintains your natural lumbar curve and shifts your weight toward the front surface of the lower abdomen, exactly where you want to center your weight and mind in the hara.

7. Relax your face and eyes and find the most comfortable posture within the context of the above instructions. This act of "centering" produces a particularly steady position. To sustain this free and relaxed condition of stability, avoid leaning in an unbalanced way, as the upper body's weight must be in equilibrium at the hara.

Muga ichi-nen ho involves gazing at an object while in a state of heightened awareness and concentration. For kado enthusiasts, a favorite flower is an ideal article to utilize for this meditation.

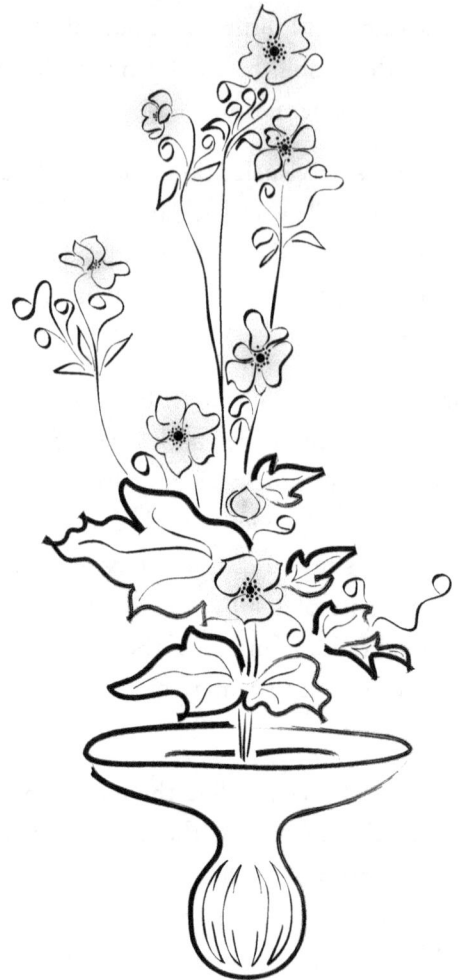

The shoka style generally expresses the dynamic growing ki of plants rooted in the earth yet stretching up toward heaven. It can be thought of as a simplified form of rikka, with which it shares an upright demeanor. In this shoka shofutai composition, only one floral element is used, Japanese anemone.

Start by aligning your posture according to the seven steps listed above. (Think of the feeling in your arm while you performed orenai te. When you did it correctly, was your arm limp? Was it stiff and tense? Most likely the sensation was one of suppleness, without excessive tension or limpness—a kind of "positive relaxation." You now need to learn how to transfer that same feeling into your entire body so that you are filled with ki.)

Gently focus your eyes on the flower. Try to position it so that you can look at it in a comfortable way and not disturb your aligned posture. Let your eyes come to rest on it softly and naturally. (Some people prefer a relaxed, half-open eye position.) Avoid staring, as this will only produce tension that inhibits coordination of body and mind and destroys the stream of ki from the eyes that is directed toward the flower. Arm tension in orenai te is similarly ineffective.

Next, bring your attention into the present moment and let the flower completely fill your mind. Actually *see* the flower, as it really is, instead of just vaguely looking at it. This focuses your mind in the present (where the flower and your body exist), which promotes the unity of mind and body. This moment of mental and physical harmony can only take place when you are in a natural and relaxed condition. While it is vital to really notice the flower, your concentration should not be forced. Aim for a sort of "relaxed concentration." To do so you'll need to focus your mind deeply on the flower without attempting to push out other thoughts and sensations. When you exclude other thoughts, you actually end up thinking more about the sensations and ideas that you are trying to avoid than about the object of your concentration. You also set up a situation in which you are in conflict with the sounds, smells, or feelings that you are trying to block out. This state of conflict ultimately conflicts with nature, since nature is everywhere. Philosophy aside, it is difficult to relax while trying to fight off all sensory impressions that do not correspond to your flower.

Instead, let your attention come to rest on the flower in a natural way. Pay attention to every part of the flower until you forget yourself and only the flower remains. This is the condition of muga ichi-nen. Self-consciousness falls away, and your flower is the "one thought." In the state of muga ichi-nen, no boundaries exist between you and nature. The mind is still, resting in harmony with the universe, and time ceases.

You've probably engaged in some act that you enjoy so deeply that you forget yourself and time is suspended. When you unite the mind and body in the moment, concentrating deeply, no self-consciousness is present, and only the action taking place fills your senses.

Another way of stating this is that when you are happy and at peace, you rarely dwell upon yourself, even on a purely physical level. For example, you're unlikely to spend the whole day conscious of your big toe unless it is injured in some way. When your toe feels fine, you don't pay much attention to it. (This, of course, does not mean that you cannot or should not be able to notice various parts of yourself.)

Flowering sculpture takes place when the unity of the artist's ki and vision combines with the ki of nature to give birth to something magical and heartfelt.

As you focus on the flower, try to find the line that divides the person that perceives the flower and the flower itself. Does this line of demarcation exist as a firm reality or is it artificially created? This is a vital inquiry, but try this meditation instead of attempting to guess an answer to the question. In an ultimate, yet still practical, sense, does a firm line exist that divides humankind from nature and one human being from another? Muga ichi-nen ho aims at a complete unification of mind, body, and nature. In such a state of harmony, which includes mind and body as well as the individual and the universe, both mind and body relax fully. Traditionally, kado has had the same objective.

Try closing your eyes at some point in your meditation. Can you still recall the details of the flower? We are so used to just glancing at the world, through the eyes of the past, that we are often not sure if we are indeed paying attention or if we only *think* that we are paying attention. Arranging flowers involves the act of genuinely *seeing*. Without this state, you will fail to sense the essential character of the plants and flowers that you plan to arrange.

You don't want to be like the man who had his television stolen while he was at work. He came home, changed clothes, prepared dinner, then plopped down on the sofa to watch one of his favorite programs. He picked up the remote control and pointed it where the TV used to be and only then discovered that it was missing. He was so used to assuming that it was there that he "saw" it even as he prepared dinner and sat on the couch. He was looking at his environment through the eyes of the past instead of actually *seeing* what was taking place in the present.

To test yourself, try turning away from the flower after some time has elapsed and attempting to draw it. Don't worry about artistic skill; the main goal is to see if you can recall the details of the flower. (This is another way of testing your powers of attention, and it is a fine and fun method of helping children to cultivate superior concentration.) Drawing and most other forms of art are actually exercises in precise observation. (For more about this concept, read *The Zen of Seeing—Seeing/Drawing as Meditation*, by Frederick Franck.) This act of "noticing" is a central element in kado as well, and it can be cultivated via meditation. In a sense, it is meditation.

PRINCIPLES OF MUGA ICHI-NEN HO

1. Coordinate mind and body while gently focusing your eyes on the subject.

2. Do not just look but actually see.

3. Concentrate until you forget yourself and only the object remains.

4. Notice all aspects of the object, then remove it from view.

5. You should still be able to visualize it clearly or draw it in detail.

Anjo Daza Ho Meditation

Many of the features of muga ichi-nen ho, such as correct posture, relaxed concentration in the present, the absence of self-consciousness, the outward movement of ki, and the benefits of the exercise, are also found in anjo daza ho meditation. You can use the same seiza, lotus, or seated positions for this method as well.

Anjo means "peaceful feeling," and *daza* refers to striking a meditation bell while in a seated posture. As you might surmise, a bell is needed for this exercise. You'll be using a metal, bowl-shaped bell called a *rin*. When the edge of this bell is hit with its accompanying wooden

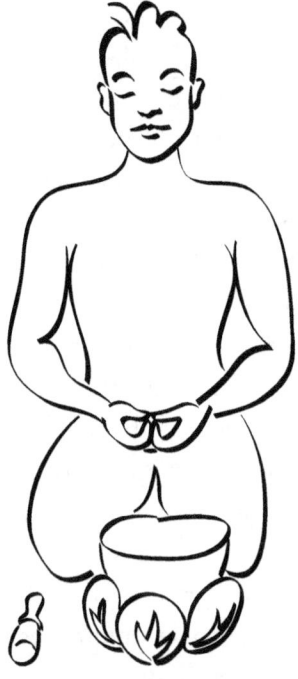

FIG. 3. When practicing anjo daza ho, strike the bell cleanly one time, and focus your attention on the sound created.

striker, a mellow gonglike note is produced. This bell, which is sometimes associated with Buddhist rituals, can sustain a fairly long tone depending on its size and the quality of the metal used, and it has a calming effect. Most Buddhist supply stores carry such a bell, and you can also contact a local Buddhist church or Asian gift shop.

To begin anjo daza ho, adopt a seated position in which you can maintain a proper posture as well as the unification of mind and body. Your eyes should be gently closed. Avoid shutting them forcefully or abruptly, as this will just produce meditation-inhibiting tension.

Strike the bell cleanly one time, and focus your attention on the sound created (Figure 3). Again, this is a "relaxed concentration." Attempting to block out other sounds and thoughts merely distracts you from the sound of the bell. Let the bell's note fill your entire mind to become the "one thought." When your mind embraces this single thought fully without trying to drive other sensory impressions out, your self is forgotten. Muga ichi-nen is achieved; no separation exists between you and the universe in which the sound resonates.

But unlike the flower in the previous exercise, the bell's tone is slowly fading . . . fading like the image of ki traveling away from you in orenai te. This can work to your advantage here. In a sense, if you think of the sound as ichi-nen, or "one thought," then as the mind follows the decreasing tone it gradually arrives at mu-nen, or "no thoughts." To use a widespread Japanese analogy, mu-nen is a mental state that is as still as a pond with no waves.

Once this single note fills your mind to form one thought, follow the decreasing waves of sound. If genuine concentration has been accomplished, as the sound waves gradually grow smaller, so too do your brain waves. In other words, it is possible to arrive at a continuously smaller and calmer pattern of waves. The bell's sound simply leads you in this direction, so it is best to think of the tone as infinitely decreasing.

As the sound waves grow infinitely small, keep following them mentally. Even when you can no longer hear the sound, let the feeling and state of mind that has been generated continue on its own. The secret is to do nothing, and then the condition of calmness will not be altered.

Since these concepts are universal, the same approach for calming the mind can be used through physical action or visualized images.

For example, even the motion of the brush in Japanese calligraphy and painting can become a vehicle for meditation. Imagine you're holding a brush above your paper. Leaving your elbow down, and in a relaxed position, you move the brush repeatedly from left to right in an arc of about a foot. As you do this, you focus your mind intently on the movement of the brush tip. Next, you gradually make the size of the arc smaller and smaller.

You may find that if you keep your mind centered on the brush tip, your thoughts will also grow "smaller" as well as calmer. In a short while, the movement will become so small that it is not outwardly observable. At this time, the mental picture of reducing movement will fall away, but a skilled practitioner of shodo will let the feeling of still-ness that has just been generated continue infinitely. If you are having trouble imagining what all of this should look like, tie a rock or relative-ly heavy object to a string. Start it swinging from side to side, then do nothing, holding your hand still. The object's arc will gradually become smaller and smaller until it seems to be hanging motionless. You can do something similar with a brush by allowing the sensation of endless reduction to continue within you.

Once shodo students get the hang of it, this method can help them calm the movement of their *fude* (brush) even when their projection of ki through the brush has not been enough. This endless-reduction approach is not only an effective means of stilling the brush and mind but has the ultimate potential to lead us to a state of transcendence that is both endless and eternal, since we cannot conceive intellectually of infinity.

You can use the infinitely decreasing bell tone to accomplish the same purpose. In fact, a similar condition can be arrived at whether you

417

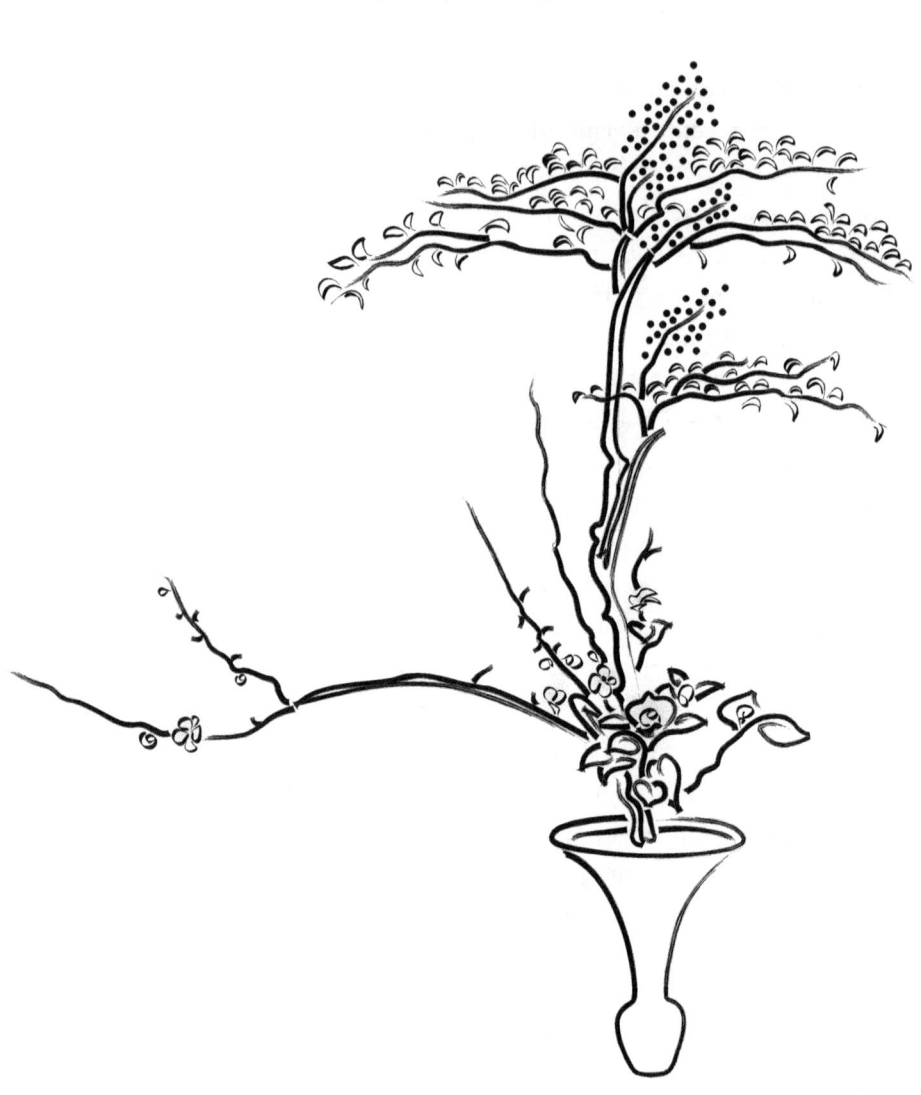

In this sanshuike or "three-material style" of shoka we see a dramatic use of nandina for the shin element, quince for soe, and camellia for tai.

make use of a decreasing sound, a decreasing physical action, or simply the mental image of endless reduction. It is the principle of infinite reduction leading to a state of doing nothing that is important, not the device that leads to it—actually, the device should eventually be abandoned when it's no longer needed.

As part of this act of doing nothing, continue to listen even when the bell's note is no longer loud enough to be heard. Unless this condition of sustained listening and attention is held after the sound has faded, calmness will be lost. When you can no longer hear the bell, what are you listening to? In a sense, you could say you are listening to the universe. At this time, let your listening expand to fill the universe until the universe or nature itself becomes the "one thought." This concept of union with the universe allows kado to transcend the mere arranging of flowers to become flower meditation.

What if you lose your concentration at some point? Simply hit the bell and start again. (Rin bells have a tone that can last for quite some time, but beginners might do well to purchase a top-quality large bell that has a particularly long sustained tone.) How long should you practice anjo daza ho and muga ichi-nen ho? That's up to you. Many people start with fifteen minutes as a standard. Using these forms of meditation before kado is an ideal means of calming the mind (to find the right asymmetrical balance for your floral arrangements more easily) and harmonizing with nature.

PRINCIPLES OF ANJO DAZA HO

1. Sit with mind and body unified.

2. Focus on the sound of the bell.

3. Mentally follow the decreasing waves to achieve muga ichi-nen.

4. As the waves become infinitely small, continue listening.

5. Let your listening expand so that your ki extends into infinite space.

The qualities you cultivate to arrive at muga ichi-nen are as important as the state that is cultivated. Although these qualities are multifaceted, one central point is the ability to concentrate the mind without having it "get stuck" anywhere or at anytime. When you focus your ki on a flower or a resonance, you cannot arrive at muga ichi-nen without learning how to deal with outside stimuli and your thoughts—all of which can distract you from the object of concentration. If your mind gets stuck on an external sound or an internal sound, it is no longer focused on the tone of the bell. If you attempt to block out these sounds, your mind is still battling them and you have set up a conflict-ridden situation.

Imagine that you are sitting in front of a busy street. Across the street you see something that captures your attention. As you watch the spectacle unfold, cars and trucks pass through your line of sight. Do you turn your head to follow each vehicle, or do you simply notice the passing objects while keeping your attention focused on what you are watching?

The bell's tone or the flower is what you are watching, while outer stimuli and thoughts are the passing cars. Notice each thought and sensation, but do not mentally comment on it or allow the mind to attach itself to it. Just continue to calmly "watch" the note of the bell and do nothing. This condition of concentration without attachment is essential for all forms of meditation. In a way, it is meditation itself.

Eventually, even the object of concentration must fall away (in this instance, the bell's tone), and only the quality of pure attention without attachment remains, resting in the eternity of the moment. It is a moment outside of the bonds of time, beyond attachment and its related suffering—a moment containing no divisions within and no barriers without. Your mind and the heart of nature are one and the same. This is kado, but it is also the essential soul of all of the Ways.

To realize such a moment, try anjo daza ho or muga ichi-nen ho before kado practice. While arranging flowers, note whether the relative, personal self is forgotten as the present moment, including the flowers before you, fills your awareness.

When is this condition lost (if ever), and what takes place at that instant? Lapses in mind and body harmony can be discovered via body language. If your psycho-physical posture is unbalanced, your floral arrangement will also lack balance. What does your posture say about you? What does your artwork express? This not to suggest that you should become self-conscious while arranging flowers—awareness and self-consciousness are not the same.

Finally, by all means enjoy your completed artwork, but don't drop the meditative condition when your arrangement is done. Take it into everyday life and use it to aid yourself and others. To help you realize this, try closing your kado session with anjo daza ho or muga ichi-nen ho, using the completed arrangement as your object of concentration.

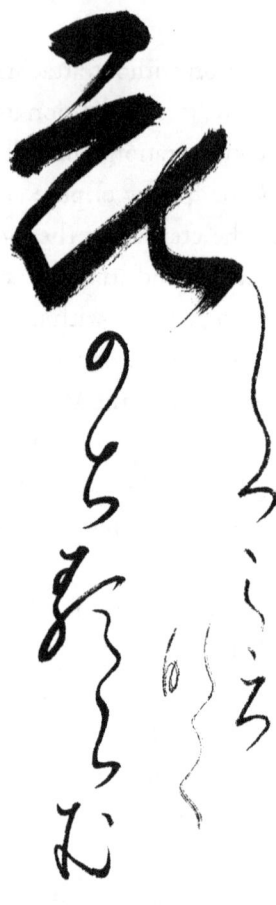

Streaming downward are
bright beams of light from above.
And the spring sun glows.
Still, I wonder why restless
cherry blossoms must float away?
KI NO TOMONORI FROM "HYAKUNIN ISSHU"

Hisakata no
hikari nodokeki
haru no hi ni
shizu kokoro naku
hano no chiru ran

Chapter 3

FUNDAMENTAL PRINCIPLES OF KADO

From the martial arts to dance to kado, particular philosophical and artistic codes are historically held in common by all traditional Japanese cultural arts. These aesthetic codes have had a deep influence on the evolution of kado. It is not an exaggeration to say that if these aesthetic principles are not understood, no great awareness of any Japanese cultural art, whether it be kado, aikido, tea, dance, or calligraphy, is possible.

A vast number of terms and concepts are associated with Japanese art, and a detailed explanation of such concepts is beyond the scope of this book. Besides, a true grasp of many of these ideas comes only through personal, hands-on experience in one of the arts of Japan. Nonetheless, the following sections describe some of the more important principles of Japanese aesthetics. Each one relates to the others to form a single, harmonious whole that is Japanese art. In fact, perhaps the most central concept in kado and other related arts is the principle of harmony itself.

Harmony

In kado, it is essential that you understand the attributes and growth patterns of the plants you are working with. Yet a mere understanding of the characteristics of a given flower is not enough to arrive at *wa* (harmony) in kado.

> The serenity and openness of a chrysanthemum
> blossom is reflected in the eye of the artist, as soon
> as he surrenders himself without reservation to the
> flower. The curved line of the mountains on the horizon
> outside the window of a Japanese home is in unison
> with the movement of the pine branch of an ikebana
> composition inside the house. Autumn outside, autumn
> in ikebana, and maturity of the artist, this would be a
> completely harmonious triad. Form and colour, flowers
> and branches, blossoms and leaves unite harmoniously
> with the container and room, with the season and the
> sentiments of the artist. Only in modern ikebana may
> we forget the principle of wa. Here dissonance appears.
> The harmony of nature is, however, underscored
> through this principle. [2]

Merging your creative ideas with the nature of the plant you're working with is vital as well. You must respect the ki of its foliage as much as you understand its growth tendencies. Skillful kado makes use of harmony in the form of a refined combination of understanding and respect. This state is reflected in the expert's relaxed and gentle handling of flowers even when he or she is bending and shaping the stems.

Likewise, the more proficient one becomes in traditional Japanese budo, the more it is possible to sense and understand an opponent's intentions. Through correct and rigorous training, the martial artist should, ideally, arrive at a heightened state of calm alertness that allows him or her to accurately comprehend the opponent's mind. But this enhanced condition of sensitivity is meaningless unless it is accompanied by an attitude of respect toward the opponent's intentions. Forcing people rarely equals an effective or efficient use of ki in budo—and the same can be said of forcing plants in kado. When both understanding and respect combine, harmony is realized in budo, and in this harmonious condition a martial arts expert can freely lead and control an attacker.

Harmony is a central aspect of shodo as well. In that art, the condition of harmony is frequently expressed through a state of dynamic balance. Balance in shodo is asymmetrical, which produces an active feeling of movement within the characters. One could liken it to a picture of a sprinter whose inclined running posture has been frozen in time by the camera. Seeing such a picture, you instantly have a sensation of movement, but this sensation is different from what you experience when viewing a photo taken of a runner at the moment he or she trips and is falling forward. Both photos show bodies inclined in the direction in which they are moving; the difference between the two is balance.

Balance in shodo can also be witnessed through a natural alternation of heavy and light brush pressure, which in turn produces an oscillation of thick and thin lines of ink. If all the brush strokes are of equal thickness the work looks stilted, unnatural, and dead. Kado, likewise, requires a natural state of asymmetrical balance. The principle of har-

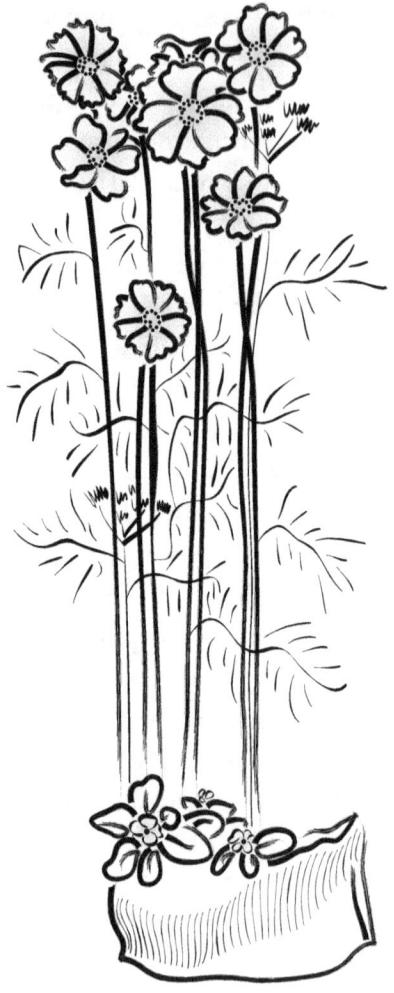

This freestyle arrangement uses a metal container and, for its central elements, periwinkle, cosmos, and patrina.

mony is a constant factor in all the Ways, though each art expresses it in its own unique manner.

Asymmetrical Balance

Asymmetrical balance is used in kado to evoke a feeling of naturalness. Since nature involves the motion of continuous change, kado should not have a static feeling—exactly what is created by using a rigid, symmetrical balance. Instead, the utilization of unevenness is endlessly variable and calls forth a dynamic feeling of movement. Kado makes use of an unequal triangular balance that you will explore more completely in this and the following chapters. As discussed in Chapter 1, balance in kado has to do with the ten-chi-jin (heaven-earth-humanity) principle in which the three elements jin (humanity), ten (heaven), and chi (earth) are all represented.

Not attempting to fill up all of the space in a composition is another form of asymmetry commonly found in Japanese art. Kado makes liberal use of empty space, which invites the imagination to complete the arrangement, thus drawing the viewer into the work of art. In other words, the unfinished asks to be finished. That which is unfinished is in harmony with life's dynamics of constant change and evolution. Again, asymmetry does not necessarily indicate a lack of balance. Just the opposite is true in kado, an art based upon a unification of opposites (in/yo, as discussed in Chapter 1) in the form of a balanced imbalance. Arriving at "unbalanced balance" can be thought of as a kado version of a Zen koan, a metaphysical question that transcends the limitations of logical thought.

The use of asymmetry, incompleteness, and unevenness can also

427

be witnessed in Japanese minimalist ink painting, brush writing, and even classical architecture.

In Japanese flower arrangement, if an overly long branch is used on one side, some shorter plant material must be used on the opposite side to create balance. In Western flower arrangement, an equally long branch might be placed on the opposite side, which would negate asymmetrical balance and evoke a rigid, static, symmetrical feeling. Kado's irregular balance makes use of combinations of contrasting elements that are in keeping with the spirit of in and yo. Basic in/yo patterns of proportion are made up of the concepts of "few vs. many" along with "large vs. small," and the fundamental number of materials utilized is odd (seven or five or three), which promotes asymmetrical balance. The viewer's eyes move from the "few-small" element of the arrangement to the "large-many" aspect, which draws him or her into the work more fully. Kado's basic proportions and number of materials are also tied into the heaven-earth-humanity trinity, or triangular balance, which you will have a chance to understand through hands-on experience later in this book.

Artlessness

Kado has been influenced by a number of the Japanese philosophies and religions that make up the traditional Japanese cultural matrix. These sources of inspiration include Zen and other forms of Buddhism, Shinto, and Dokyo. Dokyo, also known as Taoism, is not always mentioned as an influence on many Japanese arts, since its origins are in China with Lao Tsu. However, direct and indirect influence (via Zen, which originated in China through a combination of native

Taoism and Indian Buddhism) on the concept of artlessness is clear. In kado and Taoism, less is more, and noninterference with nature allows the creative process of the universe to flow through the artist. Lao Tsu wrote:

> In the pursuit of learning, every day something is acquired.
> In the pursuit of Tao, every day something is dropped.
> Less and less is done
> Until non-action is achieved.
> When nothing is done, nothing is left undone.
> The world is ruled by letting things take their course.
> It cannot be ruled by interfering. ₃

To understand what we have termed "artlessness," you will need to become familiar with several Japanese aesthetic concepts, including *wabi* and *sabi*. "Wabi" means "poverty." Dave Lowry, author of *Persimmon Wind*, wrote about the term:

> Its connotation was as negative as the English
> translation implies. Rikyu [founder of the tea ceremony]
> imbued the term with a wholly different flavor, though.
> He used wabi to mean a poverty of materialism,
> of superficial appearances. Wabi he defined as the
> minimizing of things, the better to gain a spiritual
> insight into oneself and the world around. ₄

Wabi hints at a sort of beauty perhaps best exemplified by nature or natural surroundings. Imagine a rustic lodge, standing alone in the wilderness. It is constructed of unpainted wood that has faded and aged to a soft warm color, the beauty of its grain clearly visible. Surrounding the cabin are weathered rocks covered with moss and lichens. The sense of humbleness, quiet solitude, and aged patina evoked by such an image may approach wabi. However, wabi is not to be mistaken for that which is merely soberly sedate, reserved, dull, and without character. When artists strive for wabi, but achieve only commonplace dullness, this is called *jimi* in Japanese art. Wabi transcends intellectual entanglement, all forms of self-importance and pretense, and uncovers the simple truths of nature, which underlie the diversity of relative phenomenon. Since nature is asymmetrical, uneven, even "imperfect," wabi is the impeccability of natural imperfection.

> Kado makes liberal use of empty space, which invites the imagination to complete the arrangement, thus drawing the viewer into the work of art. In other words, the unfinished asks to be finished.

In a manner of speaking, wabi is the dignity of artlessness and even deformity. When this artless, undeveloped elegance is coupled with a certain uncultured antiquity or even the illusion of this ancient attribute, Japanese artists use the term "sabi" (literally "solitude" or "lonesomeness") to describe it. In particular instances, it can also indicate an effortless quality. (Like the term "wabi," it is impossible to characterize "sabi" directly. It can only be found through genuine training in one of Japan's cultural arts.) Despite difficulties of definition, we offer the following working interpretation of sabi: it is not merely "aloneness." It is an embracing of solitariness, a relaxed and serene satisfaction in being solitary. An evening spent trapped by a torrential rain, alone in a cottage in the woods, enjoying the charged stillness and a favorite book by a woodstove—that verges upon the sensation of sabi.

Balanced imbalance, simplicity, artlessness, solitude, great age—all of these relate to wabi and sabi, which in turn are associated with the word *shibumi* (elegance) and the related term *shibui* (elegant). Shibumi connotes something astringent in taste, while shibui hints at that which is natural or dignified. In kado, a flower arrangement possesess the quality of shibumi when it creates a sensation of coolness during a scorching summer and warmth on a frigid day. Shibumi is quiet in elegance, gentle and satisfying in a manner that is not shaped exclusively by reasoning. It is the condition of being "not too much," and exemplifies artistic restraint in the highest sense.

Shibui describes the condition of being not gaudy (in color, for instance), but ample in quality. Unpolished silver or gold and the hue of ashes or bran can bring about a restrained yet finished and peaceful shibui effect. The subdued color scheme of an older woman's kimono, the spare arrangement of a Japanese guestroom, the simple clothing and implements in the tea ceremony—all can be described as shibui.

Wabi, sabi, shibumi, and shibui are traditional Japanese aesthetic concepts that we have combined for the sake of convenience under the general heading of artlessness. These ideas are most definitely presented in this book in a Japanese framework, but at their deepest level they touch something universal in the human heart that can relate to people of all cultures.

Impermanence

Sabi not only indicates a sense of aloneness, effortless action, and/or uncultured antiquity, it also relates to the universal quality of impermanence in life as well as Japanese art. Returning again to Dave Lowry's *Persimmon Wind*, we can find a clear explanation of the correlation between sabi and the ephemeral nature of existence:

> To appreciate sabi is to discover contentment in soli-
> tude. To integrate sabi into daily life is to recognize that
> all our relationships with others, even those we cherish
> and love most deeply, are limited and fleeting. Even the
> woman or man whose spouse has been at his or her side
> for fifty years feels it was but an instant when that part-
> ner dies. For Rikyu, this sensation of ephemerality was
> at the heart of the experience of chado [tea ceremony].
> No matter how beautiful the flowers arranged at the
> tokonoma or how delightful the season of the tea garden
> surrounding the hut, these will pass in an eyeblink, as
> will the moments we share with others in the hut. The
> snow outside the cabin door will melt in the morning,
> the book we savored by the fireplace will be finished. [5]

The sabi state of impermanence has been summed up frequently by exponents of tea ceremony and other Japanese cultural arts as *ichigo, ichi-e* (one encounter, one chance). In essence, when we view anoth-er's flower arrangement, or when we create our own arrangements, the mind must be in the present, as if we might never have another chance to encounter that moment—which, of course, we never do. To live the moment fully is to unify mind and body and be totally alive as opposed to merely existing.

This is the spirit of muga ichi-nen discussed in the last chapter. Muga ichi-nen and ichigo, ichi-e are related ideas that are firmly rooted in the nature of impermanence. (In fact, wabi, sabi, shibumi, and shibui, as well as other concepts and principles common to the various Ways, tend to overlap frequently, since they really describe different aspects of what is in the end a single, universal Way.) This, in turn, under-scores the value of muga ichi-nen ho as an effective meditative form for proponents of the Japanese arts, which universally regard transience as a valued aesthetic if not an actual spiritual component. Dropping self-consciousness and completely experiencing a single, fleeting moment as "one thought" is certainly comparable to the realization that life only exists at this instant and we will never have another chance to live it again.

What better art than kado to lead us to nonattachment as well as a profound awareness of the transient character of life? Flowers that you have painstakingly arranged will wither and die in a short time. Some people even wonder if there's any point in rigorously training in an art that is so impermanent. ("If you can't keep it around for a few years to enjoy and show to your friends, then what's the point? I'd rather paint and produce something lasting.")

These individuals have failed to realize that the very fact that flow-ers do not last is what makes arranging and viewing them special. These same folks suffer from the illusion that some form of permanent art exists. It does not. Beauty is in the moment, and realization of its fleet-ing nature is what encourages us to live every instant completely, with our whole minds and bodies. Someone once said, "Life is what happens when you're busy making plans"—ichigo, ichi-e indeed.

To understand the essence of nonattachment and the imperma-nent moment is to comprehend the heart of sabi, which, again, is one of the central elements in all Japanese art, including kado. Grasping the description above is, of course, not so difficult. But to truly live in the present, uniting the mind and body in a moment transcending time, goes beyond written and verbal definitions. We therefore included in Chapter 2 forms of meditation—orenai te, muga ichi-nen ho, anjo daza ho—that point to the real ever-changing rhythm of nature that cannot be experienced by a mind caught in either the past or the future. Be sure to try them, and use them in conjunction with your kado practice.

This Asian concept of impermanence has also given rise to a particular Japanese aesthetic concept called *aware*. In *Suiseki: The Japanese Art of Miniature Landscape Stones*, Felix G. Rivera defined aware as "when a moment, situation, or event evokes a more intense, nostalgic sadness connected with autumn and the vanishing of the world."[6]

That this is seen as a desirable quality (in contrast to how Westerners sometimes view the transient character of nature) is an indication of the special character of Japanese art.

Oneness with the Universe

Humanity is no more separate from the universe than a wave is separate from the ocean. Naturally, each wave is unique and only exists for a brief moment. But every wave also originates in the ocean, flows up from it, and is absorbed by the ocean again. The ocean is the wave; the wave contains the essence of the ocean. They are one.

Human beings are, in like manner, one with the universe. We contain the essential quality of the universe, or ki, within us and one could say that each person is a microcosm of the universe. You could also say this is nothing but mere words, which would be equally true. That's why this book offers substantive exercises, meditations, and compositions. Just as you cannot smell the scent of a flower via written description, you cannot deny or verify any of the material in this text merely by reading it. Actually understanding means being able to do what you claim to grasp. Theoretical understanding without firsthand experience only encourages a separation of mind and body—a conflicted condition in which the mind supposedly "knows," but the body cannot do. It leads to the illusion of comprehension instead of harmony (*wa*) with an absolute universe that is eternal and infinite. In this state of harmony, we directly perceive our similarly infinite and eternal nature. Harmony with the universe is an instant that is everlasting, beyond the shackles of time and beyond duality.

Wa in kado is arrived at when you become sensitive to the growth patterns and characteristics of the plants you are working with. Certainly this relates to specific plants and flowers that are commonly used in flower arrangement, but on a deeper level it points toward harmony with the essence, or ki, of nature itself.

Wabi and sabi are multifaceted principles that involve an asymmetrical balance that is actually nothing more than a reflection of nature. What's more, while kado does utilize set principles, this "unbalanced balance" assumes a different form in each and every arrangement. You cannot simply memorize it. True understanding of an artless balance that reflects nature comes through unity with the universe. Likewise, the simple, elegant aesthetics that are also associated with wabi are a reflection of nature, as is the sabi concept of aloneness and impermanence.

What better art than kado to lead us to nonattachment as well as a profound awareness of the transient character of life? Flowers that you have painstakingly arranged will wither and die in a short time.

435

Since these principles are derived from a genuine awareness of humankind's intimate connection with the universe, they should be ultimately true rather than contrived. In other words, they should not amount to an aesthetic based solely upon what was fashionable at a certain point in Japanese history. They never fall out of fashion, since they mirror the eternal aspect of nature. Understanding harmony, art-lessness, and impermanence is never-ending, much like the infinite universe itself, and bona fide comprehension comes as we discover and reflect these states in ourselves.

Classification of Arrangements

Various systems of kado exist, each with its own unique version of certain fundamental and ubiquitous principles, and to explore all of them in great detail is beyond the scope of this book. But within these systems are five common styles of arranging flowers: *rikka, sho-ka, nageire, moribana,* and *jiyuka* (modern freestyle). These styles of arrangement should not be confused with the schools (ryu) of flower arrangement. The styles can more accurately be thought of as different ways of arranging flowers, all of which are prevalent in many of the various ryu. But each established system will often have its own approach to the same five styles.

If you have trouble getting your hands to reconstruct what you see in this book, review the previous material relating to the coordination of body and mind. It is, of course, possible to copy the Japanese style of flower arrangement without making reference to these concepts by focusing mainly on technique and by learning to unite the mind and body through trial and error along with a large helping of intuition.

Nonetheless, if the body (hands) fail to reflect what the mind envisions, no attainment in kado (or any other activity) is possible. And since not all of us possess the same knack for quickly picking up a given art or the same degree of intuitiveness, it seems logical to experiment with the principles of mind-body connection, especially if your interest lies in using kado as a form of spiritual realization.

BASIC PRINCIPLES OF RIKKA

Rikka attempts to evoke the multifaceted character of a natural landscape, complete with mountain peaks, hills, near and distant mountain ranges, and water flowing down from the peaks, over waterfalls, through lowly fields, and into the sea. In rikka, all of these varied elements are found in a single arrangement.

Rikka, which was originally developed during the fourteenth to sixteenth centuries, has nine central parts known as *yakueda* (branches). These nine yakueda have differing lengths and angles, and consist of disparate plant materials. Jointly, they serve to emulate the diverse elements that come together harmoniously to form the natural panorama.

Primary in this panorama of beauty is the main element known as shin (humanity). The yakueda shin can have two possible forms: a branch or flower extending straight up or a limb or blossom that extends up then gracefully bends away from the center of the arrangement. (The material used, such as plant, branch, grass, or flower, is not invariably set for each of the nine yakueda.) The other yakueda begin on an imaginary line relating to shin, which runs up through the center of rikka and from which each yakueda branches out from at varying heights along the middle axis of the arrangement. Figure 4 is an example of such a rikka arrangement.

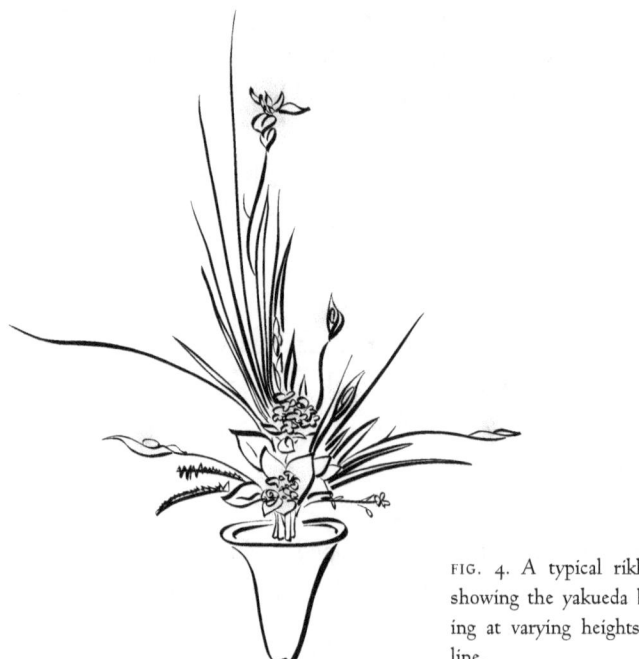

FIG. 4. A typical rikka arrangement, showing the yakueda branches emerging at varying heights from a central line.

Note the characteristic upright appearance of rikka. Complementing this erect form of arrangement is a rikka vase of sufficient height. Note that the rikka vase in Figure 5 is wider at the top than the bottom. This allows the viewer to appreciate the straight bundle of stems emerging from the water's surface (*mizugawa*) at the base of a rikka arrangement. While the bottom is narrow, it should still be wide enough to offer stability. In other words, the shape of a vase in any kado style should be practical, and it should work with the overall shape of the composition.

To hold the stems in place many beginners practice rikka using a

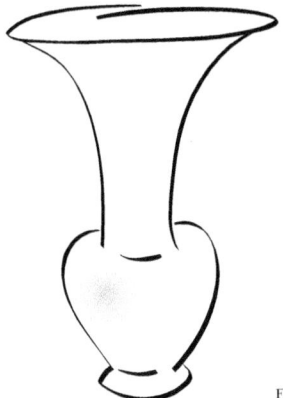

FIG. 5. A rikka vase that is wider at the top than the bottom.

kenzan (also called a "pin frog," a flat base with densely packed vertical needlepoints; see Figure 11). The kenzan rests on a bed of pebbles, with the tips of the needles beneath the lip of the vase.

Rikka flourished during the fifteenth to nineteenth centuries, and classical rikka makes use of complicated rules of arrangement stemming from this period. It also features a handed-down combination of materials and the use of traditional vases. Due to its complexity, it is valued as a means of enhancing concentration and judgment.

Contemporary rikka, on the other hand, often features a freer amalgamation of plants arranged in a simpler format and on a smaller scale that can fit into one's home or office. Even in the more creative versions of modern rikka, however, the central component can still be seen rising up from a single point. Through modern rikka, the artist can create a more personal expression of omnipresent values in nature and the peace that comes from a direct connection with the universe.

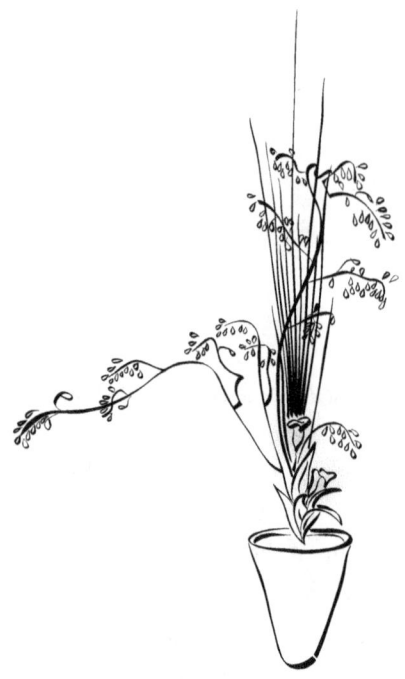

FIG. 6. A shoka shofutai arrangement has three elements. Shin is the central element that leans toward the light and thus divides the arrangement into positive and negative spaces. Soe leaves shin about midway up and angles to the rear. Tai leans toward the front.

BASIC PRINCIPLES OF SHOKA

Shoka means "living flowers," and it consists of two forms: *shoka shofutai* (Figure 6) and *shoka shimputai* (Figure 7). Shoka, in general, expresses the dynamic ki of plants that have their roots in the earth and that stretch upward toward heaven. Its upright demeanor is similar to rikka, and in some ways it can be thought of as a simplified version of rikka. The shape of shoka arrangements is therefore different from moribana, nageire, and jiyuka. And in shoka, the vase is more than a work of art—it symbolizes the origin of life.

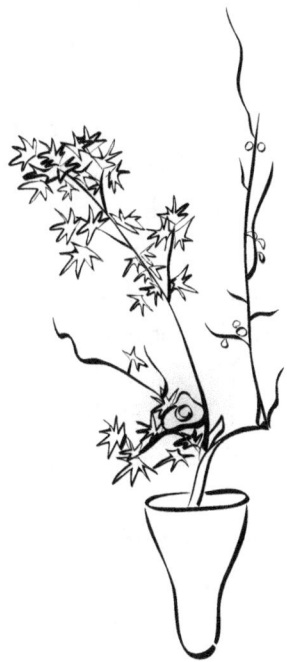

FIG. 7. A shoka shimputai arrangement consists of three main elements called shu, yo, and ashirai that respond and harmonize with each other.

Shoka shofutai is the original version of this style of arrangement, and it has three main parts: shin, soe, and tai. As you may remember from Chapter 1, these three elements are related to the ideas of heaven (ten), earth (chi), and humanity (jin).

Shoka was first set down in the late seventeenth and early eighteenth centuries. Early arrangements fixed the stems in the vase by means of four crossed sticks or a forked twig with a back crosspiece, but it is common to use a kenzan today. The height of the shin element is between two and one-half and three and one-half times the height of the vase—depending on the shape and feeling of the vase, the disposition of the floral materials, and the artist's vision. The height of the soe branch is roughly two-thirds that of shin, and tai is about one-third the height of shin.

Shin sprouts upward, leans toward the light, and, at a spot less than half its height, changes direction and curves back toward a point above the center of the container. Soe moves with shin, but at a spot below the bend it leaves the central line, angling to the rear as well as upward. Tai is placed in front of shin and opposite from soe. Its ki extends at an angle to the front, its tip normally not moving past the vase's edge. (Shin, soe, and tai are also assisted by supporting branches called *ashirai*, which are placed to the front and rear of shin, in front and rear of soe, and near tai to support and balance the part of tai that is closest to shin.)

The central shin line, additionally, serves to divide the arrangement into positive and negative elements (in/yo), thus relating shoka to the omnipresent dualism that makes up the universe. Yo is indicated by the soe, or "sunny" side, of the composition; in is reflected in the tai side that is "shady."

In 1977, Ikenobo Sen'ei Sensei developed a new form of shoka called shimputai, which can be seen as an outgrowth based on the classical rules of shoka shofutai. In shoka shofutai, the emphasis is on creating beauty through the utilization of classical rules and proportions. Shoka shimputai, in contrast, allows the artist to more freely express his or her personal feelings about the elegance hidden within each of the floral elements.

Shimputai consists of two parts—primary and secondary—whereas shofutai, as discussed above, makes use of three sections: shin, soe, and tai. The secondary shimputai element (*yo*) can be said to be the

442

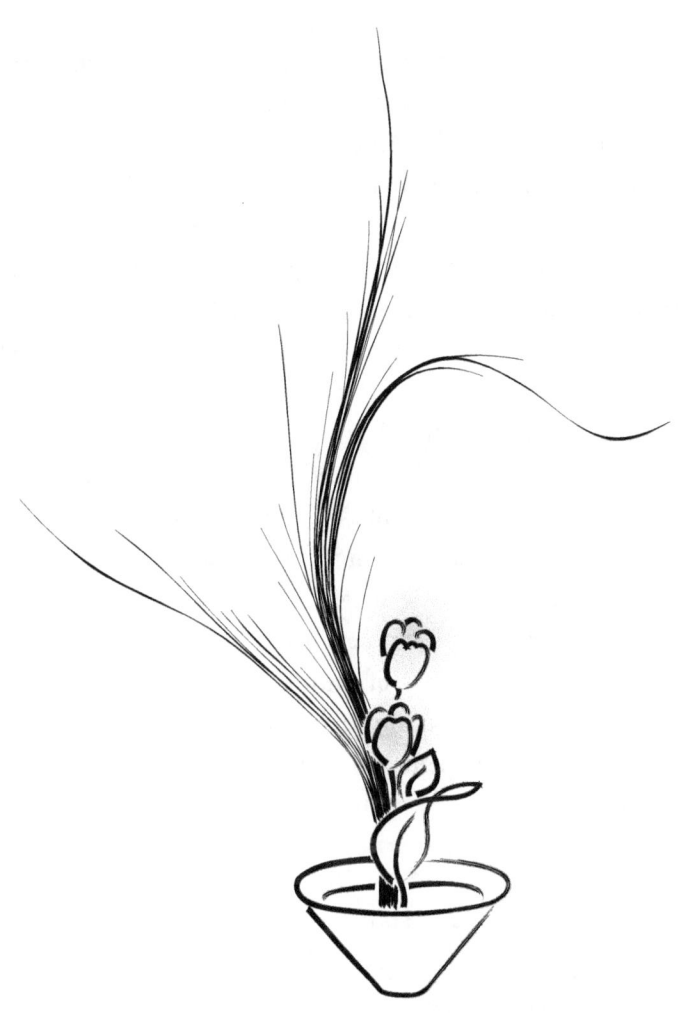

In the nishuike or "two-material style" of shoka, the taller, more dominant material typically consists of tree or shrub branches without flowers. The colorful flower material in the foreground accents the subdued quality of the non-flowering material. Here, the central elements are scotch broom and tulip.

material's "response" to the primary material (*shu*), which is chosen by the artist to best communicate what he or she wants to express in the arrangement. Essentially, your own feelings become the primary theme, and you then pick a secondary material that will respond to your main motif. To add harmony to your two main components, you can add ashirai to form a third minor aspect. In rikka and shofutai, the basic pattern of insertion of stems places woody materials toward the rear. But in shimputai, woody components may actually be in the foreground, with flowers and grasses to the back.

Both the primary and secondary portions of shimputai arise from an individual, slender base. These aspects relate to each other to form a harmony of opposites . . . much like the universe itself.

Where classical shoka shofutai is fairly strict but splendid in composition, shoka shimputai is less rigid and uses relatively few selected materials. Shimputai often has a personal theme, which is sometimes communicated through the use of a title. Shofutai can be thought of as an impersonal expression of universal harmony, while shimputai can be viewed as a personal statement of natural accord in which the compatibility between the particular ki of the plants and the individual ki of the artist assumes the forefront.

BASIC PRINCIPLES OF NAGEIRE

"Nageire" means "thrown into," and it tends to use slender, narrow-mouthed containers. Nageire and moribana arrangements share some common points, and they are often taught in relationship to each other. They first came into real prominence in the late 1800s in response to the growing influence of Western culture on Japanese homes. Like rikka and shoka, they accentuate the natural elegance of branches and flowers. However, nageire is arranged in a freer style that is a reflection of personal taste and creativity.

Nageire stems from an older method called *nageirebana* ("flowers thrown into") in which branches and flowers were freely inserted into a vase. Nageire, therefore, should present a relaxed feeling through the composition of flowers in a manner that suggests their original beauty in nature. In this system, stems are braced against the inside of the container. If needed, supporting crosspieces or other techniques can be applied to fix the stems in the correct position. When artfully executed, nageire exudes a sensation of lightness and grace.

Modern nageire (Figure 8) has three main yakueda: shin, soe, and tai. The shin element in nageire determines the overall form of the composition. Its length is normally one and one- half times the height of a tall vase. Soe is roughly three-fourths the length of shin, which it supports and responds to. Soe is placed in either the front or rear of shin to create a feeling of three-dimensional depth. Finally, tai is about one-half the length of shin. Ashirai can also be used around the base of the arrangement to add an appearance of fullness. In addition, nageire has three fundamental variations depending on the angle of the shin stem, but these variations, like many of the more technically complex details of ikebana, are beyond the scope of this book.

When creating a nageire composition, in general, the artist strives for naturalness. Less is more in nageire; though the arrangement should be potent, it should not dominate the room.

BASIC PRINCIPLES OF MORIBANA

In about 1900, Ohara Unshin Sensei developed the fundamentals for moribana (literally "piled-up flowers") arrangements. Also around

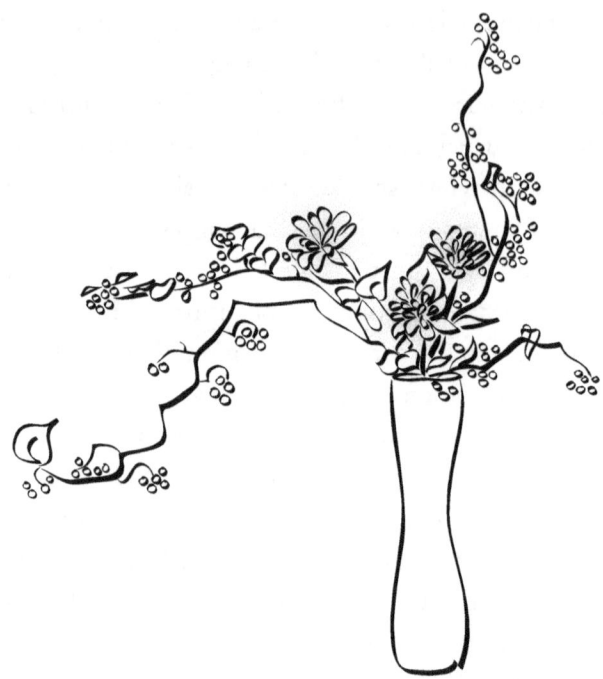

FIG. 8. A nageire arrangement is an informal style that uses three elements—shin, soe, and tai—in an attitude of lightness and grace. The container is typically tall and narrow.

this time, the kenzan, or needlepoint holder, was created, which allowed even the average person to quickly produce ikebana art.

Unlike rikka, shoka, and nageire, moribana can be made so that it is viewed from all angles. Plant materials and flowers are arranged in shallow bowls to form moribana compositions that can be made more quickly than other kado styles. Moribana has a more naturalistic style, less formal in appearance than rikka and shoka's strong upright lines.

Gradually, as Japanese interiors became more westernized through

446

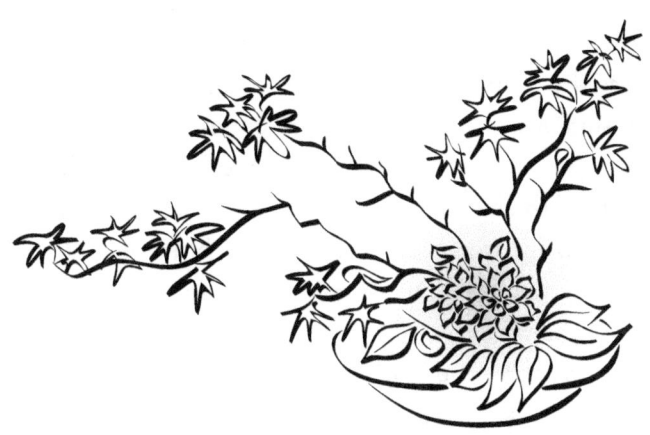

FIG. 9. Moribana arrangements are designed for the modern Japanese home and offer a more lateral rather than vertical expansiveness. Again, there are three elements that play off each other, with many variations possible depending on the selection of floral and leaf materials and their placement in the container.

the use of, for example, Western tables and chairs as opposed to tatami mats and cushions, moribana arrangements were created to add beauty to a table instead of a tokonoma alcove. Thus moribana arrangements have a more expansive, side-to-side movement of ki (Figure 9). The name "moribana" suggests a "mounding" or heaping up of materials, so as you may imagine this style gives a sensation of splendor and volume. This is in contrast to systems such as rikka and shoka that stress an extension of ki and feeling that reaches straight up toward heaven.

Nageire and moribana have somewhat varying histories and characteristics. Even today, in terms of form, vase appearance, and arranging methodologies, the two styles exhibit certain differences.

447

As is common in other forms, the yakueda in moribana are named shin, soe, and tai. Shin, as usual, is the main branch and is formed from the primary floral material of the arrangement. Its length is one and one- half times the width of the container plus the container's height. Soe reacts to shin and supports it in either the front, rear, or opposite side of the vase. Soe is about two-thirds to three-fourths as tall as shin. Tai responds to both shin and soe. It should balance the composition from front to back and from side to side. Its height is roughly one-half that of the shin element. Again, ashirai can be used to add depth and unity to the composition.

As in nageire, three moribana variations are possible, depending on the angle of shin. They are *chokutai* (standing angle), *shatai* (slant-ing angle), and *suitai* (cascading angle). These style variations can be learned from a qualified teacher.

BASIC PRINCIPLES OF JIYUKA

Jiyuka, or "freestyle flowers," is the most contemporary of the kado forms (Figure 10). Following the devastation of World War II, followers of kado sought a new approach to the arrangement of flow-ers—an approach that would allow them to create harmony in a world that had been forever changed by the havoc of bloodshed and the modernization of society. An avant-garde system—one that borrowed nonplant materials and manipulated flowers through the use of cut-ting, wire, and other techniques—arose to express harmony in current urban settings. Jiyuka has no set form or model, but it does definitely make use of universal principles found in all Japanese art and in the older variants of kado. In freestyle, the artist is not merely thinking of the flower as a flower; he or she often considers it to be a certain shape,

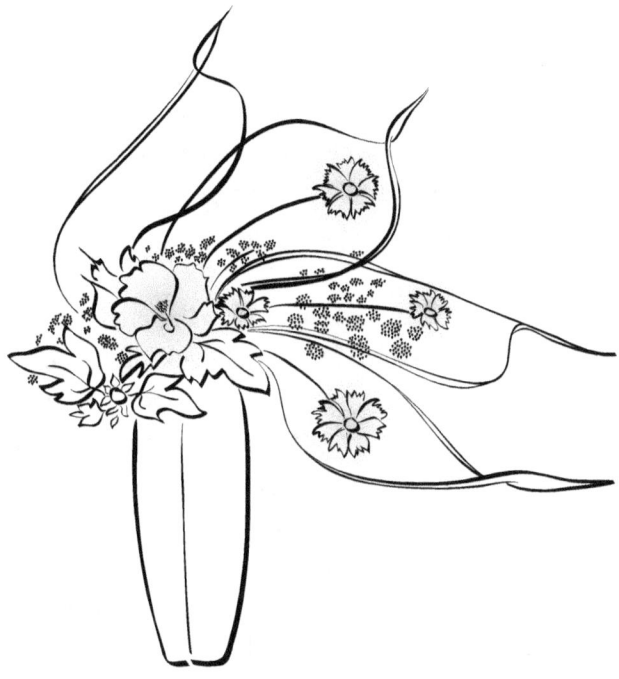

FIG. 10. Jiyuka arrangements are freestyle compositions often incorporating a simple theme. The artist blends together contrasting shapes and colors including lines, points, and surfaces to create a flower sculpture.

texture, surface, line, or mass of color. Random points, lines, shapes, and hues are arranged to create flowering sculpture. In this sense, jiyu-ka owes a debt to abstract art. The effects of shapes, colors, and forms are also used to express themes or feelings, and these are reinforced by composition titles such as *Children, Youth and Early Spring, Reverie,* and *Prayer.*

In shoka shofutai, shin, soe, and tai are arranged to create a scalene triangle. In freestyle, one also thinks of a general form. Two vertical lines create a vertical movement of ki. But twenty perpendicular lines, for example, will do more than produce an upright sensation—they will create a planed surface. This surface can be a rectangle or a square depending on the artist's intent. Straight lines of gradually increasing/ decreasing length can also be used to suggest an oval or round form. Like most art, freestyle kado makes elemental use of circles, triangles, and squares.

Freestyle also consists of three variations: vertical, horizontal, and slanting. Vertical jiyuka has an up or down ki movement. Horizontal freestyle features ki moving to the left, right, or both directions. And a slanting form has a ki movement that angles up, down, or extends to one side

Theoretical understanding without firsthand experience only encourages a separation of mind and body—a conflicted condition in which the mind supposedly "knows," but the body cannot do.

or the other, or both sides. The ki of the vertical style projects solidity, the ki action of the horizontal form expresses stability, and the ki in the slanting version gives rise to a sensation of action.

Colors can also be used in freestyle to produce differing feelings. Ikebana experts suggest the following color-sensation relationships:

white = purity, life—stillness, emptiness

black = solemnity, death—silence, nothingness

gray = modesty, repentance—solitude, plainness

red = passion, boldness—danger, revolution

orange = brave, strong emotion—health, selfishness

yellow = uplifting, cheerfulness—jealousy, lukewarm

green = repose, tranquility—intelligence, hope

blue = depth, composure—coolness, contemplation

purple = nobility, profoundness—instability, grief

brown = settled, internal—reliable, serious [7]

The container is also considered to be one of the design materials in freestyle. Stems can be fixed be using a kenzan, green floral foam, wire, and other devices. Freestyle vases must work with the abstract sculpting of lines, surfaces, mass, points, and colors . . . all tools of the freestyle artist. In jiyuka, the arranger is not limited to traditional ways of thinking about flowers and plants; new ways of looking at these materials are encouraged. But even when dissonance is deliberately created, one must still have a profound awareness of nature to produce this effect successfully, since discord is actually one of the relative aspects of an absolute harmonious universe. Coordination of mind and body is vital for any style of kado, freestyle included, and the meditative state of oneness continues to be essential.

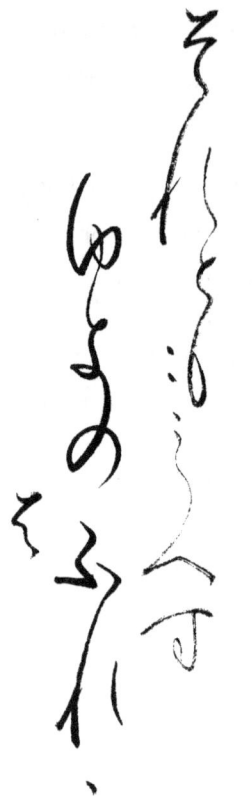
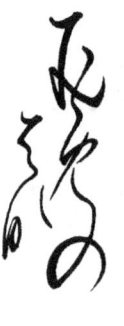
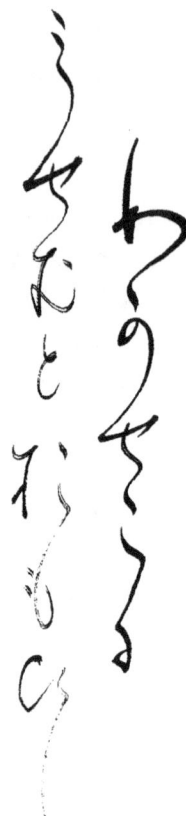

I want to give to
my child this beautiful sight—
the plum tree's blossoms.
But now that view is fading
in the newly falling snow.
AKAHITO FROM "WAKAN ROEISHU"

Waga se ko ni
misento omoishi
mume no hana
sore tomo miezu
yuki no furereba

Chapter 4

SIMPLE
EXERCISES
& EASY
ARRANGEMENTS

Now let's take a look at the basic tools you'll need to reproduce three simple flower arrangements that will appear later in this chapter. (For information on how to obtain these tools and/or a qualified teacher, see the back of this book.)

Basic Kado Tools

Quite a few supplies, including handsaws, scissors, water containers, needlepoint holders, wire, bast, florist's tape, pebbles, glass beads, and vases, can be found in the kado student's "toolbox." For this book, however, we have selected uncomplicated compositions that will not require a great number of accouterments. All you'll need here are three common items: ikebana shears, kenzan of various sizes, and perhaps some pebbles (Figure 11). Of course, a suitable vase for each arrange-

453

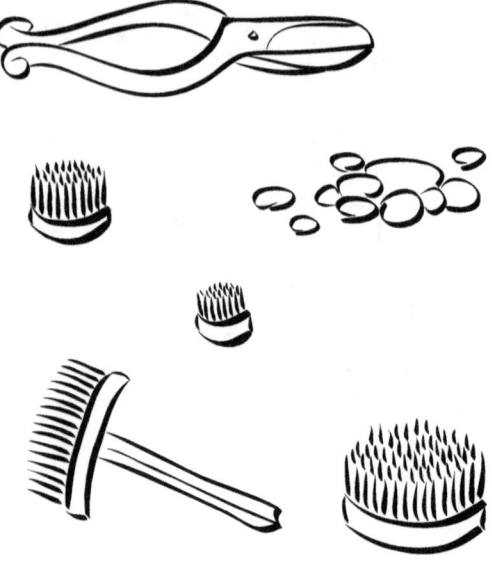

FIG. 11. The compositions in this book can all be created using some common items: hasami (shears), kenzan of various sizes, and perhaps some pebbles.

ment is also required, and we'll discuss a bit later in this chapter what makes a vase appropriate for each of the compositions.

Try to buy the highest quality tools you can find and/or afford. If no ikebana shears are available to you, Western florist's shears can be substituted. In a pinch, you can even substitute Western green floral foam (oasis) for a proper kenzan, but this isn't always going to be acceptable; buy a genuine kenzan if possible.

Basic Kado Techniques

Kado has four fundamental techniques for manipulating plant material. In certain cases, subtechniques are present, and we will explain each of these different methods and suggest exercises you can try that

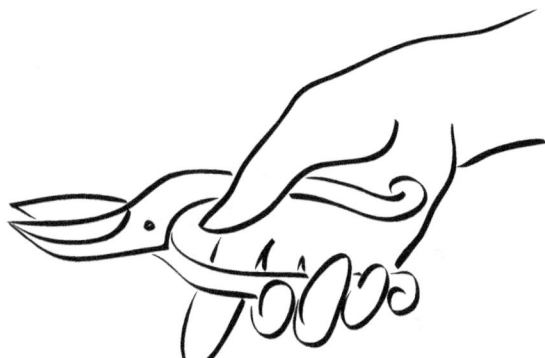

FIG. 12. Grip the hasami firmly using the last two or three fingers of the hand.

will give you firsthand experience with each main technique. This gives you the background needed to control the materials you'll be working with in the subsequent sample arrangements. Do not skip over the following information, or you will lack the proper foundation to arrange flowers.

HOLDING AND CUTTING WITH KADO SHEARS

First, you'll need to learn how to hold the *hasami* (shears). Be sure to purchase top-quality hasami if possible, and find shears that feel comfortable and balanced in your hand.

Exercise One

Try copying the grip shown in Figure 12. Grip in a firm but relaxed way, with the last two or three fingers of the hand. Your index finger is left loose or extended.

Interestingly, a similar grip is used in *kenjutsu* (classical Japanese swordsmanship) when gripping the sword. A number of jujutsu exponents use a comparable method of grasping an opponent's limbs as well.

455

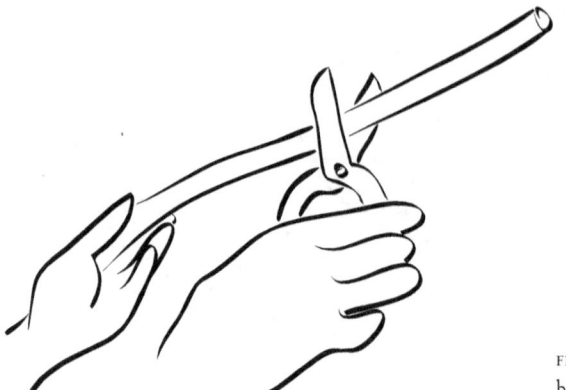

FIG. 13. Cut branches at the base of the hasami blades.

(Again, all of the various Do forms use similiar principles. We have used kado as a representative example of a single Do, but this book explores principles that correlate with all the Ways and that can be positively connected with the lives of everyone.)

Just as shodo enthusiasts sometimes take their brushes with them when not painting, holding them with the correct grip, you can "connect" with your hasami. Carry them around from time to time even when you are not engaged in kado so that you grow accustomed to their balance and feeling in your hand.

Exercise Two

Relax your hands and shoulders so that your body weight drops to the lower abdomen (hara), and calm your mind. Practice releasing and closing your grip in a smooth and fluid manner to produce a cutting action. A smooth and fluid motion can only happen when you're in a state of calmness and relaxation . . . qualities that are indispensable in kado, meditation, and everyday life.

456

Exercise Three

This drill involves cutting. Usually, you'll cut a branch or stem at an angle instead of straight across. Practice holding branches between the blades at their base and then cutting (Figure 13). Avoid cutting inefficiently with the blade tips.

Try cutting heavier branches as well. In this case, you'll need to make an introductory shallow cut followed by a deep diagonal slice. You may need to repeat this a few times with especially thick branches.

Cutting should bring out the ideal and natural form of the branch as well as shape it to fit into its role in the arrangement. Knowing what not to cut is as important as recognizing what must be removed.

TAMEKATA—SHAPING AND CURVING STEMS

To bring forth the charm of a stem's innate line or to change a stem so that its line is closer to what you desire, you'll need to learn how to bend and shape your material (*tamekata*). As you might suspect, certain plant materials can be bent easily and others cannot. Depending on what you're trying to bend, you'll choose one of the methods discussed below. Experience will help you discover which techniques work best for a given flower or plant. Always respect the ki of the plant you are working with.

Exercise Four

This technique is called *oshi-dame*. Using both thumbs, apply gradual pushing (*oshi*) pressure against the point you wish to bend. (Figure 14.) Calm your mind, and be sensitive to the material you're working with. Respect its ki, so that the stem does not break. Just as in daily life, it is possible to assert yourself without force, and this is usually the

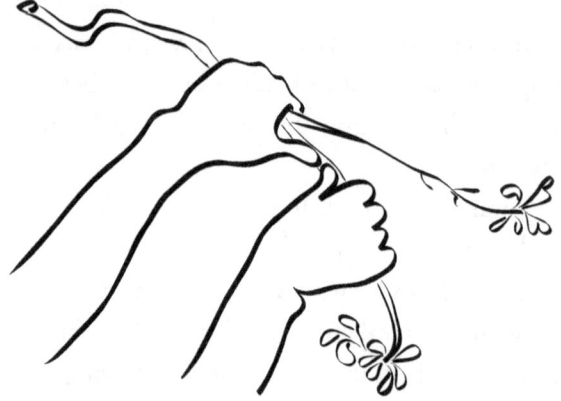

FIG. 14. Bend the branch by applying gradual pressure with the thumbs.

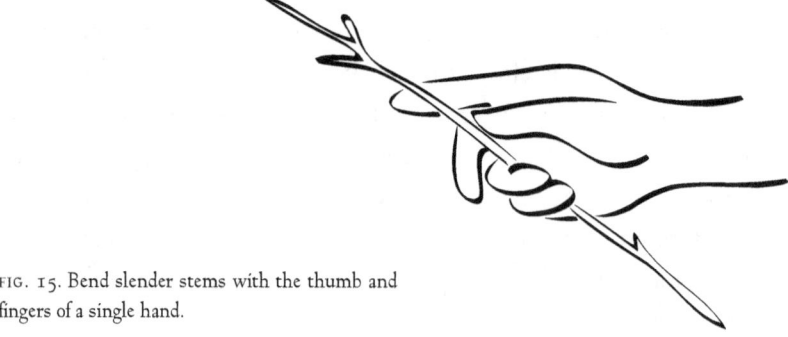

FIG. 15. Bend slender stems with the thumb and fingers of a single hand.

most efficient approach to bending stems (as well as in interpersonal relationships).

Oshi-dame works well for a variety of materials, especially heavier items. Slender stems can be bent with the thumb and fingers of a single hand, as in Figure 15. Be sure to experiment with a wide variety of plants or flowers.

458

Exercise Five

Make a slight slantways slice with your hasami in the stem. Then, similar to what is shown in Figure 14, try curving it with your hands. Place one of your thumbs over the cut to control the bend and to prevent breakage. This is called *kiri-dame*.

Make a superficial incision for a moderate curve. For a sharp curve, slice more deeply. Experiment with both approaches using a wide selection of materials.

Exercise Six

In Figure 16, note how the part of the branch to be curved is held between the hands and how it is simultaneously twisted. This technique is ideal for inflexible, brittle stems. If you have a stem that persists in returning to its initial form even after bending it with oshi-dame, then give this method a try. It is called *nejiri-dame*.

You can also use nejiri-dame if you're working with unusually twisted branches, stems, or leaves. In the case of leaf materials, you

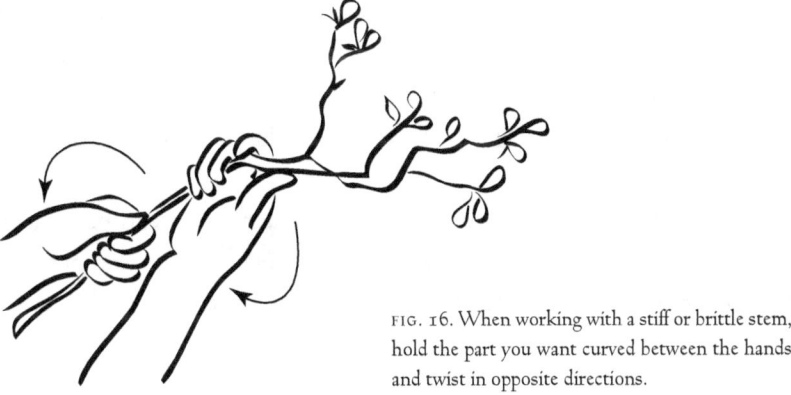

FIG. 16. When working with a stiff or brittle stem, hold the part you want curved between the hands and twist in opposite directions.

459

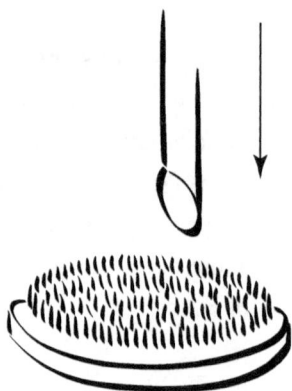

FIG. 17. Practice cutting the branch at an angle
and inserting it perpendicularly into the kenzan.

must be particularly understanding and respectful of their ki. Without
force, hold the material lightly in your hands and twist gently. Your
mind must be calm, or you'll grip too tightly and bruise the leaf surfaces. While you're trying nejiri-dame, consider what it means to spiritually put yourself in the place of the plants you're shaping.

Two more traditional methods are also used: *shigoki-dame* and wiring techniques. Shigoki-dame involves holding long leaves (or thin, hollow stems) at their base with one hand while drawing your other hand
along the length of the stem to gradually change its direction. It is an
interesting approach, one that makes use of stroking the plant in the
direction of its ki flow to gradually to lead its ki in a new direction and
thus produce a curve.

Wire is normally only used in jiyuka and rikka. It can be used to
curve stems when needed, but wiring and shigoki-dame are methods
that will not be required for the arrangements in this book.

460

TOMEKATA—FIXING MATERIALS IN PLACE

Historically, many procedures were used to hold branches and the stems of flowers in place (*tomekata*). Hefty stones with hollow, split, metallic, and symmetrical ovals; bifurcated twigs; crosspieces; and weighty metallic cylinders—all can be used to clasp materials in place. But today, the kenzan is most popular.

When you use a kenzan for fixing materials in place, make sure it is flat. Depending on the type of vase, place it between three-quarters of an inch and two inches beneath the opening of your vase. A deep, cylinder-shaped container can be laden with pebbles that rise up to within roughly two inches of the mouth of the vase. You then place your kenzan level on this pebble surface.

Exercise Seven

Pick a stem or a branch, and slice it slantways. Then insert it perpendicularly into the kenzan as in Figure 17. Next, since your materials will not invariably be fixed in an upright way, try inserting a stem so that it is inclined to one side. To do this, always initially stick in the stem vertically as before, then tilt it at the angle you wish. The cut edge always faces up, so that even inclining branches can be fixed securely in place. Stout branches can also be given added vertical incisions. This allows them to be more freely and solidly placed in the kenzan.

MIZUAGE—ENCOURAGING WATER ABSORPTION

Kado traditionally includes a variety of methods to encourage the absorption of water. This is essential for promoting flower longevity. However, many water-absorption methods (*mizuage*) are somewhat

461

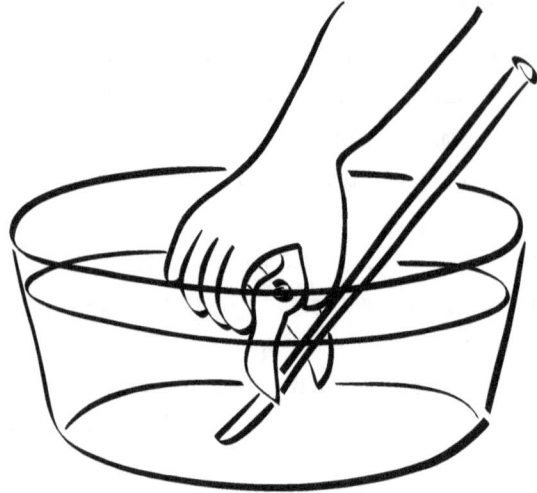

FIG. 18. Always cut the stem in a basin of water. This prevents air from entering and blocking water absorption by the plant.

difficult technically and not frequently used. We will feature only one simple mizuage procedure that has wide-ranging applicability. This easy technique, called *mizugiri* (water cutting) can be seen in Figure 18.

Exercise Eight

Place the end of a stem in a basin of water and cut the end under the water, which prevents air from entering the stem. This is vital as the entry of air into the stem can impede the absorption of water. Most flowers will benefit from this approach. (After using your hasami, be sure to dry them off or they will rust.)

Peonies, hydrangeas, roses, and certain other flowers may have difficulties with water uptake, so the end of the stem can be singed, or charred, with a flame. This form of mizuage is effective for preventing the spread of bacteria and for keeping fluids from leaving the cut stem.

Other flowers may benefit from having the cut end placed briefly (3 seconds or so) in boiling water. If milky fluid escapes from the cut stem, the stem base can be rubbed with salt. A cut end can also be crushed with the flat, closed blades of the hasami to open water arteries in the severed stem. Balloon flowers and milkbush can benefit from such treatments.

Some kado experts even make use of a flower pump for pushing water up into the stem once it is cut. Pond lilies, lotus flowers, and similar plants with big water vessels are prime candidates for this version of mizuage. Still other flowers respond well when peppermint oil or vinegar is placed in their water.

There are many different methods of mizuage, but the basic technique of mizugiri will be sufficient for experimenting with the arrangements in this chapter.

Preparing the Mind & Body for Flower Meditation

Unless the mind is calm and clear, it is difficult to accurately estimate balance and proportion in kado—just as in daily life the capacity to think acutely and judge matters effectively is determined by the depth of our clarity of mind. Hence, entering into meditation prior to the arrangement of flowers is an effective preparation for kado. Of equal importance is the ability to sustain the meditative state during the actual arranging.

Practicing muga ichi-nen ho or anjo daza ho will allow you to exercise good judgment in the way that you place flowers in your vase, because both of those exercises let you see nature as it really is and sense the movement of ki. At the same time, your concentration is

463

enhanced, making it easier to keep the mind in the present and stay focused on the task at hand. Muga ichi-nen ho has the advantage of potentially helping you connect your ki with that of the flowers and plants you'll be arranging. Try placing your materials in front of you and focusing your eyes gently on them. Sit upright in seiza or in a firm chair. Forget yourself, and allow your ki to merge with the plants you'll be working with. These plants become the "one thought," and any separation between the person who is looking and that which is gazed upon ceases. Eventually, you are led to an intimate connection with the flowers themselves. Many kado experts say that they reach a state in which the flowers "talk" to them.

Despite the effectiveness of this meditation, you may experience difficulty sustaining this condition of connection while you arrange flowers. During muga ichi-nen ho, take note of your posture, since your body acts as a counterpart to your mind. (You may want to review the principles of posture outlined in Chapter 2.) Just as in the orenai te exercise, your body should be filled with ki—it should not sag and collapse inward like a deflated balloon. Conversely, it should not be excessively upright and tense like a balloon that is about to burst. Once again, balance is needed.

A correct and natural posture (shizen-tai) is vital: one that is not tense and not limp, not rigid but not slouching, neither overly excited nor dead to the world—a state in which the mind and body are one. In this coordinated condition, the various body parts relax positively and settle downward in harmony with gravity. The upper body's weight reaches its highest point of density at your natural center of gravity and center of balance in the hara.

In meditation, your mind is in the present and your body adopts an

464

"alive posture." First, sustain this state during your meditation. Then maintain it in the midst of arranging flowers, and, finally, retain it in the midst of everyday activity.

How do you know when you've lost this unified condition? Since your body echoes your mind, notice when your posture begins to fall limp or grow tense. Either state reveals a lack of balance as well as the loss of a coordinated condition.

So what can you do if you find yourself sagging and psychologically withdrawing, or tensing up and growing agitated? Reconfirm your posture and try calming your mind at your natural center in the hara. This quick approach stills the mind and leads the body's weight to settle downward, which helps you harmonize with gravity and therefore relax dynamically.

Don't be misled by the directness and simplicity of the above suggestions. Understanding the dictionary definition of words and phrases such as "harmony," "calming the mind," and "concentration" is not always the same as grasping their true meaning. For instance, suppose we tell you to concentrate your mind at a specific point in the lower abdomen. In this case, does "concentration" mean a state in which the mind is focused on this point and nothing else? Or does it mean simply an awareness of the aforementioned point? Does this awareness involve creating an image of this point to center the mind on, or does it require merely "feeling" this point, with no specific image in the mind? And what is meant by "mind?" The brain? One's thoughts? Your feelings? No authority

> In meditation, your mind is in the present and your body adopts an "alive posture." First, sustain this state during your meditation. Then maintain it in the midst of arranging flowers, and, finally, retain it in the midst of everyday activity.

can concisely answer such questions for you. In many ways, meditation means discovering for yourself what these terms and phrases mean through direct, unbiased observation of the moment. Any assumptions stemming from your past, in the form of belief systems, prejudice, or upbringing, will only prevent you from reaching a personal and immediate perception of the true nature of existence.

Points to Remember

- Don't forget to practice anjo daza ho or muga ichi-nen ho prior to kado.

- While arranging flowers, take note of whether or not you sustain a condition in which the relative, individual self is forgotten and the present moment, as well as the flowers before you, fills your consciousness. If this state is lost, when does it happen and what takes place at that moment?

- Lapses in mind and body harmony can be detected via body language. If your psycho-physical posture is unbalanced, your floral arrangement will also lack balance. What does your posture say about you? What does your artwork say about you?

- By all means enjoy your finished artwork, but don't drop the meditative state when your arrangement is finished. Take it into daily life and use it to benefit yourself and others.

• To help you accomplish point number four, conclude your session with anjo daza ho or muga ichi-nen ho, using the finished arrangement as your point of concentration.

Arrangement One: Shoka Shofutai

MATERIALS

Seven medium-sized yellow or white spider chrysanthemums

CONTAINER

Blue ceramic vase shaped like an inverted triangle

SUBSTITUTIONS

Seven medium-sized purple or white liatris

DESCRIPTION

This arrangement is one of the simplest and most fundamental of the classical arrangements. Shoka shofutai is commonly used to introduce beginners to kado, and it can be recreated with only one item of material. In this case, the material consists of seven white spider chrysanthemums. (Other suitable chrysanthemum varieties can be found all year around, but many Japanese arrangers feel autumn produces the most outstanding flowers. No matter what the season, achieving visual balance is easiest with medium-sized flowers rather than very large or very small flower heads.)

The *kiku* (chrysanthemum) is regarded as a particularly noble

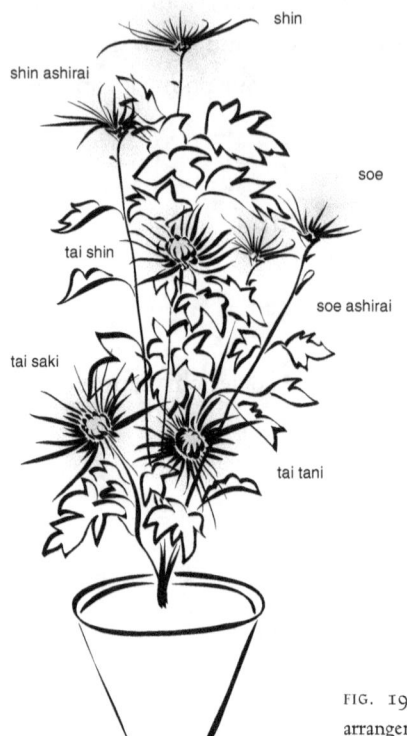

shin

shin ashirai

soe

tai shin

soe ashirai

tai saki

tai tani

FIG. 19. Composition One. A shoka shofutai arrangement using spider chrysanthemums. See the photograph on page 368.

flower in Japan. Light-colored chrysanthemums, particularly white or yellow flowers convey a sense of cheerfulness, while their dark green foliage represents repose. In general, kado experts often use light-colored flowers to project an uplifting sensation. For this purpose, chrysanthemums are ideal. The kiku was initially associated with commoners in old Japan, but its shape is copied on the sanctioned crest of the imperial family.

The composition you will be making here (shown in Figure 19)

468

is an *isshuike* arrangement, which means that only one type of flower material, in this case spider chrysanthemum, is used. Isshuike arrangements should communicate harmony and naturalness. Individual members of the arrangement should appear to be growing together, and as in nature, there should be slight variations in the size and strength of their visual impact.

Spider mums—typically consisting of various medium- to large-sized single flower heads, attractive green leaves, and tall sturdy stems—lend themselves to an isshuike arrangement. But not all flowers do. For example, carnations with their round flower heads have strong visual impact, but the flower heads sit atop spindly stems that lack leaves, which are necessary for conveying naturalness and balance. Sometimes, a flower like this is better used in another type of arrangement, such as freestyle.

Note that the stems in Figure 19 have slight curves to them. Try to pick flowers with a preexisting stem curvature, since it is sometimes hard to bend chrysanthemums without breaking them.

Again, kado does not focus exclusively on the flowers being arranged; the leaves play a central role as well. Each stem should ideally include a large number of healthy leaves. The overall appearance of the arrangement should include leaves at every level; you don't want an arrangement with many leaves in one area but bare spots elsewhere. Place stems in the arrangement first with the idea of striving for overall balance; you can trim leaves later to enhance the overall effect. Notice the variations in the density of the foliage in Figure 19 and in the photograph on page 368.

Before getting to the actual composition of this arrangement, here's a quick review of some of the general principles for shoka shofutai compositions that you'll need to keep in mind as you follow the directions in the next section.

Shoka expresses the dynamic growing ki of plants that have their roots in the earth and that stretch up toward heaven. In shoka, the vase symbolizes the origin of life. Where the stems and water meet is called the mizugiwa, and this zone is most important in representing the idea of life force pushing upward. Remove leaves and knobby growths from the stems here, up to 3 or 4 inches out of the water.

Shoka shofutai has three parts: shin, soe, and tai (heaven, earth, and humanity). The height of shin is between two and one-half and three and one-half times the height of the vase—depending on the shape of the vase, the disposition of the materials, and the artist's vision. The height of soe is roughly two-thirds that of shin, and tai is about one-third the height of shin.

Shin sprouts up, leans toward the light, and at a spot less than half its height changes direction and curves back toward a point above the center of the container. (Flower arrangements were designed for an alcove called the tokonoma. Depending upon the direction of light, an arrangement may be called either hongatte or gyakugatte. In hongatte, the light is coming from the left of the arrangement, whereas in gyaku-gatte, the light is found on the right of your composition. The central shin line additionally serves to divide the arrangement into positive and negative elements—in/yo—thus relating shoka to the dualism that makes up the universe.)

Soe moves with shin, and at a spot below the bend, leaves the central line, angling to the rear as well as up. Tai is in front of shin and opposite from soe. Its ki extends at an angle to the front, its tip not moving past the vase's edge. Shin, soe, and tai are also assisted by branches called ashirai, which are placed to the front and rear of shin, in front and rear of soe, and near tai to balance the part of tai closest to shin.

METHOD

We have numbered the various components in each of our illustrated arrangements (see Figure 20). These numbers indicate the order in which you insert the different stems into the kenzan. By using both the picture of the arrangement and the illustration of the kenzan, you should find it fairly easy to start copying the compositions in this book. If the written directions ever seem difficult to follow, take a look at the line drawings, especially the illustrations of the kenzan from above. The text should be used in conjunction with these pictures. (Bear in mind that no two arrangements will be identical, but you can still follow the same general principles to experiment with flower meditation.)

Most shoka arrangements are made in medium to tall vases with wide mouth openings. A narrow vase, which requires that the flowers be kept closer together, doesn't give you as much room to position the flowers at the proper angle or to space the flowers to illustrate depth. Once you've selected a vase, you will need to place the kenzan in it. If your vase was made for Japanese flower arrangement, it may have a built-in platform for the kenzan; just place the kenzan on the "shelf" and add water. If there's no shelf, add pebbles to provide elevation. Then, place the kenzan on, or surrounded by, the pebbles. Then add water. (Come close to the lip of your vase with the water, but stay at least a half-inch or so away.) Smooth pebbles can be placed around or over your kenzan if you like the looks of this effect.

Follow these steps to make a shoka shofutai arrangement with spi-

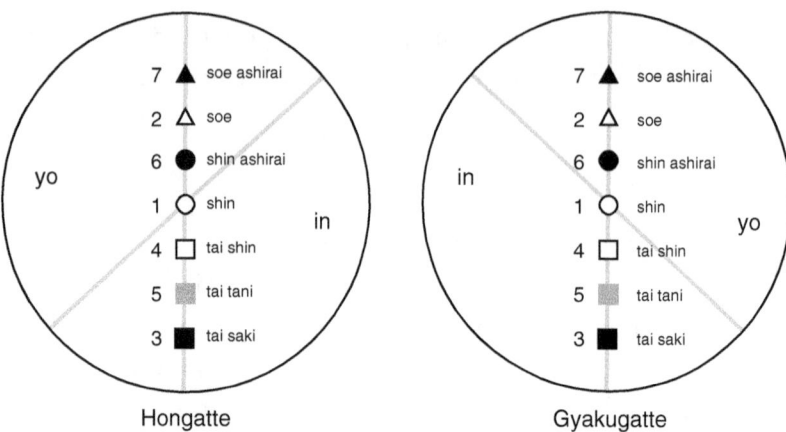

Hongatte   Gyakugatte

FIG. 20. Diagram of the order stems are inserted in the kenzan for Composition One. The view is from the top looking down and shows the different design elements and where they are placed in relation to each other. Use the corresponding illustration and the photograph to better understand how the different elements relate to each other. In hongatte, the light is from the left; in gyakugatte, the light is from the right. Shin divides the arrangement into the in (dark) and yo (light) duality.

der mums. Note that we first describe how to pick appropriate flowers to arrange, then we explain the order and method of arrangement.

1. First, select the shin flower, which should be approximately two and one-half to three times the height of the vase. Pick a large flower with strong visual impact. Find a flower stem that isn't too straight. Look for a thick stem that begins as a straight line, but curves slightly outward, then returns to the centerline. The shin flower—representing humanity and the present moment—should be just recently bloomed. If all your flowers are equally bloomed, choose flowers that meet the other criteria in terms of height, curvature, visual strength, and so on.

472

2. Next, look for the soe stem, which will need to be cut to about two-thirds the height of shin and placed at about a 45 degree angle from shin. The soe stem is placed to the rear of shin on the right side if the arrangement is a gyakugatte (sun from the right) and on the left side if the arrangement is hongatte (sun from the left). (Our arrangement in Figure 19 is gyakugatte.) Soe should curve and "look up" toward shin. Soe should also be a stem and flower with strong visual impact, but a bit less forceful than shin. The soe stem symbolizes heaven and the past and should thus incorporate a blossom in full bloom, suggesting that the flower at its peak is already on its way to decline.

3. Now find tai-saki—the first stem in the tai sequence. Tai-saki symbolizes the future and should be a bud or smaller flower, with a fresh leaf that extends forward toward the edge of the vase from just under the flower. Tai-saki, about one-third the height of shin, should also begin as a straight stem that then curves slightly, with a flower that appears to look upward toward shin.

4. Place shin, soe, and tai-saki in the kenzan according to the illustration (Figure 20). This sets the arrangement's general proportions. You may need to alter the stems slightly by cutting them. As a beginner, you should cut stems a bit on the tall side first, then readjust their height as needed. (If you cut them too short, you may be able to use them for supporting positions instead.)

473

5. Next, select tai-shin, which is about one-half the height of shin. Tai-shin should have a strong visual impact; it is a miniature version of the shin flower but with a straight stem. Place it in front of shin. Next, select tai-tani, a flower that should be in full bloom, and place it so that it looks out toward the viewer from between tai-saki and tai-shin. The Japanese word tani means "valley"; tai-tani thus provides visual contrast through a shorter stem that peeks out to the side of tai-saki and tai-shin, providing depth. Tai-tani should lean a bit, or peek out, on the same side the soe branch leans to. In the arrangement here, tai-tani leans to the right, where soe is. Place tai-tani in the kenzan as in Figure 20. The tai group is now complete.

6. Place supporting stems, or ashirai, to complete the arrangement. Select a tall straight stem to support shin; the shin-ashirai should be up to nine-tenths the height of shin. Place it directly behind shin, leaning slightly to the side opposite the soe branch.

7. Next, select a flower stem to support soe. Called the soe-ashirai, the stem should be about one-half to two-thirds the height of soe and placed directly behind it. It should support soe by leaning toward the soe branch.

Here's a quick synopsis of what you can learn from this arrangement, and some of the most important shoka concepts:

474

- It is easier to find balance if you insert the shin stem first, right in the center of the kenzan. The height of this stem should be roughly two and one-half to three times the height of the vase. But this will vary depending on the visual balance.

- Tai-saki is inserted at the front and does not extend over the edge of the vase.

- Soe should be about two-thirds the height of shin and extended outward at a 45 degree angle from shin. This angle will vary slightly due to the plant material being used. When using straighter material, as found in Arrangement One, the angle is less. As a rule of thumb, the straighter the material the less the angle.

- The tips of soe and tai should ideally be arranged to "look upward toward shin."

- Since the shin, soe, and tai positions represent present, past, and future in your arrangement, carefully consider the character of the flowers used. Shin should ideally be a half open to fully opened flower, soe a fully opened flower, and tai a bud.

- Depending on the size of the flowers, the brightness of their color, and other factors, the elements in an arrangement have different visual impacts. You can roughly quantify the visual strength of your material by rating shin as seven, soe as five, and tai as three. How a visual impact

475

is judged is open to interpretation, but this basic ratio should be kept in mind for shoka shofutai arrangments.

• Shoka arrangements, including the one presented here, typically use five, seven, or nine stems (depending on the material and its characteristics).

Look at the drawing of our completed arrangement and note the relative height differences of each component part, as well as their proportions within the arrangement. Try to re-create this as closely as possible to preserve the correct balance found in the illustration. Height, width, and proportion are precisely prescribed for balance in shoka shofutai, and no art is possible without such balance.

Arrangement Two: Jiyuka—"Arrival of Spring"

MATERIALS

Gerbera daisy
Freesia
Lemon leaf
Bear grass

CONTAINER

A ceramic bud vase

SUBSTITUTIONS

You may replace the gerbera daisy with any flower that appears to have a "face," such as a small sunflower, an anemone, or even an orchid.

Then select a small accent flower to replace the freesia for a contrasting color. Any flat green leaf material can substitute for the lemon leaf. The bear grass provides a sense movement, as can any flowing grass material, or possibly colored wire.

DESCRIPTION

Arrangement Two is an example of freestyle (Figure 21). Entitled "Arrival of Spring," it uses a type of flower with a "happy face" quality. Colors, flowers, and vase were all selected to create an uplifting mood, one of expectancy at the arrival of spring after a long winter.

In freestyle, the vase is an integral part of the arrangement and may often times be quite elaborate in shape, color, and style. A fairly generic bud vase (that is, a vase that is long and slender) was chosen for this exercise so that readers can easily duplicate the design. Although the bud vase here seems quite plain, its shape serves as a kind of "body" under the flower's head and face, and its earthy color and texture are a reminder of the earth from which emerge the beautiful flowers of spring.

In this particular design, the yellow gerbera daisy was chosen for its bright countenance that possesses a human quality, somewhat like the happy face of a child. This is typical of the way flowers for freestyle arrangments are chosen more for their color, shape, and textural qualities as unique materials, and less as true flowers. In the example of the gerbera daisy here (and this is true of most flowers in a freestyle arrangement), all the leaves are clipped off to suggest that the flower is but one visual element (among many) in an overall design.

The gerbera daisy visually dominates the composition through its size, texture, and color. It thus represents the element of "mass," one of the three design elements in freestyle (the other two being

477

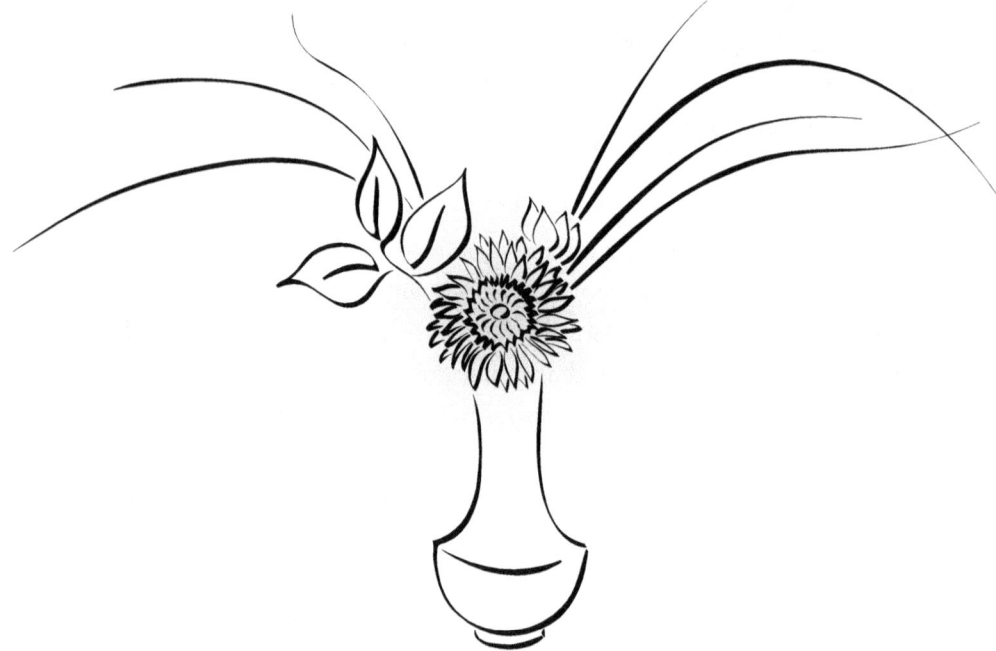

FIG. 21. Composition Two. A freestyle arrangement entitled "Arrival of Spring" that uses Gerbera daisy, freesia, lemon leaf, and bear grass. See the photograph on page 370.

"lines" and "points"). In contrast, the relatively smooth green leaves of the lemon leaf represent the design quality of "surface," providing background contrast to the richly textured daisy. The lemon leaf's cool green color also contrasts with the daisy's warm yellow, red, and brown tones.

The thin bear grass leaves, representing the design element of "lines," provide relief from the round and flat quality of the gerbera daisy and lemon leaf. Behind the gerbera daisy, accenting the arrangement

478

through its intensity of color, is the red freesia, which serves as a focal point in the design.

This composition has a simple quality partly due to its symmetry. It is balanced on each side with the same number of materials, and, in the case of the bear grass, the same material is seen on both sides. Symmetry can convey simplicity and serenity. This composition could, however, be rearranged in an asymmetrical style to impart a feeling of dynamism, complexity, and strong movement. When creating a free-style arrangement, you must consider what idea or theme you wish to convey and blend the appropriate flowers, vase, and even non-floral materials (such as colored wire) to communicate your idea.

Before you begin, let's review some of the main freestyle concepts.

In freestyle, the artist is not merely thinking of the flower as a flower; but rather, he or she considers it as a shape, texture, surface, line, or mass of color. Points, lines, shapes, and hues are arranged to create something akin to abstract art.

When two or more lines converge, various spaces are born. Materials and spaces together suggest a shape. Different shapes can express disparate feelings or themes. Titles are helpful in completing this effect.

In shoka, shin, soe, and tai create a scalene triangle. In freestyle, you give birth to a form. Two vertical lines create a vertical movement of ki. But twenty perpendicular lines will create a planed surface, much like planks on a deck. This surface can be a rectangle or a square. Straight lines of mixed length can also suggest an oval or round form. Like most art, freestyle kado uses circles, triangles, and squares.

Freestyle consists of three variations: vertical, horizontal, and slanting. Vertical jiyuka has an up or down ki movement. Horizontal has ki that moves to the left, right, or both directions. A slanting form has a ki movement that angles up, down, or extends to one side or the other, or both sides. The ki of the vertical style projects solidity, the ki of the horizontal form expresses stability, and the ki in the slanting version gives rise to a sensation of action.

Colors are used in freestyle to produce differing feelings. The container is also counted as one of the design materials.

The arrangement here is a representation of the merging of human creative ki with the ki of nature. In this synthesis of human creativity and nature, great art can be born—art that exemplifies naturalness and embodies more than just a clever idea, but which is also more than a mere carbon copy of nature.

METHOD

See the drawing of the arrangement in Figure 21 and the illustration of the vase's mouth in Figure 22 for a diagram of the insertion points and order of placement.

1. Find a suitable ceramic or colored vase suggesting a "body"; the vase should not be clear glass, as the stems will be visible. Fill the vase with water, taking care not to overfill it. Since this container has a narrow opening, you won't need green floral foam or other devices (such as a kenzan) to hold the flowers in place.

2. Select a fresh gerbera daisy taking care to examine its "face"; each flower is unique, and you should explore the feeling the flower imparts before selecting it. Gerbera daisies come in a rainbow of colors, and you'll need to harmonize your color choice with the color of the vase. The

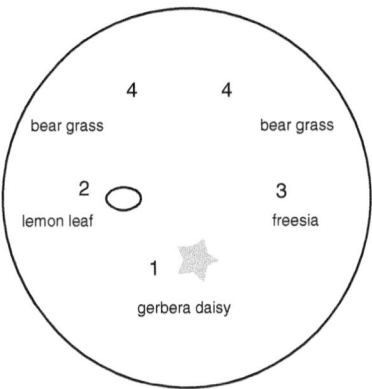

FIG. 22. Diagram of the order stems are inserted in the kenzan for Composition Two. The view is from the top looking down and shows the different design elements and where they are placed in relation to each other. Use the corresponding illustration and the photograph to better understand how the different elements relate to each other.

gerbera daisy's face must look forward, directly toward you. To obtain that effect, you may have to cut the flower short enough so that it will tilt forward a bit

3. Place some flat green leaves to the rear of the daisy; lemon leaf stems are flexible and can be bent into position easily. Cut the stems short enough so that they can be propped against the inside neck of the vase.

4. Next, add your accent color with the freesia or any small flower that can provide contrast and a small focal point.

5. The lower ends of the bear grass are often quite stiff in contrast to the tips. The lower ends don't typically shift around in the vase, but if they do, use a small piece of wire to tie them together. If the grass is excessively long, cut the tips, not the ends. The tips will lift upward from the release of weight. Select contrasting strands of grass whose thinness, thickness, length, and even color.

Arrangement Three: Moribana

MATERIALS

Two iris flowers with iris leaves
Three daffodils with their leaves

CONTAINER

A round, shallow blue ceramic vase

SUBSTITUTIONS

Tree branches, such as cherry with both leaves and buds, may be substituted for the irises. Three small tulips may be used in place of the daffodils.

DESCRIPTION

Moribana literally means "piled-up flowers," and as the name suggests, this style emphasizes flowers arranged in a mass effect. It's a naturalistic, simplified form that addresses the need for a small-scale, contemporary approach to decorating a more Western-style modern home. With the decline of the traditional Japanese-style dwelling and its related tokonoma ("decorative alcove"), less formal flower arrangements suitable for placement in various locations in the home, such as a table, are increasingly favored in Japan. Moribana, developed at the turn of the last century, serves this modern trend well.

Moribana is usually prepared in a shallow bowl with a kenzan placed off to the side or sometimes in the middle of the vase. Vases tend to be shallow and round, oval, or rectangular in shape. As with any flower arrangement, the vase must harmonize with the environment and the materials used.

In composing a moribana arrangement, keep in mind that moribana has three main elements—shin, soe, and tai. The rule for determining the height of shin is to add the diameter of the container to the height of the container and multiply by one and one-half to three times, depending on the type of material used. Another way of stating this is that the height of shin is no less than one and one-half times and no greater than three times the sum of the vase's diameter plus its height.

Soe is approximately two-thirds to three-quarters the height of shin; tai is approximately one-third to one-half the length of shin. This sounds complicated, but after a little practice you will be able "eyeball" stem lengths and judge proportions fairly easily.

The three main elements—shin, soe, and tai—should form a triangle within the vase. This triangle should not be within a single plane, but its three points should ideally create a dynamic, asymmetrical balance. Of primary visual interest is the sense of depth that the triangle creates.

Moribana stems can be inserted at greater or lesser angles for visual balance. Like nageire and shoka, moribana has a number of styles that range from a more upright to a more "leaning" style. The upright styles have fewer or smaller angles, while the more leaning styles have wider angles relative to the base of the arrangement. The style in the arrangement shown here is upright, or chokutai, which is easier for creating simple visual balance and more suitable for material, like iris, that grows in a straight, upward manner.

Arrangement Three includes only two types of material, the iris and the daffodil (Figure 23). Too many materials are difficult to harmo-

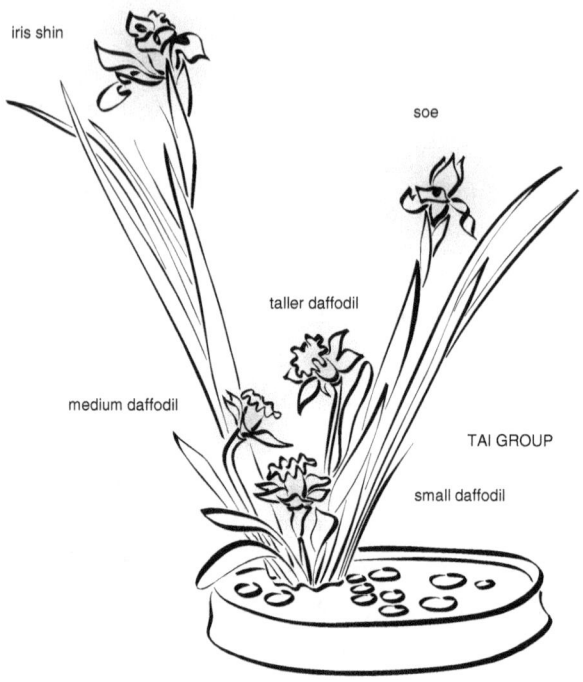

iris shin

soe

taller daffodil

medium daffodil

TAI GROUP

small daffodil

FIG. 23. Composition Three. A moribana arrangement using the flowers and leaves of iris and daffodils. See the photograph on page 374.

nize due to variations in color, shape, size, and so on. As you get more practice, you may wish to increase the number of materials to three. Kado is ultimately a study of harmony—harmony of color, shape, size, and other visual elements; harmony of mind and body; and harmony of the individual with the universe.

Our arrangement uses iris stems for both the shin and soe elements and daffodils for the tai component. Along with the iris flower stems, we incorporated iris leaves to give the arrangement a more natural character and to cover areas where the stem, even with leaves, appears bare. While the leaves may be considered the same material as the iris, they add support visually to the flower stem and can be considered an essential component of the arrangement. This is in contrast to Western flower arrangements that include a large number of flowers to provide visual fullness and completeness. Japanese flower arrangements use leaf material as supporting players, to soften the harshness of using only a few stems and flowers, while providing a "natural look."

METHOD

1. Select a shallow, round container. The larger the diameter of the container, the taller your stems will have to be. If your material is a bit short, find a vase with a smaller diameter. Place the kenzan either in the center of the vase or about one to two inches from the left side of the vase.

2. Shin should be approximately one and one-half to three times the sum of the container's diameter plus height. Do the calculation and then select an appropriately tall iris stem and trim it as needed. Place the shin stem in the center of the kenzan but lean it at an angle of about 30 degrees to the left. Place supporting leaf material in front, to the sides, and to the rear of the shin iris stem. See the diagram of the kenzan and the drawing of the completed arrangement (Figures 23 and 24).

3. For soe, select a stem approximately two-thirds to three-fourths the height of shin. Place the soe stem near the

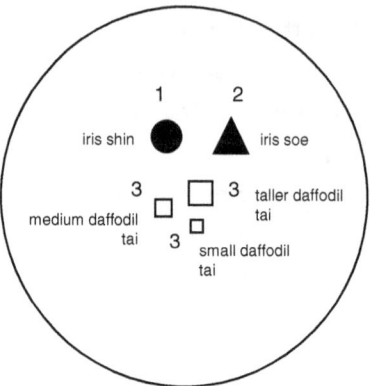

FIG. 24. Diagram of the order stems are inserted in the kenzan for Composition Three. The view is from the top looking down and shows the different design elements and where they are placed in relation to each other. Use the corresponding illustration and the photograph to better understand how the different elements relate to each other.

center of the kenzan to the right of shin. Include leaf material in front and to the rear of the stem. The angle of soe may be similar to the angle of shin for a more symmetrical harmony, or soe may be at a greater or lesser angle providing a visual counterpoint. The greater the angle, the larger the space between shin and soe. (Visually pleasing spaces between the primary elements such as shin and soe in a Japanese flower arrangement is considered an important aesthetic feature and contrasts with Western-style arrangements that often emphasize abundance through a tight clustering of blossoms.) As in the shoka arrangement, the soe stem (and the tai stems) should look toward the shin stem.

4. Tai here consists of a grouping of three bright yellow daffodils chosen to contrast with the darker purples and greens found in the shin and soe elements. These three daffodils are grouped to form a miniature moribana con-

figuration of shin, soe, and tai, repeating the theme of triangular harmony and having the same proportional characteristics as moribana arrangements. Select a daffodil to represent shin within the grouping; this largest daffodil should be approximately one-third to one-half the height of the iris shin. The other two daffodils, corresponding to soe and tai, should be about two-thirds to three-quarters and about one-third to one-half the height of the shin daffodil respectively. Insert daffodil leaves in front, to the sides, and in the rear to add naturalness and visual support to the tai grouping.

In all three of the arrangements presented in this chapter be sure to make use of the methods of cutting and bending plant materials discussed earlier. A quick reread might be in order if your stems fail to stick in the kenzan or break when you're merely trying to bend them. All of these procedures must be learned firsthand, through direct experience, time in practice, and personal experimentation. Your only "shortcut" lies in finding a qualified kado teacher—and you can find out how to do just that in the section "Sources for Instruction & Supplies."

SOURCES FOR INSTRUCTION & SUPPLIES

Now that you've read this book and tried the exercises, you'll need a skilled instructor if you'd like to proceed further. This section can help you locate a teacher as well as the art supplies required for practicing your arrangements.

How Do I Find a Teacher?

This, in many ways, is the most significant question for any student of the Japanese cultural arts. A proficient instructor is essential—books such as *The Japanese Way of the Flower* can offer information for contemplation and act as a practical supplement to hands-on training, but they are only an introduction to a given art.

Both of us—H. E. Davey and Ann Kameoka—invite you to get in touch with us if you have questions or comments about anything you've read in this book:

The Sennin Foundation Center for
Japanese Cultural Arts
1053 San Pablo Avenue
Albany, CA 94706

hedavey@aol.com
www.senninfoundation.com

Ikenobo is one of the largest, oldest, and most respected forms of ikebana, and while many other legitimate systems of kado exist, Ikenobo is also the version we are most familiar with. If you live in North America, contact Ikenobo in San Francisco for information on either teachers or art supplies:

Ikenobo Ikebana Society of America
USA Headquarters
1737 Post Street #16
San Francisco, CA 94115
Telephone: 415/567-1011

Readers outside of North America should write in English or Japanese to the Ikenobo World Headquarters in Japan:

Ikenobo Headquarters
P. O. Box 36
Nakagyo, Kyoto 604
Japan

Here are some other easy ways of locating an instructor near you:

- If a Japanese community center is nearby, try checking out their various classes. They may offer the kind of instruction mentioned in this text.

- Sometimes local colleges have classes in Japanese flower arrangement. This would be another easy place to start looking for a teacher.

- Many Buddhist churches and centers offer classes in Asian cultural arts.

- Try contacting the nearest Japanese consulate and asking for assistance.

- If none of the above resources can point you to the kind of teacher you are looking for, try talking to instructors of other Japanese art forms such as judo or tea ceremony. These teachers may know of someone who can help you.

- Make a point of getting involved in the local Japanese-American community, as this will enhance your understanding of all the Japanese arts. It can also open many doors.

Finding a capable instructor is neither quick nor easy. We both looked for several years before discovering exceptional instructors for the Japanese arts that captured our interest. Once you find a teacher, be prepared to also spend a considerable amount of time and labor studying the art. While all of this may seem a bit intimidating to you, keep in mind that the rewards are certainly equivalent to the energy expended.

What About the Internet?

While the Internet is a source for a vast amount of information about a vast number of Japanese art forms, it can also be a fount from which an equivalently vast amount of misinformation pours forth. First, visit Michi Online (home of *Michi Online: Journal of Japanese Cultural Arts*); the site offers usually reliable resources relating to a large variety of Japanese cultural arts, including kado:

www.michionline.org

Also check the following sites:

Ikebana
jin.jcic.or.jp/kidsweb/virtual/ikebana/ikebana.html

Ikebana International, San Francisco www.sf.ikebana.org/index.html

Let's Begin Ikenobo www.asianmall.com/ikenobo/about.html

Ryukoku University Ikenobo Flower Arrangement Circle www.st.rim.or.jp/~pon/ryukoku/index.html

Welcome to Sogetsu
www.tni.co.jp/sogetsu/sogetsu-e.html

Where Can I Purchase Supplies?

For the tools you need to practice any of the compositions in this book, the first place to look is your nearest garden supply store. Be certain the salesperson knows you are interested in Japanese flower arrangement. You may get a good price at the neighbor-hood garden shop, but you will rarely find a good assortment or tools of good quality.

Stores catering to aficionados of bonsai (Japanese dwarf trees) will occasionally have ikebana materials. They may also know someone who teaches flower arranging, or may even teach it themselves. Here is a sampling of places to contact:

Ichiyo Art Center
432 East Paces Ferry Road
Atlanta, GA 30305
Phone: 404-233-1846
Fax: 404-233-8012
online@ichiyoart.com
www.ichiyoart.com/index.htm

Ikebana Arts
580 North 6th Street
San Jose, CA 95112
Phone: 408-279-8342
Fax: 408-279-8345
kika@ikebana-arts.com
www.ikebana-arts.com/

Ikenobo Headquarters
P.O. Box 36
Nakagyo, Kyoto 604
Japan

Ikenobo Ikebana Society of America
USA Headquarters
1737 Post Street #16
San Francisco, CA 94115
Phone: 415-567-1011

Japanese Style
Route 1, Box 301-B
New Prague, MN 56071
Phone: 877-226-4387
Fax: 952-758-1922
sales@japanesegifts.com
www.japanesegifts.com/intro.htm

Kaki
P.O. Box 3064
Renton, WA 98056
Phone/fax: 425-255-7077
hama@kaki4u.com
www.kaki4u.com/

Shuji Ikeda Ceramics
3012 King Street
Berkeley, CA 94703

For meditation exercises you can find a small Buddhist gong in catalogs or on the Internet. Or you can contact the following address:

Soko Hardware
1698 Post Street
San Francisco, CA 94115
Phone: 415-931-5510

NOTES

1. John Stevens, *The Sword of No-Sword* (Boston: Shambhala, 1984), p. 142.

2. Shusui Komoda and Horst Pointner, *Ikebana: Spirit and Technique* (Dorset, U.K.: Blandford Press, 1980), p. 9.

3. Lao Tsu, *Tao Te Ching*, trans. Gia-Fu Feng and Jane English (New York: Vintage Books, 1972), p. 48.

4. Dave Lowry, *Persimmon Wind: A Martial Artist's Journey in Japan* (Boston: Charles E. Tuttle Company, 1998), pp. 199–200.

5. Ibid., p. 202.

6. Felix G. Rivera, *Suiseki: The Japanese Art of Miniature Landscape Stones* (Berkeley: Stone Bridge Press, 1997), p. 177.

7. Ikenobo Headquarters, *An Invitation to Ikenobo: Free Style* (Kyoto, Japan: Ikenobo Headquarters, 1999), p. 18.

Other titles in the series *An Invitation to Ikenobo* published by the Ikenobo Headquarters in Kyoto were especially helpful in the preparation of this book. Titles include *Rikka; Free Style; Nageire, Moribana, Introducing Free Style; Shoka Shimputai;* and *Shoka Shofutai.* For more on Japanese aesthetics and mind-body unification principles, see *Brush Meditation: A Japanese Way to Mind & Body Harmony* by H. E. Davey (Berkeley, California: Stone Bridge Press, 1999). Other useful titles include:

De Garis, Frederic, and H. S. K. Yamaguchi. *We Japanese.* Yokohama: Yamagata Press, 1935.

De Mente, Boye. *Everything Japanese: The Authoritative Reference on Japan Today.* Lincolnwood, Illinois: Passport Books, 1992.

Franck, Frederick. *The Zen of Seeing: Seeing Drawing as Meditation.* New York: Random House, 1973.

Okakura, Kakuzo. *The Book of Tea.* Tokyo: Kodansha International, 1991.

Koren, Leonard. *Wabi-Sabi: For Artists, Designers, Poets & Philosophers.* Berkeley: Stone Bridge Press, 1994.

Nakamura, Tempu. *Anjo Daza Kosho, Igaku kara Mita Toitsu-do* [Anjo Daza Meditation: Toitsu-do from a Medical Perspective]. Tokyo: Tempu-kai Hombu, n.d.

GLOSSARY

aiki-jujutsu: "the gentle art of pliability through union with ki," a classical Japanese martial art

anjo daza ho: "seated method to serenity via bell-ringing," a meditation developed by Nakamura Tempu Sensei

ashirai: a component in some styles of flower arrangement, used around the base of the composition, to add balance and fullness

aware: a Japanese aesthetic concept relating to a moment that evokes a nostalgic sadness connected with autumn and the vanishing of the world

budo: the martial Way

chabana: "tea flowers," a style of flower arrangement used in the tea ceremony

chado: "the Way of tea," the tea ceremony

cha no yu: tea ceremony

Do: "the Way," a spiritual path; can be pronounced "michi"

hana: "flower"

hara: "abdomen," a natural center in the lower abdomen associated with Japanese meditative forms

ichigo, ichi-e: "one encounter, one chance," a Japanese aesthetic/spiritual ideal relating to transience

ikebana: "living flowers," the art of Japanese flower arrangement

Ikenobo: the oldest system, or school, of flower arrangement

in/yo: "dark-light, negative-positive," a dualism of complementary opposites in nature (also known as yin-yang)

jiyuka: "free flowers," a free style of flower arrangement

kado: the Way of flowers

kenzan: frog pin

ki: life energy

kiri-dame: a cutting method of shaping and curving stems

komi: a forked stick used to hold flowers in a vase

mizuage: methods of encouraging water absorption

mizugiri: "water cutting," a method of encouraging water absorption

mizugiwa: the surface of the water in a vase holding a flower arrangement

moribana: "piled-up flowers," a style of flower arrangement

muga ichi-nen ho: "no self, one thought method," a form of meditation developed by Nakamura Tempu Sensei

nageire: "thrown in," a style of flower arrangement

nejiri-dame: a twisting method of shaping and curving stems

orenai te: an experiment with coordination of mind and body taught in Shin-shin-toitsu-do

oshi-dame: a pushing method of shaping and curving stems

rikka: "standing flowers," a style of flower arrangement

rin: a bowl-shaped bell associated with Japanese meditative forms

ryu: school, or "handed-down tradition"

sabi: "solitude," a Japanese aesthetic/ spiritual ideal relating to simplicity, transience, and artlessness

seiza: "correct, calm sitting," a kneeling posture associated with Japanese meditative forms

sensei: "born before," an honorific title for a teacher

shibui: "elegant," a Japanese aesthetic/spiritual ideal

shibumi: "elegance," a Japanese aesthetic/spiritual ideal

Shin-shin-toitsu-do: "The way of mind and body unification," a

form of Japanese yoga founded by Nakamura Tempu Sensei

shin-soe-tai: three main branches, or components, found in many flower arrangements (see "ten-chi-jin")

shizen-tai: a correct and natural posture

shodo: the Way of calligraphy

shoka: "living flowers," a style of flower arrangement

shoka shimputai: a modern style of shoka flower arrangement

shoka shofutai: a traditional style of shoka flower arrangement

tamekata: methods of shaping and curving stems

ten-chi-jin: "heaven-earth-humanity," three central elements in many flower arrangements

tomekata: methods of fixing materials in place

wa: harmony

wabi: poverty, a Japanese aesthetic/ spiritual ideal relating to artlessness and simplicity

wa-kei-sei-jaku: "accord-respect-purity-solitude," the maxims of the tea ceremony

yakueda: primary branches, or components, of a flower arrangement (see "shin-soe-tai")

About the Authors

H. E. DAVEY

H. E. Davey is the Director of the Sennin Foundation Center for Japanese Cultural Arts (www.senninfoundation.com), which offers instruction in Japanese systems of yoga, martial arts, healing arts, and fine arts. His introduction to the arts of Japan came via traditional martial arts. Since the age of five, he has studied jujutsu extensively in the USA and Japan. He has received the title of Kyoshi from the Kokusai Budoin, a Tokyo-based international federation. Kokusai Budoin defines Kyoshi as comparable to a "Master's Certificate" and equivalent to modern ranks of sixth- to eighth-degree black belt. He also serves on the Board of Directors of the Shudokan Martial Arts Association (www.smaa-hq.com).

In middle school, Mr. Davey began studying Shin-shin-toitsu-do, a system of Japanese yoga and meditation founded by Nakamura Tempu Sensei. He is thought to be the only American member of Tempu-kai, an organization established by Mr. Nakamura, and he hass practiced in Japan and the USA under Nakamura Sensei's senior disciples, including Sawai Atsuhiro Sensei and Hashimoto Tetsuichi Sensei. Mr. Davey has also received extensive instruction in Nakamura Sensei's methods of bodywork and healing with ki ("life energy"), which he also teaches.

Mr. Davey also studied shodo, or Japanese brush writing and ink painting, for twenty years under the late Kobara Ranseki Sensei of Kyoto. Mr. Davey holds the top rank in Ranseki Sho Juku shodo and exhibits each year in Japan. He has received numerous honors in these exhibitions, including Jun Taisho ("Associate Grand Prize").

H. E. Davey's articles on Japanese arts and his artwork have appeared in various American and Japanese magazines and newspapers. He is the author of *Unlocking the Secrets of Aiki-jujutsu* (McGraw-Hill) and five books with Stone Bridge Press.

ANN KAMEOKA

Ann Kameoka is the coauthor of *The Japanese Way of the Flower: Ikebana as Moving Meditation.* She began studying Ikenobo kado, the oldest form of Japanese flower arrangement, in 1988. She has studied under several top Ikenobo teachers, and she received teaching certification in 1998. Her exceptional floral art has been in several notable exhibitions in Northern California.

Ms. Kameoka also began studying the Shin-shin-toitsu-do system of Japanese yoga and meditation in the early 1980's. She has studied under H. E. Davey and Hashimoto Tetsuichi Sensei, one of the world's most advanced teachers of this discipline. She has obtained teaching credentials in Shin-shin-toitsu-do and related healing arts and has taught these art forms in the San Francisco Bay Area.

Ms. Kameoka is also a member of the Board of Advisors for the Sennin Foundation, Inc., a nonprofit organization that promotes Japanese cultural arts. She maintains the website Michi Online: Journal of Japanese Cultural Arts (www.michionline.org).

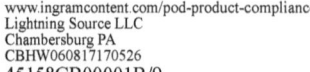